THE ARCTIC
*p 139*

GERMANY &
THE ALPINE STATES
*pp 58-59*

THE LOW
COUNTRIES
*pp 50-51*

Iceland
*p 49*

NORTHERN EUROPE
*pp 48-49*

RUSSIA & KAZAKHSTAN
*pp 76-77*

EUROPEAN RUSSIA
*pp 68-69*

THE BRITISH
ISLES
*pp 25-40*
*pp 52-53*

CENTRAL
EUROPE
*pp 62-63*

EUROPE
*pp 44-69*

ASIA
*pp 72-91*

FRANCE
*pp 54-55*

EASTERN
EUROPE
*pp 66-67*

ITALY
*pp 60-61*

SOUTHEAST
EUROPE
*pp 64-65*

TURKEY &
THE CAUCASUS
*pp 78-79*

CENTRAL
ASIA
*pp 82-83*

EAST
ASIA
*pp 86-87*

JAPAN &
KOREA
*pp 84-85*

SPAIN &
PORTUGAL
*pp 56-57*

Gibraltar
*p 40*

Malta
*p 70*

THE
MEDITERRANEAN
*pp 70-71*

Cyprus
*p 70*

Israel
*p 81*

SOUTHWEST
ASIA
*pp 80-81*

SOUTH
ASIA
*pp 88-89*

Ryukyu
Islands
*p 83*

PACIFIC

OCEAN

NORTH AFRICA
*pp 122-123*

WEST AFRICA
*pp 124-125*

EAST
AFRICA
*pp 126-127*

Andaman
& Nicobar
Islands
*p 89*

SOUTHEAST
ASIA
*pp 90-91*

SOUTHWEST
PACIFIC
*pp 136-137*

AFRICA
*pp 118-129*

AUSTRALASIA
& OCEANIA
*pp 130-137*

Samoa
*p 136*

SOUTHERN
AFRICA
*pp 128-129*

INDIAN

OCEAN

AUSTRALIA
*pp 132-133*

NEW ZEALAND
*pp 134-135*

ANTARCTICA
*p 138*

# student
# ATLAS

DK PUBLISHING, INC.
LONDON • NEW YORK • MUNICH • MELBOURNE • DELHI
www.dk.com

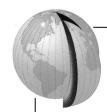

A DORLING KINDERSLEY BOOK
www.dk.com

EDUCATIONAL CONSULTANTS
Dr. David Lambert, Institute of Education, University of London, David R Wright, BA MA

TEACHER REVIEWERS
US: Ramani DeAlwis; UK: Kevin Ball, Pat Barber, Stewart Marson

DORLING KINDERSLEY CARTOGRAPHY

MANAGING EDITOR          MANAGING ART EDITOR
Lisa Thomas              Philip Lord

PROJECT EDITORS                      PROJECT DESIGNERS
Debra Clapson, Wim Jenkins, Jill Hamilton (US)   Rhonda Fisher, Karen Gregory

EDITORIAL CONTRIBUTORS               DESIGNERS
Thomas Heath, Kevin McRae, Constance Novis,   Carol Ann Davis, David Douglas Nicola Liddiard
Iris Rossoff (US), Siobhan Ryan

MANAGING CARTOGRAPHER        SENIOR CARTOGRAPHIC EDITOR
David Roberts                Roger Bullen

CARTOGRAPHERS
Pamela Alford, James Anderson, Sarah Baker-Ede, Dale Buckton,
Tony Chambers, Jan Clark, Martin Darlison, Sally Gable, Jeremy Hepworth,
Michael Martin, Simon Mumford, John Plumer, Julie Turner, Jane Voss, Peter Winfield

DATABASE MANAGER        DIGITAL MAPS CREATED IN DK CARTOPIA BY
Simon Lewis             Phil Rowles, Rob Stokes

PLACENAMES DATABASE TEAM    EDITORIAL DIRECTION
Natalie Clarkson, Julia Lynch   Andrew Heritage

PICTURE RESEARCH     PRODUCTION
Louise Thomas        David Proffit

First American Edition, 1998.
Reprinted with Revisions, 1999.
Second Edition (revised) 2002, Reprinted 2003.

Published in the United States by DK Publishing Inc.
375 Hudson Street, New York, New York, 10014

A Penguin Company

Copyright © 1998, 1999, 2002, 2003 Dorling Kindersley Limited, London.

All rights reserved under the International and Pan-American Copyright Conventions. No part of this publication may be
reproduced, stored in a retrieval system, or transmitted in any form, or by any means, electronic, mechanical, photocopying,
recording, or otherwise, without the prior written permission of the copyright holder.

Student Atlas.
    p.  cm.
    Summary: Maps, illustrations and text describe various aspects of
countries of the world including physical features, population,
standards of living, natural resources, industries, environmental
issues and climate.
    ISBN 0-7894-9052-8
    1. Children's atlases.   [1. Atlases.]  I. DK Publishing, Inc.
G1021 .S78 1998   <G&M>
912--DC21                              97-45730
                                       CIP
                                       MAPS

Reproduction by Colourscan, Singapore, and The Printed Word, London.
Printed and bound in Slovakia by TBB s.r.o.

ACKNOWLEDGMENTS

The publishers are grateful for permission to reproduce the following photographs:
t=top, b=bottom, a=above, l=left, r=right, c=center

Axiom: J Spaull 92br. Bridgeman Art Library: Hereford Cathedral, Trustees of the Hereford Mappa Mundi 8tr.
J Allan Cash: 120cr. Bruce Coleman Ltd: C Ott 28cr (below); Dr E Pott 4bc; H Reinhard 19cr; J Murray 130bl; Peter Terry
19crr. Colourific: Black Star/R Rogers 113br; Frank Herrmann 119bc. Comstock: 17tc. James Davis Travel Photography: 44tr,
119tr. Robert Harding Picture Library: 6tr (below), 21c, 21cr, 22br, 92cr (above), 28bl, 30cr, 30br, 31bl, 38tr, 118bl; A Tovy
120br; Adam Woolfitt 62br; C Bowman 112tr; Charcrit Boonson 90cr (below); David Lomax 20tr; Franz Joseph Land 19tr; G
Boutin 120cl (below); G Renner 17c, 118cr(above); Gavin Hellier 31tr; Geoff Renner 39cr (above); H P Merten 23tl; Jane
Sweeney 23bl; Louise Murray 93tr; Peter Scholey 91tr; Robert Francis 29cr; Schuster/Keine 62cr (above); Simon Westcott 90br.
Hutchison Library: A Zvoznikov 19cl; J Nowell 93bl; R Ian Lloyd 10cl. Image Bank: Carlos Navajas 17bl; M Isy-Schwart 17bc;
P Grumann 64cr (below); Steve Proehl 30cr (below); Terje Rakke 17br. Images Colour Library: 19c, 62cr (below), 118br.
Impact: Jeremy Nicholl 121cl (below); Mark Henley 20bl; Paul O'Driscoll 63cr; Robin Lubbock 118br. Frank Lane Picture
Agency: D Smith 19bc; W Wishiewsli 17cr. Magnum: Chris Steele Perking 120tr (below); Ian Berry 64br; Jean Gaumy 65cl.
N.A.S.A: 9tc. N.H.P.A: M Wendler 4cl, 110bl. Oxford Scientific Films: Konrad Wothe 19tc; L Gould 4tr; Nobert Rosing 28cl.
Panos Pictures: Alain le Garsheur 92cr; Alain le Garsmeur 31cl (below); Alberto Arzoz 63cr; Bruce Paton 121bl; Jeremy Hartley
120bl; Maria Luiza M Cavalho 112cl (below); Paul Smith 111cr; Rhodri Jones 113bl; Ron Gilling 119cr; Trygve Bolstad 22bl.
Edward Parker: 17cr (above). Pictor International: 4tc, 10bc, 18tr, 20br, 36bc, 38br. Planet Earth Pictures: J Waters 113bc.
South American Pictures: Robert Francis 29br; Tony Morrison 110cr, 111cl. Spectrum Colour Library: 29br. Frank Spooner
Pictures: Gamma/E Baitel 91cl. Still Pictures: J Frebet 113cr; R Seitre 90cr (above). Tony Stone Images: 17tr, 112cl; A Sacks
28cr; Alan Levenson 92cr; Charles Thatcher 39tr; D Austen 131cr; D Hanson 17cl; Donald Johnson 62bc; Earth Imaging 6tr
(above); G Johnson 90bl; H Strand 113tr; Hans Schlapfer 38bc; J Jangoux 19bcr; J Warden 110bc; John Garrett 121br; L Resnick
121tr; Larry Ulrich 37br; P Chesley 130tr; Paul Chesley 36br; Randy Wells 19br; Robert Frerck 65tr; Tom Walker 36bl; Tony
Craddock 65cr. Telegraph Colour Library: 29tr. Travel Ink: Colin Marshall 22bc. Trip: A Kuznetsov 92bc; H Rogers 90cr; M
Barlow 112bl; N Ray 10tr; Robert Belbin 92bl; V Kolpakov 93cr (below); V Sidoropolev 64cr; W Jacobs 130c. World Pictures:
131tr. ZEFA Picture Library: 19bcl, 19cll, 63bc; Bramaz 30bl; Damm 119bl; Heilman 110cr (below); K Siewert 110cl; Kitchen
19bll; Sunak 91cr; Surpress 111tr. Jacket: Front cover image: Science Photo Library/NOAA

# CONTENTS

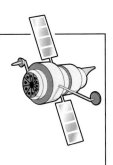

# AMAZING EARTH

**Earth is unique** among the nine planets that circle the Sun. It is the only one that can support life, because it has enough oxygen in its atmosphere and plentiful water. In fact, seen from space, the Earth looks almost entirely blue. This is because about 70% of its surface is under water, submerged beneath four huge oceans: the Pacific, Atlantic, Indian and Arctic oceans. Land makes up about 30% of the Earth's surface. It is divided into seven landmasses of varying shapes and sizes called continents. These are, from largest to smallest: Asia, Africa, North America, South America, Antarctica, Europe, and Australia.

## WATERY WORLD

The Earth's oceans and seas cover more than 142 million sq miles – that is twice the surface of Mars and nine times the surface of the moon.

Beneath the ocean waves lies the biggest and most unexplored landscape on Earth. Here are coral reefs, enormous, open plains, deep canyons, and the longest mountain range on Earth – the Mid-Atlantic Ridge – which stretches almost from pole to pole.

## THE SHAPE OF THE EARTH

**Photographs taken from space** by astronauts in the 1960s, and more recently from orbiting satellites, have proven beyond doubt what humans had worked out long ago – that the Earth is shaped like a ball. But it is not perfectly round. The force of the Earth's rotation makes the world bulge very slightly at the Equator and go a little flat at the North and South Poles. So the Earth is actually a flattened sphere, or a "geoid."

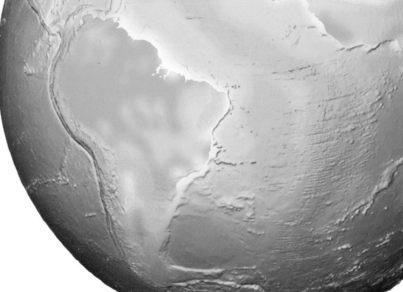

### HEIGHTS AND DEPTHS

The Pacific Ocean contains the deepest places on the Earth's surface – the ocean trenches. The very deepest is Challenger Deep in the Mariana Trench which plunges 36,060 ft into the Earth's crust. If Mount Everest, the highest point on land at 29,029 ft, was dropped into the trench, its peak wouldn't even reach the surface of the Pacific.

### WATER

Over 97% of the Earth's water is salt water. The total amount of salt in the world's oceans and seas would cover all of Europe to a depth of three miles. Less than 3% of the Earth's water is fresh. Of this, 2.24% is frozen in ice sheets and about 0.6% is stored underground as groundwater. The remainder is in lakes and rivers.

### COASTS

The total length of the Earth's coastlines is more than 300,000 miles – that is the equivalent of 12 times around the globe. A high percentage of the world's people live in coastal zones: of the ten most populated cities on Earth, eight are situated on estuaries or the coast.

### BIODIVERSITY

Today, almost six hundred million humans, approximately one million animal species, and 355,000 known plant species depend on the air, water, and land of planet Earth.

## WET EARTH

Tropical rain forests grow in areas close to the Equator, where it is wet and warm all year round. Although they cover just 7% of the Earth's land, these thick, damp forests form the richest ecosystems on the planet. More plant and animal species are found here than anywhere else on Earth.

## DRY EARTH

Deserts are among the most inhospitable places on the planet. Some deserts are scorching hot, others are freezing cold, but they have one thing in common – they are all dry. Very few plant and animal species can survive in these harsh conditions. The world's coldest and driest continent, Antarctica (*left*), is a cold desert.

### VANISHING FORESTS

10,000 years ago, thick forests covered about half of the Earth's land surface. Today, 33% of those forests no longer exist, and more than half of what remains has been dramatically altered. During the 20th century, more than 50% of the Earth's rain forests have been felled.

# DIFFERENT WORLD VIEWS

**Because the Earth is round**, we can only see half of it at any one time. This half is called a hemisphere, which means "half a sphere." There are always two hemispheres – the half that you see and the other half that you don't see. Two hemispheres placed together will always make a complete sphere.

# PLANET WATER, PLANET LAND

**The Earth can also be divided** into land and water hemispheres. The land hemisphere shows most of the land on the Earth's surface. The water hemisphere is dominated by the vast Pacific Ocean – from this view, the Earth appears to be almost entirely covered by water.

Equator 0°
North Pole
NORTH AMERICA
EUROPE
AFRICA
SOUTH AMERICA

### NORTH AND SOUTH

The Equator is an imaginary line drawn around the middle of the Earth, where its circumference is greatest. If we cut along the Equator, the Earth separates into two hemispheres: the Northern and Southern Hemispheres. Most of the Earth's land is the Northern Hemisphere. Europe and North America are the only continents that lie entirely in the northern hemisphere. Australia and Antarctica are the only continents that lie entirely in the southern hemisphere.

The Southern Hemisphere contains three of the Earth's four great oceans: the Pacific, Indian, and Arctic Oceans.

Prime Meridian (0°)
North Pole
NORTH AMERICA
EUROPE
SOUTH AMERICA
AFRICA
180°

### EAST AND WEST

The Earth can also be divided along two other imaginary lines – the Prime Meridian (0°) and 180° – which run opposite each other between the North and South Poles. This creates eastern and western hemispheres. The continents in the eastern hemisphere are traditionally called the Old World, while those in the western hemisphere – the Americas – were named the New World by the Europeans who explored them in the 15th century.

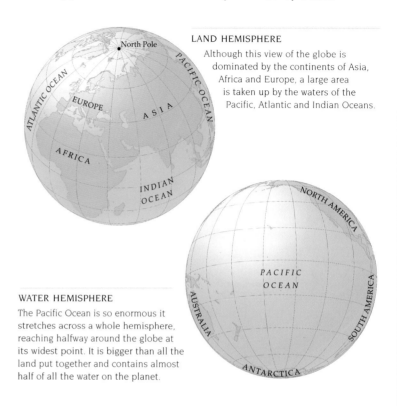

North Pole
ATLANTIC OCEAN
EUROPE
PACIFIC OCEAN
ASIA
AFRICA
INDIAN OCEAN

### LAND HEMISPHERE

Although this view of the globe is dominated by the continents of Asia, Africa and Europe, a large area is taken up by the waters of the Pacific, Atlantic and Indian Oceans.

NORTH AMERICA
PACIFIC OCEAN
AUSTRALIA
SOUTH AMERICA
ANTARCTICA

### WATER HEMISPHERE

The Pacific Ocean is so enormous it stretches across a whole hemisphere, reaching halfway around the globe at its widest point. It is bigger than all the land put together and contains almost half of all the water on the planet.

## THE SEASONS

**As the Earth orbits the Sun**, it is also spinning around an imaginary line called its axis, which joins the North and South Poles. The Earth's axis is not quite at right angles to the Sun, but tilts over at an angle of 23.5°. As a result, each place gradually moves closer to the Sun and then farther away from it again. Summer in the Northern Hemisphere is when the north is closest to the Sun. In winter, the Northern Hemisphere tilts away from the Sun, receiving far less heat and light. In the Southern Hemisphere the seasons are reversed, with summer in December and winter in June.

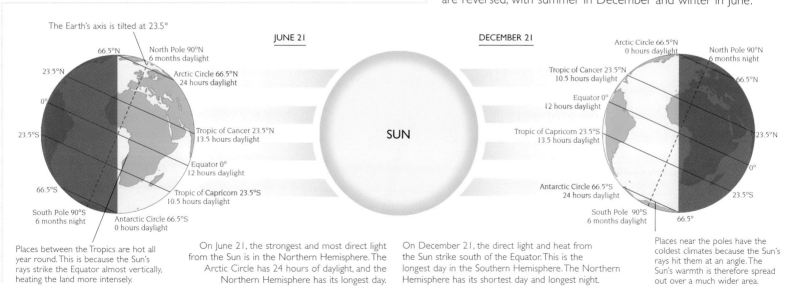

The Earth's axis is tilted at 23.5°
66.5°N
23.5°N
North Pole 90°N
6 months daylight
Arctic Circle 66.5°N
24 hours daylight
0°
23.5°S
Tropic of Cancer 23.5°N
13.5 hours daylight
Equator 0°
12 hours daylight
66.5°S
Tropic of Capricorn 23.5°S
10.5 hours daylight
South Pole 90°S
6 months night
Antarctic Circle 66.5°S
0 hours daylight

JUNE 21

SUN

DECEMBER 21

Arctic Circle 66.5°N
0 hours daylight
North Pole 90°N
6 months night
Tropic of Cancer 23.5°N
10.5 hours daylight
66.5°N
Equator 0°
12 hours daylight
Tropic of Capricorn 23.5°S
13.5 hours daylight
23.5°N
Antarctic Circle 66.5°S
24 hours daylight
0°
South Pole 90°S
6 months daylight
66.5°
23.5°S

Places between the Tropics are hot all year round. This is because the Sun's rays strike the Equator almost vertically, heating the land more intensely.

On June 21, the strongest and most direct light from the Sun is in the Northern Hemisphere. The Arctic Circle has 24 hours of daylight, and the Northern Hemisphere has its longest day.

On December 21, the direct light and heat from the Sun strike south of the Equator. This is the longest day in the Southern Hemisphere. The Northern Hemisphere has its shortest day and longest night.

Places near the poles have the coldest climates because the Sun's rays hit them at an angle. The Sun's warmth is therefore spread out over a much wider area.

# MAPPING THE WORLD

The main purpose of a map is to show, or locate, where things are. The only truly accurate map of the whole world is a globe – a round model of the Earth. But a globe is impractical to carry around, so mapmakers (cartographers) produce flat paper maps instead. Changing the globe into a flat map is not simple. Imagine cutting a globe in half and trying to flatten the two hemispheres. They would be stretched in some places, and squashed in others. In fact, it is impossible to make a map of the round Earth on flat paper without some distortion of area, distance, or direction.

## MODELS OF THE WORLD

Satellite images can show the whole world as it appears from space. However, this image shows only one half of the world, and is distorted at the edges.

A globe (right) is the only way to illustrate the shape of the Earth accurately. A globe also shows the correct positions of the continents and oceans and how large they are in relation to one another.

## LATITUDE

We can find out exactly how far north or south, east or west any place is on Earth by drawing two sets of imaginary lines around the world to make a grid. The horizontal lines on the globe below are called lines of latitude. They run from east to west. The most important is the Equator, which is given the value 0°. All other lines of latitude run parallel to the Equator. and are numbered in degrees either north or south of the Equator.

North Pole – 90°N

The value of each line of latitude increases from 0° to 90° as you move towards the North or South Poles.

90° 80°
70°
60°
50°
40°
30°
20°
10°
0° —— Equator 0°
10°
20°
30°
40°
50°
60°

South Pole – 90°S

Lines of latitude are measured from the center of the Earth. An angle is then measured from here in relation to the Equator.

One degree of latitude is approximately 70 miles.

Lines of latitude divide the world into "slices" of equal thickness on either side of the Equator.

## LONGITUDE

The vertical lines on the globe below run from north to south between the poles. They are called lines of longitude. The most important passes through Greenwich, England, and is numbered 0°. It is called the Prime Meridian. All other lines of longitude are numbered in degrees either east or west of the Prime Meridian. The line directly opposite the Prime Meridian is numbered 180°.

180°

120°
110°
100° 90° 80° 70° 60° 50° 40° 30° 20° 10° 0°
20°
10°

Prime Meridian – 0°

Lines of longitude are also measured from the center of the Earth. This time, the angle is taken in relation to the Prime Meridian.

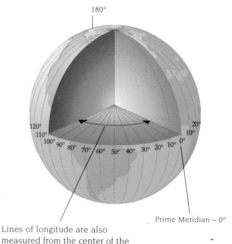

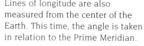

Lines of longitude divide the world into segments, like those of an orange – wide near the Equator, but narrow at the poles.

## WHERE ON EARTH?

When lines of latitude and longitude are combined on a globe, or as here, on a flat map, they form a grid. Using this grid, we can locate any place on land, or at sea, by referring to the point where its line of latitude intersects with its line of longitude. Even when a place is not located exactly where the lines cross, you can still find its approximate position.

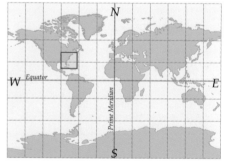

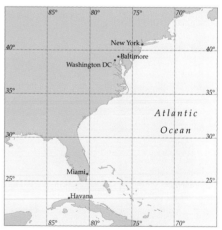

The map above is of the eastern US. It is too small to show all the lines of latitude and longitude, so they are given at intervals of 5°. Miami is located at about 26° north of the Equator and 80° west of the Prime Meridian. We write its location 26°N 80°W.

# MAKING A FLAT MAP FROM A GLOBE

**Cartographers use a technique** called projection to show the Earth's curved surface on a flat map. Many different map projections have been designed. The distortion of one feature – either area, distance, or direction – can be minimized, while other features become more distorted. Cartographers must choose which of these things it is most important to show correctly for each map that they make. Three major families of projections can be used to solve these questions.

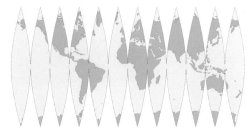

To make a globe, the Earth is divided into segments or "gores"' along lines of longitude.

## 1 CYLINDRICAL PROJECTIONS

These projections are "cylindrical" because the surface of the globe is transferred onto a surrounding cylinder. This cylinder is then cut from top to bottom and "rolled out" to give a flat map. These maps are very useful for showing the whole world.

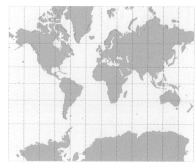

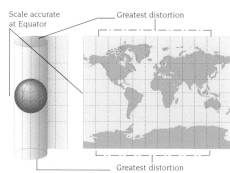

The cylinder touches the globe at the Equator. Here, the scale on the map will be exactly the same as it is on the globe. At the northern and southern edges of the cylinder, which are farthest away from the surface of the globe, the map is most distorted. The Mercator projection (*above*), created in the 16th century, is a good example of a cylindrical projection.

Scale accurate at Equator — Greatest distortion

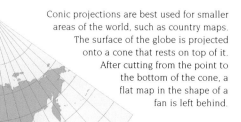

Greatest distortion

## 2 AZIMUTHAL PROJECTIONS

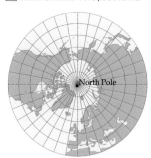

North Pole

New Delhi

Azimuthal projections put the surface of the globe onto a flat circle. "Azimuthal" means that the direction or "azimuth" of any line coming from the center point of that circle is correct. Azimuthal maps are useful for viewing hemispheres, continents, and the polar regions. Mapping any area larger than a hemisphere gives great distortion at the outer edges of the map.

Accurate scale at central point — Greatest distortion

The circle only touches the globe's surface at one central point. The scale is only accurate at this point and becomes less and less accurate the farther away the circle is from the globe. This kind of projection is good for maps centering on a major city or on one of the poles.

## 3 CONIC PROJECTIONS

Conic projections are best used for smaller areas of the world, such as country maps. The surface of the globe is projected onto a cone that rests on top of it. After cutting from the point to the bottom of the cone, a flat map in the shape of a fan is left behind.

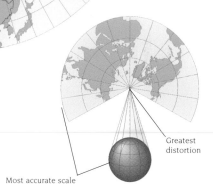

The conic projection touches the globe's surface at one latitude. This is where the scale of the map will be most accurate. The parts of the cone farthest from the globe will be the most distorted and are usually omitted from the map itself.

Greatest distortion

Most accurate scale

# PROJECTIONS USED IN THIS ATLAS

The projections that are appropriate for showing maps at a world, continental, or country scale are quite different. The projections for this atlas have been carefully chosen. They are ones that show areas as familiar shapes that are distorted as little as possible.

## 1 World Maps

**The Wagner VII** projection is used for our world maps as it shows all the countries at their correct sizes relative to one another.

## 2 Continents

**The Lambert Azimuthal Equal Area** is used for continental maps. The shape distortion is relatively small and countries retain their correct sizes relative to one another.

## 3 Countries

**The Lambert Conformal Conic** shows countries with as little distortion as possible. The angles from any point on the map are the same as they would be on the surface of the globe.

# HOW MAPS ARE MADE

New technologies have revolutionized mapmaking. Computers and information from satellites have replaced drawing boards and drafting pens, and the process of creating new maps is now far easier. But mapmaking is still a skilled and often time-consuming process. Information about the world must be gathered, sorted, and checked. The cartographer must make decisions about the function of the map and what information to select in order to make it as clear as possible.

### THE MAPPA MUNDI

Maps have been made for thousands of years. The 13th-century Mappa Mundi, meaning "known world" shows the Mediterranean Sea and the Don and Nile rivers. Asia is at the top, with Europe on the left, and Africa to the right. The oceans are shown as a ring surrounding the land. The map reflects a number of biblical stories.

## HISTORICAL MAP MAKING

This detailed hand-drawn map of the southern coast of Spain was made in about 1750. The mountains are illustrated as small hills and the labels have been hand lettered.

For centuries, maps were drawn by hand. Very early maps were no more than a pictorial representation of what the surface of the ground looked like. Where there were hills, pictures were drawn to represent them. Later maps were drawn using information gathered by survey teams. They would carefully mark out and calculate the height of the land, the positions of towns, and other geographical features. As knowledge and techniques improved, maps became more accurate.

## NEW TECHNIQUES

Computers make it easier to change map information and styles quickly. This map of the southern coast of Spain, made in 1997 has been made using digital terrain modeling (see below) and traditional cartography.

Today, cartographers have access to far more data about the Earth than in the past. Satellites collect and process information about its surface. This is called remote-sensed data. Further information may be drafted in the traditional way. Locations can be verified by GPS (Global Positioning Systems) linked to satellites. Computers are now widely used to combine different kinds of map information. Any computerized map is produced using a GIS (Geographical Information System).

## MODERN MAPMAKING

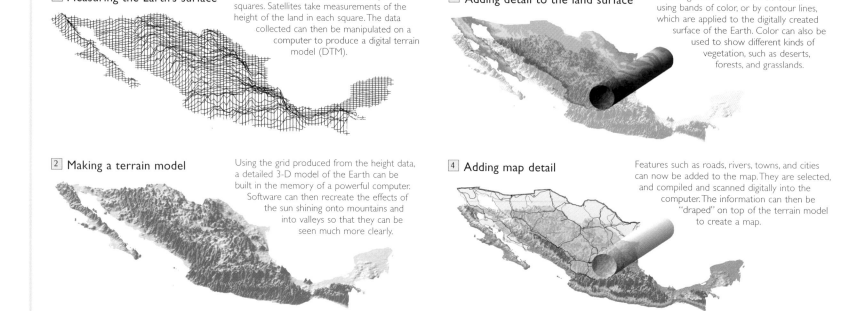

1 Measuring the Earth's surface

The surface of the Earth is divided up into squares. Satellites take measurements of the height of the land in each square. The data collected can then be manipulated on a computer to produce a digital terrain model (DTM).

2 Making a terrain model

Using the grid produced from the height data, a detailed 3-D model of the Earth can be built in the memory of a powerful computer. Software can then recreate the effects of the sun shining onto mountains and into valleys so that they can be seen much more clearly.

3 Adding detail to the land surface

The height of the land can be shown using bands of color, or by contour lines, which are applied to the digitally created surface of the Earth. Color can also be used to show different kinds of vegetation, such as deserts, forests, and grasslands.

4 Adding map detail

Features such as roads, rivers, towns, and cities can now be added to the map. They are selected, and compiled and scanned digitally into the computer. The information can then be "draped" on top of the terrain model to create a map.

## SHOWING INFORMATION ON A MAP

A map is a **selective diagram** of a place. It is the cartographer's job to decide what kind of information to show on a map. They can choose to highlight certain kinds of features – such as roads, rivers, and land height. They can also show other features such as sea depth, place names, and borders that would be impossible to see either on the ground or from a photograph. The information that can be shown on a map is influenced by a number of factors, most notably by its scale.

This is a satellite photograph of the harbor area of Rio de Janeiro in Brazil. Although you can see the bay and where most of the housing is, it is impossible to see roads or get any sense of the position of places relative to one another.

This is a map of the same area as you can see in the photograph. Much of the detail has been greatly simplified. Towns are named and marked; contours indicate the height of the land; and roads, railroads and borders between districts have been added.

## SCALE

To make a map of an area it needs to be greatly reduced in size. This is known as drawing to scale. The scale of the map shows us by how much the area has been reduced. The smaller the scale, the greater the area of land that can be shown on the map. There will be far less detail and the map will not be as accurate. The maps below show the different kinds of information that can be shown on maps of varying scales.

When using a map to work out what areas or distances are in reality, we need to refer to the scale of that particular map. Map scales can be shown in several ways.

## WAYS TO SHOW SCALE

**1** Representative fraction

One unit on the map would be equal to 1,000,0000 units on the ground.

1:1,000,000

**2** Linear scale

The line is marked off in units which represent the real distances of the map, given in both miles and kilometers.

SCALE BAR

0 km   10   20

0 miles   10   20

**3** Statement of scale

It means that 1 inch on the map represents 1 mile on the ground.

1 inch represents 1 mile

LONDON 1:21,000,000

This small-scale map shows the position of London in relation to Europe. Very little detail can be seen at this scale – only the names of countries and the largest towns.

LONDON 1:5,500,000

At a scale of 1 to 5,500,000 you can see the major road network in the southeast of the UK. Many towns are named and you can see the difference in size and status.

LONDON 1:900,000

This map is at a much larger scale. You can see the major roads that lead out from London and the names of many suburbs, places of interest, and airports.

LONDON 1:12,500

This is a street map of central London. The streets are named, as are places of interest, train and subway stations. The scale is large enough to show plenty of detail.

# READING MAPS

Maps use a unique visual language to convey a great deal of detailed information in a relatively simple form. Different features are marked out using special symbols and styles of print. These symbols are explained in the key to the map and you should always read a map alongside its key or legend. This page explains how to look for different features on the map and how to unravel the different layers of information that you can find on it.

## PHYSICAL FEATURES

All the regional and country maps in this atlas are based on a model of the Earth's surface. The computer-generated relief gives an accurate picture of the surface of the land. Colors are used to show the relative heights of the land; green is for low-lying land, and yellows, browns, and grays are for higher land. Water features like streams, rivers, and lakes are also shown.

### 1 WATER FEATURES

On this map extract, the blue lines show a number of rivers, including the Salween and the Irrawaddy. The Irrawaddy forms a huge delta, splitting into many streams as it reaches the sea.

### 2 RELIEF

These mountains are in the north of Southeast Asia. The underlying relief on the map and the colored bands help you to see the height of the land.

## HUMAN FEATURES

Maps also reveal a great deal about the human geography of an area. In addition to showing the location of towns and roads, different symbols can tell you more about the size of towns and the importance of a road. Borders between countries or regions can only be seen on a map.

## 3 BORDERS

Borders on the map are marked by a thick purple line. The boundary between Laos and Vietnam is in sparsely populated mountainous terrain, with the border generally running along a mountain range.

### KEY TO MAP SYMBOLS

**BOUNDARIES**

| | |
|---|---|
| ━━━ | Full international border |
| ┅┅┅ | Disputed border |

**COMMUNICATION FEATURES**

| | |
|---|---|
| | Major road |
| | Minor road |
| ✈ | Railroad |
| | International airport |

**DRAINAGE FEATURES**

| | |
|---|---|
| | Major river |
| | Minor river |
| ⬯ | Lake |
| ▭ | Wetland |

**LANDSCAPE FEATURES**

| | |
|---|---|
| △ | Mountain |

**POPULATED PLACES**

| | |
|---|---|
| ∘ | Less than 50,000 |
| ○ | 50,000–100,000 |
| ⊙ | 100,000–500,000 |
| ▣ | Greater than 500,000 |
| ● | Capital city |

**NAMES**

| | |
|---|---|
| **MYANMAR** | Country |
| PARACEL ISLANDS (disputed by China, Taiwan, & Vietnam) | Dependent territory |
| **JAKARTA** | Capital city |
| **Sarawak** | Cultural region |
| *Chin Hills* | Landscape feature |
| *Puncak Jaya 16,535ft* | Mountain/pass |
| *Red River* | River/lake |
| *Java Sea* | Sea feature |

## 4 SETTLEMENTS

The symbol for a settlement can tell you its position, population, and political status. Most towns are shown by a circle or a square. These represent the size of their population. Where the dot for a town is colored red, this shows that it is a capital city such as Kuala Lumpur in Malaysia.

### LAND HEIGHT / SEA DEPTH

| LAND HEIGHT | SEA DEPTH |
|---|---|
| Above 13,120ft | 0–820ft |
| 6,560–13,120ft | 820–1,640ft |
| 3,280–6,560ft | 1,640–3,280ft |
| 1,640–3,280ft | 3280–6,560ft |
| 820–1,640ft | 6,560ft–9,840ft |
| 330–820ft | 9,840–13,120ft |
| 0–330ft | Below 13,120ft |

**CITIES AND TOWNS**

| | |
|---|---|
| ▣ | Over 500,000 people |
| ⊙ | 100,000–500,000 |
| ○ | 50,000–100,000 |
| ∘ | Less than 50,000 |

## FINDING PLACES

### Alphanumeric grid references

All the maps in this book are indexed using their alphanumeric grid reference – for example, G4. To find a place you must first look up its page number and then its grid reference. Read the letters and numbers off the bottom and side of the grid. Using rulers held at right angles to one another you will find the point where the lines meet. The place will be located within this square.

### Latitude and longitude references

The lines of latitude and longitude are known as graticules. They are shown on the map as thin blue lines with the value of their latitude or longitude given as a blue number at the edge of the map.

## 5 ROADS AND RAILROADS

**a** The major road and railroad links between Hue and Nha Trang hug the Vietnamese coast. A string of coastal towns is often connected by road and rail in this manner.

Chiang Mai, in northern **b** Thailand, is linked to the capital Bangkok to the south by railroad and road. At Chiang Mai, the mountains are too high for the railroad to continue, and only roads go north into Myanmar.

# USING THE ATLAS

This Atlas has been designed to develop map-reading skills and to introduce readers to a wide range of different maps. It also provides a wealth of detailed geographic information about the world today. The Atlas is divided into four sections: **Learning Map Skills**; **The World About Us**, covering global geographic patterns; the **World Atlas**, dealing with the world's regions and an **Index-Gazetteer**.

## LEARNING MAP SKILLS

Maps show the Earth – which is three-dimensional – in just two dimensions. This section shows how maps are made; how different kinds of information are shown on maps; how to choose what to put on a map and the best way to show it. It also explains how to read the maps in this Atlas.

## THE WORLD ABOUT US

These pages contain a series of world maps that show important themes, such as physical features, climate, life zones, population, and the world economy, on a global scale. They give a worldwide picture of concepts that are explored in more detail later in the book.

Text introduces themes and concepts in each spread.

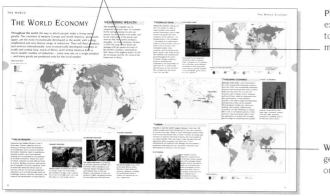

Photographs illustrate examples of places or topics shown on the main map.

World maps show geographic patterns on a global scale.

Introduction to projections: different projections and how they work.

Choosing the best projections: the map projections used in this book.

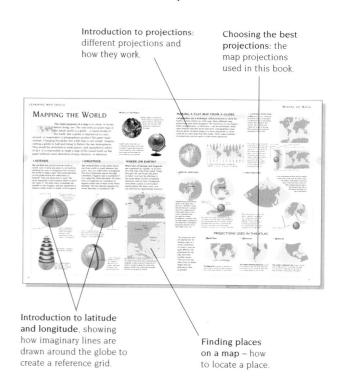

Introduction to latitude and longitude, showing how imaginary lines are drawn around the globe to create a reference grid.

Finding places on a map – how to locate a place.

## CONTINENTAL MAPS

A cross section through the continent shows the relative height of certain features.

A detailed physical map of the continent shows major natural geographic features, including mountains, lakes and rivers.

Photographs and locator maps illustrate the main geographic regions and show you where they are.

The industry map shows the main industrial towns and cities and the main industries in each continent. It also shows the wealth of each country, relative to the rest of the world.

### CONTINENTAL GEOGRAPHY PAGES

Humans have colonized and changed all the continents except Antarctica. These pages show the factors which have affected this process: climate, the availability of resources such as coal, oil and minerals, and varying patterns of land use. Mineral resources are directly linked to many industries, and most agriculture is governed both by the quality of the land and the climate.

The climate map shows the main types of climate across the continent and where the hottest and coldest, wettest and driest places are.

### CONTINENTAL PAGES

These pages show the physical shape of each continent and the impact that humans have made on the natural landscape – building towns and roads and creating borders between countries. They show where natural features such as mountain ranges and rivers have created physical boundaries, and where humans have created their own political boundaries between states.

The political map of the continent shows country boundaries and country names.

The mineral resources map shows where the most important reserves of minerals, including coal and precious metals, are found.

The land use map shows different types of land and the main kinds of farming that take place in each area.

# REGIONAL MAPS

**The main part of the Atlas** contains detailed maps of countries and regions. Each of these is accompanied by a series of small thematic maps, models, and charts, which give information about the climate, where people live, how they use the land, the different kinds of industry, and important environmental issues.

## TERRAIN MODEL

A computer-generated landscape model shows what the land really looks like. There are no roads or towns to mask the physical geography of the country or region. Mountain ranges, plains, and river basins can be easily seen.

## COLORED THUMB TAGS

Each section has its own color code.

- Learning Map Skills
- The World About Us
- Europe
- Asia
- North America
- South America
- Africa
- Australasia and Oceania
- Antarctica and the Arctic

## CLIMATE MAPS

These maps show the temperature and rainfall patterns in January and July. Colored bands indicate temperatures: blue for low temperatures, orange for high ones. Rainfall is represented by black lines with a number giving the average amount of rain. These are called isohyets.

**Isohyets** show the rainfall patterns in inches per year. The areas between the lines are either over or under the figures shown on the ishohyets.

JULY — The hottest areas are colored orange.

JANUARY

Less than 2

Here the rainfall is between 2 and 4 inches per year.

## LOCATOR GLOBE

This shows the location of the country or region both within its continent and in relation to the rest of the world.

EUROPE — Eastern Europe

NORTH AMERICA · ASIA · AFRICA · SOUTH AMERICA · AUSTRALASIA AND OCEANIA · ANTARCTICA

## MAP GRID

Each main map has a grid. Using the grid will help you to find a place on the map. Grid references are expressed as letters (running from left to right across the frame), and numbers (running from the top to the bottom of the frame), for example, A 4, G 6. Everything on the map is referenced in the **Index-Gazetteer** at the back of the book.

### EASTERN EUROPE

BELARUS, MOLDOVA, ROMANIA, UKRAINE

## REGIONAL MAPS

The main map on each regional page shows the main topographical features of the area: the height of the land, the major roads, the rivers, and lakes. It also shows the main cities and towns in the region – represented by different symbols.

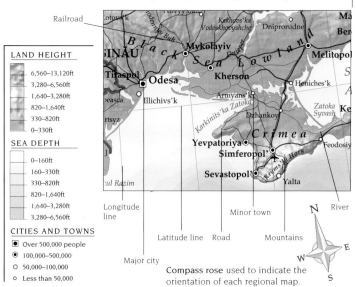

Railroad

**LAND HEIGHT**
- 6,560–13,120ft
- 3,280–6,560ft
- 1,640–3,280ft
- 820–1,640ft
- 330–820ft
- 0–330ft

**SEA DEPTH**
- 0–160ft
- 160–330ft
- 330–820ft
- 820–1,640ft
- 1,640–3,280ft
- 3,280–6,560ft

**CITIES AND TOWNS**
- ■ Over 500,000 people
- ◉ 100,000–500,000
- ○ 50,000–100,000
- ○ Less than 50,000

Longitude line

Latitude line · Road · Mountains

Major city

Minor town

River

Compass rose used to indicate the orientation of each regional map.

## THEMATIC MAPS

These small maps show various aspects of the geography of the country or region. The environment maps cover topics such as the effects of pollution. Industry, land use, and population maps locate the major industries, types of agriculture, and the distribution of population.

**Diagrams are used** to show the geographic information on the map statistically.

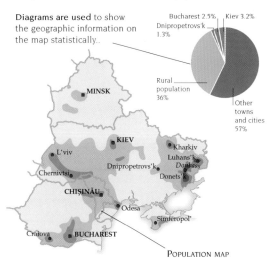

Bucharest 2.5%
Kiev 3.2%
Dnipropetrovs'k 1.3%
Rural population 36%
Other towns and cities 57%

MINSK · KIEV · L'viv · Dnipropetrovs'k · Chernivtsi · Donets'k · Luhans'k · Kharkiv · Donbass · CHIŞINĂU · Odesa · Simferopol' · Craiova · BUCHAREST

POPULATION MAP

INDUSTRY MAP

Kiev · Kharkiv · Kremenchuk · Dnipropetrovs'ke · Kryyvy Rih

LAND USE MAP

Kiev · Kharkiv · Dnipropetrovs'k · Donets'k

ENVIRONMENT MAP

Kiev · Kharkiv · Dnipropetrovs'k · Donets'k · Dnieper

# THE PHYSICAL WORLD

**This map shows** the main physical features of the world: the mountain ranges, the great rivers and lakes, deserts, grassland plains, seas, and oceans. No human settlements are named on this map – only the physical or landscape features.

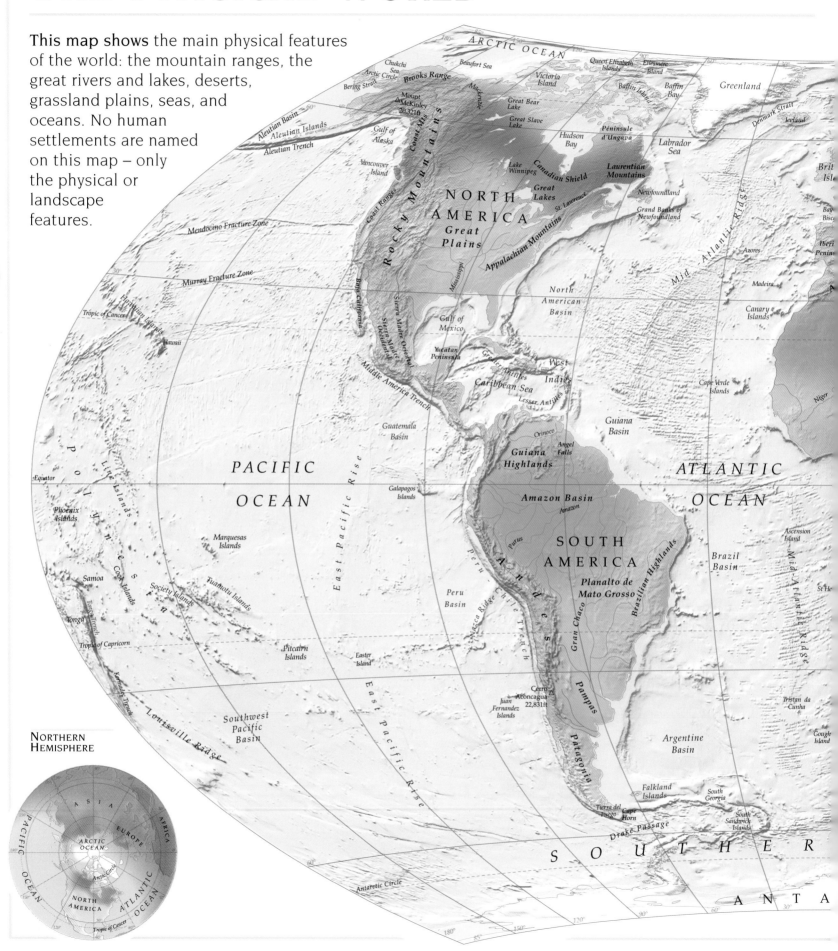

NORTHERN
HEMISPHERE

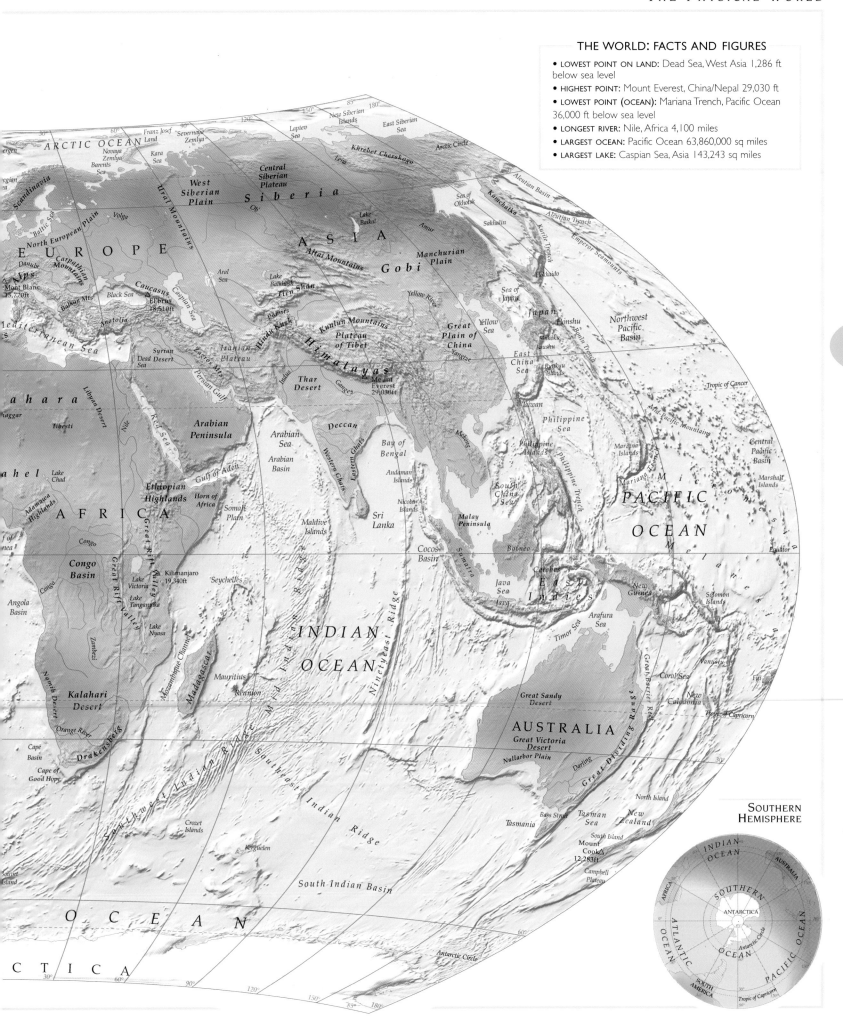

### THE WORLD: FACTS AND FIGURES

- **LOWEST POINT ON LAND:** Dead Sea, West Asia 1,286 ft below sea level
- **HIGHEST POINT:** Mount Everest, China/Nepal 29,030 ft
- **LOWEST POINT (OCEAN):** Mariana Trench, Pacific Ocean 36,000 ft below sea level
- **LONGEST RIVER:** Nile, Africa 4,100 miles
- **LARGEST OCEAN:** Pacific Ocean 63,860,000 sq miles
- **LARGEST LAKE:** Caspian Sea, Asia 143,243 sq miles

SOUTHERN
HEMISPHERE

# THE EARTH'S STRUCTURE

The shape and position of the Earth's oceans and continents make a familiar pattern. This is just the latest in a series of forms that the Earth has taken in the hundreds of millions of years since its creation. Massive forces inside the Earth cause the continents and oceans to move apart and together again, forming larger landmasses and then breaking them apart – a process known as plate tectonics. The movement is very slow – but over millions of years, the changes can be enormous.

## DYNAMIC EARTH

The heart of the Earth is a solid core of iron surrounded by several layers of very hot – sometimes liquid – rock. The crust is relatively thin and is made up of a series of "plates" that fit closely together. Movement of the molten rock deep within the mantle of the Earth causes the plates to move, creating changes in the surface features of the Earth.

### THE EARTH'S PLATES

Continental plate

Oceanic plate

Plate boundary or margin

Continental and oceanic plates are tectonic plates – made from crustal rock on which continents or oceans float

### INSIDE THE EARTH

Rocky crust

Inner core – made of iron

Outer core – liquid iron and nickel

Mantle – made from solid and molten rock

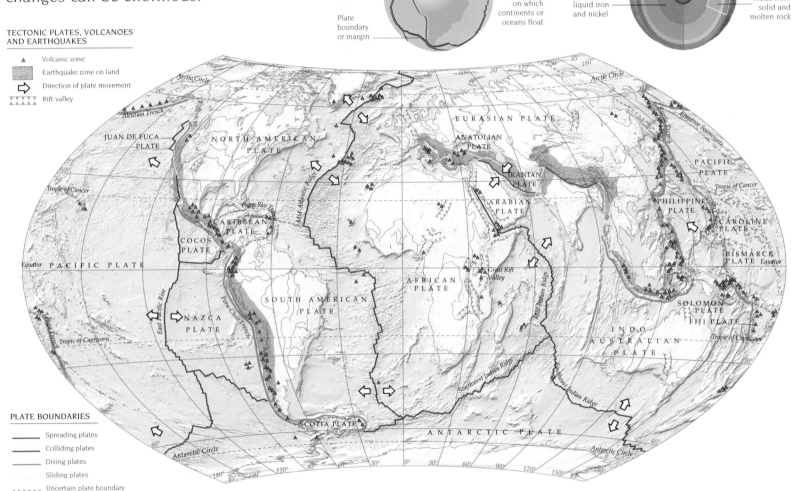

TECTONIC PLATES, VOLCANOES AND EARTHQUAKES

▲ Volcanic zone

Earthquake zone on land

⇨ Direction of plate movement

Rift valley

PLATE BOUNDARIES

Spreading plates

Colliding plates

Diving plates

Sliding plates

Uncertain plate boundary

## PLATE BOUNDARIES

The point where two plates meet is known as a plate boundary. As the Earth's plates move together or apart or slide alongside one another, the great forces that result cause great changes in the landscape. Mountains can be created, earthquakes occur, and there may be frequent volcanic eruptions.

## SPREADING PLATES

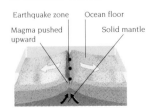

Earthquake zone

Ocean floor

Magma pushed upward

Solid mantle

As plates move apart, magma rises through the outer mantle. When it cools, it forms new crust. The Mid-Atlantic Ridge is caused by spreading plates.

## COLLIDING PLATES

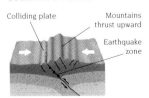

Colliding plate

Mountains thrust upward

Earthquake zone

When two plates bearing landmasses collide with one another, the land is crumpled upward into high mountain peaks such as the Alps and the Himalayas.

## DIVING PLATES

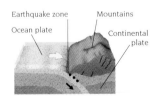

Earthquake zone

Mountains

Ocean plate

Continental plate

When an ocean-bearing plate collides with a continental plate it is forced downward under the other plate and into the mantle. Volcanoes occur along these boundaries.

## SLIDING PLATES

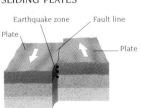

Earthquake zone

Fault line

Plate

Plate

As two plates slide past each other, great friction is set up along the fault line that lies between them. This can lead to powerful earthquakes.

## SHAPING THE LANDSCAPE

**The Earth's surface** is made from solid rock or water. The land is constantly reshaped by external forces. Water flowing as rivers or in the oceans erodes and deposits material to create valleys and lakes and to shape coastlines. When water is built up and compressed into solid sheets of ice, it can erode more deeply, creating deeper, wider valleys. Wind also has a powerful effect: stripping away vegetation and transporting rock particles vast distances.

### RIVERS

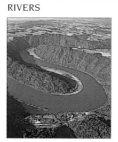

Most rivers have their sources in mountain areas. They flow fast through the mountains, eroding deep V-shaped valleys. As they reach flatter areas they begin to meander in great loops, both eroding and then depositing rock particles as they slow down.

### GLACIERS

In cold areas, close to the poles or on mountaintops, snow is built up into rivers of ice called glaciers. They move slowly, eroding deep U-shaped valleys. When the glacier melts, ridges of eroded rock called moraines are left at the sides and end of the glacier.

### SEA ACTION

The oceans change the landscape in two major ways. They batter cliffs, causing rock to break away and the land to retreat, and they carry eroded material along the coast, to make beaches and sandbars.

### WIND

Wind can erode and break down rock into smaller boulders and stones and eventually into sand. Desert sand dunes are shaped by the force of the wind and vary from ripples to hills 650 ft high.

### LANDSLIDES

Heavy rain can loosen soil and rock beneath the surface of slopes. As this moves, the top layers slip, forming heaps of rubble at the base of the slope.

## THE WORLD'S OCEANS

**Just over two-thirds of the Earth's surface** is covered by water and more than 98% of this water is contained in the oceans. Movements within the Earth shape the ocean floor in the same way they do the land surface, creating mountain ranges, trenches, and plateaus, and changing the shape and size of the oceans. The difference between an ocean and a sea is simply its size; oceans are much bigger.

### POLAR OCEANS

The Southern and Arctic Oceans contain large icebergs that have broken away from the ice shelf.

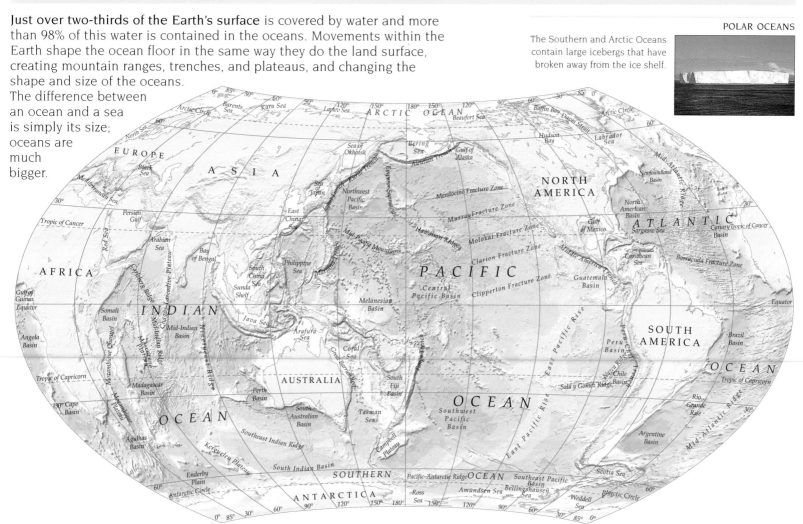

### INDIAN OCEAN

The Indian Ocean covers about 20% of the world's surface. Ocean swells, starting deep in the Southern Ocean, often cause flooding in Sri Lanka and the Maldives.

### PACIFIC OCEAN

The Pacific is the largest and deepest ocean in the world. It contains an arc of volcanic islands, including Japan, Indonesia, and New Guinea, known as the "Ring of Fire."

### ATLANTIC OCEAN

The Atlantic Ocean was formed about 180 million years ago. The land that now forms Europe and Africa pulled apart from the Americas to create an ocean 1,900 miles wide.

# CLIMATE AND LIFE ZONES

This map shows the different climates found around the world. Climates are particular combinations of temperature and humidity. Climates are affected by latitude, the height of the land, winds, and ocean currents. Climates can change, but not overnight. Weather is local and consists of short-term events such as thunderstorms, hurricanes, and blizzards.

### HURRICANES

Hurricanes are violent cyclonic windstorms, driven by heat energy gathered from tropical seas. The Caribbean islands and the east coast of the US are particularly prone to hurricanes.

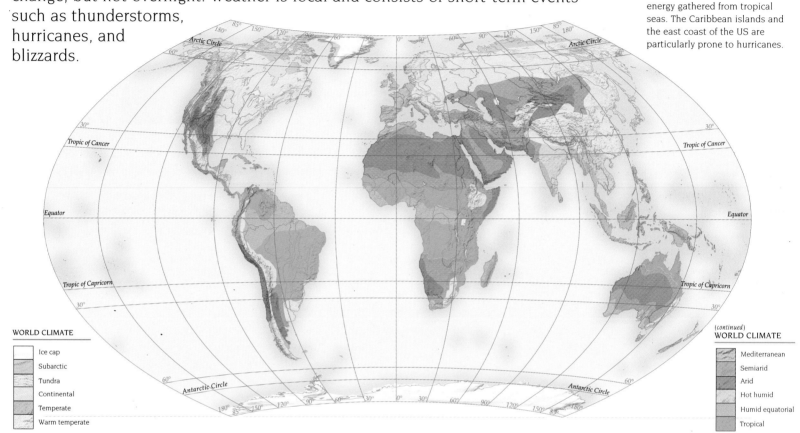

**WORLD CLIMATE**

- Ice cap
- Subarctic
- Tundra
- Continental
- Temperate
- Warm temperate

*(continued)*
**WORLD CLIMATE**

- Mediterranean
- Semiarid
- Arid
- Hot humid
- Humid equatorial
- Tropical

## WINDS

**All over the Earth** there are a series of large-scale wind patterns called prevailing winds that have a direct effect on weather and climate. The direction of the wind depends on global air pressure. Winds travel from areas of high pressure to areas of low pressure. The westerlies, polar easterlies, and northeast and southeast trade winds are all prevailing winds. The Equator is known for its light winds – referred to as the Doldrums. Changes in the direction of the prevailing winds can have a serious impact on the weather all over the planet.

**WINDS**

- Cool wind
- Warm wind

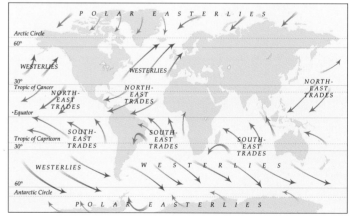

## OCEAN CURRENTS

**Ocean currents** help distribute heat around the Earth and have a great influence on climate. Convection currents circulate massive amounts of warm and cold water around the oceans. Warm water is moved away from the tropics to higher latitudes and cold water is moved toward the tropics.

**OCEAN CURRENTS AND SURFACE TEMPERATURES**

- Cold currents
- Warm currents
- El Niño

| | |
|---|---|
| | 68 – 86°F |
| | 50 – 68°F |
| | 32 – 50°F |
| | Seawater 28° – 32°F |
| | Sea ice (average) below 28°F |

# LIFE ZONES

**The map below shows** the Earth divided into different biomes – also called biogeographical regions. The combination of climate, the type of landscape, and the plants and animals that live there are used to classify a region. Similar biomes are found in very different places around the world.

## POLAR REGIONS

The North and South Poles are permanently covered by ice. Only a few plants and animals can live here.

## TUNDRA

Tundra is flat, cold, and dry, with few trees. Plants such as mosses and lichens grow close to the ground.

### DESERTS
Very little rain falls in desert areas, whether they are hot deserts such as the Sahara or cold deserts like the Gobi.

### CONIFEROUS FORESTS
Tall coniferous trees such as pine and spruce, with spines or needles instead of leaves, grow in the far north of Scandinavia, Canada, and the Russian Federation.

### BROADLEAF FORESTS
Broadleaf or deciduous forests once covered temperate regions over most of the Northern Hemisphere. They contain trees of many varieties – all of which shed their leaves every year.

### TEMPERATE RAIN FORESTS
Evergreen, broadleaved trees need a warmer, wetter climate than deciduous trees. They are known as temperate rain forests.

### MEDITERRANEAN
Close to the shores of the Mediterranean Sea, the vegetation consists mainly of herbs, shrubs, and drought-resistant trees.

## BIOME TYPES

- Mountains
- Polar regions
- Tundra
- Tropical rain forests
- Dry woodlands
- Savanna
- Temperate grasslands

*(continued)*
## BIOME TYPES

- Mediterranean
- Coniferous forests
- Temperate rain forests
- Broadleaf forests
- Cold deserts
- Hot deserts
- Wetlands

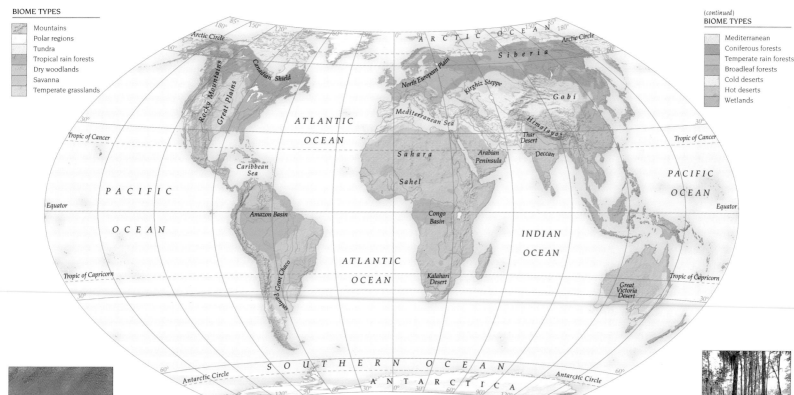

### TEMPERATE GRASSLANDS
Grasslands cover the central areas of the continents. They are known in the middle latitudes as prairies, steppe, and pampas.

### SAVANNA
The savanna consists of woodland interspersed with grassland. These regions lie between the tropical rain forest and hot desert regions.

### DRY WOODLANDS
Dry woodlands are found at the edge of grasslands. They contain small trees and shrubs adapted to dry conditions.

### TROPICAL RAIN FORESTS
Around the Equator, where temperatures are high and there is plenty of rain, tropical rain forests flourish. Trees grow continuously and are tall with huge, broad leaves.

### WETLANDS
Low-lying swamps and marshes are known as wetlands. They are often home to a rich variety of animal, plant, and bird species.

# WORLD POPULATION

*Favelas* – or shanty towns – have grown up many South American cities because of overcrowding.

**There are now nearly six billion people** on Earth. The population has increased to more than three times that of 1900. Before that date, the number of people increased slowly because people were born and died at similar rates. With improved living conditions, better medical care, and more efficient food production, more people survived to adulthood, and the population began to grow much faster. If growth continues at the present rate, the world's population is likely to reach 8.5 billion by the year 2020.

## POPULATION STRUCTURES

**Measuring the numbers** of old and young people gives the age structure of a country or continent. If there are large numbers of young people and a high birthrate, the population is said to be youthful – as is the case in many African, Asian, and South American countries. If the birthrate is low but many people survive into old age, the population distribution is said to be aging – this is true of much of Europe, Japan, Canada, and the US. Extreme events like wars can distort the population, leading to a loss of population in certain age groups.

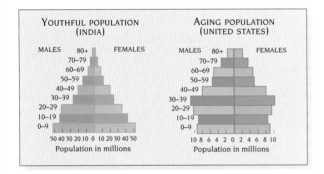

YOUTHFUL POPULATION (INDIA)

MALES — 80+ — FEMALES
70–79
60–69
50–59
40–49
30–39
20–29
10–19
0–9
50 40 30 20 10 0  0 10 20 30 40 50
Population in millions

AGING POPULATION (UNITED STATES)

MALES — 80+ — FEMALES
70–79
60–69
50–59
40–49
30–39
20–29
10–19
0–9
10 8 6 4 2 0  2 4 6 8 10
Population in millions

## POPULATION DENSITY

**The main map** (*center*) and the map below both show population density – the number of people who live in a given area. The map below shows the average population density per country. You can see that European countries and parts of Asia are very densely populated. The large map shows where people actually live. While the average population density in Brazil and Egypt is quite low, the coasts of Brazil and the areas close to the Nile River in Egypt are very densely populated.

### DENSE POPULATION

Huge crowds near the Haora Bridge in Calcutta, India – one of the world's most densely populated cities.

POPULATION DENSITY

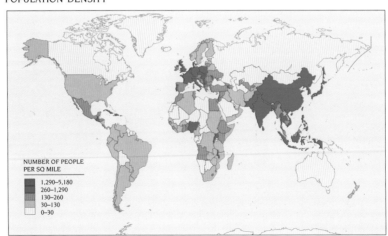

NUMBER OF PEOPLE PER SQ MILE

1,290–5,180
260–1,290
130–260
30–130
0–30

### SPARSE POPULATION

The cold north of Canada has one of the lowest population densities in the world. Some people live in extreme isolation, separated from others by lakes and forests.

## URBAN GROWTH

The 20th century has seen a huge increase in the number of people living in urban areas. This has led to more large cities and the development of some "super cities" such as Mexico City and Tokyo, each with more than 20 million people. In 1900, only about 10% of the population lived in cities. Now it is closer to 50% and soon the figure may be nearer two in three people. Some continents are far more "urbanized" than others: in South America nearly 80% of people live in cities, whereas in Africa the figure is only about 30%.

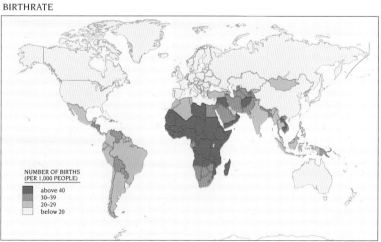

POPULATION DENSITY
(People per sq mile)

- Below 3
- 3–13
- 13–29
- 30–51
- 52–130
- 131–260
- 261–520
- Above 520

## LEVELS OF URBANIZATION

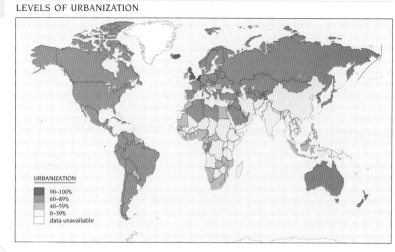

URBANIZATION
- 90–100%
- 60–89%
- 40–59%
- 0–39%
- data unavailable

## POPULATION GROWTH

The rate of population growth varies dramatically between the continents. Europe has a large population but it is increasing slowly. Africa is still sparsely populated, but in some countries such as Kenya, the population is growing very rapidly, increasing pressure on the land. China and India have the world's largest populations. Both countries now have laws designed to curb the birthrate.

### CONTROLLING GROWTH

In 1980, fewer than 25% of women in less-developed countries used birth control. Education programs and more widely available contraceptives are thought to have doubled this figure. But many families still have no access to contraception.

### AN AGING POPULATION

In some countries, a low birthrate and an increasingly long-lived elderly population have greatly increased the ratio of old people to younger people, putting a strain on health and social services. For example, in Japan, most people can now expect to live to at least 80 years of age.

## BIRTHRATE

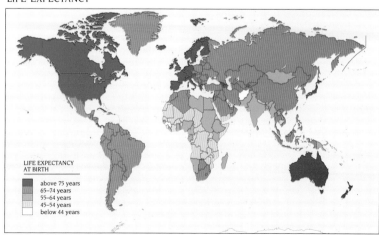

NUMBER OF BIRTHS
(PER 1,000 PEOPLE)
- above 40
- 30–39
- 20–29
- below 20

## LIFE EXPECTANCY

LIFE EXPECTANCY
AT BIRTH
- above 75 years
- 65–74 years
- 55–64 years
- 45–54 years
- below 44 years

# THE WORLD ECONOMY

Throughout the world, the way in which people make a living varies greatly. The countries of western Europe and North America, along with Japan, are the most economically developed in the world, with a long-established and very diverse range of industries. They sell their products and services internationally. Less economically developed countries in south and central Asia, much of Africa, and Central America have a much smaller number of industries – some may rely on a single product – and many goods are produced only for the local market.

## MEASURING WEALTH

The wealth of a country can be measured in several ways: for example, by the average annual income per person; by the volume of its trade; and by the total value of the goods and services that the country produces annually – its Gross Domestic Product or GDP. The map below shows the average GDP per person for each of the world's countries, expressed in $US. Most of the highest levels of GDP are in Europe and the US; most of the lowest are in Africa.

WORLD ECONOMIES

Average GDP per capita (in $US)

- Above 5,000
- 2,000–5,000
- 600–2,000
- Below 600
- Data unavailable

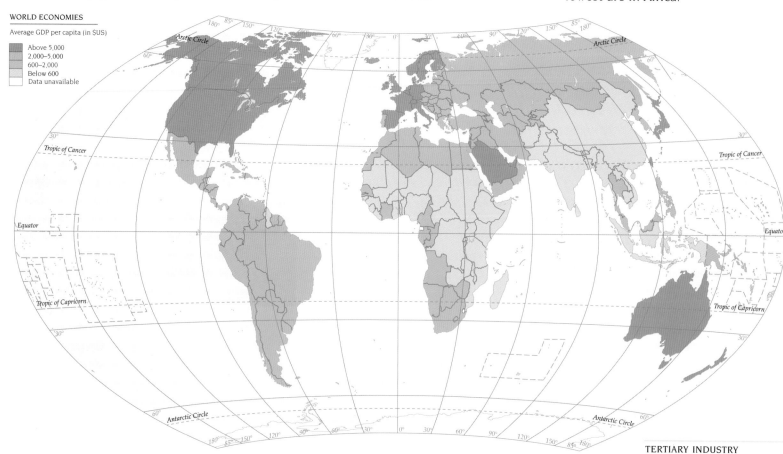

## TYPES OF INDUSTRY

Industries are usually defined in one of three ways. Primary industries such as farming or mining involve the production of raw materials such as food or minerals. Secondary industries make or manufacture finished products out of raw materials: clothing and car manufacture are examples of secondary industries. People who work in tertiary industries provide different kinds of services. Banking, insurance, and tourism are all examples of tertiary industries. Some economically advanced nations such as Germany and the US now have quaternary industries, such as biotechnology which are knowledge-creation industries, devoted to the research and development of new products.

### PRIMARY INDUSTRY

Tobacco leaves are picked and laid out for drying in Cuba, one of the world's great producers of cigars. Many countries rely on one or two high-value "cash crops" like tobacco to earn foreign currency.

### SECONDARY INDUSTRY

This skilled Thai weaver is producing an intricately patterned silk fabric on a hand loom. Fabric manufacture is an important industry throughout South and Southeast Asia. In India and Pakistan, vast quantities of cotton are produced in highly mechanized factories, but many fabrics are still hand woven.

### TERTIARY INDUSTRY

The City of London is one of the world's great finance centers. Branches of many banks and insurance companies, including the world-famous Lloyds of London, are clustered into the City's "square mile."

## PATTERNS OF TRADE

Almost all countries trade goods with one another in order to obtain products they cannot produce themselves, and to make money from goods they have produced. Some countries – for example those in the Caribbean – rely mainly on a single export, usually a food or mineral, and can suffer a loss of income when world prices drop. Other countries, such as Germany and Japan, export a vast range of both raw materials and manufactured goods throughout the world. A number of huge companies, known as multinational corporations, are responsible for more than 70% of world trade, with divisions all over the world. They include firms like Exxon, Coca Cola, and IBM.

### CONTAINER SHIPS

Many products are transported around the world on container ships. Containers are of a standard size so that they can be efficiently transported to their destinations. Some ships are specially designed to carry perishable goods such as fruit and vegetables.

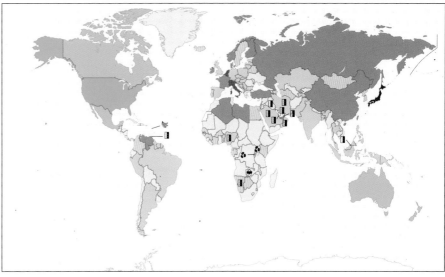

BALANCE OF TRADE (MILLIONS $US)

| | Surplus | | Deficit | |
|---|---|---|---|---|
| ■ | Over 30,000 | | 1,000–9,999 | 0–999 |
| ■ | 10,000–29,000 | | 0–999 | 1,000–9,999 |
| | | | 10,000–29,999 | Below 30,000 | Data unavailable |

COUNTRIES RELIANT ON ONE EXPORT

oil/petroleum    coffee
bananas    copper

## DEVELOPING ECONOMIES

Although world trade is still dominated by the more economically developed countries, since the 1970s, less economically developed countries have increased their share of world trade from less than 10% to nearly 20%. Countries such as Brazil, Mexico, Malaysia, and South Korea, aided by investment from their governments or from wealthier countries, were able to begin manufacturing and exporting a wide variety of goods. These products include cars, electronics, clothing, and footwear. Multinational companies can take advantage of cheaper labor costs to manufacture goods in these countries. Moves are being made to limit the exploitation of workers who are paid very low wages for producing luxury goods.

### ASIAN "TIGER" ECONOMIES

The economies of Malaysia, Taiwan, and South Korea boomed in the late 1980s, attracting investment for buildings such as the Petronas Towers (*above*).

## TOURISM

Tourism is now the world's largest industry. More than 500 million people travel both abroad and in their own countries as tourists each year. People in more developed countries have more money and leisure time to travel. Tourism can bring large amounts of cash into the local economy, but local people do not always benefit. They may have to take low-paid jobs and experience great intrusions into their lives. Tourist development and pollution may damage the environment – sometimes destroying the very attractions that led to the development of tourism in the first place.

### ECOTOURISM

These tourists are being introduced to a giant tortoise, one of the many unique animals found in the Galapagos Islands. A number of places with special animals and ecosystems have introduced programs to teach visitors about them. This not only educates people about the need to safeguard these environments, but brings in money to help protect them.

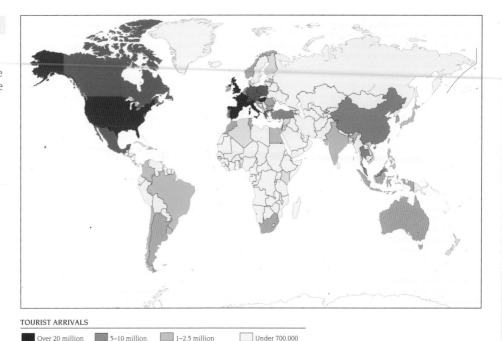

TOURIST ARRIVALS

| | | |
|---|---|---|
| Over 20 million | 5–10 million | 1–2.5 million | Under 700,000 |
| 10–20 million | 2.5–5 million | 700,000–1 million | Data unavailable |

# BORDERS AND BOUNDARIES

There are more countries in the world today than ever before – over 190 – whereas in 1950, there were only 82. Since then, many former European colonies and Soviet states have become independent. The establishment of borders for each of these countries has often been the subject of disagreement.

## Military borders
At the end of wars, new borders are often drawn up between the countries – frequently along cease-fire lines. They may remain there for many years. At the end of the Korean War in 1953, North and South Korea were divided close to the 38° line of latitude. This border has remained heavily fortified.

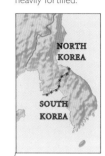

## The longest border
The border between the US and Canada is the longest continuous border in the world. It cuts through the center of the Great Lakes. West of the Great Lakes, the border runs along the 49° line of latitude.

## Enclaves
If part of a country's territory has become separated from the rest of the country, and is surrounded by foreign territory, it is called an enclave. Kaliningrad is part of the Russian Federation, but is cut off from it by Lithuania and Belarus.

## River borders
Over one-sixth of the world's national borders are formed by rivers. Long stretches of the Danube River form natural borders in southeastern Europe.

ARCTIC OCEAN

EUROPE ASIA

NORTH AMERICA

ATLANTIC OCEAN

PACIFIC OCEAN

AFRICA

PACIFIC OCEAN

SOUTH AMERICA

ATLANTIC OCEAN

INDIAN OCEAN

AUSTRALASIA AND OCEANIA

## Mountain borders
Mountain ranges such as the Pyrenees, Alps, and Himalayas form natural borders between many countries. In the Andes, border disputes between Chile and Argentina centered on finding the highest point in the mountain range that divided them.

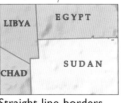

## Straight line borders
The borders of many countries in Africa and other former colonial territories are straight lines. This was the simplest solution for colonial administrators, who often knew little of the country's geography or population.

## Lake boundaries
Countries that lie next to lakes usually place their borders in the middle of the lake. Complicated agreements between colonial powers led to the awkward division of Lake Nyasa in Africa.

## Territorial disputes
There are still many disputed territories and borders. One of the most serious territorial disputes is between India and Pakistan, over Jammu and Kashmir, which has led to three wars since 1947.

# THE ATLAS
## OF THE
# WORLD

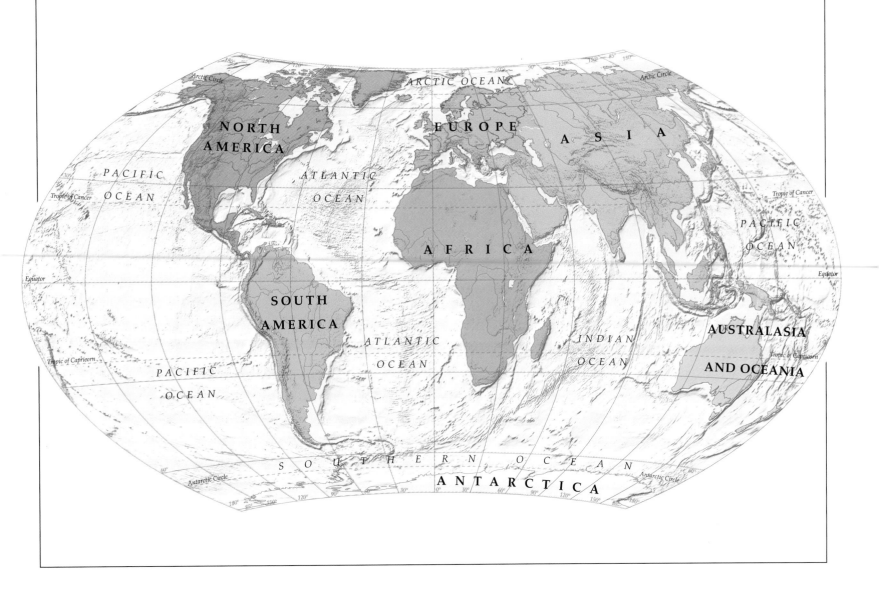

ARCTIC OCEAN

Arctic Circle

NORTH
AMERICA

EUROPE

A S I A

PACIFIC
OCEAN

ATLANTIC
OCEAN

Tropic of Cancer

Tropic of Cancer

PACIFIC
OCEAN

AFRICA

Equator

Equator

SOUTH
AMERICA

ATLANTIC
OCEAN

INDIAN
OCEAN

AUSTRALASIA

Tropic of Capricorn

Tropic of Capricorn

PACIFIC
OCEAN

AND OCEANIA

S O U T H E R N    O C E A N

Antarctic Circle

Antarctic Circle

ANTARCTICA

# THE NATIONS OF THE WORLD

**The world is divided** into 192 independent countries and about 60 overseas territories or dependencies. The largest country is the Russian Federation covering 6,592,000 sq miles; the smallest is Vatican City in Rome, with an area of 0.17 sq miles.

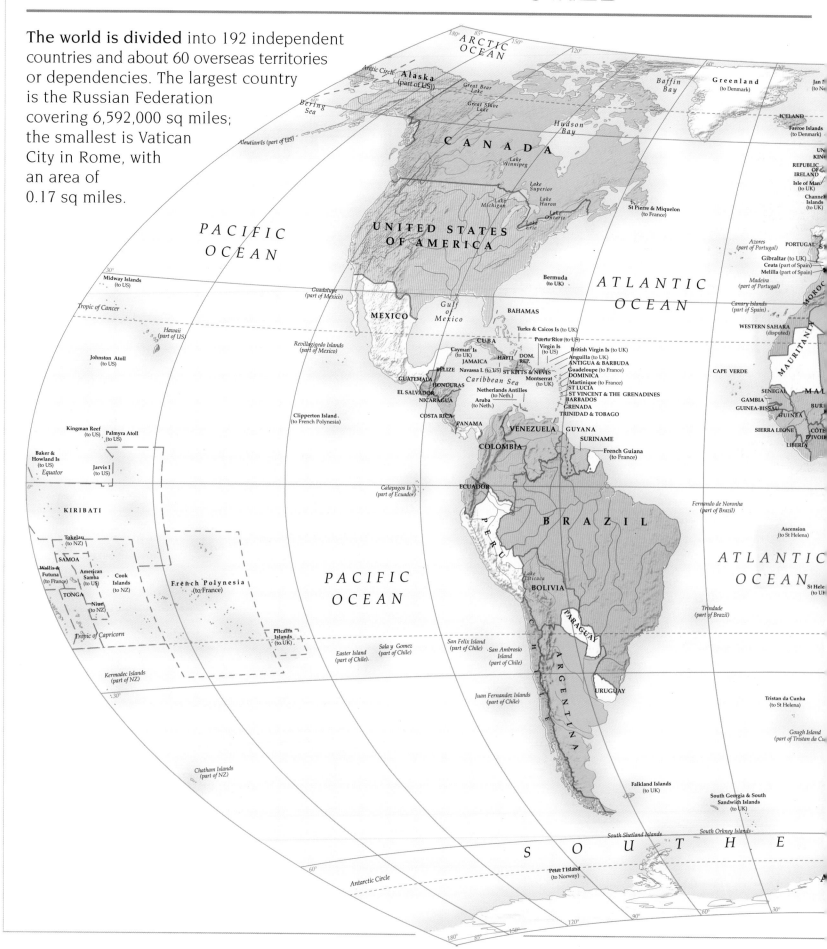

ARCTIC OCEAN

Arctic Circle
Alaska (part of US)
Great Bear Lake
Great Slave Lake
Hudson Bay
Baffin Bay
Greenland (to Denmark)
Jan M (to Ne
ICELAND
Faeroe Islands (to Denmark)

Bering Sea
Aleutian Is (part of US)

C A N A D A
Lake Winnipeg
Lake Superior
Lake Michigan
Lake Huron
Lake Ontario
Lake Erie

PACIFIC OCEAN

UNITED STATES OF AMERICA

St Pierre & Miquelon (to France)

UN KING
REPUBLIC OF IRELAND
Isle of Man (to UK)
Channel Islands (to UK)

Midway Islands (to US)
Tropic of Cancer
Guadalupe (part of Mexico)

Bermuda (to UK)

ATLANTIC OCEAN

Azores (part of Portugal)
PORTUGAL S
Gibraltar (to UK)
Ceuta (part of Spain)
Melilla (part of Spain)
Madeira (part of Portugal)

MOROC

Hawaii (part of US)

MEXICO
Gulf of Mexico
BAHAMAS

Canary Islands (part of Spain)

Johnston Atoll (to US)

Revillagigedo Islands (part of Mexico)

Turks & Caicos Is (to UK)
Puerto Rico (to US)
CUBA
Cayman Is (to UK)
JAMAICA
HAITI DOM. REP.
Virgin Is (to US)
British Virgin Is (to UK)
Anguilla (to UK)
ANTIGUA & BARBUDA
Guadeloupe (to France)
DOMINICA
Montserrat (to UK)
Martinique (to France)
ST LUCIA
ST VINCENT & THE GRENADINES
BARBADOS
GRENADA
TRINIDAD & TOBAGO

WESTERN SAHARA (disputed)

MAURITANIA

CAPE VERDE

BELIZE Navassa I. (to US) ST KITTS & NEVIS
GUATEMALA
HONDURAS
EL SALVADOR
NICARAGUA
Netherlands Antilles (to Neth.)
Aruba (to Neth.)

MAL

SENEGAL
GAMBIA
GUINEA-BISSAU
GUINEA
BUR

Clipperton Island (to French Polynesia)

COSTA RICA
PANAMA

SIERRA LEONE
CÔTE D'IVOIR
LIBERIA

VENEZUELA GUYANA
SURINAME
COLOMBIA
French Guiana (to France)

Kingman Reef (to US) Palmyra Atoll (to US)

Baker & Howland Is (to US)
Jarvis I (to US)
Equator

Galapagos Is (part of Ecuador)
ECUADOR

Fernando de Noronha (part of Brazil)

Ascension (to St Helena)

KIRIBATI

B R A Z I L

ATLANTIC OCEAN

Tokelau (to NZ)

P E R U

SAMOA
Wallis & Futuna (to France)
American Samba (to US)
Cook Islands (to NZ)
French Polynesia (to France)
TONGA
Niue (to NZ)

PACIFIC OCEAN

Lake Titicaca
BOLIVIA

St Hele (to UK)

Trindade (part of Brazil)

Pitcairn Islands (to UK)

PARAGUAY

C H I L E
A R G E N T I N A

Tropic of Capricorn
Sala y Gomez (part of Chile)
San Felix Island (part of Chile)
San Ambrosio Island (part of Chile)

URUGUAY

Easter Island (part of Chile)

Kermadec Islands (part of NZ)

Juan Fernandez Islands (part of Chile)

Tristan da Cunha (to St Helena)

Gough Island (part of Tristan da C

Chatham Islands (part of NZ)

Falkland Islands (to UK)

South Georgia & South Sandwich Islands (to UK)

S O U T H E

South Shetland Islands
South Orkney Islands

A

Antarctic Circle
Peter I Island (to Norway)

26

# CONTINENTAL NORTH AMERICA

**North America is the world's** third largest continent, stretching from icy Greenland to the tropical Caribbean. The first people came from Asia more than 20,000 years ago. Their descendants spread across the continent, ate fish, meat, and wild and cultivated plants, and developed a wide variety of cultures and languages. About 500 years ago, immigrants from Europe, Africa, and Asia began to arrive in North America, bringing their own languages and cultures to the "New World."

4,600 miles

3,540 miles

## CROSS SECTION THROUGH NORTH AMERICA

Rocky Mountains · Great Plains · Great Lakes · Appalachian Mountains

W — 3,200 miles — E

The land rises from the Pacific Ocean to the Rocky Mountains. Farther east, the continent flattens into the Great Plains and the freshwater Great Lakes – gouged out by glaciers at the end of the last Ice Age. The Appalachian Mountains are older than the Rockies, and are very worn down.

## PHYSICAL NORTH AMERICA

**The high peaks of the Rocky Mountains** of Canada and the US tower above the lower mountains of the western coasts. These ranges stretch from the icy north of Alaska, south to Mexico and Central America. The heart of the continent is flatter, and much of it is drained by the mighty Mississippi-Missouri river system.

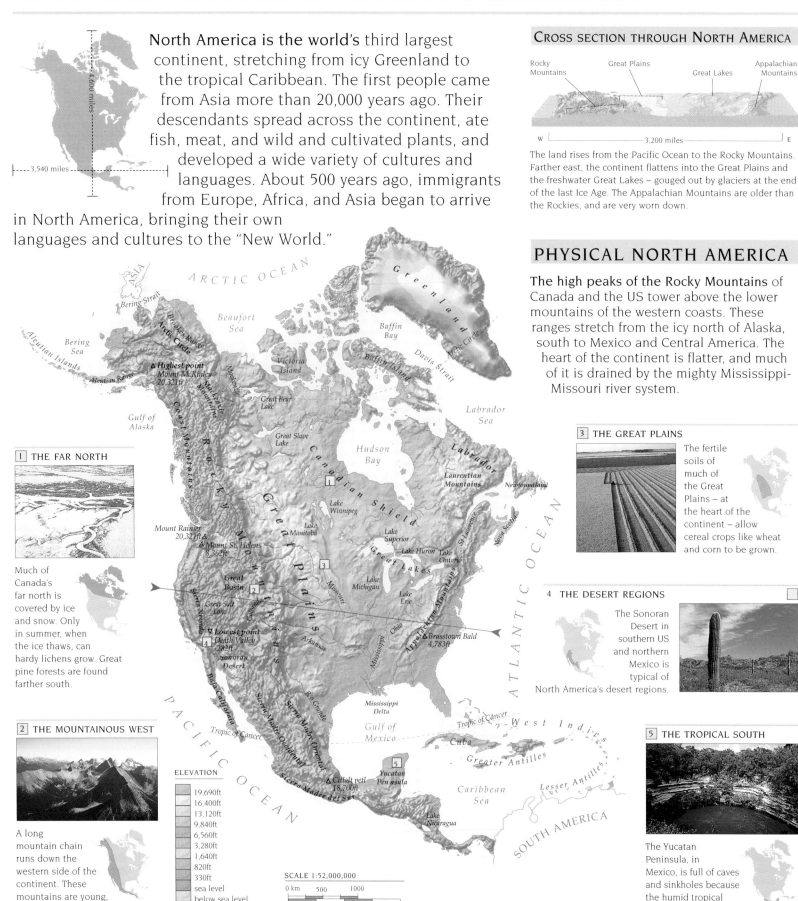

### 1 THE FAR NORTH

Much of Canada's far north is covered by ice and snow. Only in summer, when the ice thaws, can hardy lichens grow. Great pine forests are found farther south.

### 2 THE MOUNTAINOUS WEST

A long mountain chain runs down the western side of the continent. These mountains are young, and are still being formed.

### 3 THE GREAT PLAINS

The fertile soils of much of the Great Plains – at the heart of the continent – allow cereal crops like wheat and corn to be grown.

### 4 THE DESERT REGIONS

The Sonoran Desert in southern US and northern Mexico is typical of North America's desert regions.

### 5 THE TROPICAL SOUTH

The Yucatan Peninsula, in Mexico, is full of caves and sinkholes because the humid tropical climate accelerates erosion.

ASIA · ARCTIC OCEAN · Greenland · Bering Strait · Beaufort Sea · Baffin Bay · Arctic Circle · Brooks Range · Arctic Circle · Aleutian Islands · Bering Sea · △ Highest point Mount McKinley 20,321ft · Victoria Island · Baffin Island · Davis Strait · Aleutian Range · Mackenzie Mountains · Mackenzie · Great Bear Lake · Labrador Sea · Gulf of Alaska · Coast Mountains · Great Slave Lake · Hudson Bay · Labrador · Laurentian Mountains · Newfoundland · Rocky Mountains · Canadian Shield · Lake Winnipeg · Mount Rainier 20,321ft △ · Lake Manitoba · Lake Superior · St. Lawrence · Nova Scotia · △ Mount St. Helens 8,362ft · Great Lakes · Lake Huron · Lake Ontario · Great Basin · Sierra Nevada · Missouri · Lake Michigan · Lake Erie · Great Salt Lake · Colorado · ▽ Lowest point Death Valley -282ft · Arkansas · Ohio · Appalachian Mountains · △ Brasstown Bald 4,783ft · Sonoran Desert · Mississippi · ATLANTIC OCEAN · Baja California · Rio Grande · Sierra Madre Occidental · Mississippi Delta · Gulf of Mexico · Tropic of Cancer · West Indies · PACIFIC OCEAN · Tropic of Cancer · Cuba · Greater Antilles · Lesser Antilles · Sierra Madre Oriental · △ Citlaltpetl 18,700ft · Yucatan Peninsula · Caribbean Sea · Sierra Madre del Sur · Lake Nicaragua · SOUTH AMERICA

**ELEVATION**

19,690ft
16,400ft
13,120ft
9,840ft
6,560ft
3,280ft
1,640ft
820ft
330ft
sea level
below sea level
cross section

**SCALE 1:52,000,000**

0 km — 500 — 1000

0 miles 250 — 500 — 750 — 1000

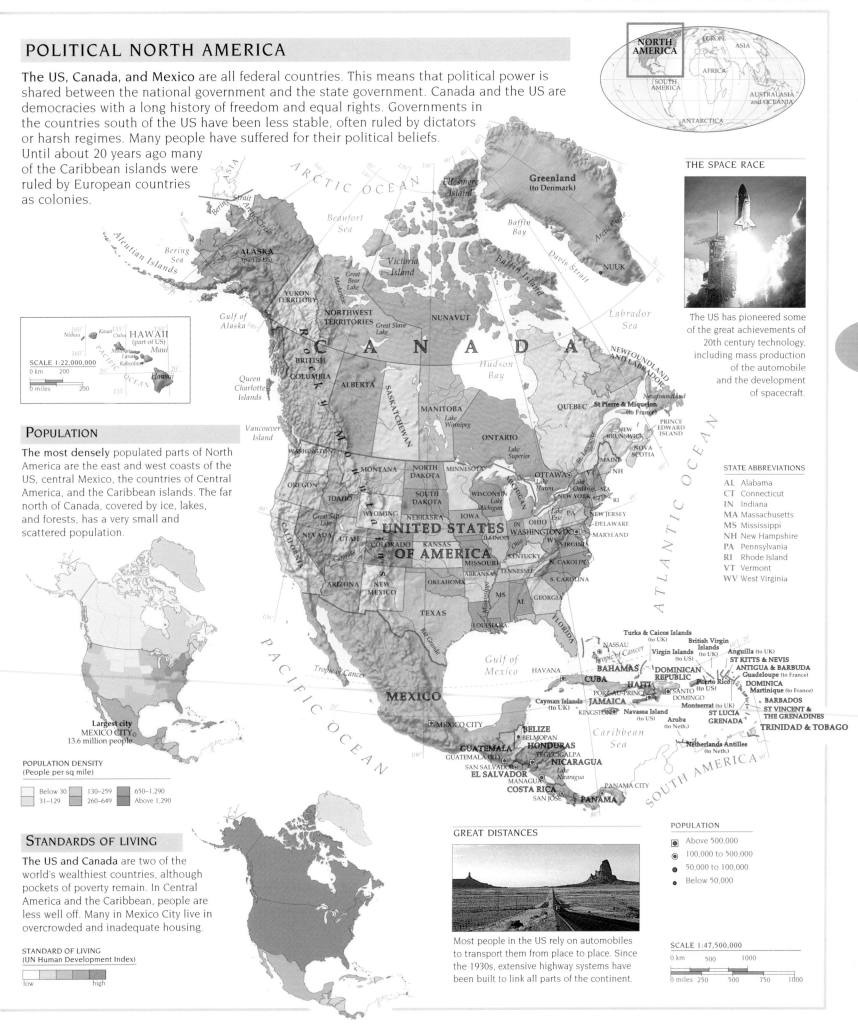

# POLITICAL NORTH AMERICA

**The US, Canada, and Mexico** are all federal countries. This means that political power is shared between the national government and the state government. Canada and the US are democracies with a long history of freedom and equal rights. Governments in the countries south of the US have been less stable, often ruled by dictators or harsh regimes. Many people have suffered for their political beliefs. Until about 20 years ago many of the Caribbean islands were ruled by European countries as colonies.

## THE SPACE RACE

The US has pioneered some of the great achievements of 20th century technology, including mass production of the automobile and the development of spacecraft.

## POPULATION

**The most densely** populated parts of North America are the east and west coasts of the US, central Mexico, the countries of Central America, and the Caribbean islands. The far north of Canada, covered by ice, lakes, and forests, has a very small and scattered population.

Largest city
MEXICO CITY
13.6 million people

POPULATION DENSITY
(People per sq mile)

| | | |
|---|---|---|
| Below 30 | 130–259 | 650–1,290 |
| 31–129 | 260–649 | Above 1,290 |

## STANDARDS OF LIVING

**The US and Canada** are two of the world's wealthiest countries, although pockets of poverty remain. In Central America and the Caribbean, people are less well off. Many in Mexico City live in overcrowded and inadequate housing.

STANDARD OF LIVING
(UN Human Development Index)

low          high

## GREAT DISTANCES

Most people in the US rely on automobiles to transport them from place to place. Since the 1930s, extensive highway systems have been built to link all parts of the continent.

STATE ABBREVIATIONS

AL  Alabama
CT  Connecticut
IN  Indiana
MA  Massachusetts
MS  Mississippi
NH  New Hampshire
PA  Pennsylvania
RI  Rhode Island
VT  Vermont
WV  West Virginia

POPULATION

◉ Above 500,000
◎ 100,000 to 500,000
● 50,000 to 100,000
• Below 50,000

SCALE 1:47,500,000

0 km   500   1000
0 miles  250  500  750  1000

SCALE 1:22,000,000
0 km       200
0 miles       200

# NORTH AMERICAN GEOGRAPHY

**Canada and the US are among** the world's wealthiest countries. They have rich natural resources, good farmland, and thriving, varied industries. The range of different industries in Mexico is growing, but other Central American countries and the Caribbean islands rely on one or two important cash crops and tourism for most of their incomes. They have a lower standard of living than the US and Canada.

## MINERAL RESOURCES

**North America still has** large amounts of mineral resources. Canada has important nickel reserves, Mexico is renowned for its silver, and bauxite – used to make aluminum – is found in Jamaica. Oil and gas are plentiful, particularly in the Arctic northwest by the Beaufort Sea, and farther south by the Gulf of Mexico.

MINERAL RESOURCES
Bauxite
Copper
Iron
Nickel
Phosphates
Uranium
Silver
Oil/gas field
Coal field

## INDUSTRY

**The US and Canada** have an extremely wide range of industries, from mining and the processing of farm produce, to heavy and light manufacturing and service industries like banking. A variety of goods are produced, including airplanes, cars, and computers. Oil exports and machine assembly are Mexico's main industries. In Central America and the Caribbean nations, most industry is based on agricultural produce.

ARCTIC OCEAN
ASIA
Greenland
(to Denmark)
Bering Sea
Beaufort Sea
Baffin Bay
US
Labrador Sea
Gulf of Alaska
CANADA
Hudson Bay
INDUSTRY
Aerospace
Brewing
Car/vehicle manufacturing
Chemicals
Coal
Defense
Engineering
Film industry
Finance
Food processing
High-tech industry
Iron and steel
Oil and gas
Pharmaceuticals
Printing and publishing
Research and development
Shipbuilding
Textiles
Timber processing
GNP per capita (US$)
Below 1,999
2,000-4,999
5,000-9,999
10,000-19,999
20,000-24,999
Above 25,000
Industrial center
Vancouver
Calgary
Seattle
Winnipeg
Portland
PACIFIC OCEAN
Montréal
Toronto
Minneapolis
Boston
Buffalo
UNITED STATES OF AMERICA
Detroit
New York
Chicago
Cleveland
Pittsburgh
Philadelphia
Baltimore
San Francisco
Denver
Kansas City
Saint Louis
Los Angeles
San Diego
Tulsa
Phoenix
Birmingham
Atlanta
ATLANTIC OCEAN
Dallas
El Paso
Ciudad Juarez
Houston
New Orleans
Tampa
Miami
Gulf of Mexico
DOMINICAN REPUBLIC
Monterrey
BAHAMAS
Havana
Puerto Rico
(to US)
West Indies
San Juan
CUBA
HAITI
Port-au-Prince
Santo Domingo
MEXICO
Guadalajara
JAMAICA
Mexico City
Puebla
Caribbean Sea
TRINIDAD & TOBAGO
Port-of-Spain
BELIZE
GUATEMALA
HONDURAS
Guatemala City
San Salvador
NICARAGUA
Managua
EL SALVADOR
COSTA RICA
San José
Panama City
PANAMA
SOUTH AMERICA

### TIMBER PROCESSING

Huge tracts of forest are found across the north of the continent; over 40% of Canada is covered by forest. Timber is processed to make paper in cities such as Portland and Vancouver.

### HIGH-TECH INDUSTRY

The Santa Clara Valley, just south of San Francisco, is also known as Silicon Valley because of the number of firms producing computer hardware and software and microelectronics that have set up in the area.

### FOOD PROCESSING

Jamaica has been famous for its rum since the 16th century. Syrup is extracted from sugarcane, which is then fermented to make rum.

### MANUFACTURING

Mexico has many car assembly plants, like this Volkswagen plant. Labor costs in Mexico are low, making it cheap to assemble cars here.

## CLIMATE

Much of northern Canada lies within the Arctic Circle and is permanently covered by ice or the sparse vegetation known as tundra. Southern Canada and much of central US have a continental climate, with hot summers and cold winters. The southern parts of the US, Central America, and the Caribbean have a hot, humid tropical climate. The islands and the eastern and central states of the US often experience hurricane-force winds, waterspouts, and tornadoes.

**EXTREME WEATHER EVENTS**

Symbols indicate climatic extremes

Coldest place
NORTHICE (Greenland)
Temp. -87°F

Wettest place
HENDERSON LAKE (BC, Canada)
Annual rainfall 262 in

Hottest place
DEATH VALLEY (CA, USA)
Temp. 135°F

Driest place
BATAQUES (Mexico)
Annual rainfall 1.2 in

**CLIMATE**

- Ice cap
- Tundra
- Subarctic
- Cool continental
- Warm temperate
- Mediterranean
- Semiarid
- Arid
- Humid equatorial
- Tropical
- Hot humid

NORTH AMERICA

### NORTH AMERICA'S HOTTEST PLACE

Death Valley in California is the hottest and driest place in the US. Strong, dry winds sweep through the valley, constantly reshaping the sand and salt deposits that cover its floor.

## LAND USE AND AGRICULTURE

On the Great Plains of Canada and the US, vast quantities of cereal crops, including corn and wheat, grow in the fertile soils. Cattle are also raised on great ranches throughout these regions and on the foothills of the Rocky Mountains. In California, vegetables and fruits are grown with the aid of irrigation. Bananas, coffee, and sugarcane are grown for export in Central America and the Caribbean, while sorghum and corn are grown as subsistence crops.

### BANANA PLANTATION

Banana plantations are common in the Caribbean and Central America. The fruit is grown for local consumption and for export to the US and Europe, where they are valued for their flavor and nutritional qualities.

### FISHING

The Grand Banks off the eastern coast of Canada were once home to almost limitless fish stocks. Overfishing has reduced the number of fish to very low levels. Quotas limiting the numbers of fish caught help the numbers to rise.

**LAND USE AND AGRICULTURE**

- Cattle
- Poultry
- Pigs
- Reindeer
- Sheep
- Bananas
- Cereals
- Citrus fruits
- Coffee
- Corn
- Cotton
- Fishing
- Fruit
- Peanuts
- Rice
- Shellfish
- Soybeans
- Sugarcane
- Timber
- Tobacco
- Vineyards
- Cropland
- Desert
- Forest
- Ice cap
- Mountain region
- Pasture
- Tundra
- Wetland
- Major conurbation

# WESTERN CANADA

ALBERTA, BRITISH COLUMBIA, MANITOBA, NORTHWEST
TERRITORIES, NUNAVUT, SASKATCHEWAN, YUKON TERRITORY

**The first inhabitants** of Canada's western provinces
were Native Americans. By the late 1800s, the Canadian
Pacific Railroad was completed and European settlers
moved west, turning most of the prairie into huge grain
farms. North of the prairies lie the vast, empty territories
that have significant Native American populations.
In 1999, part of the Northwest Territories, known as
Nunavut, became a self-governing Inuit homeland.

## FARMING AND LAND USE

**More than** 20% of the world's wheat is
grown in Canada's prairie provinces:
Manitoba, Alberta, and
Saskatchewan. Beef cattle
graze on the ranches
of Alberta and British
Columbia. Fruits,
especially apples,
flourish in the sheltered
southern valleys of British
Columbia, and Pacific
salmon, and herring are
caught off the west coast.

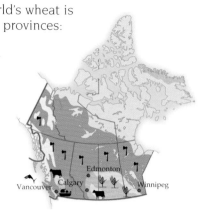

### LAND USE

Pasture 5%
Cropland 4%
Forest 38%
Other (including mountains) 53%

### FARMING AND LAND USE

- Cattle
- Fishing
- Cereals
- Fruit
- Timber
- Major conurbation

- Pasture
- Cropland
- Forest
- Mountain region
- Barren
- Tundra

## INDUSTRY

**The major industries** in the prairie provinces
are related to agriculture, such as meat-
processing in Manitoba. Alberta has
huge reserves of fossil fuels, and the
other provinces are rich in minerals,
including zinc, nickel, silver, and
uranium. British Columbia's
economy depends on
manufacturing, especially
automobiles, chemicals, and
machinery, along
with paper and
timber industries.

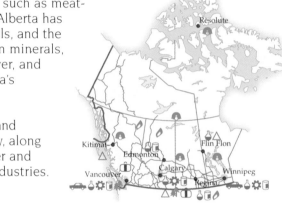

Resolute
Kitimat
Edmonton
Flin Flon
Vancouver
Calgary
Winnipeg
Regina

### STRUCTURE OF INDUSTRY (Canada)

Primary 3%
Services 66%
Manufacturing 31%

### INDUSTRY

- Car manufacturing
- Chemicals
- Engineering
- Food processing
- Metal refining
- Oil and gas
- Mining
- Timber processing
- Tourism
- Major industrial center / area
- Major road

## THE LANDSCAPE

**The prairie provinces** are mostly flat. Occasionally, the
level plains are broken up by river valleys such as that
of the Qu'Appelle in Saskatchewan. In the west, the
jagged peaks and steep passes of the Rocky Mountains
are covered in snow for months on end. West of the
Rockies, the land descends sharply toward the coast of
British Columbia. The far north is covered by dense
forests and many glacial lakes.

### The Arctic

Most of Canada's northern
islands are within of the
Arctic Circle. They are
covered by ice year-round.

**Mount Logan** (B 5)
Mount Logan is Canada's
tallest peak. It rises 19,551 ft.

### Glacial lakes

The plains are
covered by
thousands of
lakes, many of
which are vast.
They are the
remains of great
glacial lakes left
after the last
Ice Age.

## ENVIRONMENTAL ISSUES

**Across the north of the region**, the ground is permanently
frozen. This is called permafrost. Building on this frozen
surface is very difficult, because the heat from houses or
roads can cause the ground to melt, and subside.
Many of the extensive forests in
British Columbia are used for
commercial lumbering. The
province produces more than
half of Canada's timber.

### ENVIRONMENTAL ISSUES

- Lumbering activity
- Permafrost zone
- Major industrial center

Vancouver
Winnipeg

### Islands and inlets (C 6, C 7)

The British Columbia coast is peppered
with islands and fjordlike inlets, created
by the force of the Pacific Ocean.

### River valleys

Prairie river valleys such as the Qu'Appelle (F 7)
(meaning "who calls") were cut by glacial
meltwater thousands of years ago.

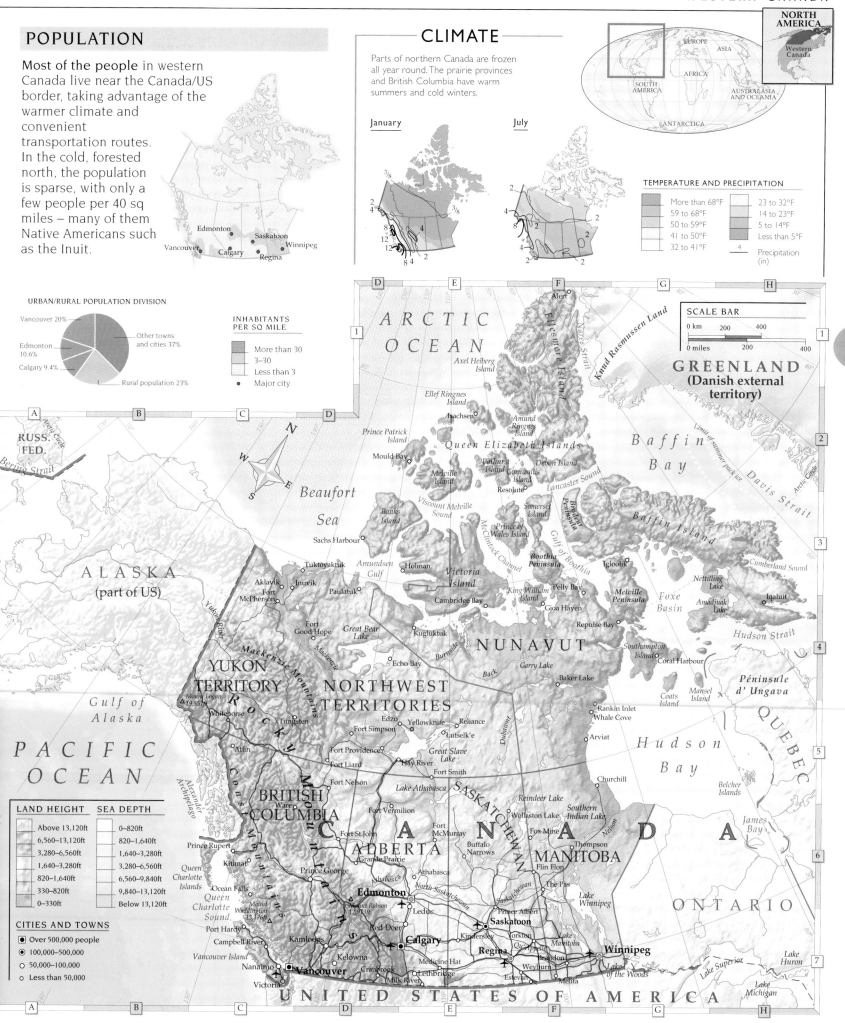

## POPULATION

**Most of the people** in western Canada live near the Canada/US border, taking advantage of the warmer climate and convenient transportation routes. In the cold, forested north, the population is sparse, with only a few people per 40 sq miles – many of them Native Americans such as the Inuit.

Edmonton
Saskatoon
Winnipeg
Vancouver
Calgary
Regina

URBAN/RURAL POPULATION DIVISION

Vancouver 20%
Other towns and cities 37%
Edmonton 10.6%
Calgary 9.4%
Rural population 23%

INHABITANTS PER SQ MILE

More than 30
3–30
Less than 3
● Major city

## CLIMATE

Parts of northern Canada are frozen all year round. The prairie provinces and British Columbia have warm summers and cold winters.

January

July

TEMPERATURE AND PRECIPITATION

More than 68°F
59 to 68°F
50 to 59°F
41 to 50°F
32 to 41°F

23 to 32°F
14 to 23°F
5 to 14°F
Less than 5°F
4 Precipitation (in)

NORTH AMERICA
Western Canada

EUROPE
ASIA
AFRICA
SOUTH AMERICA
AUSTRALASIA AND OCEANIA
ANTARCTICA

SCALE BAR
0 km    200    400
0 miles    200    400

RUSS. FED.
Bering Strait
Arctic Circle

ALASKA
(part of US)

PACIFIC OCEAN

Gulf of Alaska

ARCTIC OCEAN

Beaufort Sea

Axel Heiberg Island
Ellesmere Island
Alert
Knud Rasmussen Land
Nares Strait
Limit of summer pack ice
Baffin Bay
Davis Strait
Arctic Circle

GREENLAND
(Danish external territory)

Ellef Ringnes Island
Isachsen
Amund Ringnes Island
Prince Patrick Island
Queen Elizabeth Islands
Mould Bay
Bathurst Island
Cornwallis Island
Devon Island
Resolute
Lancaster Sound
Somerset Island
Boothia Peninsula
Brodeur Peninsula
Baffin Island
Nettilling Lake
Cumberland Sound
Iqaluit

Banks Island
Viscount Melville Sound
Melville Island
Prince of Wales Island
McClintock Channel
King William Island
Gulf of Boothia
Igloolik
Melville Peninsula
Foxe Basin
Amadjuak Lake

Sachs Harbour
Tuktoyaktuk
Amundsen Gulf
Holman
Victoria Island
Pelly Bay
Gjoa Haven
Repulse Bay
Southampton Island
Coral Harbour
Hudson Strait
Péninsule d' Ungava

Aklavik
Inuvik
Fort McPherson
Paulatuk
Cambridge Bay
Kugluktuk

Yukon River
Fort Good Hope
Great Bear Lake
Echo Bay
Burnside
Back
Garry Lake
Baker Lake
Coats Island
Mansel Island

Mackenzie Mountains
Mackenzie
NUNAVUT

YUKON TERRITORY
Mount Logan 19,551ft
Whitehorse
Tungsten
Atlin

NORTHWEST TERRITORIES
Edzo
Yellowknife
Reliance
Dubawnt
Rankin Inlet
Whale Cove
Arviat

Fort Simpson
Lutselk'e
Great Slave Lake
HUDSON BAY

QUEBEC

Fort Providence
Fort Liard
Hay River
Fort Smith
Churchill

Fort Nelson
Lake Athabasca
SASKATCHEWAN
Reindeer Lake
Southern Indian Lake
Wollaston Lake
Fox Mine
Nelson

BRITISH COLUMBIA
Ware
Fort St. John
Fort McMurray
Buffalo Narrows
Flin Flon
Thompson

Prince Rupert
Kitimat
ALBERTA
Grande Prairie
Athabasca
North Saskatchewan
CANADA
MANITOBA

Queen Charlotte Islands
Prince George
Athabasca
Edmonton
Leduc
Saskatchewan
The Pas
Lake Winnipeg

ONTARIO
James Bay
Belcher Islands

Ocean Falls
Mount Robson 12,913ft
Red Deer
Prince Albert
Saskatoon
Lake Manitoba

Queen Charlotte Sound
Mount Waddington 13,176ft
Port Hardy
Campbell River
Kamloops
Kelowna
Calgary
Kindersley
Yorkton
Qu'Appelle
Regina
Brandon
Winnipeg
Lake of the Woods
Lake Superior
Lake Huron

Vancouver Island
Nanaimo
Vancouver
Victoria
Cranbrook
Lethbridge
Medicine Hat
Milk River
Weyburn
Estevan
Melita
Lake Michigan

Alexander Archipelago
Coast Mountains
Rocky Mountains

UNITED STATES OF AMERICA

LAND HEIGHT
Above 13,120ft
6,560–13,120ft
3,280–6,560ft
1,640–3,280ft
820–1,640ft
330–820ft
0–330ft

SEA DEPTH
0–820ft
820–1,640ft
1,640–3,280ft
3,280–6,560ft
6,560–9,840ft
9,840–13,120ft
Below 13,120ft

CITIES AND TOWNS
◙ Over 500,000 people
◉ 100,000–500,000
○ 50,000–100,000
○ Less than 50,000

33

# EASTERN CANADA

NEW BRUNSWICK, NEWFOUNDLAND AND LABRADOR,
NOVA SCOTIA, ONTARIO, PRINCE EDWARD ISLAND, QUEBEC

**The first towns** built by European settlers grew up in the maritime provinces, close to the rich fishing grounds of the Atlantic Ocean. In recent years, people have migrated to cities along the St. Lawrence River and near the Great Lakes. Although most Canadians speak English, people in Quebec speak mainly French and have sought independence from the rest of Canada.

## INDUSTRY

**In the maritime provinces** the traditional fishing industry has declined, causing unemployment. However, Newfoundland has a thriving food processing industry. Ontario and Quebec have a wide range of industries, including the generation of hydroelectricity, mining, and chemicals, car manufacturing and fruit canning in the great cities. Large amounts of wood pulp and paper are also produced.

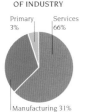

STRUCTURE OF INDUSTRY

Primary 3%
Services 66%
Manufacturing 31%

INDUSTRY

| | | | |
|---|---|---|---|
| 🚗 | Car manufacturing | 🛠 | Timber processing |
| | Chemicals | 💻 | High-tech industry |
| | Fish processing | | Tourism |
| | Food processing | | Major industrial center / area |
| | Hydroelectric power | | |
| △ | Metal refining | — | Major road |
| | Mining | | |

## FARMING AND LAND USE

The best farmland lies on the flat, fertile plains close to the St. Lawrence River and on the strip of land between Lake Erie and Lake Ontario. It is used to grow fruits such as grapes, cherries, and peaches, and to raise cattle. Nova Scotia has fruit farms, and the rich red soils of Prince Edward Island produce a big potato crop. The vast forests that grow across the north are a major source of timber.

LAND USE

Pasture 2%    Cropland 2%
Other (including mountains) 32%
Forest 64%

FARMING AND LAND USE

| | | | |
|---|---|---|---|
| 🐄 | Cattle | | Pasture |
| 🐟 | Fishing | | Cropland |
| 🦞 | Fruit | | Forest |
| ☘ | Potatoes | | Tundra |
| 🌲 | Timber | ● | Major conurbation |

## ENVIRONMENTAL ISSUES

**Acid rain** caused by emissions from factories in the US and along the St. Lawrence River destroys forests and kills marine life. Several huge new hydroelectric power projects are planned for James Bay on Hudson Bay, which will flood huge areas of land. Overfishing in the Atlantic has led to limits being set on the number of fish that can be caught.

ENVIRONMENTAL ISSUES

| | |
|---|---|
| 🐟 | Depleted fish stocks |
| | Major dam |
| ☠ | Urban air pollution |
| | Affected by acid rain |
| ● | Major industrial center |

## THE LANDSCAPE

**A huge, ancient mass of rock** called the Canadian Shield lies beneath much of eastern Canada. It is covered by low hills, rocky outcrops, thousands of lakes, and huge areas of forest. Much of the Canadian Shield is permanently frozen. The St. Lawrence River flows out of Lake Ontario and into the Atlantic Ocean. It is surrounded by rolling hills and flat areas of very fertile farmland.

### Scoured by ice
About 20,000 years ago, Labrador and northern Quebec were completely covered by ice. The glaciers scraped hollows in the rock beneath. When the ice melted, lakes were left in the hollows that remained.

### Lake Superior (B 5)
Lake Superior is the largest freshwater lake in the world. It covers an area of 32,150 sq miles and lies between Canada and the USA.

### St. Lawrence River (E 5)
The St. Lawrence River is 2,350 miles long. Parts of it have become silted up, causing it to be braided into many different channels. Between December and mid-April the river freezes over.

### Highlands
The highlands of New Brunswick, Nova Scotia, and Newfoundland are the most northerly part of the Appalachian mountain chain.

### The Bay of Fundy (F 5)
This bay has the world's highest tides. It is shaped like a funnel, and as the Atlantic flows into it, the ever narrowing shores cause the water level to rise 20–50 ft at every high tide.

NORTH
AMERICA

Eastern
Canada

## POPULATION

Colonists from both France and Britain settled in Canada from the early 1600s onward. Ontario and the maritime provinces are English speaking. Quebec is the center of French settlement; 75% of the people there have French as a first language. Most people in eastern Canada now live in large towns and cities close to the St. Lawrence River.

Thunder Bay
St. John's
Québec
**OTTAWA** Montréal
Toronto Halifax
Windsor London

URBAN/RURAL POPULATION DIVISION

Toronto 20.2%
Montréal 16%
Ottawa 4.8%
Rural population 24%
Other towns and cities 35%

INHABITANTS PER SQ MILE
More than 260   ■ Capital city
130–260   ● Major city
3–130
Less than 3

## CLIMATE

Winters are very cold, but warm winds from the Gulf of Mexico can bring hot summers to southern Ontario and the areas bordering the St. Lawrence River.

January
July

TEMPERATURE AND PRECIPITATION
More than 68°F
59 to 68°F
50 to 59°F
41 to 50°F
32 to 41°F
23 to 32°F
5 to 23°F
-13 to 5°F
Less than -13°F
—4— Precipitation (in)

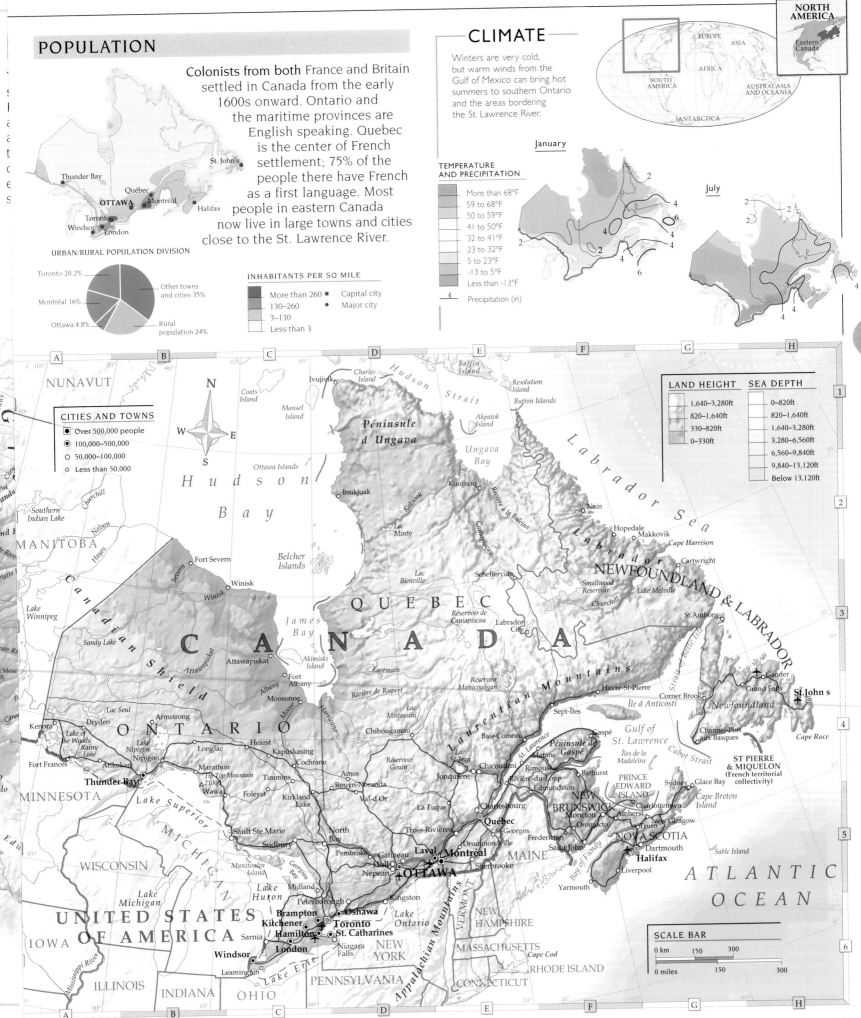

CITIES AND TOWNS
● Over 500,000 people
◉ 100,000–500,000
○ 50,000–100,000
○ Less than 50,000

LAND HEIGHT    SEA DEPTH
1,640–3,280ft    0–820ft
820–1,640ft      820–1,640ft
330–820ft        1,640–3,280ft
0–330ft          3,280–6,560ft
                 6,560–9,840ft
                 9,840–13,120ft
                 Below 13,120ft

SCALE BAR
0 km    150    300
0 miles    150    300

# UNITED STATES OF AMERICA

**From a sparsely populated** "unknown" territory in the 16th century, the US has built on its natural strengths – immense tracts of fertile land and great mineral resources – to become the world's most powerful nation. Its global success was fueled by a hardworking immigrant population, exploiting their land of opportunity and sustained by the ideals of liberty and democracy that continue to bind the American people.

## WASHINGTON DC

Washington DC is the administrative capital of the US. All national government is based here, centered on the White House, an 18th-century building on Pennsylvania Avenue that is the official residence of the US president. Congress, composed of the Senate and the House of Representatives, meets in the Capitol.

## THE FIFTY STATES

**The US is a federation** of 50 states. Following the 1776 Revolutionary War, 13 former colonies formed the core of the new nation. Expansion continued southward and westward, aided by the Louisiana Purchase in 1803, which added former French lands to the Union. By 1867, with the purchase of Alaska, the modern shape of the US was nearly complete. Alaska and Hawaii were admitted as states in 1959.

ARCTIC OCEAN
RUSSIAN FEDERATION
ALASKA
Anchorage
CANADA
Juneau
PACIFIC OCEAN
SCALE 1:54,000,000
0 km 600
0 miles 600

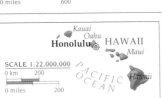

Kauai
Oahu
Honolulu ⊙ HAWAII
Maui
SCALE 1:22,000,000
0 km 200
0 miles 200
PACIFIC OCEAN
Hawaii

CANADA
PACIFIC OCEAN
Seattle
Olympia
WASHINGTON
Spokane
Portland
Salem
Eugene
OREGON
MONTANA
Helena
NORTH DAKOTA
Bismarck
Boise
IDAHO
SOUTH DAKOTA
Pierre
Sioux Falls
WYOMING
Reno
NEVADA
Sacramento
Carson City
Concord
San Francisco
Stockton
San Jose
Fresno
CALIFORNIA
Bakersfield
Salt Lake City
UTAH
Cheyenne
UNITED STATES
Denver
COLORADO
Colorado Springs
Pueblo
NEBRASKA
Oma
Lincol
KANSA
Wich
Las Vegas
Simi Valley
Los Angeles
Long Beach
Riverside
San Diego
ARIZONA
Phoenix
Tucson
Santa Fe
Albuquerque
NEW MEXICO
Amarillo
Oklaho
City
OKLAHOM
Lubbock
Dalla
Fort Worth
El Paso
TEXAS
Austin
San Antonio
Corpus
Christi
MEXICO
Rocky Mountains

## NEW YORK

The first skyscrapers in New York were built at the beginning of the 20th century. The intricate Manhattan skyline has become a symbol of US urban culture throughout the world.

## STARS AND STRIPES

The 13 stripes of the US flag represent the 13 colonies that formed the first states of the Union. Each star symbolizes one of the current states; as states are admitted to the union, the number of stars increases.

## ANCIENT CIVILIZATIONS

Evidence of some of the oldest cultures in the US can still be found in the Southwest. Peoples such as the Hopi and Hohokam farmed and built settlements (pueblos) here.

NORTH AMERICA
Eastern Canada

## POPULATION

Colonists from both France and Britain settled in Canada from the early 1600s onward. Ontario and the maritime provinces are English speaking. Quebec is the center of French settlement; 75% of the people there have French as a first language. Most people in eastern Canada now live in large towns and cities close to the St. Lawrence River.

Thunder Bay · St. John's · Québec · **OTTAWA** · Montréal · Halifax · Toronto · Windsor · London

URBAN/RURAL POPULATION DIVISION

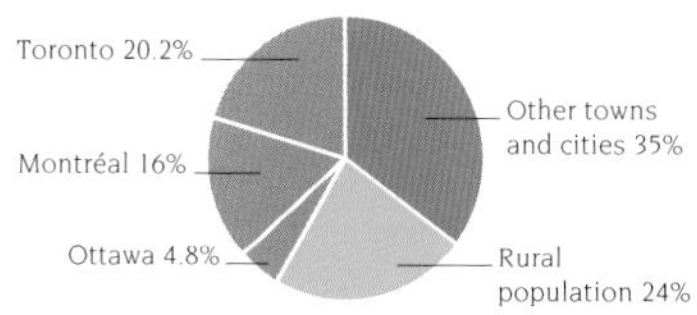

Toronto 20.2% · Montréal 16% · Ottawa 4.8% · Other towns and cities 35% · Rural population 24%

INHABITANTS PER SQ MILE
- More than 260
- 130–260
- 3–130
- Less than 3
- ■ Capital city
- ● Major city

## CLIMATE

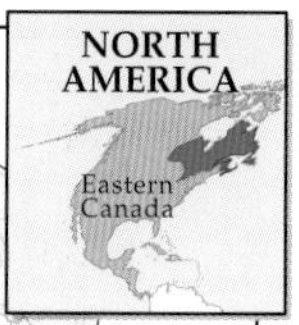

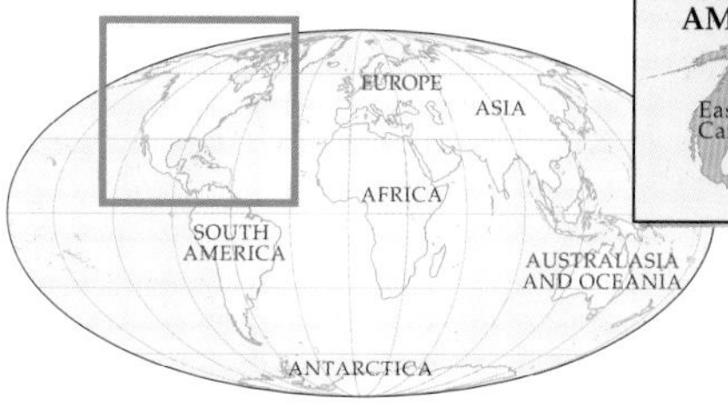

Winters are very cold, but warm winds from the Gulf of Mexico can bring hot summers to southern Ontario and the areas bordering the St. Lawrence River.

TEMPERATURE AND PRECIPITATION
- More than 68°F
- 59 to 68°F
- 50 to 59°F
- 41 to 50°F
- 32 to 41°F
- 23 to 32°F
- 5 to 23°F
- -13 to 5°F
- Less than -13°F
- 4 Precipitation (in)

January · July

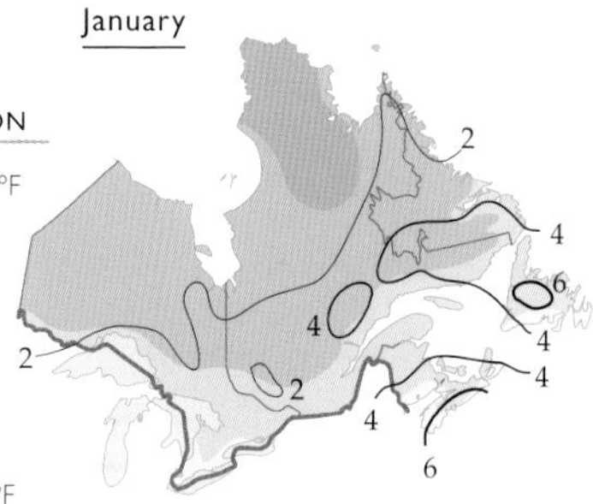

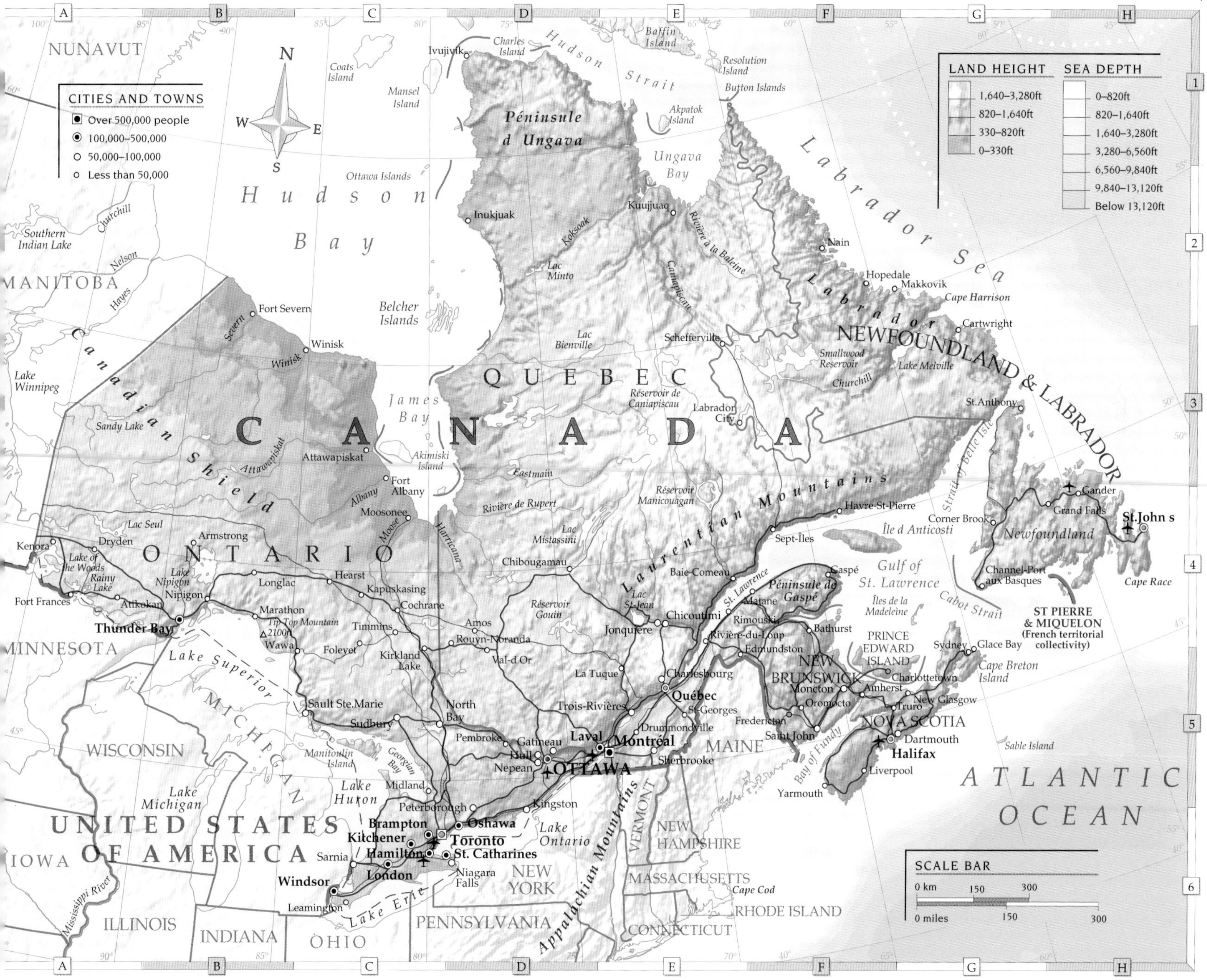

CITIES AND TOWNS
- Over 500,000 people
- 100,000–500,000
- 50,000–100,000
- Less than 50,000

LAND HEIGHT
- 1,640–3,280ft
- 820–1,640ft
- 330–820ft
- 0–330ft

SEA DEPTH
- 0–820ft
- 820–1,640ft
- 1,640–3,280ft
- 3,280–6,560ft
- 6,560–9,840ft
- 9,840–13,120ft
- Below 13,120ft

SCALE BAR
0 km 150 300
0 miles 150 300

(Map of Eastern Canada showing provinces NUNAVUT, MANITOBA, ONTARIO, QUEBEC, NEWFOUNDLAND & LABRADOR, NEW BRUNSWICK, NOVA SCOTIA, PRINCE EDWARD ISLAND, United States, Hudson Bay, James Bay, Labrador Sea, Atlantic Ocean, Gulf of St. Lawrence, with cities including Thunder Bay, Toronto, Ottawa, Montréal, Québec, Halifax, St. John's, and many others.)

# THE PHYSICAL US

**The United States of America** covers the broad central portion of North America, from the northern border with Canada to Mexico in the dry desert south, and includes the mountainous northwestern state of Alaska and the distant volcanic islands of Hawaii. The US has large areas of fertile land at its heart, flanked by the high Rocky Mountains in the west and the ancient Appalachians in the east.

## CROSS SECTION THROUGH THE US

Cascade Range | Rocky Mountains | Great Plains | Mississippi Basin | Bars and spits on East Coast

W — 2,807 miles — E

The highest points in the US are found in the wide belt of mountains in the west. Rising from the sea are the coastal ranges of the Cascades and Sierra Nevada, while the Rocky Mountains are farther inland. The terrain drops away to the east, down across the Great Plains and Mississippi Basin, toward the Appalachians and the East Coast.

## THE LANDSCAPE OF THE US

Coastal mountains rise from the Pacific coast, dropping inland to the deserts and salt lakes of the Great Basin. The high Rocky Mountains are new mountains, formed by the collision of two of Earth's tectonic plates. Much of the central US is flat, consisting of a series of undulating, often virtually featureless plains known as the Great Plains. The Appalachian Mountains in the East are much older, lower, and more eroded than the Rockies. The Great Lakes, the world's largest freshwater lakes, lie on the US–Canada border.

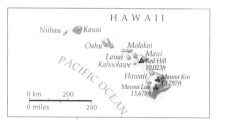

### HAWAII

Niihau, Kauai, Oahu, Molokai, Lanai, Maui, Red Hill 10,023ft, Kahoolawe, Hawaii, Mauna Kea 13,797ft, Mauna Loa 13,678ft

0 km 200
0 miles 200

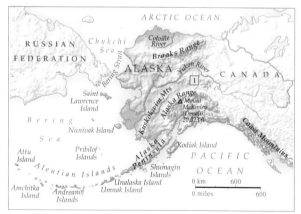

ARCTIC OCEAN

RUSSIAN FEDERATION | Chukchi Sea | Colville River | Brooks Range | ALASKA | Yukon River | CANADA

Saint Lawrence Island | Kuskokwim Mts | Alaska Range | Mount McKinley (Denali) 20,323ft | Coast Mountains

Bering Sea | Nunivak Island | Kodiak Island | PACIFIC OCEAN

Attu Island | Pribilof Islands | Alaska Peninsula | Shumagin Islands

Aleutian Islands | Amchitka Island | Andreanof Islands | Unalaska Island | Umnak Island

0 km 600
0 miles 600

### LAND HEIGHT

Above 13,120ft
6,560–13,120ft
3,280–6,560ft
1,640–3,280ft
820–1,640ft
330–820ft
0–330ft
Below sea level

*(Main map of western US showing physical features including Cascade Range, Columbia Basin, Rocky Mountains, Sierra Nevada, Great Basin, Colorado Plateau, Mojave Desert, Sonoran Desert, with Canada to the north and Mexico to the south)*

Cape Flattery, Mount Olympus 7,965ft, Glacier Peak 10,541ft, Columbia River, Franklin D.Roosevelt Lake, Mount Rainier 14,409ft, Flathead Lake, Missouri River, Fort Peck Lake, Columbia Basin, Snake River, Clearwater Mountains, Mount Hood 11,235ft, Blue Mountains, Salmon River, Musselshell River, Mount Jefferson 10,495ft, Hells Canyon, Salmon River Mountains, Borah Peak 12,660ft, Yellowstone Lake, Yellowstone River, Cloud Peak 13,165ft, Devils Tower, Harney Basin, Malheur Lake, Hyndman Peak 12,076ft, Grand Teton 13,769ft, Gannett Peak 13,802ft, Upper Klamath Lake, Mount Shasta 14,159ft, Goose Lake, Fremont Peak 13,743ft, Cape Blanco, Honey Lake, Humboldt River, Great Salt Lake, Bear Lake, Great Divide Basin, Cape Mendocino, Pyramid Lake, Great Basin, Kings Peak 13,526ft, Uinta Mountains, Flaming Gorge Reservoir, Point Arena, Lake Tahoe, Great Salt Lake Desert, Utah Lake, Walker Lake, Wheeler Peak 13,060ft, Sevier Lake, White River, Roan Plateau, Mono Lake 13,139ft, Boundary Peak, Delano Peak 12,171ft, Mount Elbert 14,432ft, North Palisade 14,241ft, Colorado Lake Powell, Mount Peale 12,719ft, Uncompahgre Peak 14,307ft, Mount Whitney 14,495ft, Death Valley, Owens Lake, Lake Mead, Virgin River, Grand Canyon, Colorado Plateau, San Juan River, Blanca Peak 14,343ft, Wheeler Peak 13,159ft, Channel Islands, Mojave Desert, Humphreys Peak 12,634ft, Painted Desert, Little Colorado River, Salton Sea, Colorado River, Sonoran Desert, Gila River, Verde River, Baldy Peak 11,404ft, Sierra Blanca Peak 11,972ft, Sacramento Mountains, Chiricahua Peak 9,796ft, Guadalupe Peak 8,749ft, Rio Grande, Emory Peak, MEXICO

SCALE BAR

0 km 100 200
0 miles 100 200

### 1 ALASKA

Alaska's far north is frozen solid for most of the year. Rivers can flow only during the short summer, when heat from the weak sun melts the surface ice.

### 2 DESERTS

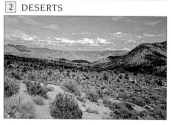

The Great Basin in the Rocky Mountains is made up of many shallow, salty lakes, deserts, and scrubby vegetation like tumbleweed.

### 3 MOUNTAINS

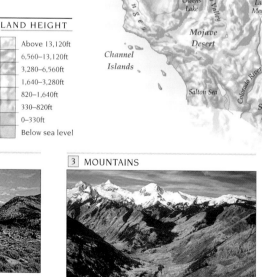

The Rocky Mountains form a spine running up the western side of the US. The mountains continue north through Canada, into Alaska.

NORTH AMERICA

USA

# CLIMATE

The climate of the US is generally temperate and continental – with warm summers and cold winters. Humid, subtropical climates occur only in Hawaii and the Florida keys. In contrast, much of Alaska has a freezing arctic climate. On the Pacific Coast, warm, moist air from the ocean creates a milder climate, but the coastal mountains prevent this air from reaching the interior – making most of the central US very dry. Extreme weather events are common in the central US, including sudden tornadoes, blizzards, and hailstorms.

CLIMATE
- Subarctic
- Cool continental
- Temperate
- Warm temperate
- Semiarid
- Arid
- Tropical

**Wettest place**
Waialeale, Kauai, Hawaii
Annual rainfall 460in

**Coldest place**
Prospect Creek, Alaska
Temp. -80°F

**Hottest and driest place**
Death Valley (California, USA)
Temp. 134°F
Annual rainfall 1.63in

**EXTREME WEATHER EVENTS**

Symbols indicate climatic extremes

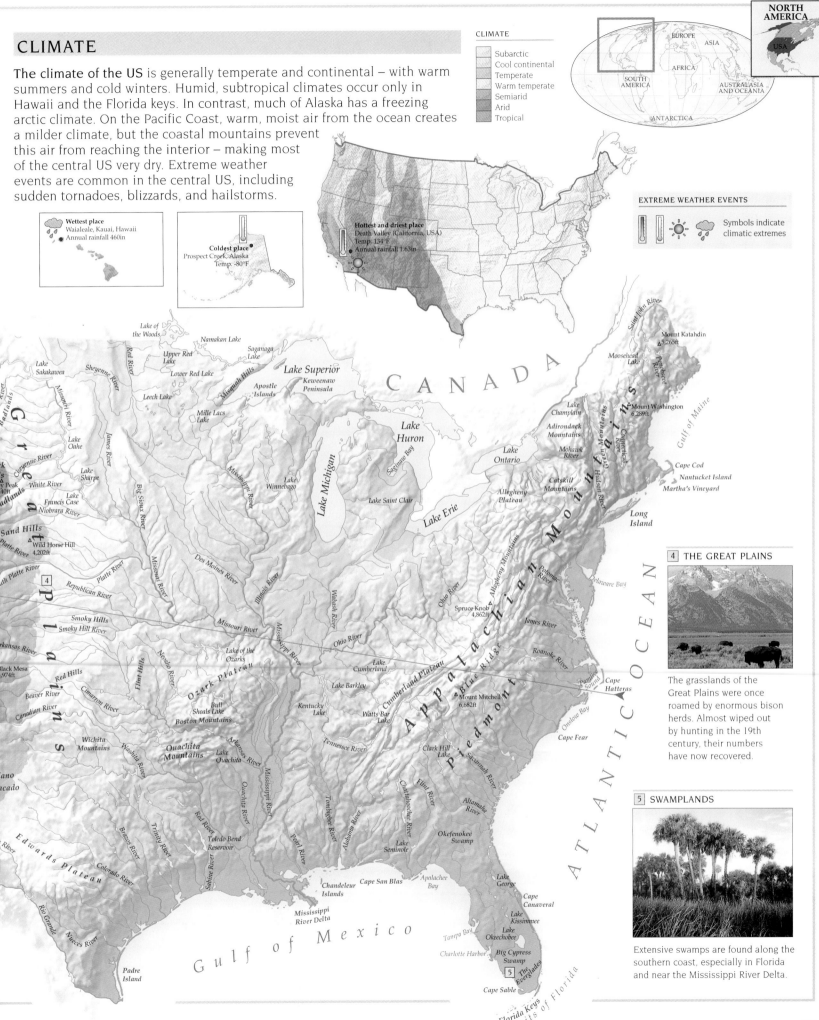

**4 THE GREAT PLAINS**

The grasslands of the Great Plains were once roamed by enormous bison herds. Almost wiped out by hunting in the 19th century, their numbers have now recovered.

**5 SWAMPLANDS**

Extensive swamps are found along the southern coast, especially in Florida and near the Mississippi River Delta.

# UNITED STATES OF AMERICA

From a sparsely populated "unknown" territory in the 16th century, the US has built on its natural strengths – immense tracts of fertile land and great mineral resources – to become the world's most powerful nation. Its global success was fueled by a hardworking immigrant population, exploiting their land of opportunity and sustained by the ideals of liberty and democracy that continue to bind the American people.

WASHINGTON DC

Washington DC is the administrative capital of the US. All national government is based here, centered on the White House, an 18th-century building on Pennsylvania Avenue that is the official residence of the US president. Congress, composed of the Senate and the House of Representatives, meets in the Capitol.

## THE FIFTY STATES

The US is a federation of 50 states. Following the 1776 Revolutionary War, 13 former colonies formed the core of the new nation. Expansion continued southward and westward, aided by the Louisiana Purchase in 1803, which added former French lands to the Union. By 1867, with the purchase of Alaska, the modern shape of the US was nearly complete. Alaska and Hawaii were admitted as states in 1959.

ARCTIC OCEAN

RUSSIAN FEDERATION

ALASKA

CANADA

Anchorage

Juneau

SCALE 1:54,000,000
0 km          600
0 miles          600

PACIFIC OCEAN

Kauai
Oahu
Honolulu  HAWAII
Maui

SCALE 1:22,000,000
0 km          200
0 miles          200

PACIFIC OCEAN

Hawaii

NEW YORK

The first skyscrapers in New York were built at the beginning of the 20th century. The intricate Manhattan skyline has become a symbol of US urban culture throughout the world.

STARS AND STRIPES

The 13 stripes of the US flag represent the 13 colonies that formed the first states of the Union. Each star symbolizes one of the current states; as states are admitted to the union, the number of stars increases.

ANCIENT CIVILIZATIONS

Evidence of some of the oldest cultures in the US can still be found in the Southwest. Peoples such as the Hopi and Hohokam farmed and built settlements (pueblos) here.

CANADA

PACIFIC OCEAN

Olympia  Seattle
WASHINGTON  Spokane
Portland
Salem
Eugene

OREGON

MONTANA
Helena

Boise
IDAHO

Rocky

WYOMING

Salt Lake City

NORTH DAKOTA
Bismarck

SOUTH DAKOTA
Pierre
Sioux Falls

Cheyenne

NEBRASKA
Oma
Lincol

Reno  NEVADA
Sacramento
Carson City

UNITED  STATE

Concord
San  Stockton
Francisco  San Jose

Fresno

CALIFORNIA

Bakersfield

Las Vegas

UTAH

Mountains

COLORADO
Denver
Colorado Springs
Pueblo

KANSA
Wich

Simi Valley
Los Angeles
Long Beach  Riverside

San Diego

ARIZONA

Phoenix

Tucson

Santa Fe
Albuquerque

NEW MEXICO

El Paso

OKLAHOM

Amarillo
Oklaho City

Lubbock

Dallas
Fort Worth

TEXAS

Austin

MEXICO

San Antonio

Corpus Christi

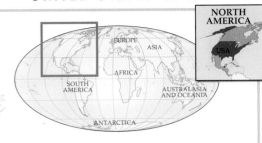

## POPULATION

**The US has** the most varied population in the world. The original native population has been swollen by peoples from all corners of Europe, many seeking a new life away from poverty and persecution; by Africans whose ancestors were brought to the US as slaves; and during the later half of the 20th century, by people from South America, the Caribbean, and many parts of Asia – particularly the countries on the edge of the Pacific Ocean.

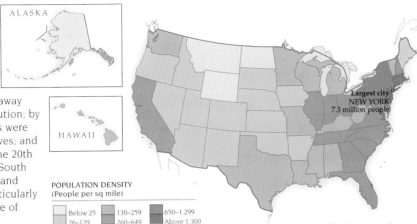

ALASKA

HAWAII

Largest city
NEW YORK
7.3 million people

**POPULATION DENSITY**
(People per sq mile)

Below 25
26–129
130–259
260–649
650–1,299
Above 1,300

SCALE 1:15,500,000

0 km   200   400
0 miles   200   400

**POPULATION**

▣ Above 500,000
◉ 100,000 to 500,000
● 50,000 to 100,000
• Below 50,000

### ALL AMERICANS

These children are all American citizens, regardless of their race, culture, or their parents' nationality. They show the diversity of the US, whose many different peoples came to North America for a variety of reasons.

### THE GOOD LIFE

Since the beginning of the 1980s many people have moved to the northwest Pacific states, Oregon and Washington, drawn by a more leisurely lifestyle and proximity to the magnificent countryside.

### URBAN DECAY

As industry and middle-class people have moved out of city centers into suburban areas, many inner cities have become run down, with restricted health services and delapidated amenities.

## STANDARDS OF LIVING

**Cheap and abundant food,** spacious homes equipped with labor-saving devices, and easy access to beautiful scenery for leisure activities enable many people in the US to enjoy the highest standard of living in the world. In some inner-city areas, however, unemployment has led to poverty and homelessness with related social problems. Illegal immigrants, members of minority ethnic groups, and certain isolated rural dwellers are among the less privileged people in the US.

CANADA

MAINE

Lake Superior

MINNESOTA

MICHIGAN

VERMONT

Augusta

Montpelier

NEW HAMPSHIRE

Saint Paul

WISCONSIN

Minneapolis

Lake Michigan

Lake Huron

Concord

Boston

MASSACHUSETTS

Lake Ontario   Albany

NEW YORK   Hartford   Providence

Madison   Lansing

Milwaukee

Buffalo

RHODE ISLAND

CONNECTICUT

IOWA

Detroit

Lake Erie

Cleveland

Newark

New York

Des Moines

Chicago

Toledo

PENNSYLVANIA

Trenton

NEW JERSEY

Davenport

INDIANA

OHIO

Pittsburgh

Harrisburg   Philadelphia

Baltimore   Dover

DELAWARE

OF AMERICA

Columbus

Indianapolis

Springfield

Cincinnati

WEST VIRGINIA

Annapolis

WASHINGTON DC

MARYLAND

Kansas City

Jefferson City

ILLINOIS

Saint Louis

Louisville

Frankfort

Charleston

Richmond

opeka

MISSOURI

Evansville

VIRGINIA

Norfolk

KENTUCKY

Springfield

Raleigh

Nashville

NORTH CAROLINA

TENNESSEE

Charlotte

lsa

ARKANSAS

Memphis

Columbia

SOUTH CAROLINA

Little Rock

Atlanta

Birmingham

MISSISSIPPI

GEORGIA

Appalachian Mountains

ATLANTIC OCEAN

ALABAMA

Columbus

Savannah

Shreveport

Jackson

Montgomery

LOUISIANA

Houston

Baton Rouge

Mobile

New Orleans

Tallahassee

Jacksonville

FLORIDA

Orlando

Tampa

Saint Petersburg

*Gulf of Mexico*

Fort Lauderdale

Miami

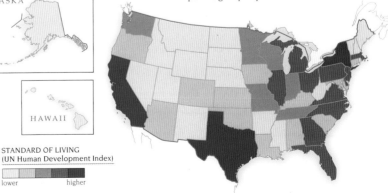

ALASKA

HAWAII

**STANDARD OF LIVING**
(UN Human Development Index)

lower          higher

# US: THE NORTHEASTERN STATES

CONNECTICUT, DELAWARE, MAINE, MASSACHUSETTS, NEW HAMPSHIRE, NEW JERSEY, NEW YORK, PENNSYLVANIA, RHODE ISLAND, VERMONT

The dynamic 200-year boom of the northeastern states has been the result of a combination of factors. Between 1855 and 1924, over 20 million people poured into the region from all over the world, hoping to build a new life. Natural resources, including coal and iron, fueled new industries and fertile farmland provided food for the region's growing population. The "gateway" cities of the Atlantic seaboard, New York and Boston, enabled manufacturers to export their goods worldwide.

## INDUSTRY

Boston, New York, and Philadelphia are international centers of industry and commerce. Electronics and communications are growing throughout the Northeast alongside traditional industries such as fishing and wood products. Tourism is vital for the northeastern states, particularly along the Atlantic coast.

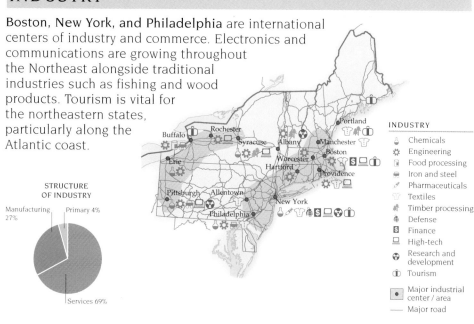

STRUCTURE OF INDUSTRY

Manufacturing 27%
Primary 4%
Services 69%

INDUSTRY

- Chemicals
- Engineering
- Food processing
- Iron and steel
- Pharmaceuticals
- Textiles
- Timber processing
- Defense
- Finance
- High-tech
- Research and development
- Tourism
- Major industrial center / area
— Major road

## ENVIRONMENTAL ISSUES

The high level of industry and the large population puts great pressure on the environment. Air pollution from automobiles and industry led to poor air quality in many cities and caused acid rain. The problem is worse toward the Great Lakes, where severe lake pollution has occurred.

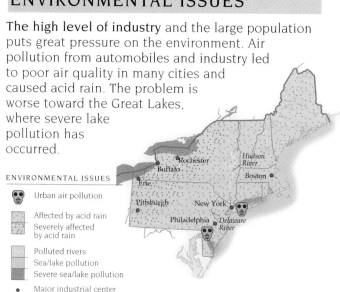

ENVIRONMENTAL ISSUES

- Urban air pollution
- Affected by acid rain
- Severely affected by acid rain
- Polluted rivers
- Sea/lake pollution
- Severe sea/lake pollution
- Major industrial center

## FARMING AND LAND USE

The varied landscape of the northeastern states supports a great range of farming. Livestock, including cattle, horses, poultry, and pigs, are raised throughout the region. The main crops are fruits and vegetables. Fishing is important, especially off the Atlantic coast of Maine.

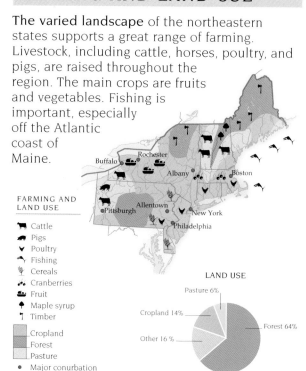

FARMING AND LAND USE

- Cattle
- Pigs
- Poultry
- Fishing
- Cereals
- Cranberries
- Fruit
- Maple syrup
- Timber
- Cropland
- Forest
- Pasture
- Major conurbation

LAND USE

Pasture 6%
Cropland 14%
Other 16 %
Forest 64%

## THE LANDSCAPE

The Appalachian and Adirondack Mountains form a barrier between the marshy lowlands of the Atlantic coast and the lowlands farther west. The interior consists of rolling hills, fertile valleys, and thousands of lakes created by the movement of glaciers.

### Appalachians (E 3)
The Appalachian Mountains, which run through most of this region, are the eroded remnants of peaks that were once much higher.

### Rocky coastline (G 3)
The coast of Maine is made up of rocky bays, islands, and inlets. If the shoreline were stretched out, it would be 2,500 miles long.

### Adirondacks (E 3)
The Adirondacks are a broad, wide mountain range, formed when older rocks were forced into a "dome" shape by movements in the Earth's crust many millions of years ago.

### Long Island Sound (F 5)
Long Island Sound is a river valley that was drowned by rising sea levels.

### Finger Lakes (D 3)
The long, narrow Finger Lakes lie in upper New York state. They were cut by glaciers.

### Delaware Bay (D 6)
Deep bays such as Delaware Bay are often surrounded by salt marshes and barrier beaches that create ideal breeding conditions for a wide variety of birds and animals.

NORTH AMERICA
US: The Northeastern States

# POPULATION

**The areas along the eastern seaboard** were settled by some of the earliest European colonists. The Northeast is now one of the most densely populated parts of the US. A few of the largest cities in the US, such as New York and Philadelphia, are in this region, but in the six states known as New England many towns and cities have populations of less than 30,000 inhabitants.

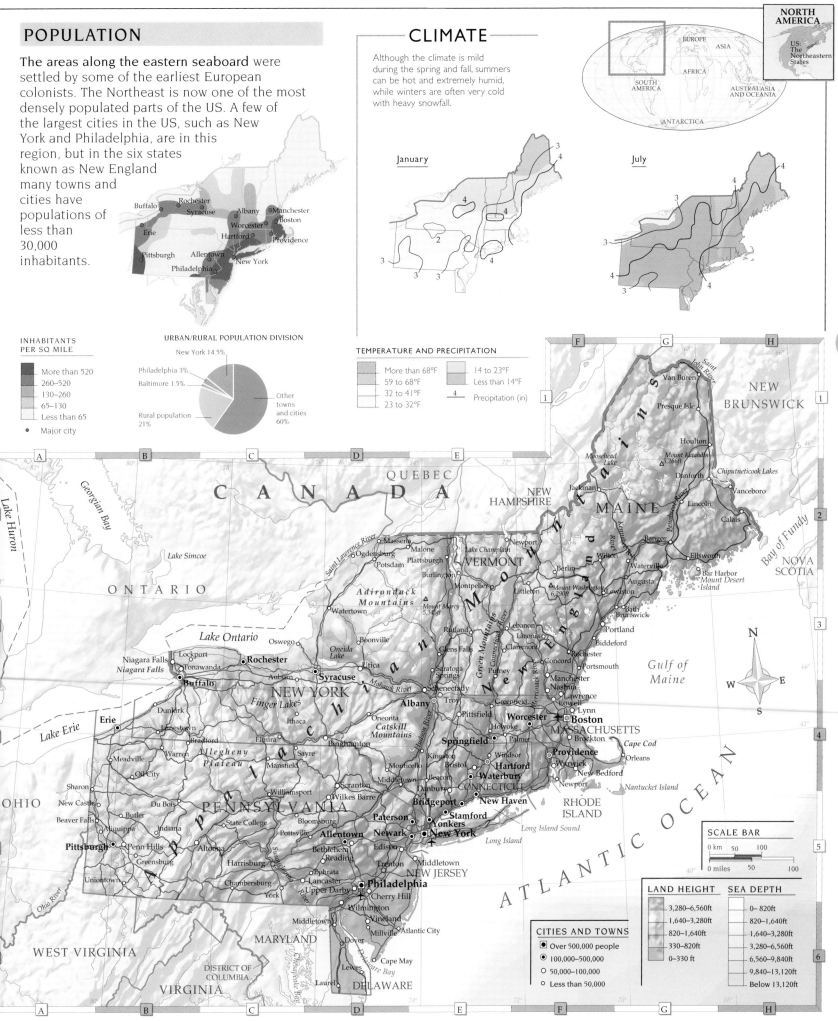

Buffalo · Rochester · Syracuse · Albany · Manchester · Boston · Worcester · Hartford · Providence · Erie · Pittsburgh · Allentown · Philadelphia · New York

## INHABITANTS PER SQ MILE

- More than 520
- 260–520
- 130–260
- 65–130
- Less than 65
- ● Major city

## URBAN/RURAL POPULATION DIVISION

- New York 14.5%
- Philadelphia 3%
- Baltimore 1.5%
- Rural population 21%
- Other towns and cities 60%

# CLIMATE

Although the climate is mild during the spring and fall, summers can be hot and extremely humid, while winters are often very cold with heavy snowfall.

January

July

## TEMPERATURE AND PRECIPITATION

- More than 68°F
- 59 to 68°F
- 32 to 41°F
- 23 to 32°F
- 14 to 23°F
- Less than 14°F
- —4— Precipitation (in)

EUROPE · ASIA · AFRICA · NORTH AMERICA · SOUTH AMERICA · AUSTRALASIA AND OCEANIA · ANTARCTICA

QUEBEC

CANADA

NEW HAMPSHIRE

VERMONT

MAINE

NEW BRUNSWICK

Van Buren
Presque Isle
Houlton
Moosehead Lake
Mount Katahdin △5,266ft
Danforth
Chiputneticook Lakes
Vanceboro
Jackman
Lincoln
Calais

Lake Huron

Georgian Bay

Lake Simcoe

ONTARIO

Lake Ontario

Massena
Ogdensburg
Potsdam
Malone
Plattsburgh
Lake Champlain
Newport
Burlington
Montpelier
Berlin
Littleton
Mount Washington 6,290ft
Wilton
Waterville
Augusta
Lewiston
Bath
Brunswick
Bar Harbor
Mount Desert Island
Bangor
Ellsworth

NOVA SCOTIA

Bay of Fundy

Gulf of Maine

Adirondack Mountains
Mount Marcy 5,345ft
Watertown
Oswego
Boonville
Oneida Lake
Utica
Rutland
Lebanon
Claremont
Concord
Rochester
Portsmouth
Portland
Biddeford
Glens Falls
Saratoga Springs
Putney
Manchester
Nashua
Schenectady
Mohawk River
Albany
Troy
Greenfield
Lawrence
Lowell
Lynn

New England Mountains
Green Mountains
Connecticut River
Hudson River
Merrimack River

Niagara Falls
Lockport
Tonawanda
Rochester
Syracuse
Auburn
NEW YORK
Finger Lakes
Buffalo
Dunkirk
Erie
Jamestown
Ithaca
Oneonta
Catskill Mountains
Binghamton
Pittsfield
Worcester
Holyoke
Boston
MASSACHUSETTS
Brockton
Cape Cod
Springfield
Palmer
Providence
Orleans
Lake Erie

Appalachian Mountains

Meadville
Warren
Bradford
Allegheny Plateau
Oil City
Mansfield
Sayre
Elmira
Kingston
Windsor
Bristol
Hartford
Waterbury
CONNECTICUT
New Haven
Newport
RHODE ISLAND
Nantucket Island
Danbury
Bridgeport
Stamford
Yonkers
New York

Monticello
Beacon
Middletown
Scranton
Wilkes Barre
Williamsport
Paterson
Newark
Edison
Bloomsburg
Allentown
Bethlehem
Reading
Trenton
Middletown
Long Island Sound
Long Island

OHIO

Sharon
New Castle
Beaver Falls
Aliquippa
Pittsburgh
Penn Hills
Greensburg
Butler
Indiana
State College
Altoona
Pottsville
Harrisburg
PENNSYLVANIA
Uniontown
Chambersburg
Lancaster
York
Upper Darby
Philadelphia
Cherry Hill
Wilmington
Vineland
Millville
Atlantic City
NEW JERSEY
Susquehanna River
Delaware River

WEST VIRGINIA

VIRGINIA

MARYLAND

DISTRICT OF COLUMBIA

DELAWARE

Dover
Lewes
Cape May
Laurel
Chesapeake Bay
Delaware Bay

ATLANTIC OCEAN

N W E S

## SCALE BAR

0 km 50 100
0 miles 50 100

## LAND HEIGHT

- 3,280–6,560ft
- 1,640–3,280ft
- 820–1,640ft
- 330–820ft
- 0–330 ft

## SEA DEPTH

- 0– 820ft
- 820–1,640ft
- 1,640–3,280ft
- 3,280–6,560ft
- 6,560–9,840ft
- 9,840–13,120ft
- Below 13,120ft

## CITIES AND TOWNS

- ■ Over 500,000 people
- ⊙ 100,000–500,000
- ○ 50,000–100,000
- ○ Less than 50,000

# US: THE SOUTHERN STATES

ALABAMA, ARKANSAS, DISTRICT OF COLUMBIA, FLORIDA, GEORGIA, KENTUCKY, LOUISIANA, MARYLAND, MISSISSIPPI, NORTH CAROLINA, SOUTH CAROLINA, TENNESSEE, VIRGINIA, WEST VIRGINIA

**The southern states** suffered great devastation and poverty as a result of the Civil War (1861–65). Recovery has come with the discovery and exploitation of resources and the development of major commercial and industrial centers. Yet these states retain the vibrant mix·of cultures that reflect their French, Spanish, English, and African heritage.

## INDUSTRY

**Tourism is a major industry** in the "sunbelt" states, especially Florida, and many people move to the area when they retire to enjoy the climate. Oil and gas are extracted along the coast of the Gulf of Mexico, and there are many related chemical industries. Textiles are still produced in North and South Carolina, but aerospace and other high-tech industries have been established as well.

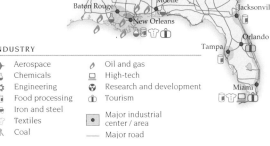

### STRUCTURE OF INDUSTRY

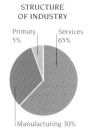

Primary 5%
Services 65%
Manufacturing 30%

### INDUSTRY

- ✈ Aerospace
- ⚗ Chemicals
- ⚙ Engineering
- ▤ Food processing
- ▦ Iron and steel
- 👕 Textiles
- ⚒ Coal
- ⬤ Oil and gas
- ▢ High-tech
- ◉ Research and development
- 🏛 Tourism
- ▣ Major industrial center / area
- —— Major road

## POPULATION

**Creoles, descended from** Spanish and French colonizers, and Cajuns, of French-Canadian ancestry, live in the south of this region. Florida has a large Hispanic population, increased by migration from the Caribbean. In the early 20th century, five million black people, the descendants of slaves, left the South for cities in the North.

### INHABITANTS PER SQ MILE

- More than 520
- 260–520
- 130–260
- 65–130
- Less than 65
- ▪ Capital city
- ● Major city

### URBAN/RURAL POPULATION DIVISION

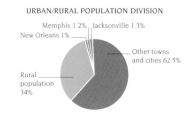

Memphis 1.2%   Jacksonville 1.3%
New Orleans 1%
Other towns and cities 62.5%
Rural population 34%

## FARMING AND LAND USE

**Cotton is still the South's main crop,** but many old cottonfields are now pastures where all types of livestock are raised. Florida is famous for citrus fruits, while Georgia is renowned for peanuts. Sugarcane, soybeans, tobacco, corn, fruits, and rice are grown in other areas.

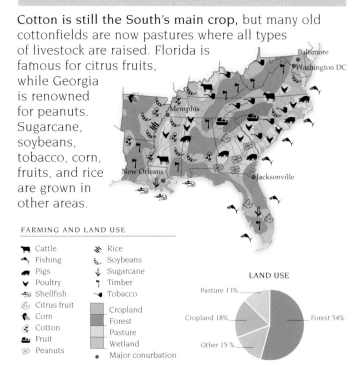

### FARMING AND LAND USE

- 🐄 Cattle
- 🐟 Fishing
- 🐖 Pigs
- 🐓 Poultry
- 🦐 Shellfish
- 🍊 Citrus fruit
- 🌽 Corn
- Cotton
- Fruit
- Peanuts
- 〰 Rice
- Soybeans
- Sugarcane
- Timber
- Tobacco
- Cropland
- Forest
- Pasture
- Wetland
- ● Major conurbation

### LAND USE

Pasture 13%
Cropland 18%
Forest 54%
Other 15 %

## THE LANDSCAPE

**The South is a land of contrasts,** the uplands of the Appalachians, the foothills of the Piedmont, and low-lying coastal regions are all featured. The interior lowlands are drained by the Mississippi. Florida is dotted with thousands of lakes and is home to The Everglades, a giant sawgrass swamp.

**Mississippi River (C 4)**
A major transportation artery, the Mississippi was an essential route in opening up the interior region. With its main tributary, the Missouri, it is nearly 3,800 miles long, making it the world's third-longest river.

**Kentucky Bluegrass (E 2)**
The gently rolling bluegrass landscape of northern Kentucky is ideal horse- and livestock-raising country.

**Barrier beaches (I 3)**
Sandy barrier beaches and islands line the eastern and southern coasts, along with sheltered lagoons and salt marshes.

**The Everglades (G 8)**
The Everglades cover 5,000 sq miles and support abundant wild animals and plants, many unique to the area.

**Thermal springs (B 4)**
Hot Springs National Park in Arkansas has 47 thermal springs and is a popular tourist and health resort. Visitors relax here in the hot water that trickles from the hillsides.

**Tennessee River (D 4)**
The Tennessee River is 625 miles long. Dams along the river generate hydro-electricity to provide most of the region's energy needs.

**Limestone caves (E 4)**
Cathedral Caverns in Alabama is a collection of enormous limestone caves. The main entrance is more than 1,000 ft high and 150 ft wide.

# ENVIRONMENTAL ISSUES

**Factories in the Great Lakes region** have contributed to the large blanket of acid rain across the northern part. Toward the south, hurricanes sweep in from the Atlantic Ocean and Gulf of Mexico during the hurricane season, which lasts from May to October each year.

ENVIRONMENTAL ISSUES
- Path of recent, devastating hurricane
- Affected by acid rain
- Polluted river

NORTH AMERICA
US: The Southern States

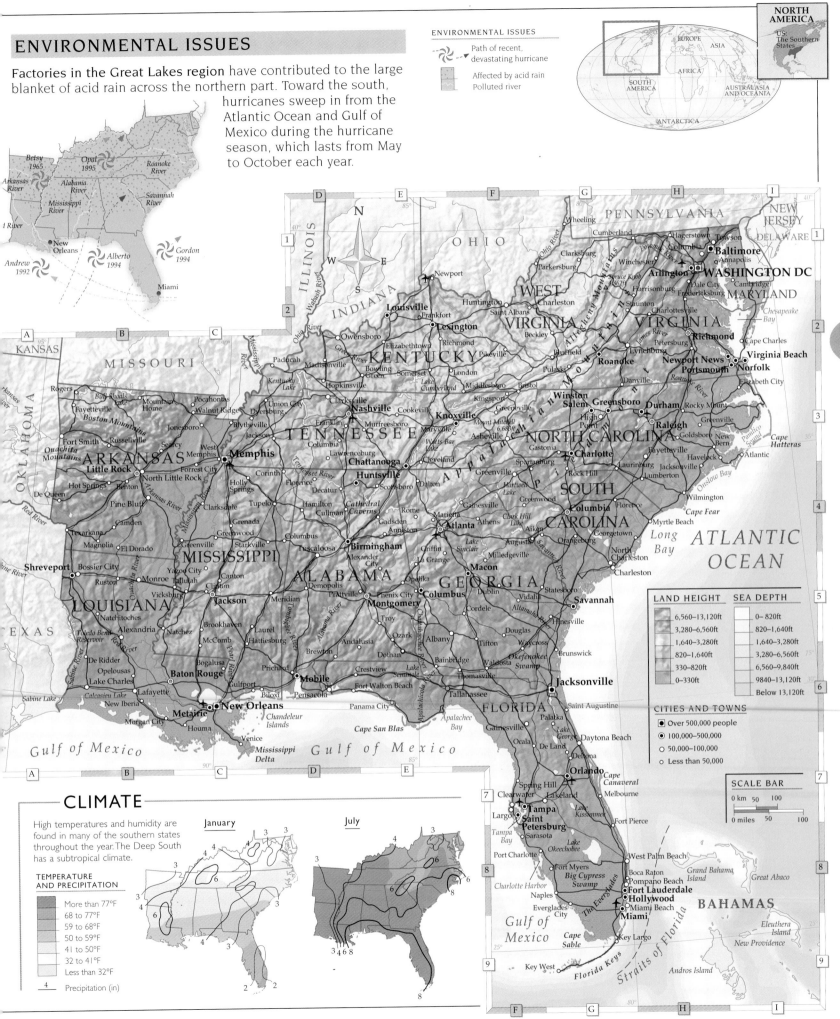

## CLIMATE

High temperatures and humidity are found in many of the southern states throughout the year. The Deep South has a subtropical climate.

January

July

TEMPERATURE AND PRECIPITATION
- More than 77°F
- 68 to 77°F
- 59 to 68°F
- 50 to 59°F
- 41 to 50°F
- 32 to 41°F
- Less than 32°F

— 4 — Precipitation (in)

LAND HEIGHT
- 6,560–13,120ft
- 3,280–6,560ft
- 1,640–3,280ft
- 820–1,640ft
- 330–820ft
- 0–330ft

SEA DEPTH
- 0–820ft
- 820–1,640ft
- 1,640–3,280ft
- 3,280–6,560ft
- 6,560–9,840ft
- 9840–13,120ft
- Below 13,120ft

CITIES AND TOWNS
- Over 500,000 people
- 100,000–500,000
- 50,000–100,000
- Less than 50,000

SCALE BAR
0 km   50   100
0 miles   50   100

# US: THE GREAT LAKES STATES

ILLINOIS, INDIANA, MICHIGAN, OHIO, WISCONSIN

**Good transportation links**, excellent farmland, and a wealth of natural resources drew settlers from Europe and the south and east of the US to the Great Lakes states during the late 19th century. By the 1930s, they had become one of the world's most prosperous industrial and agricultural regions. In recent years, the decline in traditional heavy industries has hit some cities hard, leading to unemployment and a rising crime rate.

## POPULATION

The Great Lakes states are one of the most densely populated parts of the US. Many of the largest cities in this region – Chicago, Detroit, and Milwaukee – grew up on the banks of the lakes and are connected to each other and the rest of the US by an impressive road and rail network.

INHABITANTS PER SQ MILE
- More than 520
- 260–520
- 130–260
- 65–130
- Less than 65
- ● Major city

URBAN/RURAL POPULATION DIVISION

Detroit 2.4%
Chicago 7%
Indianapolis 1.6%
Other towns and cities 63%
Rural population 26%

## CLIMATE

Plentiful rainfall waters the agricultural lands. In winter, strong winds sweep across the lakes, and water close to the shore may freeze.

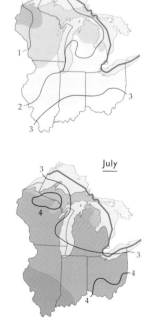

January

July

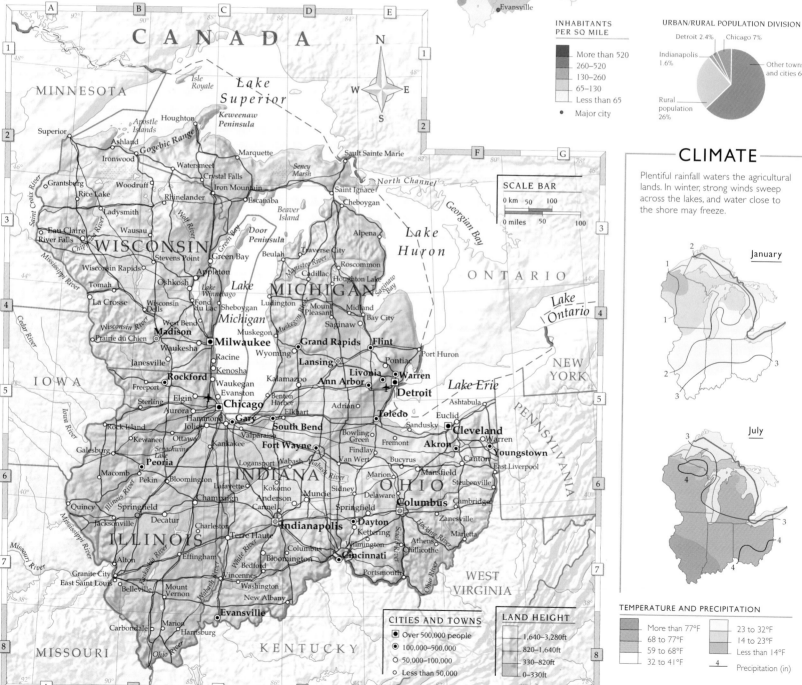

SCALE BAR

0 km 50 100

0 miles 50 100

CITIES AND TOWNS
- ■ Over 500,000 people
- ◉ 100,000–500,000
- ◎ 50,000–100,000
- ○ Less than 50,000

LAND HEIGHT
- 1,640–3,280ft
- 820–1,640ft
- 330–820ft
- 0–330ft

TEMPERATURE AND PRECIPITATION
- More than 77°F
- 68 to 77°F
- 59 to 68°F
- 32 to 41°F
- 23 to 32°F
- 14 to 23°F
- Less than 14°F
- 4 Precipitation (in)

# FARMING AND LAND USE

Michigan is renowned for its cherries and apples. Corn and soybeans are the main crops produced in the region's southern states. Livestock-rearing includes pig and poultry farms – many very large – in Illinois, Indiana, and Ohio. Cattle rearing and dairy farming are common in Michigan and Wisconsin.

LAND USE

Pasture 8%
Other 16%
Cropland 47%
Forest 29%

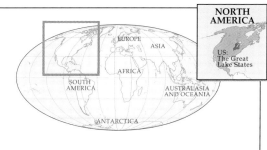
NORTH AMERICA
US: The Great Lake States

### FARMING AND LAND USE
- Cattle
- Pigs
- Poultry
- Corn
- Fruit
- Soybeans
- Timber
- Cropland
- Forest
- Pasture
- • Major conurbation

# INDUSTRY

The US automobile industry grew up on the banks of the Great Lakes, supported by the manufacture of iron and steel. Both industries have suffered in recent years from competition from cheap foreign imports. Meat packing has moved out from cities such as Chicago closer to the farms. New industries which have developed since the 1970s include electronics, service, and finance industries.

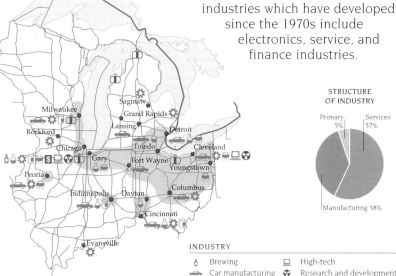

STRUCTURE OF INDUSTRY

Primary 5%
Services 57%
Manufacturing 38%

### INDUSTRY
- Brewing
- Car manufacturing
- Chemicals
- Engineering
- Food processing
- Iron and steel
- Finance
- High-tech
- Research and development
- Tourism
- Major industrial center / area
- Major road

# THE LANDSCAPE

Until about 10,000 years ago, much of this region was covered by great ice sheets that extended south to Illinois and Ohio. When the ice melted the Great Lakes were left in large hollows that the ice had scoured. The ice sheets changed the course of many rivers, so today most rivers flow south into the Misissippi/Missouri River system.

### Lakes and marshes (B3)
Wisconsin is scattered with thousands of smaller lakes and many marshy areas. Like the Great Lakes, they were formed by erosion by the retreating ice at the end of the last Ice Age.

### Underground water
In northern Illinois much of the water is pumped from underground reservoirs. In some places, the water table has dropped by 700 ft over the last century, so many areas now face a water shortage.

### Moraines
When the last ice age ended, the retreating ice sheets left long ridges and piles of rock to the south of Lake Michigan. Some of these ridges, known as moraines, can be up to 300 ft high.

### Limestone region
Limestone in the hills of southern Indiana has been dissolved by acid rainwater. This has produced features such as sinkholes and underground caves.

### Lake Erie (F5)
Lake Erie is the shallowest of the Great Lakes. Its average depth is about 62 ft. Storms that sweep across from Canada have eroded its shores and caused the silting of its harbors.

# ENVIRONMENTAL ISSUES

The heavy industries on the banks of the Great Lakes have caused terrible pollution over the last century. Industrial effluent has polluted the lakes themselves, and factory emissions have led to severely acidic rain, which affects forests and lakes both here and farther away in Canada.

### ENVIRONMENTAL ISSUES
- Urban air pollution
- Affected by acid rain
- Severely affected by acid rain
- Polluted rivers
- Lake pollution
- Severe lake pollution
- • Major industrial center

# US: THE CENTRAL STATES

IOWA, KANSAS, MINNESOTA, MISSOURI, NEBRASKA, NORTH DAKOTA, OKLAHOMA, SOUTH DAKOTA

**The prairie states** of the central US became one of America's richest agricultural regions in the mid-19th century. Despite the "Dustbowl" crisis of the 1930s, which led many farmers to leave their ruined lands, agriculture is still crucial to the economy, and most people still live in rural areas rather than large cities.

## FARMING AND LAND USE

**Wheat and corn** grow on the fertile plains. Kansas is the leading grower of wheat in the entire US, while Iowa is the leader in corn, soybeans, and livestock. Irrigation projects to combat drought are crucial in large areas. Livestock – including cattle in vast herds; pigs, particularly in Iowa, the Dakotas, and Nebraska; sheep; and turkeys – are raised throughout these states.

LAND USE

Other 11%
Forest 11%
Cropland 44%
Pasture 34%

FARMING AND LAND USE

- Cattle
- Pigs
- Poultry
- Sheep
- Corn
- Soybeans
- Wheat
- Cropland
- Forest
- Pasture
- Wetland
- ● Major conurbation

## INDUSTRY

**Industries related to agriculture**, such as food processing and the production of farm machinery, are traditional in these states but high-tech industries – such as aeronautical engineering – are increasing and large aerospace plants are found in Wichita and Saint Louis. Oil and gas are extracted in great quantities toward the south of the region, especially in Oklahoma and Kansas.

STRUCTURE OF INDUSTRY

Primary 9%
Services 60%
Manufacturing 31%

INDUSTRY

- ✈ Aerospace
- Car manufacturing
- Chemicals
- Engineering
- Food processing
- Iron and steel
- Textiles
- Oil and gas
- S Finance
- ⊡ Major industrial center / area
- — Major road

## THE LANDSCAPE

**Most of the eastern edge** of this region is marked by the Mississippi River, while the Missouri bisects it, running from northwest to southeast. The Great Plains cover most of this area, gradually rising toward the Rocky Mountains at the far western edge of the Central States.

### The Badlands (A 4)
The Badlands cover an area of about 2,000 sq miles in South Dakota. Heavily eroded by wind and water, almost nothing grows there.

### Minnesota
Minnesota is filled with lakes, hills strewn with boulders, and mineral-rich deposits that have been left behind by the scouring movement of glaciers.

### Chimney Rock (A 5)
Chimney Rock stands 500 ft above the plains. It is a remnant of an ancient land surface that was eroded by the North Platte River.

## ENVIRONMENTAL ISSUES

**Intensive agriculture** requires large quantities of water to grow crops. Overintensive use of the land has destroyed the balance of soil and water in the past, leading to fertile farmland being turned into useless areas of "Dustbowl." These states have a great underground store of water known as the Ogallala Aquifer, but overextraction for irrigation is reducing the amount of available water.

James River
Minneapolis
Saint Paul
Niobrara River
Platte River
Missouri River
Mississippi River
Kansas City
Ogallala Aquifer
Saint Louis
Arkansas River

ENVIRONMENTAL ISSUES

- Urban air pollution
- Affected by acid rain
- Aquifer
- Polluted river
- Risk of desertification
- ● Major industrial center

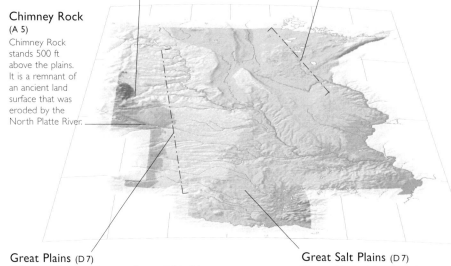

### Great Plains (D 7)
Little more than a century ago the great flat plains that cover most of these states were home to wild grasses and massive herds of buffalo. In areas where lack of water has made farming impossible, large tracts of land are being allowed to return to grassland.

### Great Salt Plains (D 7)
These arid salt plains cover about 45 sq miles of northern Oklahoma. An ancient salt lake once occupied the area. When the salt evaporated, only the salt flats were left.

NORTH AMERICA

US: The Central States

## POPULATION

**The inhabitants are largely** the descendants of Europeans who came to the region in the late 1800s. The entire region is primarily rural, with enormous tracts of land devoted to growing crops. North Dakota has no city with a population greater than 100,000.

**URBAN/RURAL POPULATION DIVISION**

Saint Louis 1.8%   Kansas City 2.2%
Minneapolis 1.5%
Other towns and cities 53.5%
Rural population 41%

**INHABITANTS PER SQ MILE**

- More than 130
- 65–130
- Less than 65
- Major city

Minneapolis · Saint Paul
Des Moines · Cedar Rapids · Davenport
Topeka · Kansas City
Wichita · Saint Louis
Tulsa
Oklahoma City

## CLIMATE

The Central States have a continental climate, with hot, dry summers and long, cold winters. Unreliable rainfall can be a problem for farmers on the Great Plains.

January
0.5   1   1
0.5   1
0.5

July
2   3
2
4
2   3
2

**TEMPERATURE AND PRECIPITATION**

| | |
|---|---|
| More than 77°F | 23 to 32°F |
| 68 to 77°F | 14 to 23°F |
| 59 to 68°F | 5 to 14°F |
| 50 to 59°F | Less than 5°F |
| 41 to 50°F | 4 Precipitation (in) |
| 32 to 41°F | |

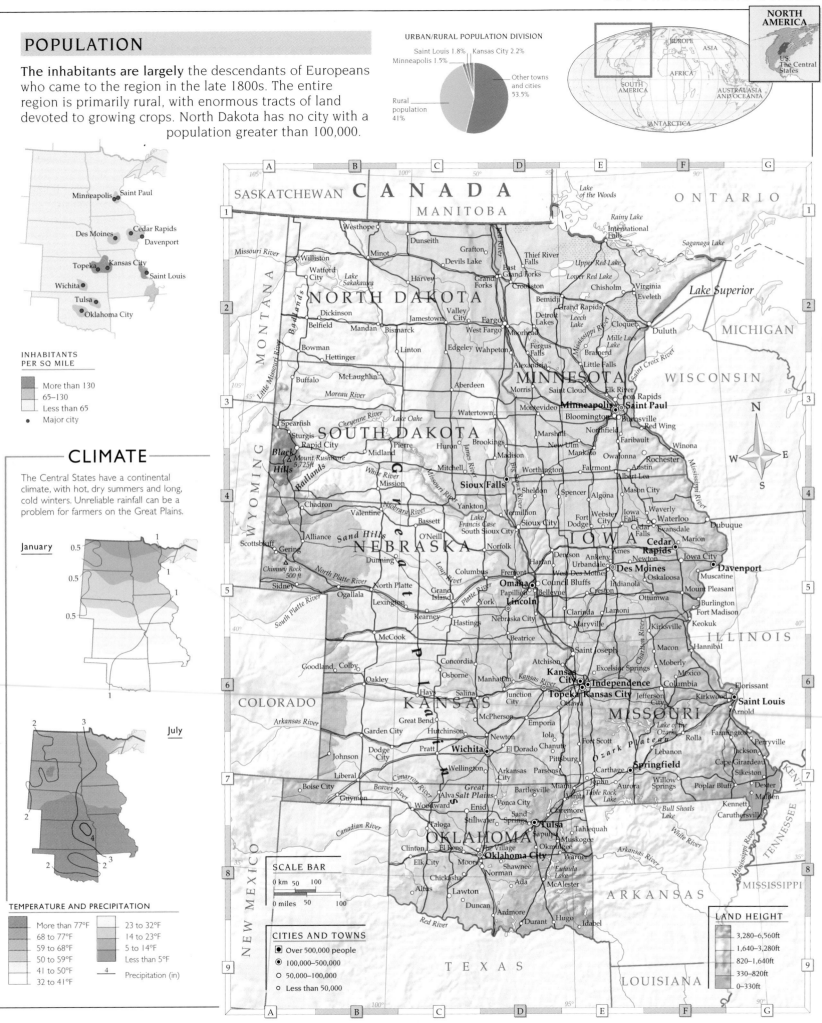

SASKATCHEWAN   CANADA   MANITOBA   ONTARIO
Lake of the Woods
Rainy Lake
Saganaga Lake
International Falls
Upper Red Lake
Lower Red Lake
Lake Superior
MONTANA
Westhope   Dunseith   Grafton   Thief River Falls
Williston   Minot   Devils Lake   East Grand Forks   Virginia   Eveleth
Watford City   Missouri River   Harvey   Grand Forks   Crookston   Chisholm
Lake Sakakawea   Bemidji   Grand Rapids
NORTH DAKOTA   Detroit Lakes   Leech Lake   Brainerd   Cloquet   Duluth   MICHIGAN
Dickinson   Valley City   Fargo   Moorhead   Mille Lacs Lake
Belfield   Mandan   Bismarck   Jamestown   West Fargo   Fergus Falls   Little Falls
Bowman   Linton   Edgeley   Wahpeton   Alexandria   Saint Croix River   WISCONSIN
Hettinger   MINNESOTA
Buffalo   McLaughlin   Aberdeen   Morris   Saint Cloud   Elk River   Coon Rapids
Moreau River   Watertown   Montevideo   Minneapolis   Saint Paul
Spearfish   Cheyenne River   Lake Oahe   Bloomington   Burnsville   Red Wing
Sturgis   SOUTH DAKOTA   Brookings   Marshall   Northfield   Faribault   Winona
Rapid City   Pierre   Huron   New Ulm   Owatonna   Rochester
Black Hills   Midland   Madison   Mankato   Fairmont   Austin   Albert Lea
Mount Rushmore 5,725ft   Mitchell   Worthington   Sheldon   Mason City
Badlands   White River   James River   Sioux Falls   Spencer   Algona   IOWA
Mission   Missouri River   Iowa Falls   Waverly   Dubuque
Chadron   Vermillion   Fort Dodge   Webster City   Waterloo   Cedar Falls   Marion
Valentine   Niobrara River   Yankton   Sioux City   Evansdale   Cedar Rapids
Bassett   Lake Francis Case   South Sioux City   Ames   Iowa City
Alliance   Sand Hills   O'Neill   Ankeny   Newton
Scottsbluff   NEBRASKA   Norfolk   Denison   Harlan   Urbandale   Des Moines   Davenport
Gering   Columbus   Fremont   West Des Moines   Indianola   Muscatine
Chimney Rock 500 ft   Dunning   Loup River   Omaha   Council Bluffs   Creston   Oskaloosa   Mount Pleasant
North Platte River   North Platte   Grand Island   Papillion   Bellevue   Ottumwa   Burlington
Sidney   Ogallala   Lexington   York   Lincoln   Clarinda   Lamoni   Fort Madison
South Platte River   Kearney   Hastings   Nebraska City   Maryville   Kirksville   Keokuk
McCook   Beatrice   ILLINOIS
COLORADO   Saint Joseph   Macon   Hannibal
Goodland   Colby   Concordia   Atchison   Excelsior Springs   Moberly
Oakley   Osborne   Manhattan   Kansas River   Kansas City   Independence   Mexico   Columbia
Hays   Salina   Junction City   Topeka   Kansas City   Jefferson City   Kirkwood   Saint Louis
KANSAS   Ottawa   MISSOURI   Arnold   Florissant
Great Bend   McPherson   Emporia   Lake of the Ozarks   Rolla   Farmington
Garden City   Hutchinson   Newton   Iola   Fort Scott   Lebanon   Perryville
Johnson   Pratt   Wichita   El Dorado   Chanute   Pittsburg   Ozark Plateau   Jackson   Cape Girardeau
Dodge City   Arkansas City   Parsons   Carthage   Springfield   Sikeston
Liberal   Wellington   Miami   Joplin   Willow Springs   Poplar Bluff   Dexter
Boise City   Beaver River   Cimarron River   Salt Plains   Bartlesville   Vinita   Aurora   Bull Shoals Lake   Kennett   Malden
Guymon   Woodward   Enid   Ponca City   Table Rock Lake   Caruthersville
Canadian River   Alva   Sand Springs   Claremore   Arkansas River   White River   TENNESSEE
Taloga   Stillwater   Sapulpa   Tulsa   Tahlequah   KENTUCKY
OKLAHOMA   Clinton   El Reno   The Village   Muskogee   Okmulgee
NEW MEXICO   Elk City   Moore   Oklahoma City   Shawnee   Warner   Eufaula Lake   MISSISSIPPI
Chickasha   Norman   Ada   McAlester   ARKANSAS
Altus   Lawton   Duncan   TEXAS   LOUISIANA
Ardmore   Durant   Hugo   Idabel
Red River

**SCALE BAR**
0 km 50 100
0 miles 50 100

**CITIES AND TOWNS**
- Over 500,000 people
- 100,000–500,000
- 50,000–100,000
- Less than 50,000

**LAND HEIGHT**
- 3,280–6,560ft
- 1,640–3,280ft
- 820–1,640ft
- 330–820ft
- 0–330ft

47

# US: THE SOUTHWESTERN STATES

ARIZONA, NEW MEXICO, TEXAS

**Large parts of the southwestern states** were purchased from Mexico in 1848. This land of expansive plateaus, spectacular canyons, prairies, and deserts is home to several distinct peoples, whose customs and traditions are still practiced. The Navaho and Hopi own one-third of the land in Arizona, and the ruins of thousand-year-old cliff dwellings built by the Anasazi people are still preserved there today.

## ENVIRONMENTAL ISSUES

**Desertification is a serious problem** in the southwestern states. Lack of water combined with intensive farming has allowed soils to erode. Drought is held at bay by irrigation, but falling water table levels are a cause for concern. New Mexico was the site for many of the earliest nuclear weapons tests, and some places remain contaminated.

ENVIRONMENTAL ISSUES
- Urban air pollution
- Former nuclear test site
- Desert area
- Risk of desertification
- Polluted river
- Major industrial center

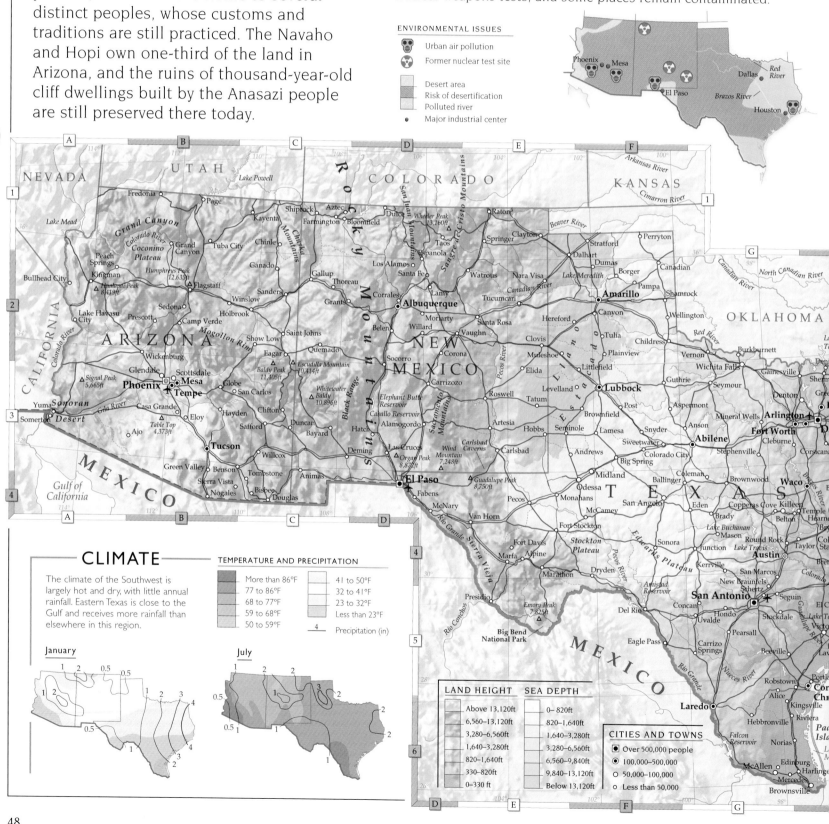

NORTH
AMERICA
US:
The Southwestern
States

## THE LANDSCAPE

The arid, mountainous **Colorado Plateau** covers nearly half of Arizona, dipping toward the south to form desert basins. Parts of northern New Mexico are forested, but the south consists primarily of semiarid plains. Eastern Texas is bordered by the waters of the Gulf of Mexico, and the farmland of this area is well watered. Western Texas is covered by the Llano Estacado and, in the south, much of the land is arid.

### Big Bend (E5)
Big Bend National Park gets its name from the 90° bend that the Rio Grande makes there.

### Invading sea
The crust of southeastern Texas is warping, causing the land to subside and allowing the sea to invade. Hurricanes make the situation worse.

### Grand Canyon (B1)
The Grand Canyon is a dramatic gorge cut in the rock by the Colorado River. It is about 217 miles long, 418 miles wide, and up to one mile deep.

### Carlsbad Caverns (B3)
Carlsbad Caverns are a series of underground caves, consisting of a three-level chain of limestone chambers studded with towering stalactites and stalagmites. They are millions of years old.

### Rio Grande (G5)
The Rio Grande, or "Great River" forms all of the border between Texas and Mexico. It flows from its source high up in the Rocky Mountains, to the Gulf of Mexico.

## INDUSTRY

**Mining and related industries** are one of the most important sources of income in the Southwest. Great deposits of oil lie under about 65% of Texas; copper and coal are mined in Arizona and New Mexico. Defense-related industries, including NASA have encouraged the development of many high-tech companies in Texas – and high-tech is also growing in larger cities such as Santa Fe and Phoenix.

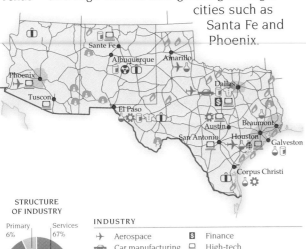

STRUCTURE OF INDUSTRY
Primary 6%
Services 67%
Manufacturing 27%

INDUSTRY
- ✈ Aerospace
- 🚗 Car manufacturing
- Chemicals
- ⚙ Engineering
- Food processing
- Mining
- Oil and gas
- ⚙ Defense
- 💲 Finance
- High-tech
- Research and development
- Tourism
- Major industrial center / area
- — Major road

SCALE BAR
0 km 100
0 miles 100

## FARMING AND LAND USE

**Many cattle and sheep ranches** have been set up on the open plateaus. Fruit and vegetables, grown in hothouses and cotton, hay, and wheat are among the major crops. Beef cattle and broiler chickens are raised on huge farms while sheep graze the drier parts of Texas. Extensive irrigation has made farming possible in even the most arid areas.

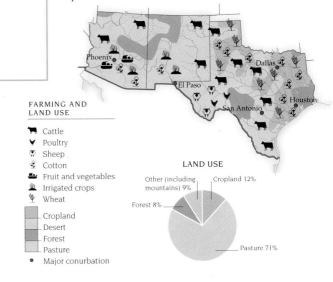

FARMING AND LAND USE
- Cattle
- Poultry
- Sheep
- Cotton
- Fruit and vegetables
- Irrigated crops
- Wheat
- Cropland
- Desert
- Forest
- Pasture
- • Major conurbation

LAND USE
Other (including mountains) 9%
Cropland 12%
Forest 8%
Pasture 71%

## POPULATION

**The descendants of Mexican** and Spanish settlers and numerous groups of Native Americans live in the southwestern states. The great cities of Texas grew up on income from cattle-ranching and the oil industry. Much of Arizona and New Mexico is sparsely populated, but today people are moving to these states to escape the cold winters elsewhere.

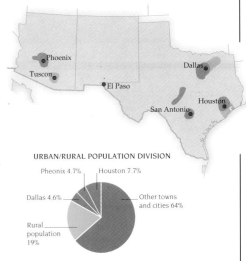

INHABITANTS PER SQ MILE
- More than 130
- 65–130
- Less than 65
- • Major city

URBAN/RURAL POPULATION DIVISION
Pheonix 4.7%
Houston 7.7%
Dallas 4.6%
Other towns and cities 64%
Rural population 19%

49

# US: THE MOUNTAIN STATES

COLORADO, IDAHO, MONTANA, NEVADA, UTAH, WYOMING

**These states are home** to some of the nation's most fantastic landscapes: endless treeless plains, craggy peaks, incredible desert landforms, and the salt flats of Utah. Although this was one of the last regions of the US to be settled, great mineral reserves have been exploited here in recent years, and new industries have grown up in some of the larger cities. Utah is the headquarters of the Mormon religion.

## INDUSTRY

**Rich mineral reserves,** including coal, oil, and gas, are mined throughout the region and forests are a source of good-quality timber. In the larger cities of Colorado and Utah, growing industries include high-tech computer firms. Many tourists are drawn to this region to ski in the resorts of Colorado and to explore the wilderness.

**STRUCTURE OF INDUSTRY**

Manufacturing 23%
Primary 7%
Services 70%

**INDUSTRY**
- Chemicals
- Food processing
- Textiles
- Coal
- Mining
- Oil and gas
- Timber processing
- Gambling
- High-tech
- Research and development
- Tourism
- Major industrial center / area
- Major road

## FARMING AND LAND USE

**In the southern** mountain states, cattle ranching is the main form of farming. Wheat and corn are grown in the eastern states, and the fertile soils of the Snake River valley in Idaho produce large crops of potatoes and many other vegetables. The northern states have many large commercial forests.

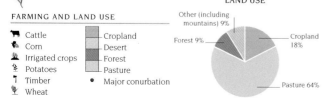

**FARMING AND LAND USE**
- Cattle
- Corn
- Irrigated crops
- Potatoes
- Timber
- Wheat
- Cropland
- Desert
- Forest
- Pasture
- Major conurbation

**LAND USE**
Other (including mountains) 9%
Forest 9%
Cropland 18%
Pasture 64%

## POPULATION

**Colorado, with the growing city of** Denver, is the most populous of the mountain states. In other states, people have settled close to sources of water such as Great Salt Lake in Utah. Many towns have less than 10,000 people and are far apart.

**INHABITANTS PER SQ MILE**
- More than 130
- 65–130
- Less than 65
- Major city

**URBAN/RURAL POPULATION DIVISION**
- Las Vegas 4%
- Denver 6%
- Salt Lake City 2%
- Other towns and cities 64%
- Rural population 24%

## THE LANDSCAPE

**The great Rocky Mountains** and many smaller mountain ranges cover almost all of this region. Only eastern Montana is not mountainous. Here western parts of the Great Plains rise to meet the mountains. Parts of the southern mountain states are very arid with spectacular scenery, including blocklike *mesas*, formed by erosion.

**Continental Divide**
From this watershed, crossing the Lewis Range, rivers flow in different directions across North America. Some flow east to Hudson Bay, some south to the Gulf of Mexico and others west to the Pacific Ocean.

**Yellowstone National Park (D 3)**
Yellowstone was set up in 1872 as the first national park in the US. Water from hot springs has deposited minerals as it cools, forming white rock terraces close to the springs.

**Snake River (C 4)**

**Great Plains (E 2)**

**North Platte River (F 4)**

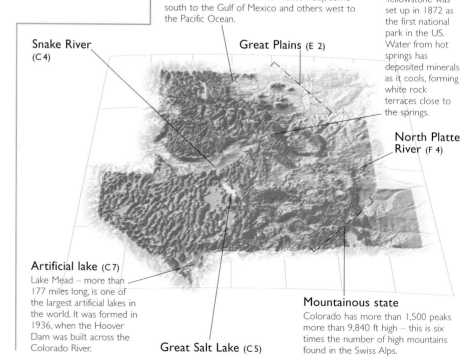

**Artificial lake (C 7)**
Lake Mead – more than 177 miles long, is one of the largest artificial lakes in the world. It was formed in 1936, when the Hoover Dam was built across the Colorado River.

**Great Salt Lake (C 5)**

**Mountainous state**
Colorado has more than 1,500 peaks more than 9,840 ft high – this is six times the number of high mountains found in the Swiss Alps.

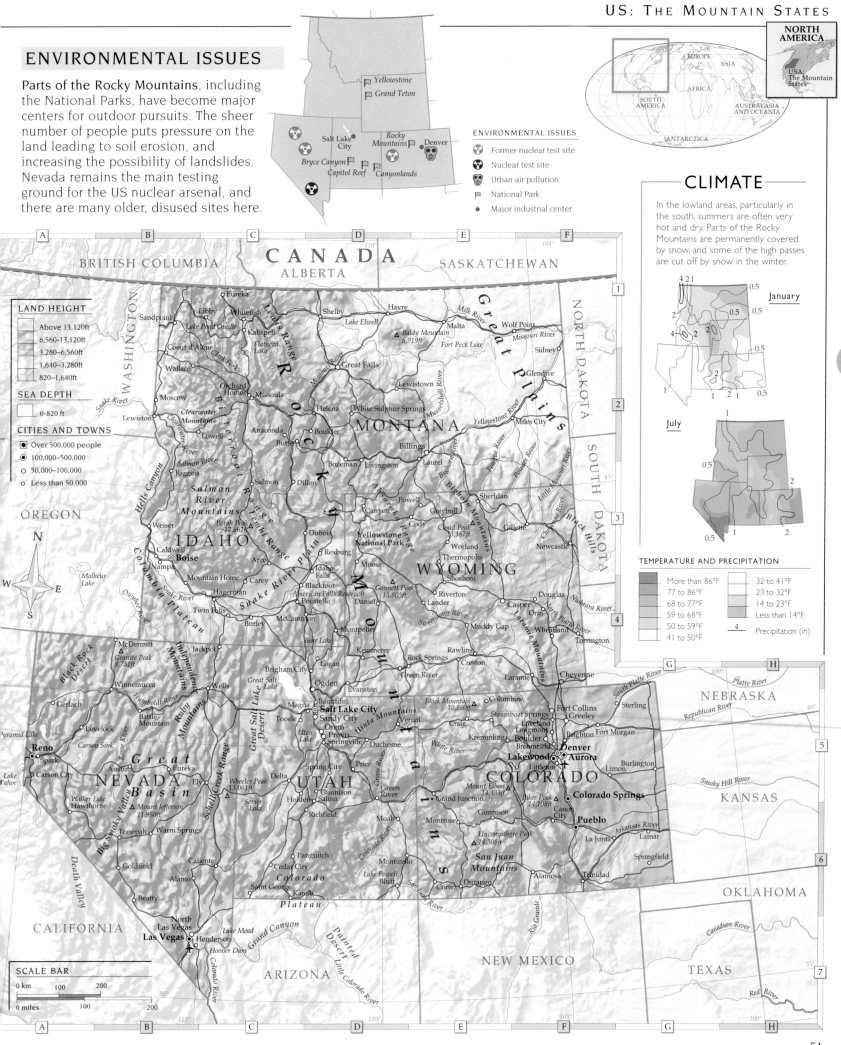

# ENVIRONMENTAL ISSUES

Parts of the Rocky Mountains, including the National Parks, have become major centers for outdoor pursuits. The sheer number of people puts pressure on the land leading to soil erosion, and increasing the possibility of landslides. Nevada remains the main testing ground for the US nuclear arsenal, and there are many older, disused sites here.

NORTH AMERICA

ENVIRONMENTAL ISSUES
- Former nuclear test site
- Nuclear test site
- Urban air pollution
- National Park
- Major industrial center

## CLIMATE

In the lowland areas, particularly in the south, summers are often very hot and dry. Parts of the Rocky Mountains are permanently covered by snow, and some of the high passes are cut off by snow in the winter.

January

July

TEMPERATURE AND PRECIPITATION
- More than 86°F
- 77 to 86°F
- 68 to 77°F
- 59 to 68°F
- 50 to 59°F
- 41 to 50°F
- 32 to 41°F
- 23 to 32°F
- 14 to 23°F
- Less than 14°F
- 4 — Precipitation (in)

LAND HEIGHT
- Above 13,120ft
- 6,560-13,120ft
- 3,280-6,560ft
- 1,640-3,280ft
- 820-1,640ft

SEA DEPTH
- 0-820 ft

CITIES AND TOWNS
- Over 500,000 people
- 100,000-500,000
- 50,000-100,000
- Less than 50,000

# US: THE PACIFIC STATES

## CALIFORNIA, OREGON, WASHINGTON

The earliest European visitors to the West Coast were fur-trappers and miners, but the Gold Rush of 1849 brought in the first major wave of settlers. Drawn by tales of the beautiful scenery, pleasant climate, and fertile valleys, more people arrived on the newly built railroads. People from all over the world are still moving into this region, seeking jobs in the dynamic economy and the famous laid-back lifestyle.

## INDUSTRY

The Pacific States are the center of the high-tech computer industry with Silicon Valley between San Francisco and San Jose, and electronics industries growing in Portland and Seattle. Other major industries include research and development for the defense industry, filmmaking in Los Angeles, food processing and lumbering. Tourism is well developed throughout the Pacific States.

### STRUCTURE OF INDUSTRY

Primary 6%
Services 68%
Manufacturing 25%

### INDUSTRY

| | | | |
|---|---|---|---|
| ✈ | Aerospace | ✹ | Film industry |
| 🜀 | Chemicals | 🖳 | High-tech |
| ✿ | Engineering | ◉ | Research and development |
| 🏭 | Food processing | ✆ | Tourism |
| 🏭 | Iron and steel | ▪ | Major industrial center / area |
| ⚓ | Shipbuilding | | |
| ♈ | Textiles | — | Major road |
| 🌲 | Timber processing | | |

## FARMING AND LAND USE

California's Central Valley and the river valleys of Washington and Oregon provide ideal conditions for a wide range of fruit and vegetables, including citrus fruit and grapes. Poultry farming is widespread in the northwest and there are many large cattle ranches. Millions of acres of commercial forest are located in this region.

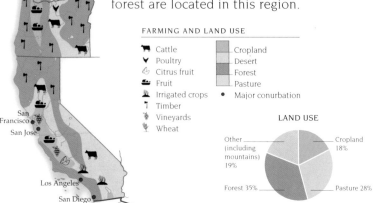

### FARMING AND LAND USE

| | | | |
|---|---|---|---|
| 🐄 | Cattle | | Cropland |
| ✔ | Poultry | | Desert |
| 🍊 | Citrus fruit | | Forest |
| 🍓 | Fruit | | Pasture |
| ⚜ | Irrigated crops | ● | Major conurbation |
| ⵋ | Timber | | |
| ❧ | Vineyards | | |
| ⚘ | Wheat | | |

### LAND USE

Other (including mountains) 19%
Cropland 18%
Forest 35%
Pasture 28%

## ENVIRONMENTAL ISSUES

Some of the great national parks of the US, including Yosemite and Sequoia, are found here. The immense numbers of visitors put great pressure on the landscape. Water is in short supply in large parts of California, and desertification, caused by overintense farming methods, is a problem. Wind farms have been set up on the hills above the San Joaquin valley to provide alternative energy.

### ENVIRONMENTAL ISSUES

| | | | |
|---|---|---|---|
| ⚑ | National park | | Desert area |
| 😷 | Urban air pollution | | Risk of desertification |
| | | | Severe risk of desertification |
| 🌀 | Wind farm | | Polluted rivers |
| | | ● | Major industrial center |

## THE LANDSCAPE

The Coast and Cascade ranges run north–south through Oregon and Washington while further south, the high Sierra Nevada run along California's eastern fringes. Two broad valleys, the Sacramento and San Joaquin, are known as the Central Valley, and form a trough beneath the Sierra Nevada. The south is extremely dry – Death Valley is the hottest place in the entire US.

### Northern rain forest (B2)

The ocean-facing side of the Olympic Mountains receives 142 in of rain every year, supporting the only true temperate rain forest in the Northern Hemisphere.

### Hells Canyon (D3)

Hells Canyon is North America's deepest gorge. Running through part of Oregon, it was created as the Snake River cut down through the land.

### Volcanic eruption (B2)

Mount St. Helens erupted in 1980, killing 57 people and destroying a vast area.

### San Andreas Fault

The San Andreas Fault runs for 650 miles underneath California. When both sides of the fault move at different rates, tremors and earthquakes result.

### Hottest place (D7)

In 1913, Death Valley set the record for the highest temperature ever recorded in the US, at 134° F.

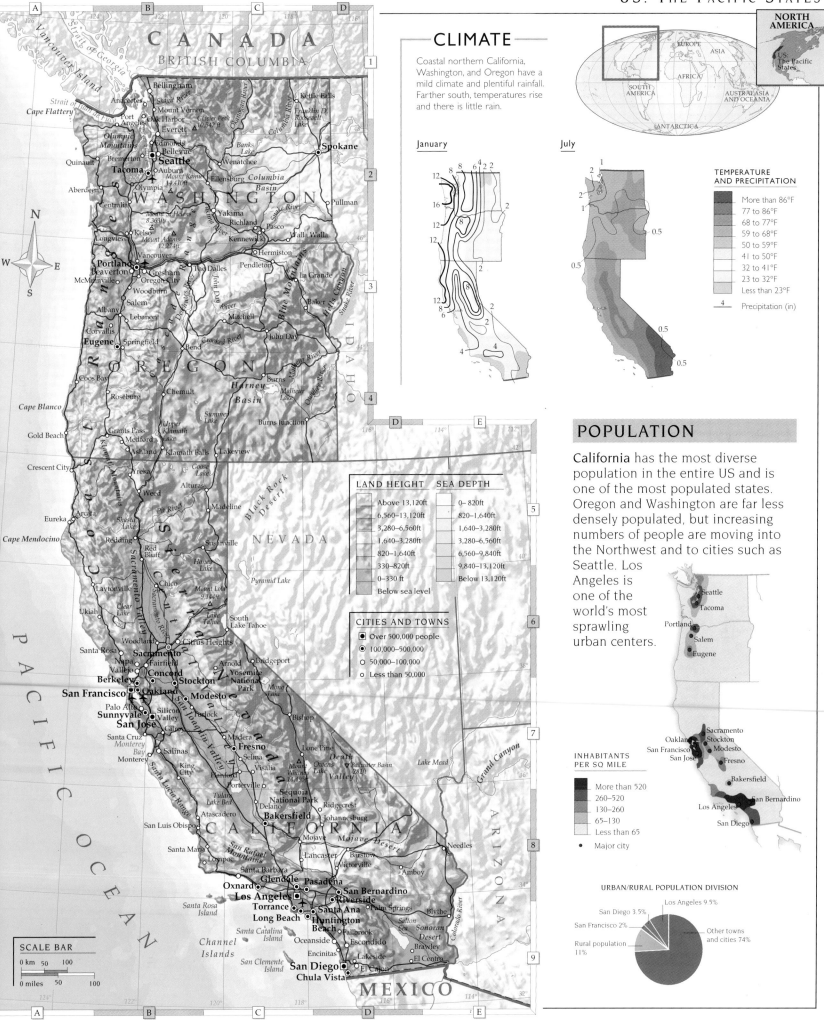

NORTH AMERICA
US: The Pacific States

## CLIMATE

Coastal northern California, Washington, and Oregon have a mild climate and plentiful rainfall. Farther south, temperatures rise and there is little rain.

January

July

TEMPERATURE AND PRECIPITATION

- More than 86°F
- 77 to 86°F
- 68 to 77°F
- 59 to 68°F
- 50 to 59°F
- 41 to 50°F
- 32 to 41°F
- 23 to 32°F
- Less than 23°F
- 4 — Precipitation (in)

LAND HEIGHT

- Above 13,120ft
- 6,560–13,120ft
- 3,280–6,560ft
- 1,640–3,280ft
- 820–1,640ft
- 330–820ft
- 0–330 ft
- Below sea level

SEA DEPTH

- 0– 820ft
- 820–1,640ft
- 1,640–3,280ft
- 3,280–6,560ft
- 6,560–9,840ft
- 9,840–13,120ft
- Below 13,120ft

CITIES AND TOWNS

- Over 500,000 people
- 100,000–500,000
- 50,000–100,000
- Less than 50,000

## POPULATION

**California** has the most diverse population in the entire US and is one of the most populated states. Oregon and Washington are far less densely populated, but increasing numbers of people are moving into the Northwest and to cities such as Seattle. Los Angeles is one of the world's most sprawling urban centers.

INHABITANTS PER SQ MILE

- More than 520
- 260–520
- 130–260
- 65–130
- Less than 65
- • Major city

URBAN/RURAL POPULATION DIVISION

Los Angeles 9.5%
San Diego 3.5%
San Francisco 2%
Rural population 11%
Other towns and cities 74%

SCALE BAR
0 km   50   100
0 miles   50   100

# ALASKA

A **magnificent land** of mountains, forests, and snowfields, with rich oil and mineral reserves, Alaska was purchased from Russia for $1 million in 1867. Just over half a million people live here, many drawn by the oil industry. Some of Alaska's native peoples like the Aleuts and Inupiaq still live by hunting and fishing.

## ENVIRONMENTAL ISSUES

**Much of northern Alaska** is covered by permafrost (permanently frozen ground). The Trans-Alaskan Pipeline, which brings oil from Prudhoe Bay to Valdez, was built above ground to stop the permafrost melting. A number of major oil spills have threatened Alaska's unique envrionment.

Trans-Alaskan Pipeline

Prudhoe Bay

Valdez

Exxon Valdez 1993

**ENVIRONMENTAL ISSUES**

- ⛴ Major oil spill
- --- Oil pipeline
- ⛏ Oil wells
- Permafrost zone
- ● Major town

## INDUSTRY

Prudhoe Bay

Anchorage

Valdez

Juneau

**The Alaskan economy** is dominated by the oil business. The oilfields of Alaska are of a similar size to those in the Persian Gulf. Minerals including gold are mined in the mountains, and paper products are exported to countries on the Pacific Rim.

**INDUSTRY**

- Chemicals
- Mining
- Oil and gas
- Timber processing
- ⊙ Major industrial center
- — Major road

## FARMING AND LAND USE

Anchorage

**Salmon are caught** in great numbers in the waters of the north Pacific. Much of the state – more than 5.5 million acres – is covered by forest which is commercially lumbered. Most food must be imported, although fruit is grown in hothouses near the larger cities.

**FARMING AND LAND USE**

- ↘ Fishing
- 🦀 Fruit
- ↑ Timber
- Barren
- Forest
- Mountains
- Tundra
- ● Major conurbation

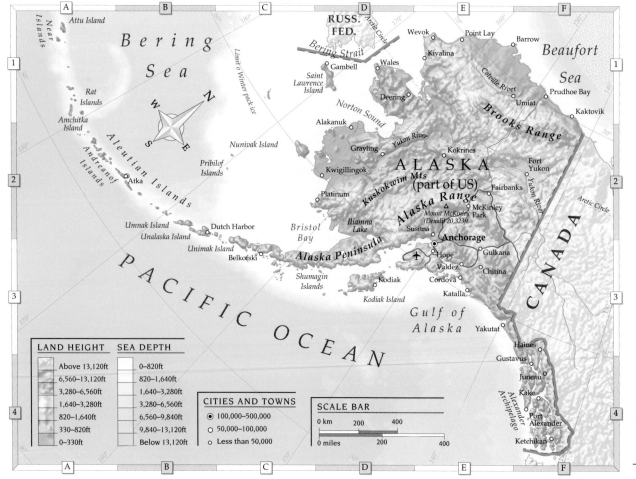

RUSS. FED.

Bering Strait

Attu Island

Near Islands

Bering Sea

Rat Islands

Amchitka Island

Andreanof Islands

Aleutian Islands

Atka

Umnak Island

Unalaska Island

Dutch Harbor

Unimak Island

Belkofski

Nunivak Island

Pribilof Islands

Saint Lawrence Island

Gambell

Wales

Deering

Alakanuk

Grayling

Kwigillingok

Platinum

Bristol Bay

Iliamna Lake

Shumagin Islands

Kodiak

Kodiak Island

Alaska Peninsula

Norton Sound

Wevok

Kivalina

Point Lay

Barrow

Beaufort Sea

Coleville River

Umiat

Prudhoe Bay

Kaktovik

Brooks Range

Kokrines

Yukon River

ALASKA (part of US)

Kuskokwim Mts

Alaska Range

Mount McKinley (Denali) 20,323ft

McKinley Park

Fort Yukon

Fairbanks

Yukon River

Arctic Circle

CANADA

Susitna

Anchorage

Hope

Valdez

Gulkana

Chitina

Cordova

Katalla

Gulf of Alaska

Yakutat

Haines

Gustavus

Juneau

Kake

Alexander Archipelago

Port Alexander

Ketchikan

PACIFIC OCEAN

**LAND HEIGHT**
- Above 13,120ft
- 6,560–13,120ft
- 3,280–6,560ft
- 1,640–3,280ft
- 820–1,640ft
- 330–820ft
- 0–330ft

**SEA DEPTH**
- 0–820ft
- 820–1,640ft
- 1,640–3,280ft
- 3,280–6,560ft
- 6,560–9,840ft
- 9,840–13,120ft
- Below 13,120ft

**CITIES AND TOWNS**
- ⊙ 100,000–500,000
- ○ 50,000–100,000
- ○ Less than 50,000

**SCALE BAR**
0 km 200 400
0 miles 200 400

## CLIMATE

Parts of northern Alaska are frozen year-round and can be cut off entirely in the winter. Summers are milder – especially in the Aleutians.

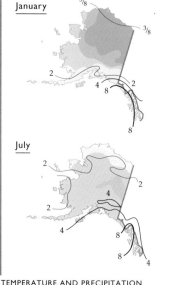

January

July

**TEMPERATURE AND PRECIPITATION**
- More than 59°F
- 50 to 59°F
- 41 to 50°F
- 32 to 41°F
- 23 to 32°F
- 14 to 23°F
- 5 to 14°F
- Less than 5°F
- —4— Precipitation (in)

# HAWAII

Hawaii is the 50th US state. It lies far from the mainland in the middle of the Pacific Ocean. The island chain was formed by volcanoes, only one of which, Mauna Loa, remains active today. The islands' indigenous peoples are Polynesians, but continued immigration means that they now make up only 2% of the population.

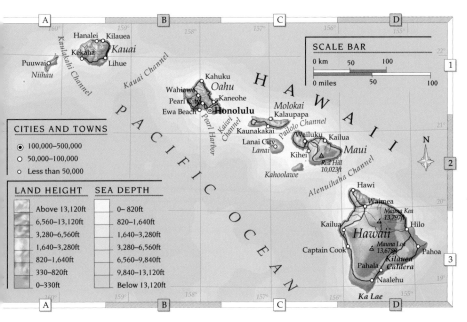

### CITIES AND TOWNS
- ◉ 100,000–500,000
- ○ 50,000–100,000
- ○ Less than 50,000

### LAND HEIGHT
- Above 13,120ft
- 6,560–13,120ft
- 3,280–6,560ft
- 1,640–3,280ft
- 820–1,640ft
- 330–820ft
- 0–330ft

### SEA DEPTH
- 0–820ft
- 820–1,640ft
- 1,640–3,280ft
- 3,280–6,560ft
- 6,560–9,840ft
- 9,840–13,120ft
- Below 13,120ft

SCALE BAR

## INDUSTRY AND LAND USE

Tourism is the most important industry in Hawaii, accounting for one in every three jobs. The naval base at Pearl Harbor also provides jobs for numerous people. The many large plantations grow sugarcane, bananas, and tropical fruit for export.

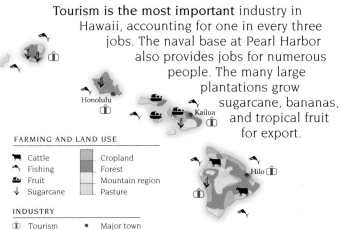

### FARMING AND LAND USE
- Cattle
- Fishing
- Fruit
- Sugarcane
- Cropland
- Forest
- Mountain region
- Pasture

### INDUSTRY
- Tourism
- Major town

## ENVIRONMENTAL ISSUES

Climatic occurrences, combined with the growth of tourism, have an adverse effect on the indigenous flora and fauna. Eruptions from Mauna Loa are an accepted risk for the population.

### ENVIRONMENTAL ISSUES
- Tourist resort
- Volcanic eruption
- Major town

Mauna Loa – 1984
Kilauea – 1983

# US OVERSEAS TERRITORIES

America's overseas territories have traditionally been seen as strategically or economically important. In most cases, the local population has been given a say in deciding whether it wants to govern itself. A US commonwealth territory has a greater level of independence than a US unincorporated or external territory. The US has 13 overseas territories: the four largest are shown here.

### PUERTO RICO

The large island of Puerto Rico has a population of more than 3.5 million people. In recent years there have been campaigns to make it the 51st US state.

### AMERICAN SAMOA

American Samoa consists of five volcanic islands and two coral atolls in the south Pacific. The people are among the last true Polynesians.

### GUAM

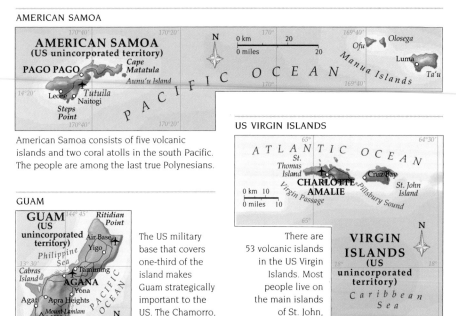

The US military base that covers one-third of the island makes Guam strategically important to the US. The Chamorro, the indigenous people, are in charge of political and social life.

### US VIRGIN ISLANDS

There are 53 volcanic islands in the US Virgin Islands. Most people live on the main islands of St. John, St. Thomas, and St. Croix, which has a vast oil refinery.

# MEXICO

Mexico is a large country with a rich mixture of traditions and cultures. The ancient civilization of the Aztecs that flourished here was crushed by Spanish invaders in the 16th century. Spain ruled Mexico until its independence in 1836, and today the country has the world's largest and fastest-growing Spanish-speaking population. Mexico is mostly dry and mountainous, and farmland is limited, so the country has to import most of the basic foods it needs to feed its people.

## FARMING AND LAND USE

Most of the land suitable for farming is planted with corn – a big part of the Mexican diet. Along the Gulf coast coffee, sugarcane, and cotton are grown on plantations for export. Parts of the dry north are irrigated to grow cotton, but most of the land is taken up by large cattle ranches. Fishing, especially for shellfish such as lobster and shrimp is important in coastal areas.

**FARMING AND LAND USE**

- 🐂 Cattle
- 🐟 Fishing
- ☕ Coffee
- 🌽 Corn
- Cotton
- Shellfish
- ↓ Sugarcane
- Timber

- Cropland
- Desert
- Forest
- Pasture
- Wetland
- • Major conurbation

**LAND USE**

- Cropland 13%
- Pasture 39%
- Forest 26%
- Other 22%

## THE LANDSCAPE

Much of Mexico is made up of a high plateau. The climate there is very dry and varies between true desert in the north, and semidesert farther south. The plateau is separated from the coastal plains by two long, rugged mountain chains: the Eastern Sierra Madre and the Western Sierra Madre. Toward the south, the mountain ranges join, meeting in the region of high volcanic peaks that surround Mexico City.

**The Rio Grande (D 2)**
This river flows from Colorado in the US and forms much of Mexico's northern border. It crosses a vast arid area on its way to the Gulf of Mexico.

**Earthquakes and volcanoes**
Volcanic activity is common in Mexico. Popocatépetl (F 5) and Volcán El Chichónal (G 5) have erupted recently, and Mexico City was hit by a devastating earthquake in 1985.

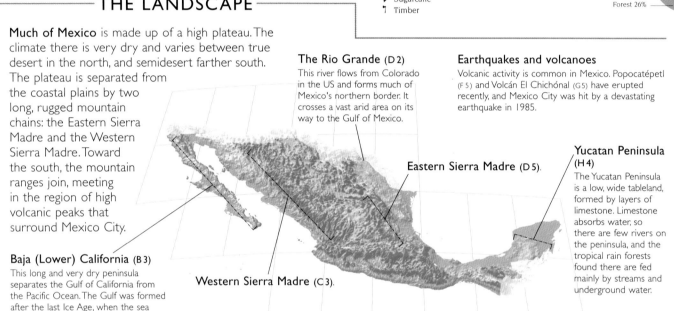

**Eastern Sierra Madre (D 5)**

**Yucatan Peninsula (H 4)**
The Yucatan Peninsula is a low, wide tableland, formed by layers of limestone. Limestone absorbs water, so there are few rivers on the peninsula, and the tropical rain forests found there are fed mainly by streams and underground water.

**Baja (Lower) California (B 3)**
This long and very dry peninsula separates the Gulf of California from the Pacific Ocean. The Gulf was formed after the last Ice Age, when the sea rose to flood a major rift valley.

**Western Sierra Madre (C 3)**

## POPULATION

Most of the north is sparsely populated due to the hot, dry climate and lack of cultivable farmland. As people have migrated from the countryside in search of work, the cities have grown dramatically; almost 75% of Mexicans now live in urban areas. Mexico City is home to almost a quarter of the population and is one of the world's largest cities.

**INHABITANTS PER SQ MILE**
- More than 520
- 260–520
- 130–260
- Less than 130
- ■ Capital city
- • Major city

**URBAN/RURAL POPULATION DIVISION**
- Mexico City 21.6%
- Guadalajara 2.4%
- Monterrey 2%
- Other towns and cities 48%
- Rural population 26%

## ENVIRONMENTAL ISSUES

Fast, unplanned growth has led to poor sanitation and water supplies in Mexico City, while the wall of mountains that surrounds the city traps pollution from cars and factories, giving it some of the world's worst air pollution. Much of Mexico's tropical rainforest has been felled, leading to increased soil erosion. Land clearance farther north is also causing desertification.

**ENVIRONMENTAL ISSUES**
- 🌋 Volcanic eruption
- Urban air pollution
- Risk of desertification
- Deforested areas
- Remaining tropical forests
- • Major industrial center

**CALIFORNIA**

Tijuana  Mexicali  San I
Rosarito  Ensenada

Isla Cedros  Bahía Sebastián Vizcaín
Guerrero Negro

Tropic of Cancer

Isla Clarión

NORTH
AMERICA

# INDUSTRY

**Oil and gas** on the Gulf coast are the biggest source of income. Mexico is also rich in other minerals; it is the world's top silver producer. Manufacturing is centered around Mexico City and along the US border, where mainly foreign-owned factories assemble products for export. Tourism is increasing throughout Mexico.

**STRUCTURE OF INDUSTRY**

Primary 8%
Services 64%
Manufacturing 28%

**INDUSTRY**

- 🚗 Car manufacturing
- Electronics
- ⚙ Engineering
- Food processing
- Iron and steel
- Oil refining
- Textiles
- Mining
- Oil and gas
- Tourism
- Major industrial center / area
- Major road

# CLIMATE

Northern Mexico and the peninsula of Baja California are dry, hot, and largely desert. Toward the south, rainfall increases, especially in July. Moist, warm conditions allow rain forests to grow.

January

July

**TEMPERATURE AND PRECIPITATION**

- More than 86°F
- 77 to 86°F
- 68 to 77°F
- 59 to 68°F
- 50 to 59°F
- 41 to 50°F
- Less than 41°F
- 4 — Precipitation (in)

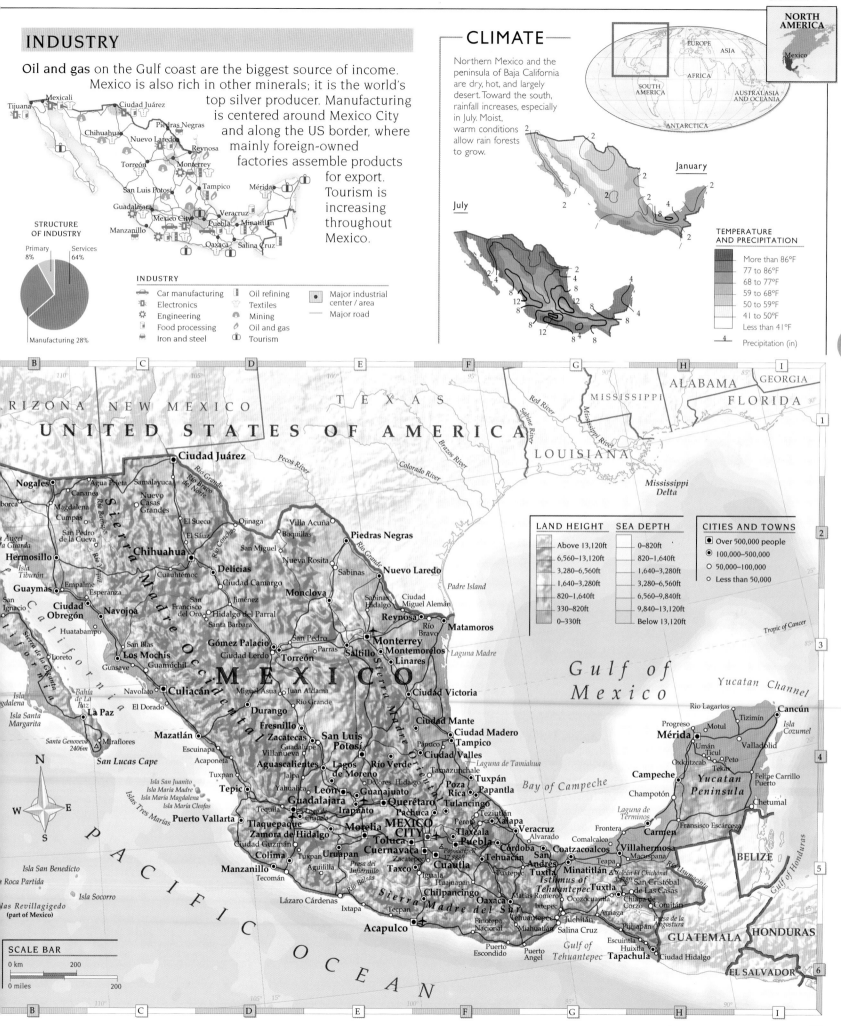

**LAND HEIGHT**
- Above 13,120ft
- 6,560–13,120ft
- 3,280–6,560ft
- 1,640–3,280ft
- 820–1,640ft
- 330–820ft
- 0–330ft

**SEA DEPTH**
- 0–820ft
- 820–1,640ft
- 1,640–3,280ft
- 3,280–6,560ft
- 6,560–9,840ft
- 9,840–13,120ft
- Below 13,120ft

**CITIES AND TOWNS**
- ■ Over 500,000 people
- ● 100,000–500,000
- ○ 50,000–100,000
- ○ Less than 50,000

**SCALE BAR**
0 km        200
0 miles      200

# CENTRAL AMERICA

BELIZE, COSTA RICA, EL SALVADOR, GUATEMALA, HONDURAS, NICARAGUA, PANAMA

**Central America lies** on a narrow bridge of land which links North and South America. All the countries here, except Belize, were once governed by Spain. Today, most of their people are *mestizos* – a mix of the original Maya Indian inhabitants and Spanish settlers. The hot, steamy climate is ideal for growing tropical crops, such as coffee and bananas, which are exported worldwide.

## FARMING AND LAND USE

**About half of all** the agricultural products grown here are exported. The Pacific coast has fertile, well-watered land suitable for growing cotton and sugarcane. In the central highlands are big coffee plantations and ranches where beef cattle are raised. Bananas grow well along the humid Caribbean coastal plain, and shrimp and lobster are caught offshore.

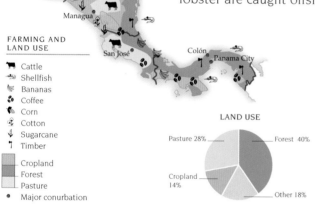

**FARMING AND LAND USE**

- 🐂 Cattle
- 🦐 Shellfish
- 🍌 Bananas
- ☕ Coffee
- 🌽 Corn
- Cotton
- Sugarcane
- Timber

- Cropland
- Forest
- Pasture
- • Major conurbation

**LAND USE**

Pasture 28%
Forest 40%
Cropland 14%
Other 18%

## ENVIRONMENTAL ISSUES

**Central America's rain forests** are rapidly being cut down for timber and to make way for farmland and land for building. Over half of Guatemala's forests have been felled, mostly in the last 30 years. The situation is also bleak in Honduras, Costa Rica, and Nicaragua. Central America lies in a volcanically active zone, and the line of volcanoes running through the region have erupted many times this century.

▲ Volcán Tacaná 1986
▲ Volcán de Fuego 1974
Volcán de Izalco 1958
Volcán Cerro Negro 1995
▲ Volcán Concepcion 1986
▲ Volcán Arenal 1995

**ENVIRONMENTAL ISSUES**
- ▲ Volcanic eruption
- Deforested areas
- Remaining forests

## POPULATION

**Central America's people** live mainly in the valleys of the central highlands or along the Pacific coastal plains. Despite the threat of volcanic eruptions and earthquakes, towns and cities were developed in these areas because of the fertile volcanic soils found there. Just over half the population still lives in rural areas, mostly in small villages or remote settlements, but the cities have expanded rapidly and overcrowding has become a serious problem.

BELMOPAN
GUATEMALA CITY
TEGUCIGALPA
SAN SALVADOR
MANAGUA
SAN JOSÉ
PANAMA CITY

**INHABITANTS PER SQ MILE**
- More than 130
- 52–130
- Less than 52
- ■ Capital city

**URBAN/RURAL POPULATION DIVISION**

San Salvador 3.3%
Tegucigalpa 3.2%
Managua 3.5%
Other towns and cities 37%
Rural population 53%

## THE LANDSCAPE

**The Sierra Madre** in the north and the Cordillera Central to the south form a mountainous ridge that stretches down most of Central America. Along the Pacific coast north of Panama is a belt of more than 40 active volcanoes. The mountains are broken by valleys and basins with large, fertile areas of rich, volcanic soil.

**Coral reef (C 2)**
Off the coast of Belize is a 180-mile-long coral reef – the second longest in the world. Its waters contain spectacular marine life. In places, the reef has become built up into dozens of small sandy islands called cayes.

**Sierra Madre (A 3)**

**The Mosquito Coast (E 4)**
The Mosquito Coast is a remote area of tropical rain forests, lagoons, and rivers lined with mangroves. Most of it is uninhabited by humans, but there is a huge variety of animal species, including monkeys and alligators.

**Lake Nicaragua (E 5)**
This large freshwater lake contains about 400 islands, some of which are active volanoes like Volcán Concepcion. The lake is also home to the world's only freshwater sharks.

**Cordillera Central (G 6)**

**Panama Canal (H 6)**
The Panama Canal links the Atlantic and Pacific oceans along a distance of 51 miles. Half of its route passes through Lake Gatún, a freshwater lake that acts as a reservoir for the canal, providing water to operate the locks.

MEXICO
Yucatán
Carmen
Río Usumacinta
Barillas
Jacaltenango
Chajul
GUA
Huehuetenango
Nebaj
Volcán Tacaná 13,429'
Santa Cruz del Quichéo
Quezaltenango
San Marcos
GUATEMALA CITY
Champerico
San José

## CLIMATE

Temperatures are high all year round, although in January the Caribbean side of Central America is cooler and wetter than the Pacific side. Summers are generally much wetter, especially in the Sierra Madre in Guatemala and on the Pacific coasts of Costa Rica and Panama.

**TEMPERATURE AND PRECIPITATION**

- More than 77°F
- 68 to 77°F
- Less than 68°F
- —4— Precipitation (mm)

January

July

NORTH AMERICA

EUROPE  ASIA
AFRICA
SOUTH AMERICA  Central America
AUSTRALASIA AND OCEANIA
ANTARCTICA

## INDUSTRY

Coffee, fish, and timber processing, fruit exporting, and textile-weaving are typical of the small-scale industries found in Central America. Most industries are based in the capital cities and larger towns. In Panama, many people work at the Panama Canal, which is one of the world's busiest shipping routes. The country is also a major financial center, with many banking and insurance companies.

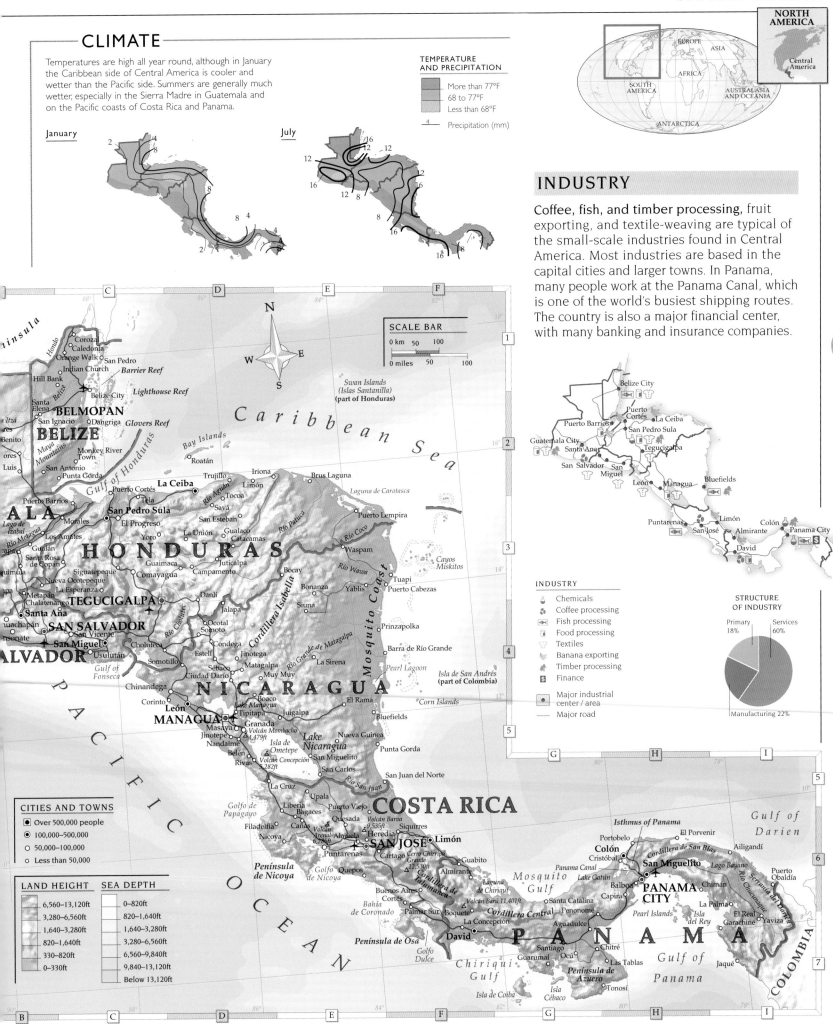

**INDUSTRY**

- 🧪 Chemicals
- ☕ Coffee processing
- 🐟 Fish processing
- 🥫 Food processing
- 👕 Textiles
- 🍌 Banana exporting
- 🌲 Timber processing
- Ⓢ Finance
- ⊙ Major industrial center / area
- — Major road

**STRUCTURE OF INDUSTRY**

Primary 18%
Services 60%
Manufacturing 22%

**CITIES AND TOWNS**
- ■ Over 500,000 people
- ◉ 100,000–500,000
- ○ 50,000–100,000
- ○ Less than 50,000

**LAND HEIGHT      SEA DEPTH**

| LAND HEIGHT | SEA DEPTH |
|---|---|
| 6,560–13,120ft | 0–820ft |
| 3,280–6,560ft | 820–1,640ft |
| 1,640–3,280ft | 1,640–3,280ft |
| 820–1,640ft | 3,280–6,560ft |
| 330–820ft | 6,560–9,840ft |
| 0–330ft | 9,840–13,120ft |
|  | Below 13,120ft |

# THE CARIBBEAN

**The Caribbean Sea** is enclosed by an arc of many hundreds of islands, islets, and offshore reefs that reach from Florida in the US, round to Venezuela in South America. From 1492, Spain, France, Britain, and the Netherlands claimed the islands as colonies. Most of the islands' original inhabitants were wiped out by disease and a wide mixture of peoples – of African, Asian, and European descent – now make up the population. The islands are prone to earthquakes, hurricanes, and volcanic eruptions.

## THE LANDSCAPE

### The Bahamas
The Bahamas are low-lying islands formed from limestone rock. Their coastlines are fringed by coral reefs, lagoons, and mangrove swamps. Some of the bigger islands are covered by forests.

**The islands are formed** from two main mountain chains: the Greater Antilles, which are part of a chain running from west to east, and the Lesser Antilles, which run from north to south. The mountains are now almost submerged under the Atlantic Ocean and Caribbean Sea. Only the higher peaks reach above sea level to form islands.

### Hispaniola (F 4)
Two countries, Haiti and the Dominican Republic, occupy the island of Hispaniola. The land is mostly mountainous, broken by fertile valleys.

### Cuba (C 3)
Cuba is the largest island in the Antilles. Its landscape is made up of wide, fertile plains with rugged hills and mountains in the southeast.

### The Lesser Antilles
Most of these small volcanic islands have mountainous interiors. Barbados and Antigua and Barbuda are flatter, with some higher volcanic areas. Monserrat was evacuated in 1997, following volcanic eruptions on the island.

## FARMING AND LAND USE

**Agriculture is an important source of income**, with over half of all produce exported. Many islands have fertile, well-watered land and large areas are set aside for commercial crops such as sugarcane, tobacco, and coffee. Some islands rely heavily on a single crop; in Dominica, bananas provide over half the country's income. Cuba is one of the world's biggest sugar producers.

| FARMING AND LAND USE | |
|---|---|
| | Cattle |
| | Fishing |
| | Bananas |
| | Coffee |
| | Shellfish |
| | Sugarcane |
| | Tobacco |
| | Cropland |
| | Forest |
| | Pasture |
| • | Major conurbation |

## ENVIRONMENTAL ISSUES

**The islands of the Caribbean** are often under threat from hurricane storm systems which sweep in from the Atlantic Ocean between May and October. The winds can reach speeds of up to 156 miles per hour, devastating everything that lies in their path and causing severe flooding. The storms themselves are enormous; a hurricane can extend outward for 406 miles from its calm center, which is known as the "eye."

## TOURISM

**Tourism is thriving** in the Caribbean, often bringing more income to the region than other, traditional industries. Long sandy beaches, clear, warm waters, and the climate are the main attractions. In Cuba and the Dominican Republic, tourism is expanding at some of the fastest rates in North America. As hotel complexes and new roads and airports are developed, the environment is often damaged. Local people who work in the industry often receive little of the extra cash brought in by the tourists.

| TOURISM | |
|---|---|
| | Major tourist destinations |

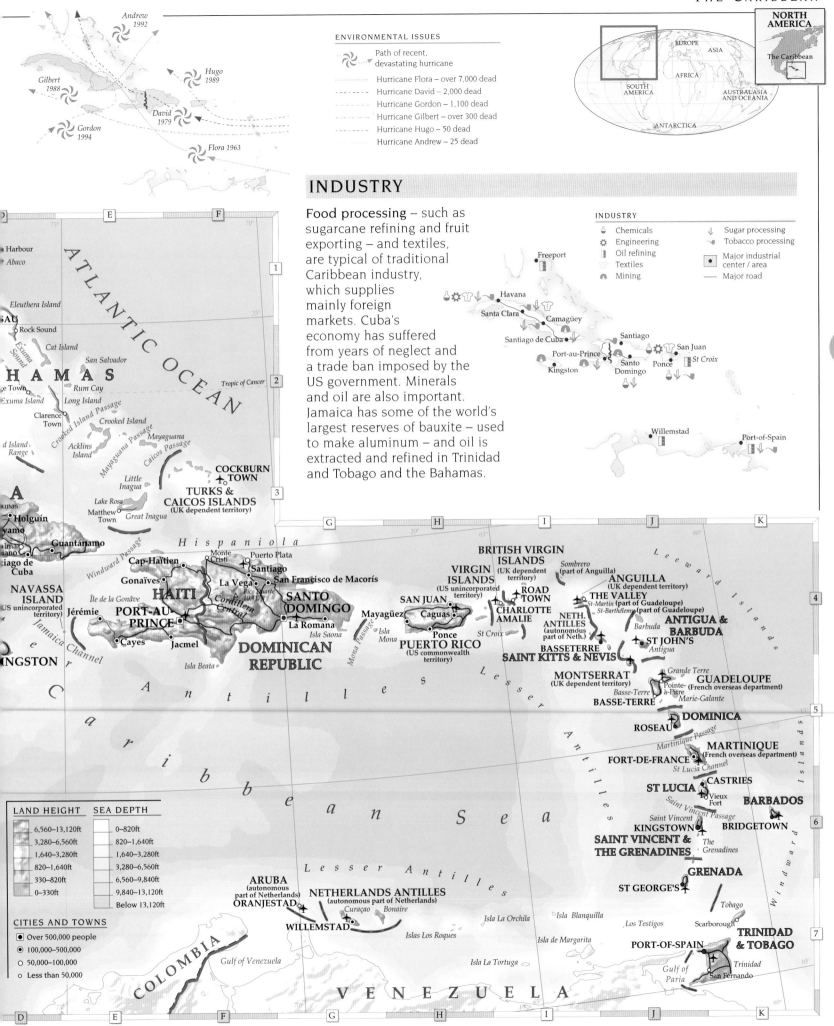

NORTH AMERICA

The Caribbean

EUROPE
ASIA
AFRICA
SOUTH AMERICA
AUSTRALASIA AND OCEANIA
ANTARCTICA

**ENVIRONMENTAL ISSUES**

- Path of recent, devastating hurricane
- Hurricane Flora – over 7,000 dead
- Hurricane David – 2,000 dead
- Hurricane Gordon – 1,100 dead
- Hurricane Gilbert – over 300 dead
- Hurricane Hugo – 50 dead
- Hurricane Andrew – 25 dead

Andrew 1992
Hugo 1989
Gilbert 1988
David 1979
Gordon 1994
Flora 1963

## INDUSTRY

Food processing – such as sugarcane refining and fruit exporting – and textiles, are typical of traditional Caribbean industry, which supplies mainly foreign markets. Cuba's economy has suffered from years of neglect and a trade ban imposed by the US government. Minerals and oil are also important. Jamaica has some of the world's largest reserves of bauxite – used to make aluminum – and oil is extracted and refined in Trinidad and Tobago and the Bahamas.

**INDUSTRY**

- Chemicals
- Engineering
- Oil refining
- Textiles
- Mining
- Sugar processing
- Tobacco processing
- Major industrial center / area
- Major road

Freeport
Havana
Santa Clara
Camagüey
Santiago de Cuba
Santiago
San Juan
St Croix
Port-au-Prince
Ponce
Kingston
Santo Domingo
Willemstad
Port-of-Spain

**LAND HEIGHT**
- 6,560–13,120ft
- 3,280–6,560ft
- 1,640–3,280ft
- 820–1,640ft
- 330–820ft
- 0–330ft

**SEA DEPTH**
- 0–820ft
- 820–1,640ft
- 1,640–3,280ft
- 3,280–6,560ft
- 6,560–9,840ft
- 9,840–13,120ft
- Below 13,120ft

**CITIES AND TOWNS**
- Over 500,000 people
- 100,000–500,000
- 50,000–100,000
- Less than 50,000

ATLANTIC OCEAN
BAHAMAS
Harbour
Abaco
Eleuthera Island
Rock Sound
Cat Island
San Salvador
Exuma Sound
Exuma Island
Long Island
Rum Cay
Clarence Town
Crooked Island Passage
Crooked Island
Mayaguana
Acklins Island
Mayaguana Passage
Caicos Passage
Little Inagua
Caicos Islands
Lake Rosa
Matthew Town
Great Inagua
Tropic of Cancer

COCKBURN TOWN
TURKS & CAICOS ISLANDS (UK dependent territory)

Holguín
yamo
Guantánamo
Santiago de Cuba
NAVASSA ISLAND (US unincorporated territory)
Windward Passage
Hispaniola
Cap-Haïtien
Monte Cristi
Puerto Plata
Santiago
San Francisco de Macorís
Gonaïves
La Vega
HAITI
Île de la Gonâve
Pico Duarte 10,417ft
Cordillera Central
SANTO DOMINGO
PORT-AU-PRINCE
Jérémie
DOMINICAN REPUBLIC
La Romana
Isla Saona
Cayes
Jacmel
Isla Beata
Jamaica Channel
KINGSTON
Caribbean Sea
Lesser Antilles
Antilles

Mayagüez
Caguas
SAN JUAN
Ponce
PUERTO RICO (US commonwealth territory)
Mona Passage
Isla Mona
St Croix
BRITISH VIRGIN ISLANDS (UK dependent territory)
Sombrero (part of Anguilla)
VIRGIN ISLANDS (US unincorporated territory)
ROAD TOWN
CHARLOTTE AMALIE
NETH. ANTILLES (autonomous part of Neth.)
BASSETERRE
SAINT KITTS & NEVIS
ANGUILLA (UK dependent territory)
THE VALLEY
St-Martin (part of Guadeloupe)
St-Barthélemy (part of Guadeloupe)
Barbuda
ANTIGUA & BARBUDA
ST JOHN'S
Antigua
MONTSERRAT (UK dependent territory)
Leeward Islands
Grande Terre
GUADELOUPE (French overseas department)
Pointe-à-Pitre
Basse-Terre
BASSE-TERRE
Marie-Galante
DOMINICA
ROSEAU
Martinique Passage
MARTINIQUE (French overseas department)
FORT-DE-FRANCE
St Lucia Channel
ST LUCIA
CASTRIES
Vieux Fort
Saint Vincent Passage
BARBADOS
Saint Vincent
KINGSTOWN
SAINT VINCENT & THE GRENADINES
The Grenadines
BRIDGETOWN
GRENADA
ST GEORGE'S
Windward Islands
Tobago
Scarborough
TRINIDAD & TOBAGO
PORT-OF-SPAIN
Trinidad
Gulf of Paria
San Fernando

ARUBA (autonomous part of Netherlands)
ORANJESTAD
NETHERLANDS ANTILLES (autonomous part of Netherlands)
WILLEMSTAD
Curaçao
Bonaire
Isla La Orchila
Isla Blanquilla
Los Testigos
Islas Los Roques
Isla de Margarita
COLOMBIA
Gulf of Venezuela
Isla La Tortuga
VENEZUELA

61

# CONTINENTAL EUROPE

**Europe is the world's** second smallest continent, occupying the western tip of the vast Eurasian landmass. To the north and west are old highlands, with the high peaks of the Alps in the south. Most people live on the densely populated North European Plain, which extends from southern England, through northern France, across Germany into Russia.

## CROSS-SECTION THROUGH EUROPE

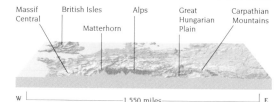

In the west, the land rises up from the Atlantic coast toward the Massif Central in France, and the high peaks of the Alps. Between the Alps and the Carpathian Mountains is the Great Hungarian Plain, where the Danube River flows on its way to the Black Sea.

## PHYSICAL EUROPE

**The ancient mountains** of northwest Europe were scoured and smoothed by glaciers in the last Ice Age. The Alps are newer and more jagged – pushed up when Africa collided with Europe. In between is the North European Plain, where thick layers of fertile soils allow many different crops to be grown.

### 1 THE FROZEN NORTH

Europe's northern coastline stretches deep into the Arctic Circle. Here in Norway, icebergs drift into the deep, wide-bottomed fjords.

### THE NORTH EUROPEAN PLAIN 2

The North European Plain has low, rolling hills and plains. Much of the area is cultivated and used for growing crops like wheat and sugarbeet.

### 3 ANCIENT HIGHLANDS

Some of the world's oldest rocks are found in northwest Europe. Erosion by glaciers in the last Ice Age created smoothed hills like the mountains of Wales.

### 4 THE ATLANTIC COAST

On Europe's Atlantic coast, the force of waves and winds has created striking landforms like this huge sand dune in southwest France.

### THE ALPS 5

The Alps are Europe's major mountain chain. They formed about 65 million years ago. The Matterhorn is one of the most dramatic peaks.

ELEVATION

16,400ft
13,120ft
9,840ft
6,560ft
3,280ft
1,640ft
820ft
330ft
sea level
below sea level
cross section

SCALE 1:31,000,000

0 km    300    600

0 miles    300    600

# POLITICAL EUROPE

Europe's population increased rapidly during the 18th and 19th centuries, following the Industrial Revolution. In the 20th century, Europe suffered a series of wars that redrew the political map. From 1989 to 1991, communist governments in eastern Europe and the former Soviet Union collapsed, as political reform swept through the countries behind the "Iron Curtain." In western Europe, the 15 countries of the European Union are discussing closer political and economic ties.

**POPULATION**

Capital cities

- Above 500,000
- 100,000 to 500,000
- 50,000 to 100,000

**REGIONAL IDENTITY**

Throughout Europe, there is a growing call to recognize regional cultural identity. The Basque region, bordering southwest France and Spain, is one example.

**RURAL LIFE**

Away from Europe's bustling cities, traditional rural lifestyles survive. Here in the Republic of Ireland, a winter shelter is being made for cattle.

## STANDARDS OF LIVING

Living standards are generally much lower in eastern Europe than in the wealthier west. Homelessness and unemployment are still common, even in the most prosperous countries.

SCALE 1:27,500,000

0 km    300    600

0 miles    300    600

## POPULATION

More than 700 million people live in Europe, and its population is highly urbanized. In Belgium and the Netherlands, almost 90% of people live in cities. In the south and east, more people still live in rural areas. The northern countries have the smallest populations because much of the land is too cold to be habitable.

POPULATION DENSITY
(People per sq mile)

Below 129
130–259
260–389
390–519
520–779
Above 780

Largest city
MOSCOW
9.4 million people

SPREADING CITIES

Amsterdam, in the Netherlands, is part of a conurbation, a large built-up area where several towns or cities have merged together to form a single urban area.

STANDARD OF LIVING
(UN Human Development Index)

low    high

# EUROPEAN GEOGRAPHY

Europe is blessed with a temperate climate, ample mineral reserves, and good transportation links. During the 18th and 19th centuries the continent was transformed, as new methods of production made industry and farming more efficient and productive. Today, in many countries, heavy industries have been replaced by high-tech and service industries. Agriculture is still important, and many crops thrive on Europe's fertile plains.

## INDUSTRY

Western Europe has some of the world's wealthiest countries. In countries such as France, Germany, and the UK, traditional industries like iron and steel-making are now being replaced by light industries, such as electronics, and services like finance and insurance. In Eastern Europe, industry was subsidized by the communist governments for years. Many factories are old-fashioned and need investment to improve their equipment and production methods.

## MINERAL RESOURCES

Europe has few sizable reserves of metallic minerals; most were used up by industry during the last century. Oil, gas, and coal are found in large quantities – gas in the North Sea and oil in the Volga basin. Coal, although abundant, is being steadily depleted.

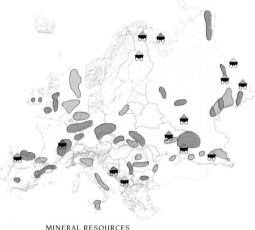

### MINERAL RESOURCES

- Bauxite
- Chromium
- Iron
- Manganese
- Nickel
- Uranium
- Oil/gas field
- Coal field

### OIL AND GAS

Oil and gas reserves are plentiful in the Russian Federation. South of Rostov-on-Don, oil is pumped from the ground and piped to nearby refineries.

### ECONOMIC ACTIVITY

- ✈ Aerospace
- 🚚 Vehicle manufacturing
- ⚗ Chemicals
- Coal
- Defense
- Electronics
- ⚙ Engineering
- Ⓢ Finance
- Food processing
- High-tech industry
- Iron and steel
- Oil and gas
- Printing and publishing
- Textiles
- Timber processing

### GNP per capita (US$)

- Below 1,999
- 2,000–4,999
- 5,000–9,999
- 10,000–19,999
- 20,000–24,999
- Above 25,000
- • Industrial center

### CAR MANUFACTURING

Germany is one of the world's largest manufacturers of cars. Companies like BMW, Mercedes-Benz, and Volkswagen export cars across the world.

### FINANCE

London is one of the most important financial centers in the world. Many banks and financial institutions have their headquarters here. At the London Stock Exchange, people buy and sell stocks and shares.

## CLIMATE

**Europe's climate is** temperate with few climatic extremes. In the far north, Europe extends into the Arctic Circle and the climate is so cold that the Baltic Sea freezes over in the winter. Toward the Atlantic coast in the west, the climate becomes wetter and warmer because of a warm ocean current, known as the Gulf Stream. Countries such as Italy and Spain that border the Mediterranean Sea have long, hot summers and low rainfall, which can sometimes lead to such problems as drought.

### EXTREME WEATHER EVENTS

Symbols indicate climatic extremes

**CLIMATE**
- Tundra
- Subarctic
- Cool continental
- Temperate/humid
- Mediterranean
- Semiarid

Arctic Circle

**Coldest place**
UST' SHCHUGOR (Russ. Fed.)
Temp. -67°F

**Driest place**
ASTRAKHAN' (Russ. Fed.)
Annual rainfall 6 in

**Hottest place**
SEVILLE (Spain)
Temp. 122°F

**Wettest place**
CRKVICE (Yugoslavia)
Annual rainfall 183 in

NORTH AMERICA · EUROPE · ASIA · AFRICA · SOUTH AMERICA · AUSTRALASIA and OCEANIA · ANTARCTICA

### THE MEDITERRANEAN CLIMATE

The mild, warm climate around the Mediterranean Sea allows olives, citrus fruits, and grapes to thrive. Long, sunny days also help the fruits ripen. Grapes are harvested and crushed to make many different wines.

## LAND USE AND AGRICULTURE

**Europe's agricultural heart** is the North European Plain, where fertile soils and ample rainfall allow a variety of crops to be grown. Wheat is the main grain crop, and a wide range of fruit and vegetables are also grown. Dairy and beef cattle are raised for their milk and meat throughout Europe. In the south, the Mediterranean climate is ideal for citrus fruits and olives. Forests cover much of northern Scandinavia, while sheep farming is common in the hills of the British Isles.

### FISHING

The north Atlantic Ocean provides a rich marine harvest for fishermen. High-quality cod and mackerel are caught in the cold, nutrient-rich waters.

### CROPLANDS

Many different crops are grown on the North European Plain. Sunflowers, wheat, and sugar beets – used to make sugar – are among the main crops grown there.

### LAND USE AND AGRICULTURE
- Cattle
- Goats
- Pigs
- Reindeer
- Sheep
- Cereals
- Citrus fruits
- Fishing
- Fruit
- Olive oil
- Potatoes
- Root crops
- Shellfish
- Sunflowers
- Timber
- Vineyards

- Cropland
- Forest
- Ice cap
- Mountain region
- Pasture
- Tundra
- Wetland
- Major conurbation

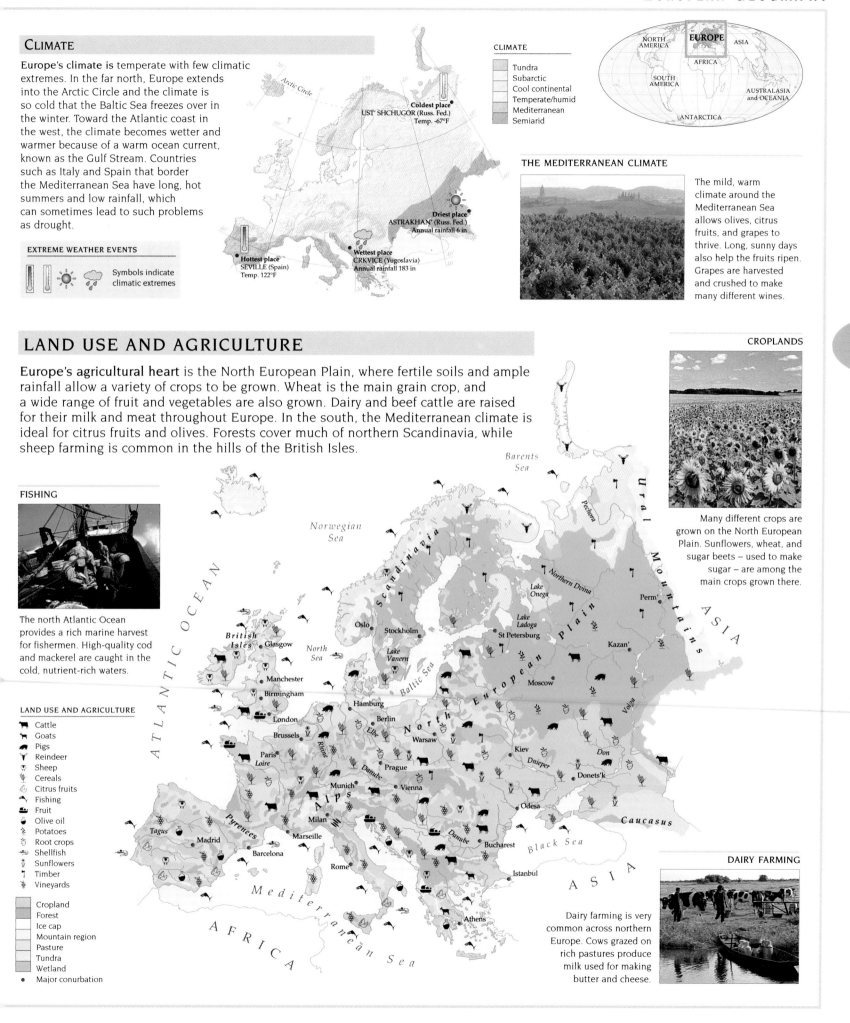

Barents Sea

Ural Mountains · ASIA

Norwegian Sea

ATLANTIC OCEAN

British Isles · Glasgow · North Sea

Manchester · Birmingham · London · Brussels · Paris · Loire · Rhine

Oslo · Stockholm · Lake Vänern · Baltic Sea · St Petersburg · Lake Ladoga · Lake Onega · Northern Dvina · Pechora · Perm'

Hamburg · Berlin · North European Plain · Moscow · Kazan' · Volga

Elbe · Warsaw · Kiev · Dnieper · Don · Donets'k

Prague · Danube · Munich · Vienna · Odesa · Caucasus

Alps · Milan · Marseille · Danube · Bucharest · Black Sea · Istanbul · ASIA

Tagus · Madrid · Barcelona · Pyrenees · Rome

Mediterranean Sea · Athens · AFRICA

### DAIRY FARMING

Dairy farming is very common across northern Europe. Cows grazed on rich pastures produce milk used for making butter and cheese.

# NORTHERN EUROPE

DENMARK, ESTONIA, FINLAND, ICELAND, LATVIA,
LITHUANIA, NORWAY, SWEDEN

**Denmark, Sweden, and Norway** are together known as Scandinavia. These countries, along with the North Atlantic island of Iceland, have similar languages and cultures. Finland has a very different language and a separate identity from its Scandinavian neighbors. Estonia, Latvia, and Lithuania, known as the Baltic states, were part of the Soviet Union until 1989, when each became an independent country.

## INDUSTRY

**In Scandinavia,** many natural resources are used in industry: timber for paper and furniture; iron ore for steel and cars; and fish and natural gas from the seas. Hydroelectric power is generated by water flowing down steep mountain slopes. The Baltic states still rely on Russia to supply their raw materials and energy.

### INDUSTRY

- 🚗 Car manufacturing
- 🝃 Chemicals
- ⚙ Engineering
- 🐟 Fish processing
- ⊢ Hydroelectric power
- ⏚ Shipbuilding
- 🌲 Timber processing
- 🏛 Tourism
- ▣ Major industrial center / area
- — Major road

#### STRUCTURE OF INDUSTRY

Primary 4%
Services 65%
Manufacturing 31%

## POPULATION

**The population is distributed** mainly along the warmer and flatter southern and coastal areas. Population totals and densities are low for all of the countries, and Iceland has the lowest population density in Europe, with just eight people per sq mile. Many Scandinavians have holiday homes on the islands, along the lake shores, or in coastal areas.

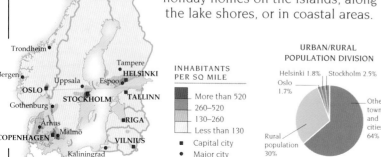

#### INHABITANTS PER SQ MILE

- More than 520
- 260–520
- 130–260
- Less than 130
- ■ Capital city
- • Major city

#### URBAN/RURAL POPULATION DIVISION

Helsinki 1.8%    Stockholm 2.5%
Oslo 1.7%
Other towns and cities 64%
Rural population 30%

## FARMING AND LAND USE

**Southern Denmark and Sweden** are the most productive areas, with pig farming, dairy farming, and crops such as wheat, barley, and potatoes. Sheep farming is important in southern Norway and Iceland. In the Baltic states, cereals, potatoes, and sugar beets are the main crops, and cattle graze on damp pasture.

### FARMING AND LAND USE

- 🐄 Cattle
- 🐟 Fishing
- 🐖 Pigs
- 🐑 Sheep
- 🌾 Cereals
- 🥕 Root crops
- 🌲 Timber
- Pasture
- Cropland
- Forest
- Ice cap
- Mountain region
- Tundra
- • Major conurbation

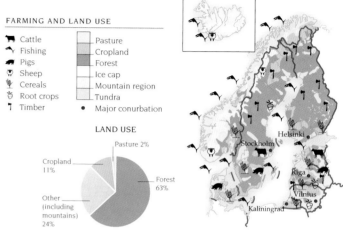

#### LAND USE

Pasture 2%
Cropland 11%
Forest 63%
Other (including mountains) 24%

## THE LANDSCAPE

**The north and west** of Scandinavia is extremely rugged and mountainous, with landscapes eroded by ice. In the south of Scandinavia the land is flatter, with fertile soils deposited by glaciers. Much of Finland, Norway, and Sweden is covered by dense forests. The Baltic states are much lower, with rounded hills and many lakes and marshes.

**The land of ice and fire.**
Iceland is one of the world's most active volcanic areas. There are about 200 volcanoes on the island, along with bubbling hot springs, mud-holes, and geysers that spurt boiling water and steam high into the air.

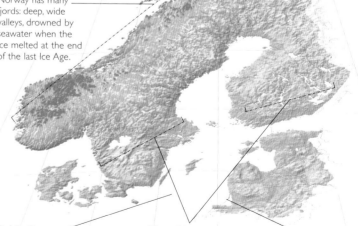

**Fjords**
Norway has many fjords: deep, wide valleys, drowned by seawater when the ice melted at the end of the last Ice Age.

**Baltic Sea (D 7)**
Ships from Finland, Sweden, and the Baltic states use the Baltic Sea as their route to the north Atlantic Ocean. In winter, much of the sea is frozen.

**Glacial lakes**
Finland and Sweden have many thousands of lakes. During the last Ice Age, glaciers scoured hollows that filled with water when the ice melted.

**Courland Spit (D 7)**
This wide sandspit runs for 62 miles along the Baltic coast of Lithuania and the Russian enclave of Kaliningra. It encloses a huge lagoon.

# ENVIRONMENTAL ISSUES

**Northern Europe** has been badly affected by industrial pollution from other parts of Europe. Polluted air moves north and mixes with the rain to create acid rain. This poisons forests and lakes, destroying the plants and animals living in them. In Norway and Sweden, electricity is produced by dams that obtain from the plentiful water supply. Hydro-electric power is a clean, alternative energy source.

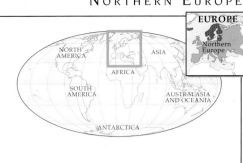

EUROPE
Northern Europe

Vatnajökull 1996
Surtsey 1963

**ENVIRONMENTAL ISSUES**
- Major dams
- Urban air pollution
- Volcanic eruption
- Affected by acid rain
- Sea pollution
- Major industrial center

## CLIMATE

Warm ocean currents flowing north along the coasts of Norway and Iceland make the climate mild and wet. Away from the sea, the climate is generally colder and drier.

January

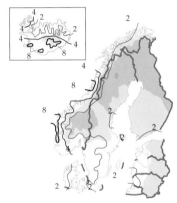

July

**TEMPERATURE AND PRECIPITATION**

| | |
|---|---|
| More than 59°F | 23 to 32°F |
| 50 to 59°F | 14 to 23°F |
| 41 to 50°F | 5 to 14°F |
| 32 to 41°F | Less than 5°F |
| | —4— Precipitation (in) |

### ICELAND

Bolungarvík
Raufarhöfn
Ísafjörður
Siglufjörður
Húsavík
Stykkishólmur
Akureyri
Seydhisfjördhur
REYKJAVIK
Neskaupstadhur
Sólfoss
Djúpivogur
Thorlákshöfn
Hvannadalshnúkur 2119m
Surtsey
Vestmannaeyjar
Faxaflói
*Norwegian Sea*
Arctic Circle
ATLANTIC OCEAN

**SCALE BAR**
0 km 100 200
0 miles 100 200

**LAND HEIGHT**
- 6,560–13,120ft
- 3,280–6,560ft
- 1,640–3,280ft
- 820–1,640ft
- 330–820ft
- 0–330ft

**SEA DEPTH**
- 0–160ft
- 160–330ft
- 330–820ft
- 820–1,640ft
- 1,640–3,280ft
- 3,280–6,560ft
- Below 6,560ft

**CITIES AND TOWNS**
- Over 500,000 people
- 100,000–500,000
- 50,000–100,000
- Less than 50,000

# THE LOW COUNTRIES

BELGIUM, LUXEMBOURG, NETHERLANDS

**Belgium, Luxembourg, and the Netherlands** are called the Low Countries because most of their land is flat and low-lying. Much of the Netherlands lies below sea level, and over hundreds of years the Dutch have built dikes and dams to prevent flooding, and have pumped water off large areas of land to reclaim them from the sea. The Low Countries are Europe's most densely populated countries, but most of their people have a high living standard.

## ENVIRONMENTAL ISSUES

Huge land reclamation projects in the Netherlands, such as the IJsselmeer project, have created some new land for agricultural use, and also for houses, roads, and open spaces. Heavy industry has caused serious air pollution in cities such as Amsterdam and Rotterdam, and added to Europe's acid rain problem.

ENVIRONMENTAL ISSUES

- Urban air pollution
- Built-up areas
- Reclaimed land
- Polluted river
- Major industrial center

## CLIMATE

The Low Countries share a similar climate, with mild winters and warm summers. Only in the upland Ardennes region does rainfall increase and temperatures decrease.

January

July

TEMPERATURE AND PRECIPITATION

- More than 59°F
- 50 to 59°F
- 41 to 50°F
- 32 to 41°F
- Less than 32°F

4 — Precipitation (in)

NETHERLANDS' TWO CAPITALS
AMSTERDAM - capital
THE HAGUE - seat of government

LAND HEIGHT
- 1,640–3,280ft
- 820–1,640ft
- 330–820ft
- 0–330ft
- Below sea level

SEA DEPTH
- 0–330ft

CITIES AND TOWNS
- Over 500,000 people
- 100,000–500,000
- 50,000–100,000
- Less than 50,000

SCALE BAR
0 km   25   50
0 miles   25   50

EUROPE
Low Countries

# POPULATION

**More than 25 million people** live in the Low Countries, and nine out of every ten people live in a town or city. The largest urban area – known as the *Randstad Holland* – is in the Netherlands. It runs in an unbroken line from Rotterdam in the south, to Amsterdam in the west. Even most rural areas in the Low Countries are densely populated.

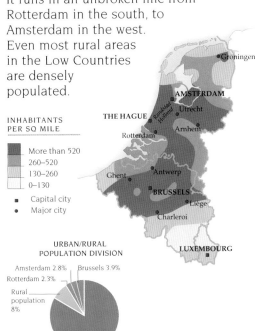

INHABITANTS
PER SQ MILE

- More than 520
- 260–520
- 130–260
- 0–130

- Capital city
- Major city

URBAN/RURAL
POPULATION DIVISION

Amsterdam 2.8%  Brussels 3.9%
Rotterdam 2.3%
Rural population 8%

Other towns and cities 83%

# FARMING AND LAND USE

The Low Countries' fertile soils and flat plains provide excellent conditions for farming. The main crops grown are barley, potatoes, and flax for making linen. In the Netherlands, much farmland is used for dairy farming. The country is also famous for growing flowers, which are exported around the world. Flowers and vegetables are grown either in open fields or in enormous greenhouses, which allow production year-round.

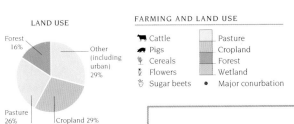

LAND USE

Forest 16%
Other (including urban) 29%
Pasture 26%
Cropland 29%

FARMING AND LAND USE

- Cattle
- Pigs
- Cereals
- Flowers
- Sugar beets
- Pasture
- Cropland
- Forest
- Wetland
- Major conurbation

# THE LANDSCAPE

The Low Countries are largely flat and low-lying. The ancient hills of the Ardennes, in the far southeast, are the only higher region. They rise to heights of more than 1,640 ft. Two major rivers – the Meuse and the Rhine – flow across the Low Countries to their mouths in the North Sea. At the coast, the Rhine deposits large quantities of sediment to form a delta.

**Polders**
In the Netherlands, land has been reclaimed from the sea since the Middle Ages by building dikes and drainage ditches. These areas of land are called polders. They are very fertile.

**Rhine River (E4)**
The River Rhine erodes and carries large amounts of sediment along its course. When it reaches the Netherlands it divides into three rivers. As they approach the North Sea, the rivers slow down, depositing the sediment to form a delta.

**Low-lying Netherlands**
Over two-thirds of the Netherlands lies at or below sea level. This makes flooding a constant threat in coastal areas.

# INDUSTRY

The Low Countries are an important center for the high-tech and electronics industries. Good transportation links to the rest of Europe allow them to sell their products in other countries. The built-up area stretching from Amsterdam in the Netherlands to Antwerp in Belgium has the greatest number of factories. Luxembourg is also an important banking center; many international banks have their headquarters in its capital city.

STRUCTURE
OF INDUSTRY

Primary 3%
Services 68%
Manufacturing 29%

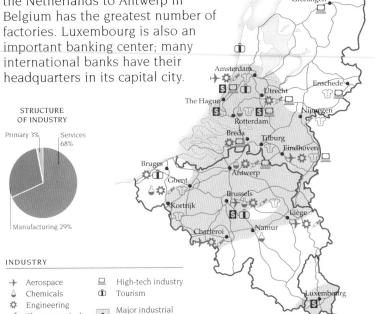

INDUSTRY

- ✈ Aerospace
- 🛢 Chemicals
- ⚙ Engineering
- Pharmaceuticals
- Textiles
- $ Finance
- 💻 High-tech industry
- 🏛 Tourism
- ▪ Major industrial center / area
- — Major road

**Flanders (B6)**
The plains of Flanders in western Belgium have fertile soils which were deposited by glaciers during the last Ice Age. They provide excellent land for growing crops.

**Heathlands**
The heathlands on the Dutch-Belgian border have thin, sandy soils. The only plants that grow well here are heathers and gorse.

**Ardennes (D8)**
The hills of the Ardennes were formed over 300 million years ago. They have many deep valleys, which have been eroded by rivers like the Meuse.

# THE BRITISH ISLES

UNITED KINGDOM, REPUBLIC OF IRELAND

**The British Isles** lie off the northwest coast of mainland Europe. They are made up of two large islands and more than 5,000 smaller ones. Politically, the region is divided into two countries: the United Kingdom – England, Wales, Scotland, and Northern Ireland – and the Republic of Ireland. Geographically, the British Isles are divided between highlands to the north and west, and lowlands to the south and east.

## THE LANDSCAPE

**Low rolling hills,** high moorlands, and small fields with high hedges are all typical of the British Isles. Ireland is known as the Emerald Isle because heavy rainfall gives it a lush, green appearance. Scotland and Wales are mountainous; the rocks forming the mountains there are some of the oldest in the world.

### Indented coastlines
The west coast of the British Isles faces the Atlantic Ocean, and more than 1,860 miles of open sea to the North American continent. Storms and high waves constantly batter the hard, rocky coastline, giving it a jagged outline.

### Ben Nevis (C 4)
This mountain is the highest point in the British Isles. It is 4,406 ft above sea level.

### The Lake District (D 5)
The Lake District National Park has England's highest peak, Scafell Pike, at 3,209 ft, its deepest lake, Wast Water (260 ft), and its largest lake, Windermere (10 miles long).

### The Pennines (D 6)
The Pennines are a chain of high hills, topped by moorland. They run for more than 250 miles, and are known as the "backbone of England."

### The Burren (A 6)
The Burren is a large area of limestone in the west of Ireland. Its flat surfaces are known as limestone "pavements." There are also many caves and sinkholes in the area.

### Rias
Rias are river valleys that have been drowned by rising sea levels. The southern coast of southwest England has many good examples.

### The Fens (E 6)
This is the flattest area in England. Much of the land here has been reclaimed from the sea.

## FARMING AND LAND USE

**The English lowlands** and the wide, flat stretches of land in East Anglia are the agricultural heartland of the United Kingdom. The country is no longer self-sufficient in food, but wheat, potatoes and other vegetables, and fruits, are widely grown. In Ireland, and in central and southern England, dairy and beef cattle feed off grassy pastures. In the hilly and mountainous areas, sheep farming is more usual.

**FARMING AND LAND USE**

| | |
|---|---|
| 🐄 Cattle | ▢ Pasture |
| 🐑 Sheep | ▨ Cropland |
| 🌾 Cereals | ▩ Forest |
| 🚜 Market gardening | ▢ Mountain region |
| 🌱 Root crops | ● Major conurbation |

**LAND USE**

Cropland 24%
Pasture 50%
Other (including urban) 17%
Forest 9%

## INDUSTRY

**The United Kingdom's** traditional industries, such as coal mining, iron- and steel-making, and textiles, have declined in recent years. Today, newer industries make cars, chemicals, and electronic and high-tech goods. Service industries, especially banking and insurance, have grown in importance. The country's most valuable natural resource is its large North Sea oil and gas fields.

**INDUSTRY**

| |
|---|
| ✈ Aerospace |
| 🚗 Car manufacturing |
| ⚗ Chemicals |
| ⚙ Engineering |
| ▽ Textiles |
| $ Finance |
| 💻 High-tech industry |
| ⛴ Tourism |
| ▣ Major industrial center / area |
| — Major road |

**STRUCTURE OF INDUSTRY**

Primary 2%
Services 67%
Manufacturing 31%

## POPULATION

**The United Kingdom** is densely populated, with most of the people living in urban areas. The southeast is the most crowded part of the country. The Scottish Highlands are less populated today than they were 200 years ago. Ireland is still mainly rural, with many Irish people making their living from farming.

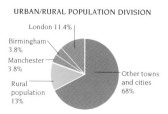

**URBAN/RURAL POPULATION DIVISION**

London 11.4%
Birmingham 3.8%
Manchester 3.8%
Rural population 13%
Other towns and cities 68%

**INHABITANTS PER SQ MILE**

- More than 520
- 260–520
- 130–260
- Less than 130
- ■ Capital city
- ● Major city

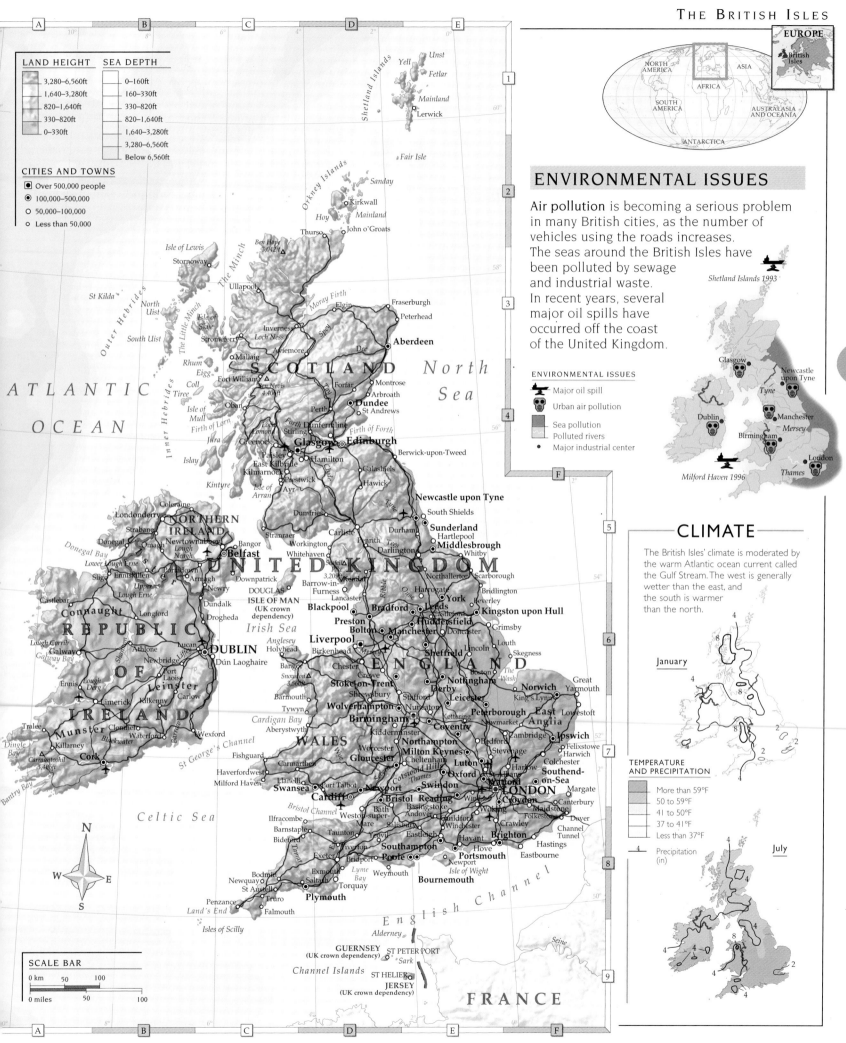

EUROPE
British Isles

NORTH AMERICA
ASIA
AFRICA
SOUTH AMERICA
AUSTRALASIA AND OCEANIA
ANTARCTICA

**LAND HEIGHT**

3,280–6,560ft
1,640–3,280ft
820–1,640ft
330–820ft
0–330ft

**SEA DEPTH**

0–160ft
160–330ft
330–820ft
820–1,640ft
1,640–3,280ft
3,280–6,560ft
Below 6,560ft

**CITIES AND TOWNS**

▣ Over 500,000 people
◉ 100,000–500,000
○ 50,000–100,000
○ Less than 50,000

## ENVIRONMENTAL ISSUES

**Air pollution** is becoming a serious problem in many British cities, as the number of vehicles using the roads increases. The seas around the British Isles have been polluted by sewage and industrial waste. In recent years, several major oil spills have occurred off the coast of the United Kingdom.

Shetland Islands 1993

**ENVIRONMENTAL ISSUES**

⬲ Major oil spill
☠ Urban air pollution
▪ Sea pollution
▫ Polluted rivers
● Major industrial center

Glasgow
Newcastle upon Tyne
Tyne
Dublin
Manchester
Mersey
Birmingham
London
Thames

Milford Haven 1996

## CLIMATE

The British Isles' climate is moderated by the warm Atlantic ocean current called the Gulf Stream. The west is generally wetter than the east, and the south is warmer than the north.

January

July

**TEMPERATURE AND PRECIPITATION**

More than 59°F
50 to 59°F
41 to 50°F
37 to 41°F
Less than 37°F

─4 Precipitation (in)

ATLANTIC OCEAN

North Sea

Shetland Islands
Yell
Unst
Fetlar
Mainland
Lerwick

Fair Isle

Orkney Islands
Sanday
Kirkwall
Hoy
Mainland
John o'Groats
Thurso

Ben Hope 3,042ft △

Isle of Lewis
Stornoway

St Kilda

North Uist
South Uist

Outer Hebrides

The Minch

The Little Minch

Ullapool
Inverness
Loch Ness
Stroneferry
Aviemore
Isle of Skye
Mallaig
Rhum
Eigg
Coll
Tiree
Isle of Mull
Oban
Fort of Lorn
Jura
Islay
Kintyre
Isle of Arran

Inner Hebrides

Moray Firth
Elgin
Spey
Fraserburgh
Peterhead

**SCOTLAND**

**Aberdeen**

Dee
Forfar
Montrose
Arbroath
**Dundee**
St Andrews
Perth
Ben Nevis 4,406ft △
Loch Lomond
Forth
Stirling
Dunfermline
Firth of Forth
Greenock
**Glasgow**
**Edinburgh**
Paisley
Hamilton
East Kilbride
Kilmarnock
Prestwick
Galashiels
Ayr
Hawick
Berwick-upon-Tweed

Clyde

Dumfries

**Newcastle upon Tyne**
South Shields
Tyne
**Sunderland**
Hartlepool
**Middlesbrough**
Whitby
Tees
Darlington
Durham
Penrith
Carlisle
Workington
Whitehaven
Scarborough
Northallerton
Scalfell Pike 3,209ft △
Bridlington
Harrogate

Coleraine
Londonderry
Strabane
**NORTHERN IRELAND**
Newtownabbey
Bangor
Donegal
Omagh
Lough Neagh
**Belfast**
Enniskillen
Armagh
Portadown
Newry
Downpatrick
Upper Lough Erne
Lower Lough Erne
Sligo
Castlebar

**UNITED KINGDOM**

**REPUBLIC**

Donegal Bay

Connaught

Lough Corrib
**DUBLIN**
Galway
Galway Bay
Athlone
Lucan
Newbridge
Dún Laoghaire
Ennis
Lough Derg
**OF**
Port Laoise
Longford
Drogheda
Dundalk
Leinster
Carlow
Kilkenny

**IRELAND**

Limerick
Munster
Clonmel
Blackwater
Waterford
Wexford
Dingle Bay
Carrauntoohil 3,406ft △
Killarney
Tralee
**Cork**

Bantry Bay

ISLE OF MAN
DOUGLAS
(UK crown dependency)

Irish Sea

Barrow-in-Furness
Kendal
Lancaster
**Blackpool**
**Preston**
**Bolton**
**Bradford**
**Leeds**
**York**
Castleford
Beverley
**Kingston upon Hull**
Grimsby
Louth
**Huddersfield**
**Manchester**
Doncaster
**Liverpool**
Birkenhead
**Sheffield**
Lincoln
Skegness
Bangor
Holyhead
Anglesey
Chester
Crewe
Mersey
**ENGLAND**
Boston
Snowdon 3,560ft △
Stoke-on-Trent
**Nottingham**
The Wash
Shrewsbury
**Derby**
**Leicester**
King's Lynn
Stafford
**Norwich**
Great Yarmouth
**Wolverhampton**
Nuneaton
Peterborough
**East Anglia**
Barmouth
Kidderminster
**Birmingham**
Coventry
Newmarket
**Ipswich**
Lowestoft
Tywyn
Cambridge
Cardigan Bay
Worcester
**Northampton**
Felixstowe
Aberystwyth
**WALES**
**Milton Keynes**
Stevenage
Harwich
**Gloucester**
Cheltenham
Bedford
Colchester
Cotswold Hills
**Luton**
Harlow
**Oxford**
St Albans
Southend-on-Sea
Carmarthen
Thames
**Swindon**
Watford
Margate
Haverfordwest
Llanelli
Newport
**Bristol**
**Reading**
**LONDON**
Canterbury
Milford Haven
Port Talbot
Bath
Basingstoke
Croydon
Maidstone
Fishguard
**Swansea**
**Cardiff**
Weston-super-Mare
Andover
Woking
Folkestone
Bristol Channel
Salisbury
Guildford
Crawley
Dover
Ilfracombe
Winchester
**Brighton**
Channel Tunnel
Barnstaple
Taunton
Yeovil
Eastleigh
Havant
Hastings
Bideford
Tiverton
**Southampton**
**Portsmouth**
Hove
Eastbourne
Exmouth
Bridport
Poole
Isle of Wight
Newport
Exeter
Lyme Bay
Weymouth
**Bournemouth**
Torquay
Bodmin
Newquay
Saltash
St Austell
**Plymouth**
Penzance
Truro
Land's End
Falmouth

Celtic Sea

St George's Channel

Isles of Scilly

English Channel

Alderney

**GUERNSEY**
(UK crown dependency)
ST PETER PORT
Sark
Channel Islands
ST HELIER
**JERSEY**
(UK crown dependency)

Seine

**FRANCE**

**SCALE BAR**

0 km   50   100

0 miles   50   100

# FRANCE

ANDORRA, MONACO, FRANCE

**France has helped shape** the history and culture of Europe for centuries. Today, as a founder-member of the European Union, France is an avid supporter of the eventual political and economic integration of Europe's different countries. France is Western Europe's leading farming nation and one of the world's top industrial powers. Its cultural attractions and scenery draw tourists from around the world.

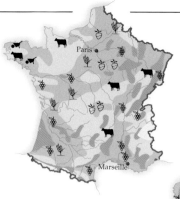

## FARMING AND LAND USE

**France is able** to produce a variety of crops because of its rich soils and mild climate. Wheat is grown in many parts of the north, along with potatoes and other vegetables. Fields of corn and sunflowers and fruit orchards are found in the south, while grapes for the famous wine industry are grown across the country. Beef and dairy cattle are grazed on low-lying pasture.

### FARMING AND LAND USE

- 🐄 Cattle
- 🌾 Cereals
- 🐖 Market gardening
- 🥕 Root crops
- 🍇 Vineyards
- Pasture
- Cropland
- Forest
- Mountain region
- Wetland
- ● Major conurbation

### LAND USE

- Cropland 35%
- Pasture 20%
- Forest 27%
- Other (including urban) 18%

## THE LANDSCAPE

**The north and west** of France is made up of mainly flat, grassy plains or low hills. Wooded mountains line the country's borders in the south and east, and much of central France is taken up by the Massif Central, an enormous plateau cut by deep river valleys and scattered with extinct volcanoes. Three major rivers, the Loire, Seine, and Garonne, drain the lowland basins.

### Paris Basin

The Paris Basin is a saucer-shaped hollow made up of layers of hard and soft rock, covered with very fertile soils. It runs across about 38,600 sq miles of northern France.

### Alps (E 5)

The western end of the European Alpine mountain chain stretches into southeast France. The French Alps can be crossed by several passes, which give access to Italy and Switzerland.

### Normandy

The coast of Normandy is lined with high chalk cliffs.

## INDUSTRY

**France is one of the world's** top manufacturing nations, with a variety of both traditional and high-tech industries. Cars, machinery, and electronic products are exported worldwide, along with luxury goods such as perfumes, fashions, and wines. Fossil fuels provide some energy, but France is currently the world's second-biggest producer of nuclear power.

### STRUCTURE OF INDUSTRY

- Primary 4%
- Services 63%
- Manufacturing 33%

### INDUSTRY

- ✈ Aerospace
- 🚗 Car manufacturing
- 🧪 Chemicals
- ⚙ Engineering
- 👕 Textiles
- 💻 High-tech industry
- 🧳 Tourism
- ▪ Major industrial center / area
- — Major road

### Pyrenees (C 7)

These mountains form a natural barrier between France and Spain. Several peaks reach heights of over 9,480 ft. The Pyrenees are difficult to cross, due to their height, and because they have few low passes.

### Massif Central (D 5)

This vast granite plateau was formed over 200 million years ago. Volcanic activity here stopped only within the last 10,000 years, and the region's rounded hills are the worn-down remains of volcanic mountains.

### Mont Blanc (E 5)

This mountain in the French Alps is the tallest in Western Europe. It is 15,771 ft high.

### Camargue (D 7)

The Camargue is an area of marshes, pastures, sand dunes, and salt flats at the mouth of the Rhône River. Rare animal and plant species are found there.

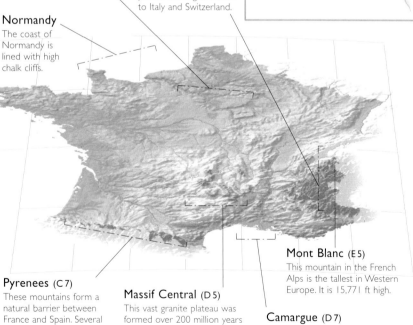

## POPULATION

**In the past 50 years,** most people have moved from the countryside into urban areas. Paris and its suburbs, the industrial cities, and the Côte d'Azur in the southeast are the most economically developed parts of France and now have the biggest populations.

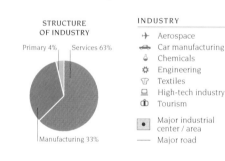

### URBAN/RURAL POPULATION DIVISION

- Paris 16.6%
- Lyon 2.3%
- Marseille 1.5%
- Rural population 26%
- Other towns and cities 53.6%

### INHABITANTS PER SQ MILE

- More than 520
- 260–520
- 130–260
- Less than 130
- ▪ Capital city
- ● Major city

EUROPE

# ENVIRONMENTAL ISSUES

Many of France's coastal areas have been polluted by industry and tourism. The French government has recently introduced policies that aim to protect the country's environment. France's reliance on nuclear energy – 75% of its electricity is generated by nuclear power – causes it to suffer less from the pollution caused by burning fossil fuels than many other countries in Europe.

NORTH AMERICA · AFRICA · SOUTH AMERICA · ASIA · AUSTRALASIA AND OCEANIA · ANTARCTICA

**ENVIRONMENTAL ISSUES**

- Nuclear power station
- Sea pollution
- Polluted rivers
- Major industrial center

Seine · Paris · Lille · Loire · Saône · Bordeaux · Lyon · Garonne · Rhône · Marseille

## CLIMATE

In winter, the coldest areas of France are the mountains of the Massif Central and the Alps. Summers are hottest on the Mediterranean coast.

**TEMPERATURE AND PRECIPITATION**

- More than 68°F
- 59 to 68°F
- 50 to 59°F
- 41 to 50°F
- 32 to 41°F
- 23 to 32°F
- Less than 23°F

4 — Precipitation (in)

January

July

### Map of France

UNITED KINGDOM

**SCALE BAR**
0 km 50 100
0 miles 50 100

English Channel

GUERNSEY (UK crown dependency)
Channel Islands
JERSEY (UK crown dependency)

Alderney
Golfe de St-Malo
Baie de la Seine

Île d'Ouessant · Brest · Morlaix · Landerneau · Plérin · St-Brieuc · Dinan · Iroise · Quimper · Pontivy · Loudéac · Concarneau · Quimperlé · Hennebont · Vannes · Lorient · Auray

Belle Île · la Baule-Escoublac · St-Nazaire · Nantes · Rezé

Bay of Biscay

Île d'Yeu · Challans · les Herbiers · la Roche-sur-Yon · les Sables-d'Olonne · Fontenay-le-Comte · Île de Ré · la Rochelle · Rochefort · Île d'Oléron · Saintes · Royan

Channel Tunnel · Strait of Dover · Calais · Dunkerque · Boulogne-sur-Mer · St-Omer · Lille · Tourcoing · Roubaix · le Portel · Berck-Plage · Artois · Douai · Valenciennes · Abbeville · Arras · Cambrai · Dieppe · Albert · Hirson · Charleville-Mézières · Fécamp · Amiens · Beauvais · Noyon · Laon · Sedan · le Havre · Picardy (Picardie) · Barentin · Rouen · Oise · Compiègne · Bayeux · Caen · Lisieux · Louviers · Évreux · Senlis · Pontoise · Château-Thierry · Reims · Châlons-en-Champagne · Coutances · St-Lô · Avranches · Alençon · Argenteuil · Nanterre · PARIS · Créteil · Versailles · Antony · Melun · Fontainebleau · Marne · Bar-le-Duc · Granville · St-Malo · Normandy (Normandie) · Fougères · Chartres · Nemours · Troyes

BELGIUM · GERMANY · LUXEMBOURG · Leie · Sambre · Meuse · Ardennes · Thionville · Metz · Hagondange · Moselle · Lorraine · Nancy · Saverne · Haguenau · Schiltigheim · Alsace · Strasbourg · Toul · St-Dié · Sélestat · Colmar · Épinal · Vosges · Chaumont · Langres · St-Louis · Belfort · Montbéliard · Audincourt · Mulhouse · Vesoul · Cernay

Morlaix · Brittany (Bretagne) · Rennes · Maine · Vitré · Laval · le Mans · Sarthe · Île-de-France · Redon · Châteaubriant · la Flèche · Orléans · Vendôme · Châteaudun · Angers · Trélazé · Touraine · Tours · Orléanais · Blois · Olivet · Saumur · Anjou · Cholet · Thouars · Berry · Bourges · Cosne-Cours-sur-Loire · Côte d'Or · Auxerre · Yonne · Burgundy (Bourgogne) · Dijon · Châtellerault · Châteauroux · Nevers · Nivernais · Morvan · Besançon · Franche-Comté · Beaune · Dôle · Pontarlier

Poitou · Niort · Poitiers · Vienne · Creuse · Bourbonnais · Montluçon · Moulins · Digoin · Chalon-sur-Saône · Lons-le-Saunier · Jura

SWITZERLAND · Lake Geneva · Thonon-les-Bains · Bourg-en-Bresse · Amberieu-en-Bugey · Annecy · Mont Blanc 15,771ft

Limoges · Limousin · Guéret · Marche · Riom · Vichy · Thiers · Roanne · Tarare · St-Claude · Cognac · Charente · Angoulême · Charente · Clermont-Ferrand · Ussel · Issoire · Puy de Sancy 6,185ft · Auvergne · Lyon · Villeurbanne · Vienne · Chamonix · Savoie · Annecy · Col du Mont Cenis 6,834ft · Lille Saint Bernard Pass 7,179ft

Médoc · Coutras · Mérignac · Pessac · Libourne · Bergerac · Périgueux · Dordogne · Tulle · Brive-la-Gaillarde · Aurillac · St-Flour · le Puy · St-Étienne · St-Chamond · Voiron · St-Egrève · Grenoble · Massif · Central · Briançon · Col de Montgenèvre 6,070ft

Bordeaux · Arcachon · la Teste · Isle · Dordogne · Lot · Figeac · Cahors · Rodez · Mende · Valence · Privas · Ardèche · Montélimar · Drôme · Dauphiné · Gap · Po · ITALY

Marmande · Houilles · Agen · Moissac · Aveyron · Albi · Carmaux · Tarn · Alès · Orange · Bollène · Sorgues · Digne · Mont-de-Marsan · Castelsarrasin · Montauban · Gaillac · Graulhet · Cévennes · Languedoc · Nîmes · Avignon · Tarascon · Manosque · Salon-de-Provence · Provence

Aquitaine · Dax · Marmande · Landes · Garonne · Auch · Armagnac · Gascony (Gascogne) · Toulouse · Tarn · Montpellier · Frontignan · Béziers · Sète · Agde · Arles · Aix-en-Provence · Aubagne · Nice · Antibes · Cannes · le Cannet · MONACO

Anglet · Bayonne · Biarritz · Orthez · Pau · Lourdes · Tarbes · St-Gaudens · Balaïtous 10,312ft · Auch · Castelnaudary · Carcassonne · Narbonne · Marseille · Six-Fours-les-Plages · la Seine-sur-Mer · Toulon · Îles d'Hyères · Côte d'Azur · Hyères · la Ciotat

SPAIN · Ebro · ANDORRA LA VELLA · ANDORRA · Pamiers · Foix · Limoux · Perpignan · Roussillon · Pyrenees · Gulf of Lion

**LAND HEIGHT**
- Above 13,120ft
- 6,560–13,120ft
- 3,280–6,560ft
- 1,640–3,280ft
- 820–1,640ft
- 330–820ft
- 0–330ft

**SEA DEPTH**
- 0–160ft
- 160–330ft
- 330–820ft
- 820–1,640ft
- 1,640–3,280ft
- 3,280–6,560ft
- Below 6,560ft

**CITIES AND TOWNS**
- Over 500,000 people
- 100,000–500,000
- 50,000–100,000
- Less than 50,000

Gulf of Gascony

Ligurian Sea · Mediterranean Sea · Corsica (Corse) · Bastia · Monte Cinto 8,871ft · Monte Incudine 7,008ft · Ajaccio · Sartène · Bonifacio · Strait of Bonifacio · Sardinia (Sardegna) (part of Italy) · Scale: same as main map · Tyrrhenian Sea

Corsica (Corse) · Bastia · Monte Cinto 8,878ft · Ligurian Sea

# SPAIN AND PORTUGAL

PORTUGAL, SPAIN

**Spain and Portugal** occupy the Iberian Peninsula, which is cut off from the rest of Europe by the Pyrenees. Over the centuries, Iberia has been invaded and settled by many different peoples. The Moors, who arrived from North Africa in the 8th century, ruled much of Spain for almost 800 years, and their influence can still be seen in Spanish culture. Portugal is one of the poorest countries in western Europe, but Spain's economy is rapidly expanding.

## FARMING AND LAND USE

Cereals, especially wheat and barley, are Iberia's chief crops. In the dry south of Spain, the land is irrigated to citrus fruits, particularly oranges, and a variety of vegetables. In both countries, olive trees and vineyards occupy large areas of land; olive oil and wine are important exports. Cork oak trees from Iberia's forests supply 80% of the world's cork.

### FARMING AND LAND USE
- 🐑 Sheep
- 🌾 Cereals
- 🍋 Citrus fruit
- 🫒 Olive oil
- 🍇 Vineyards
- ♣ Cork
- ☐ Pasture
- ☐ Cropland
- ■ Forest
- ☐ Mountain region
- ● Major conurbation

### LAND USE
Other 10% · Cropland 39% · Forest 33% · Pasture 18%

## INDUSTRY

**Madrid, Barcelona,** and the northern ports are Spain's industrial centers. Here, iron ore from Spanish mines is used to make steel, and factories produce cars, machinery, and chemicals. Portugal exports textiles, clothing, and footwear, along with fish, such as sardines and tuna, caught off the Atlantic coast. In both countries, tourism is very important to the economy.

### STRUCTURE OF INDUSTRY
Primary 5% · Services 62% · Manufacturing 33%

### INDUSTRY
- 🚗 Car manufacturing
- Chemicals
- ⚙ Engineering
- Fish processing
- Shipbuilding
- Textiles
- Mining
- Tourism
- ▣ Major industrial center / area
- — Major road

## POPULATION

**In the first half** of the 20th century, most Spaniards lived in villages or small towns scattered around the country. Today, tourism and industry have drawn most of the population to the cities and coastal areas. Most Portuguese still live in rural areas along the coast or in the river valleys, but the cities are growing fast.

### URBAN/RURAL POPULATION DIVISION
Madrid 7.8% · Barcelona 6.8% · Lisbon 3.4% · Other towns and cities 52% · Rural population 30%

### INHABITANTS PER SQ MILE
- More than 520
- 260–520
- 130–260
- Less than 130
- ■ Capital city
- ● Major city

## THE LANDSCAPE

**Most of inland Spain is taken up** by the Meseta, a dry, almost treeless plateau surrounded by steep mountain ranges. The only lowlands, apart from narrow strips along the Mediterranean coast, are the valleys of the Ebro, Tagus, Guadiana, and Guadalquivir Rivers. Portugal's coast is lined by wide plains. Inland, the Tagus River divides the country in two. To the north the land is hilly and wooded; to the south it is low-lying and drier.

**Westward-flowing rivers**
The Duero, Tagus, and Guadalquivir Rivers flow across the Meseta on their courses to the Atlantic Ocean.

**Ebro River** (E2)
The Ebro River carries vital irrigation water to Spain's northeastern plains before flowing into the Mediterranean Sea.

**Cordillera Cantábrica** (C1)
These rugged, forested mountains rise on Spain's Atlantic coast. They form the northern edge of the Meseta.

**The Pyrenees** (F2)
These high mountains form a natural boundary with France.

**Duero River** (D2)

**Tagus River** (B4)

**The Meseta**
Much of this vast plateau of ancient rock is covered with dry, dusty high plains. It has thin soils and is mainly used to graze sheep and goats.

**Sierra Morena** (C5)
The southern end of the Meseta is marked by this low range of mountains.

**Guadalquivir Basin** (C5)
The Guadalquivir River has deposited layers of rich soil called alluvium on its floodplain, making this one of Spain's most fertile regions.

**Mulhacén** (D5)
Mulhacén, in the snow-capped Sierra Nevada range in southern Spain, is 11,421 ft high. It is Iberia's tallest mountain.

# ENVIRONMENTAL ISSUES

Soil erosion – where the top layer of soil has been worn away by wind and rain – has affected much of the Iberian Peninsula. This is caused by farming, combined with drought and deforestation. In Spain, a national tree-planting program has been started to combat this problem. Industrial and tourist development along the Mediterranean coast of Spain and in the Balearic Islands has damaged natural habitats on both land and sea.

**ENVIRONMENTAL ISSUES**

- Overbuilding
- Soil degradation
- Severe soil degradation
- Polluted rivers

## CLIMATE

Northern Spain is wetter and cooler than the south. On the central plateau, summers are very hot and dry, and winters often freezing. The north of Portugal is cooled by winds blowing off the Atlantic Ocean. The south is warmer, with dry, mild winters.

**TEMPERATURE AND PRECIPITATION**

- More than 77°F
- 68 to 77°F
- 59 to 68°F
- 50 to 59°F
- 41 to 50°F
- 32 to 41°F
- 23 to 32°F
- 14 to 23°F
- Less than 14°F

4 — Precipitation (in)

January

July

EUROPE

**LAND HEIGHT**

- 6,560–13,120ft
- 3,280–6,560ft
- 1,640–3,280ft
- 820–1,640ft
- 330–820ft
- 0–330ft

**SEA DEPTH**

- 0–820ft
- 820–1,640ft
- 1,640–3,280ft
- 3,280–6,560ft
- 6,560–9,840ft
- 9,840–13,120ft
- Below 13,120ft

**CITIES AND TOWNS**

- Over 500,000 people
- 100,000–500,000
- 50,000–100,000
- Less than 50,000

**SCALE BAR**

0 km 50 100

0 miles 50 100

# ITALY

ITALY, SAN MARINO, VATICAN CITY

**Italy has played** an important role in Europe since the Romans based their mighty empire here over 2,000 years ago. The famous boot shape divides into two very different halves. Northern Italy has a varied range of industries and agriculture. Beautiful cities like Venice, Florence, and Rome draw tourists from all over the world. Southern Italy is poorer and less developed than the north, with a hotter, drier climate and less productive land.

## THE LANDSCAPE

**Italy is a peninsula** jutting south from mainland Europe into the Mediterranean Sea. In northern and central Italy the land is mainly mountainous. Most of the flat land is in the Po Valley and along the eastern coast. Italy lies within an earthquake zone, which makes the land unstable, and there are also a number of active volcanoes.

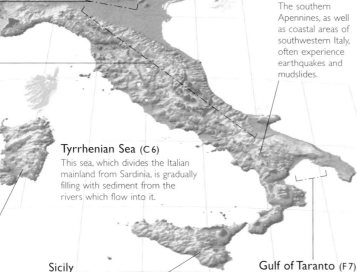

**Po Valley** (C 2)
The basin of the Po River has the best soils in Italy. Rich alluvium is washed from the mountains by the river to form a wide plain.

**Italian lakes**
Great lakes like Garda (B3) and Como (B2) fill several south-facing valleys once occupied by glaciers.

**The Dolomites** (D 2)
These high mountains are part of the same range as the Alps. They were formed 65 million years ago.

**The Apennines** (C 4)
This mountain range forms the "backbone" of Italy, dividing the rocky west coast from the flatter, sandy east coast.

**Earthquakes**
The southern Apennines, as well as coastal areas of southwestern Italy, often experience earthquakes and mudslides.

**Tyrrhenian Sea** (C 6)
This sea, which divides the Italian mainland from Sardinia, is gradually filling with sediment from the rivers which flow into it.

**Sardinia**
The island of Sardinia is made from very old rocks that were thrust up to form mountains.

**Sicily**
Sicily is the largest island in the Mediterranean. It has a famous active volcano called Mount Etna and often experiences earthquakes.

**Gulf of Taranto** (F 7)
During earthquakes, great blocks of land have broken away and sunk into the sea, forming the Gulf's square shape.

## FARMING AND LAND USE

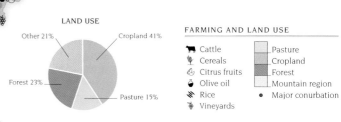

**The Po Valley is a** broad, flat plain in the north of Italy. It contains the most fertile land in the country, and wheat and rice are the main cereal crops grown here. Grapes for wine are grown everywhere in Italy. In much of the south, the land must be irrigated to support crops. Where there is enough water, citrus fruits, olives, and many kinds of tomatoes are grown.

LAND USE

Other 21%
Cropland 41%
Forest 23%
Pasture 15%

FARMING AND LAND USE
- Cattle
- Cereals
- Citrus fruits
- Olive oil
- Rice
- Vineyards
- Pasture
- Cropland
- Forest
- Mountain region
- Major conurbation

## INDUSTRY

**Italian industry is located** mainly in the north. Design is extremely important to Italians, and they are proud of the elegant designs of their furniture, clothes, and shoes. Although many firms are small, they are very efficient. Italy has few mineral resources, so it needs to import raw materials to make cars, engines, and other high-tech products.

INDUSTRY
- Car manufacturing
- Chemicals
- Iron and steel
- Textiles
- Finance
- High-tech industry
- Tourism
- Major industrial center / area
- Major road

STRUCTURE OF INDUSTRY
Primary 3%
Services 66%
Manufacturing 31%

## POPULATION

**Most of Italy's population** lives in the north, mainly in and around the Po Valley, which is home to over 25 million people. Most people here have a high standard of living. Southern Italy is much more rural: towns are smaller and life is often much harder.

URBAN/RURAL POPULATION DIVISION

Milan 1.5%   Rome 2.8%
Naples 1.2%
Rural population 31%
Other towns and cities 63.5%

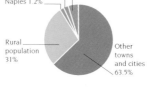

INHABITANTS PER SQ MILE
- More than 520
- 260–520
- 130–260
- 0–130
- Capital city
- Major city

EUROPE
NORTH AMERICA · ASIA · AFRICA · SOUTH AMERICA · AUSTRALASIA AND OCEANIA · ANTARCTICA
Spain and Portugal

## ENVIRONMENTAL ISSUES

Soil erosion – where the top layer of soil has been worn away by wind and rain – has affected much of the Iberian Peninsula. This is caused by farming, combined with drought and deforestation. In Spain, a national tree-planting program has been started to combat this problem. Industrial and tourist development along the Mediterranean coast of Spain and in the Balearic Islands has damaged natural habitats on both land and sea.

### ENVIRONMENTAL ISSUES

- Overbuilding
- Soil degradation
- Severe soil degradation
- Polluted rivers

Douro · Ebro · Costa Brava · Guadiana · Guadalquivir · Segura · Majorca · Ibiza · Costa Blanca · Costa del Sol

## CLIMATE

Northern Spain is wetter and cooler than the south. On the central plateau, summers are very hot and dry, and winters often freezing. The north of Portugal is cooled by winds blowing off the Atlantic Ocean. The south is warmer, with dry, mild winters.

January

July

TEMPERATURE AND PRECIPITATION
- More than 77°F
- 68 to 77°F
- 59 to 68°F
- 50 to 59°F
- 41 to 50°F
- 32 to 41°F
- 23 to 32°F
- 14 to 23°F
- Less than 14°F

4 — Precipitation (in)

LAND HEIGHT
- 6,560–13,120ft
- 3,280–6,560ft
- 1,640–3,280ft
- 820–1,640ft
- 330–820ft
- 0–330ft

SEA DEPTH
- 0–820ft
- 820–1,640ft
- 1,640–3,280ft
- 3,280–6,560ft
- 6,560–9,840ft
- 9,840–13,120ft
- Below 13,120ft

CITIES AND TOWNS
- Over 500,000 people
- 100,000–500,000
- 50,000–100,000
- Less than 50,000

SCALE BAR
0 km   50   100
0 miles   50   100

# GERMANY AND THE ALPINE STATES

AUSTRIA, GERMANY, LIECHTENSTEIN, SLOVENIA, SWITZERLAND

**Germany lies at the heart** of Europe and is the biggest industrial power in the continent. In 1945, Germany was divided into two separate countries, East and West Germany, which were reunited in 1990. To the south, the snow-capped peaks of the Alps, Europe's highest mountains, tower over the Alpine states – Switzerland, Austria, Liechtenstein, and the former Yugoslavian state of Slovenia.

## INDUSTRY

**Germany is a leading** manufacturer of cars, chemicals, machinery, and transportation equipment. Switzerland and Liechtenstein make high-value products such as watches and pharmaceuticals and provide services such as banking. The Alpine states are a popular tourist location year-round.

### INDUSTRY

- Car manufacturing
- Chemicals
- Engineering
- Iron and steel
- Shipbuilding
- Pharmaceuticals
- High-tech industry
- Tourism
- Major industrial center / area
- Major road

STRUCTURE OF INDUSTRY

Primary 1% Services 62%
Manufacturing 37%

## POPULATION

**Western and central Germany** are the most densely populated areas in this region – particularly in and around the Rhine and Ruhr valleys, where there are many industries. In the south, the steep slopes of the Alps and permanent snow cover on the higher peaks means that most large towns and cities are in scattered lowland areas.

INHABITANTS PER SQ MILE
- More than 520
- 260–520
- 130–260
- Less than 130
- Capital city
- Major city

URBAN/RURAL POPULATION DIVISION

Vienna 1.4% Berlin 3.6%
Munich 1%
Rural population 18%
Other towns and cities 76%

## FARMING AND LAND USE

**Germany produces** three-quarters of its own food. Crop farming is widespread, with cereals and root crops grown in flat, fertile areas. Cattle and pig farming supplies meat and dairy products. Across the Alps, the mountains limit farming, although grapes are grown on the warmer, south-facing slopes. The rich pastures of the lower slopes are used to graze beef and dairy cattle.

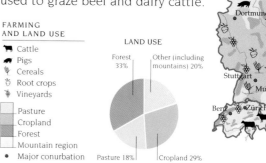

FARMING AND LAND USE
- Cattle
- Pigs
- Cereals
- Root crops
- Vineyards
- Pasture
- Cropland
- Forest
- Mountain region
- Major conurbation

LAND USE
Forest 33%
Other (including mountains) 20%
Pasture 18%
Cropland 29%

## THE LANDSCAPE

**To the north, flat plains** and heathlands surround the North Sea coast. Farther south are Germany's central uplands, which are lower and older than the jagged peaks of the Alps, which began to form about 65 million years ago. From its source in the Black Forest, the Danube River flows eastward across Germany and Austria on its course to the Black Sea. The other major river, the Rhine, flows northward.

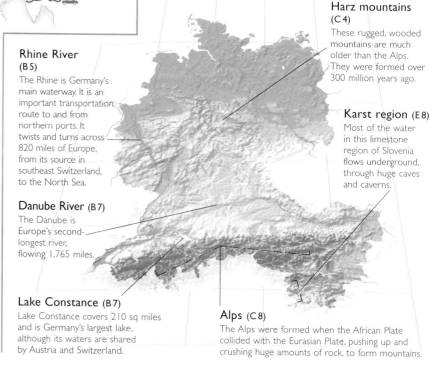

**Harz mountains (C4)**
These rugged, wooded mountains are much older than the Alps. They were formed over 300 million years ago.

**Rhine River (B5)**
The Rhine is Germany's main waterway. It is an important transportation route to and from northern ports. It twists and turns across 820 miles of Europe, from its source in southeast Switzerland, to the North Sea.

**Karst region (E8)**
Most of the water in this limestone region of Slovenia flows underground, through huge caves and caverns.

**Danube River (B7)**
The Danube is Europe's second-longest river, flowing 1,765 miles.

**Lake Constance (B7)**
Lake Constance covers 210 sq miles and is Germany's largest lake, although its waters are shared by Austria and Switzerland.

**Alps (C8)**
The Alps were formed when the African Plate collided with the Eurasian Plate, pushing up and crushing huge amounts of rock, to form mountains.

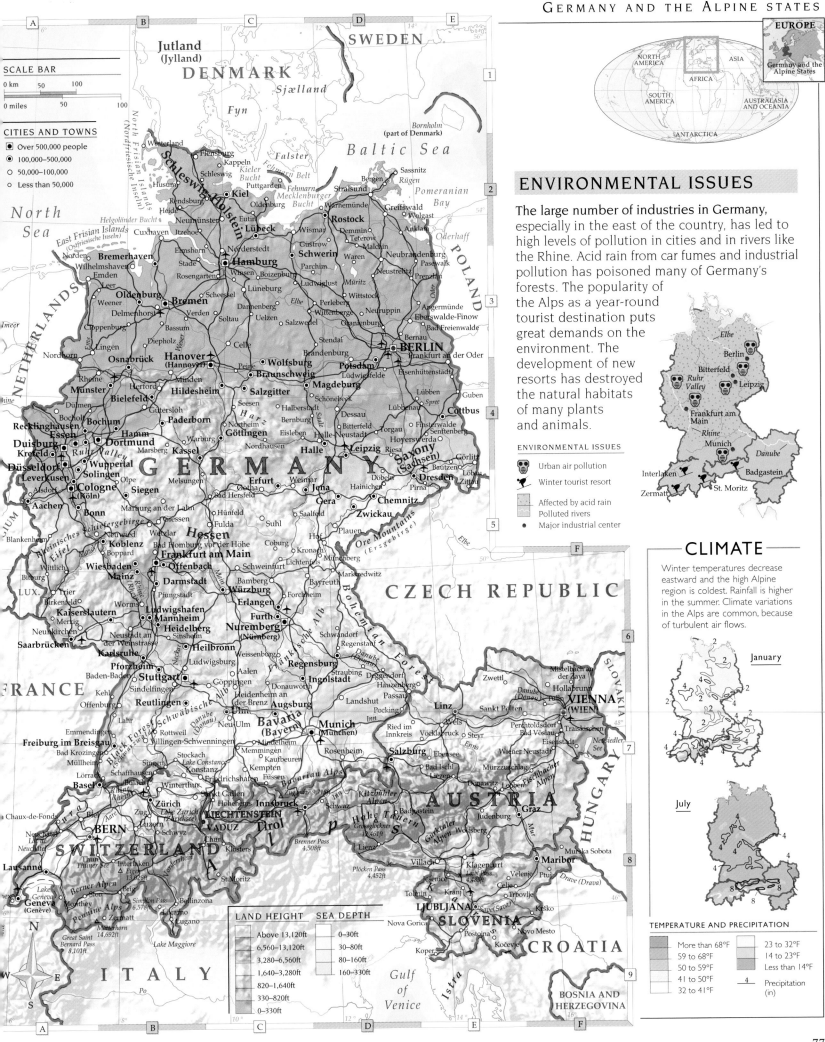

EUROPE

NORTH
AMERICA        ASIA

AFRICA

SOUTH
AMERICA

AUSTRALASIA
AND OCEANIA

ANTARCTICA

Germany and the
Alpine States

# ENVIRONMENTAL ISSUES

The large number of industries in Germany, especially in the east of the country, has led to high levels of pollution in cities and in rivers like the Rhine. Acid rain from car fumes and industrial pollution has poisoned many of Germany's forests. The popularity of the Alps as a year-round tourist destination puts great demands on the environment. The development of new resorts has destroyed the natural habitats of many plants and animals.

**ENVIRONMENTAL ISSUES**

- Urban air pollution
- Winter tourist resort
- Affected by acid rain
- Polluted rivers
- Major industrial center

# CLIMATE

Winter temperatures decrease eastward and the high Alpine region is coldest. Rainfall is higher in the summer. Climate variations in the Alps are common, because of turbulent air flows.

January

July

**TEMPERATURE AND PRECIPITATION**

| | |
|---|---|
| More than 68°F | 23 to 32°F |
| 59 to 68°F | 14 to 23°F |
| 50 to 59°F | Less than 14°F |
| 41 to 50°F | |
| 32 to 41°F | 4 — Precipitation (in) |

**SCALE BAR**

0 km   50   100
0 miles   50   100

**CITIES AND TOWNS**

- ■ Over 500,000 people
- ● 100,000–500,000
- ○ 50,000–100,000
- ○ Less than 50,000

**LAND HEIGHT    SEA DEPTH**

| | |
|---|---|
| Above 13,120ft | 0–30ft |
| 6,560–13,120ft | 30–80ft |
| 3,280–6,560ft | 80–160ft |
| 1,640–3,280ft | 160–330ft |
| 820–1,640ft | |
| 330–820ft | |
| 0–330ft | |

# ITALY

ITALY, SAN MARINO, VATICAN CITY

**Italy has played** an important role in Europe since the Romans based their mighty empire here over 2,000 years ago. The famous boot shape divides into two very different halves. Northern Italy has a varied range of industries and agriculture. Beautiful cities like Venice, Florence, and Rome draw tourists from all over the world. Southern Italy is poorer and less developed than the north, with a hotter, drier climate and less productive land.

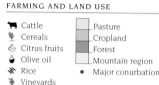

## THE LANDSCAPE

**Italy is a peninsula** jutting south from mainland Europe into the Mediterranean Sea. In northern and central Italy the land is mainly mountainous. Most of the flat land is in the Po Valley and along the eastern coast. Italy lies within an earthquake zone, which makes the land unstable, and there are also a number of active volcanoes.

### Po Valley (C 2)
The basin of the Po River has the best soils in Italy. Rich alluvium is washed from the mountains by the river to form a wide plain.

### Italian lakes
Great lakes like Garda (B3) and Como (B2) fill several south-facing valleys once occupied by glaciers.

### The Dolomites (D 2)
These high mountains are part of the same range as the Alps. They were formed 65 million years ago.

### The Apennines (C 4)
This mountain range forms the "backbone" of Italy, dividing the rocky west coast from the flatter, sandy east coast.

### Tyrrhenian Sea (C 6)
This sea, which divides the Italian mainland from Sardinia, is gradually filling with sediment from the rivers which flow into it.

### Earthquakes
The southern Apennines, as well as coastal areas of southwestern Italy, often experience earthquakes and mudslides.

### Sardinia
The island of Sardinia is made from very old rocks that were thrust up to form mountains.

### Sicily
Sicily is the largest island in the Mediterranean. It has a famous active volcano called Mount Etna and often experiences earthquakes.

### Gulf of Taranto (F 7)
During earthquakes, great blocks of land have broken away and sunk into the sea, forming the Gulf's square shape.

## FARMING AND LAND USE

**The Po Valley is a** broad, flat plain in the north of Italy. It contains the most fertile land in the country, and wheat and rice are the main cereal crops grown here. Grapes for wine are grown everywhere in Italy. In much of the south, the land must be irrigated to support crops. Where there is enough water, citrus fruits, olives, and many kinds of tomatoes are grown.

### LAND USE
Other 21%
Cropland 41%
Forest 23%
Pasture 15%

### FARMING AND LAND USE
- Cattle
- Cereals
- Citrus fruits
- Olive oil
- Rice
- Vineyards
- Pasture
- Cropland
- Forest
- Mountain region
- Major conurbation

## INDUSTRY

**Italian industry is located** mainly in the north. Design is extremely important to Italians, and they are proud of the elegant designs of their furniture, clothes, and shoes. Although many firms are small, they are very efficient. Italy has few mineral resources, so it needs to import raw materials to make cars, engines, and other high-tech products.

### INDUSTRY
- Car manufacturing
- Chemicals
- Iron and steel
- Textiles
- Finance
- High-tech industry
- Tourism
- Major industrial center / area
- Major road

### STRUCTURE OF INDUSTRY
Primary 3%
Services 66%
Manufacturing 31%

## POPULATION

**Most of Italy's population** lives in the north, mainly in and around the Po Valley, which is home to over 25 million people. Most people here have a high standard of living. Southern Italy is much more rural: towns are smaller and life is often much harder.

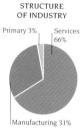

### URBAN/RURAL POPULATION DIVISION
Milan 1.5%
Rome 2.8%
Naples 1.2%
Rural population 31%
Other towns and cities 63.5%

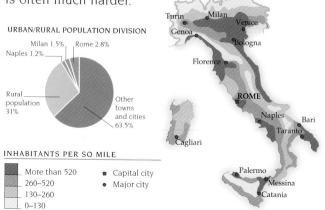

### INHABITANTS PER SQ MILE
- More than 520
- 260–520
- 130–260
- 0–130
- Capital city
- Major city

ITALY

EUROPE
Italy

# ENVIRONMENTAL ISSUES

Sewage and chemical by-products from industry have polluted the Mediterranean and Adriatic Seas. In many northern cities, severe air pollution is a health hazard. Southern Italy is subject to natural dangers like earthquakes and mudslides.

ENVIRONMENTAL ISSUES

⊚ Catastrophic earthquakes

☻ Urban air pollution

▦ Acid rain
▦ Sea pollution

• Major industrial center

# CLIMATE

The Alpine north has cold winters, often with snow. Farther south, temperatures are higher. Sicily has Italy's highest temperatures, because of the warm African winds.

January

July

TEMPERATURE AND PRECIPITATION

More than 77°F
68 to 77°F
59 to 68°F
50 to 59°F
41 to 50°F
32 to 41°F
23 to 32°F
14 to 23°F
Less than 14°F

— 4 — Precipitation (in)

SCALE BAR

0 km   40   80

0 miles   40   80

CITIES AND TOWNS

■ Over 500,000 people
◉ 100,000–500,000
○ 50,000–100,000
○ Less than 50,000

LAND HEIGHT

Above 13,120ft
6,560–13,120ft
3,280–6,560ft
1,640–3,280ft
820–1,640ft
330–820ft
0–330ft

SEA DEPTH

0–160ft
160–330ft
330–820ft
820–1,640ft
1,640–3,280ft
3,280–6,560ft
Below 6,560ft

# CENTRAL EUROPE

CZECH REPUBLIC, HUNGARY, POLAND, SLOVAKIA

**Central Europe** has been invaded many times throughout history. The countries have changed shape frequently as their borders have shifted back and forth. From the end of World War Two until 1989, they were ruled by communist governments, which were supported by the Soviet Union. In 1993, the state of Czechoslovakia voted to split into two separate nations, called the Czech Republic and Slovakia.

## INDUSTRY

**Brown coal, or lignite,** is central Europe's main fuel, and one of Poland's major exports. A variety of minerals are mined in the mountains of the Czech Republic and Slovakia. Hungary has a wide range of industries producing vehicles, metals, and chemicals, as well as textiles and electrical goods. The Czech Republic is famous for its breweries and glass-making.

STRUCTURE OF INDUSTRY

Primary 6%
Services 56%
Manufacturing 38%

INDUSTRY
- 🍶 Brewing
- 🚗 Car manufacturing
- ⚗️ Chemicals
- ⚙️ Engineering
- 🥫 Food processing
- Iron and steel
- ⛏️ Coal mining
- ⊡ Major industrial center / area
- — Major road

## ENVIRONMENTAL ISSUES

**The growth of heavy industries** that took place under communist rule has caused terrible environmental pollution in some places. Hungary's oil and Poland's brown coal have a high sulfur content. Burning these fuels to produce electricity causes air pollution, and the sulfur dioxide produced combines with moisture in the air, leading to acid rain.

ENVIRONMENTAL ISSUES
- Severe industrial pollution
- Urban air pollution
- Affected by acid rain
- Polluted rivers
- • Major industrial center

## FARMING AND LAND USE

**Central Europe's** main crops are cereals such as corn, wheat and rye, along with sugar beets and potatoes. Sweet peppers grow in Hungary, helped by the warm summers and mild winters. They are used to make paprika. Grapes are also grown, to make wine. Large areas of the plains of Hungary and Poland are used for rearing pigs and cattle. Trees for timber grow in the mountains of Slovakia and the Czech Republic.

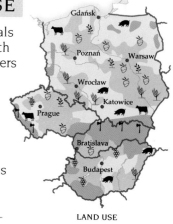

FARMING AND LAND USE
- Cattle
- Pigs
- Cereals
- Root crops
- Potatoes
- Timber
- Pasture
- Cropland
- Forest
- • Major conurbation

LAND USE

Cropland 47%
Forest 29%
Pasture 13%
Other 11%

## THE LANDSCAPE

**The high Carpathian Mountains** sweep across northern Slovakia. The lower Sudeten Mountains lie on the border of the Czech Republic and Poland. Together, these mountains form a barrier that divides the Great Hungarian Plain and the Danube River basin in the south from Poland and the vast rolling lowlands of the North European Plain.

**Pomerania** (C 2)
This is a sandy coastal area with lakes formed by glaciers. It stretches west from the River Vistula to just beyond the German border.

**Vistula River** (F 4)
Poland's largest river is the Vistula. It flows northward, passing through the capital, Warsaw, on its way to the Baltic Sea.

**North European Plain**

**Hot springs**
The Sudeten mountains (C5) are famous for their hot mineral springs. These occur where water heated deep within the Earth's crust finds its way to the surface along fractures in the rock.

**Danube River** (D 7)
The Danube River forms the border between Slovakia and Hungary for over 100 miles. It then turns south to flow across the Great Hungarian Plain.

**Great Hungarian Plain** (E 8)
This huge plain covers almost half of Hungary's land area. It is a mixture of farmland and steppe.

**Tatra Mountains** (E 6)
The Tatra Mountains are a small range at the northern end of the Carpathian Mountains. They include Gerlachovsky Stít, which is Central Europe's highest point at 8,711 ft.

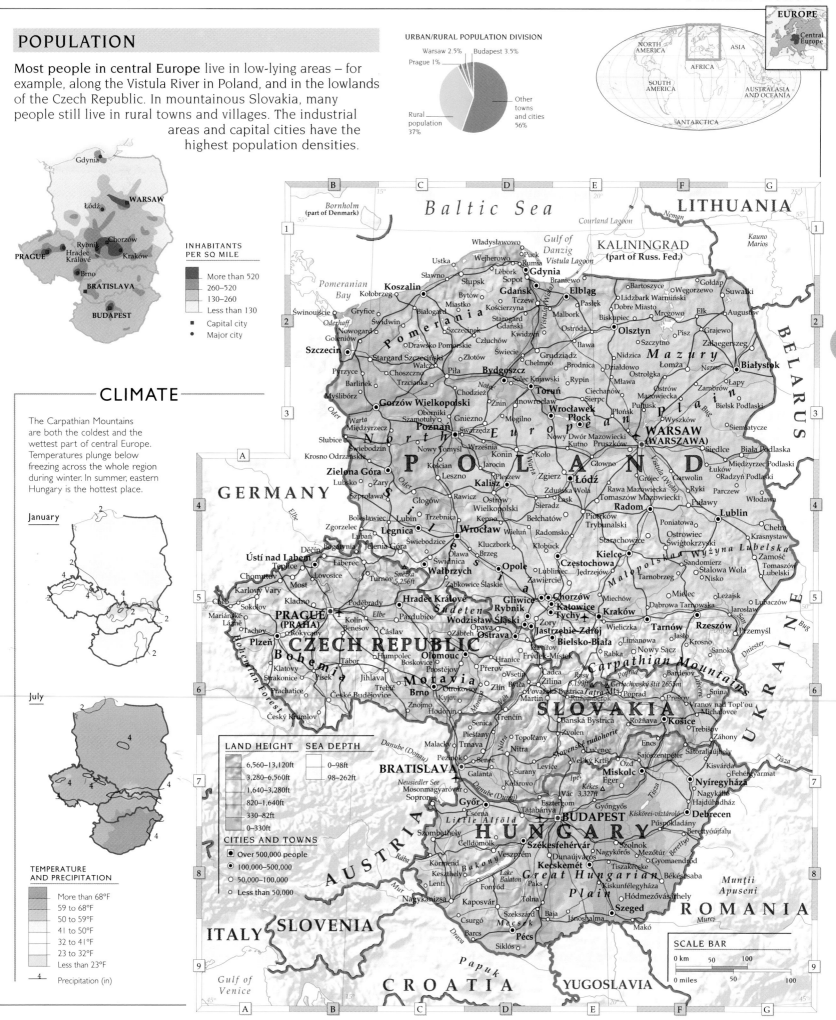

## POPULATION

Most people in central Europe live in low-lying areas – for example, along the Vistula River in Poland, and in the lowlands of the Czech Republic. In mountainous Slovakia, many people still live in rural towns and villages. The industrial areas and capital cities have the highest population densities.

**URBAN/RURAL POPULATION DIVISION**

Warsaw 2.5%
Budapest 3.5%
Prague 1%
Other towns and cities 56%
Rural population 37%

EUROPE
Central Europe

NORTH AMERICA
ASIA
AFRICA
SOUTH AMERICA
AUSTRALASIA AND OCEANIA
ANTARCTICA

**INHABITANTS PER SQ MILE**
More than 520
260–520
130–260
Less than 130
■ Capital city
● Major city

Gdynia
Łódź
WARSAW
Rybnik Chorzów
PRAGUE Hradec Králové Kraków
Brno
BRATISLAVA
BUDAPEST

## CLIMATE

The Carpathian Mountains are both the coldest and the wettest part of central Europe. Temperatures plunge below freezing across the whole region during winter. In summer, eastern Hungary is the hottest place.

January

July

**TEMPERATURE AND PRECIPITATION**
More than 68°F
59 to 68°F
50 to 59°F
41 to 50°F
32 to 41°F
23 to 32°F
Less than 23°F
—4— Precipitation (in)

**LAND HEIGHT**
6,560–13,120ft
3,280–6,560ft
1,640–3,280ft
820–1,640ft
330–82ft
0–330ft

**SEA DEPTH**
0–98ft
98–262ft

**CITIES AND TOWNS**
■ Over 500,000 people
◉ 100,000–500,000
◎ 50,000–100,000
○ Less than 50,000

**SCALE BAR**
0 km 50 100
0 miles 50 100

# SOUTHEAST EUROPE

ALBANIA, BOSNIA AND HERZEGOVINA, BULGARIA, CROATIA, GREECE, MACEDONIA, YUGOSLAVIA (SERBIA & MONTENEGRO)

Southeast Europe extends inland from the coasts of the Aegean, Adriatic, and Black Seas. Ancient Greece was the birthplace of European civilization. Albania and Bulgaria were ruled by communists for over 50 years, until the early 1990s. The rest of the region was part of a communist union of states called Yugoslavia. The collapse of this union in 1991 led to a civil war, after which five separate countries emerged.

## THE LANDSCAPE

Southeast Europe is largely mountainous, with ranges running from northwest to southeast. The Dinaric Alps run parallel to the Dalmatian coast, and the Pindus Mountains continue this line into Greece. In the Aegean Sea, the drowned peaks of an old mountain chain form thousands of islands.

### Earthquakes
Bulgaria, Greece, and Macedonia lie in earthquake zones. Major earthquakes have hit the Ionian Islands in 1953 and Macedonia in 1963.

### Great Hungarian Plain (D 1)
The Vojvodina region of Yugoslavia is the southern part of the Great Hungarian Plain. The plain is flat, and fertile soil enables crops like corn and wheat to be grown.

### Dinaric Alps (C 2)

### Balkan Mountains (F 3)
The mountains form a spur running east to west through Bulgaria and separate the two main rivers, the Danube and the Maritsa.

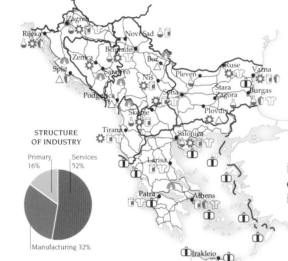

### Dalmatian coast (B 2)
The Dalmatian coast has many long, narrow islands near the shore. These were formed as the Adriatic Sea flooded the river valleys that ran parallel to the coast.

### Greek Islands

### The Peloponnese (E 6)
The Peloponnese is a mountainous peninsula linked to the Greek mainland only by a narrow strip of land called an isthmus. Here, it is the Isthmus of Corinth.

### Greek Islands
There are two groups of Greek Islands, the Ionian Islands to the west of mainland Greece, and the more numerous islands to the east in the Aegean Sea.

## FARMING AND LAND USE

Cereals like wheat, and fruits, vegetables, and grapes are grown in the fertile north of the region. The band of mountains across southeast Europe is used mainly for grazing sheep and goats. Farther south, and in coastal areas, the warm Mediterranean climate is ideal for growing grapes, olives, and tobacco.

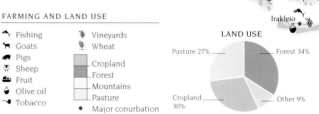

### FARMING AND LAND USE
- Fishing
- Goats
- Pigs
- Sheep
- Fruit
- Olive oil
- Tobacco
- Vineyards
- Wheat
- Cropland
- Forest
- Mountains
- Pasture
- • Major conurbation

### LAND USE
- Forest 34%
- Other 9%
- Cropland 30%
- Pasture 27%

## INDUSTRY

Mainland Greece and the many islands in the Aegean Sea are centers of a thriving tourist trade, while tourism on the Black Sea coast continues to grow. The Dalmatian coast had a small, but growing tourist industry, until the civil war in former Yugoslavia disrupted that, and other industries. Heavy industries like chemicals, engineering, and shipbuilding remain an important source of income in Bulgaria.

### STRUCTURE OF INDUSTRY
- Primary 16%
- Services 52%
- Manufacturing 32%

### INDUSTRY
- Chemicals
- Engineering
- Food processing
- Metal refining
- Shipbuilding
- Textiles
- Mining
- Tourism
- Major industrial center / area
- Major road

## POPULATION

Greece's population is mostly urban; over 50% live in the capital, Athens, and in Salonica. In Bulgaria, most people live in cities. About half of Albania's and Macedonia's people are still rural. Since the civil war, the different ethnic groups in Bosnia and Herzegovina, Yugoslavia, and Croatia have lived apart from one another.

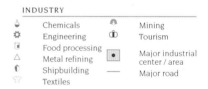

### URBAN/RURAL POPULATION DIVISION
- Belgrade 3.5%
- Athens 8%
- Sofia 2.5%
- Other towns and cities 42%
- Rural population 44%

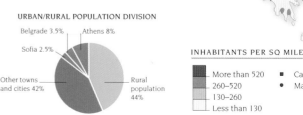

### INHABITANTS PER SQ MILE
- More than 520
- 260–520
- 130–260
- Less than 130
- ■ Capital city
- • Major city

EUROPE

Southeast Europe

# CLIMATE

Southeastern Europe's climate varies from north to south. Continental climates are found in the north; winters are cold and dry, while toward the south, winters are milder and summers much hotter. Europe's wettest place is found in the mountains in Bosnia and Herzegovina.

January

July

TEMPERATURE AND PRECIPITATION

More than 77°F
68 to 77°F
59 to 68°F
50 to 59°F
41 to 50°F
32 to 41°F
23 to 32°F
Less than 23°F

4 — Precipitation (in)

NORTH AMERICA
SOUTH AMERICA
ASIA
AFRICA
AUSTRALASIA AND OCEANIA
ANTARCTICA

## CITIES AND TOWNS

■ Over 500,000 people
◉ 100,000–500,000
○ 50,000–100,000
∘ Less than 50,000

SCALE BAR

0 km   50   100
0 miles   50   100

# ENVIRONMENTAL ISSUES

**Emissions from industry** and traffic fumes have polluted the air in Athens and Zagreb. In Athens, smog caused by exhausts can become so severe on some days that the use of cars is banned. Earthquakes are common, Macedonia's capital city, Skopje, was badly hit in 1963, and Bulgaria's rundown Kozloduy nuclear power station lies within the earthquake zone.

## ENVIRONMENTAL ISSUES

◎ Catastrophic earthquake
⚏ Unstable nuclear reactor
☻ Urban air pollution
   Water pollution
   Polluted river
• Major town

## LAND HEIGHT

6,560–13,120ft
3,280–6,560ft
1,640–3,280ft
820–1,640ft
330–820ft
0–330ft

## SEA DEPTH

0–160ft
160–330ft
330–820ft
820–1,640ft
1,640–3,280ft
3,280–6,560ft
Below 6,560ft

# EASTERN EUROPE

BELARUS, MOLDOVA, ROMANIA, UKRAINE

**Much of Eastern Europe,** which extends north from the Danube River and the Black Sea, is covered by open grasslands called steppe. Ukraine's excellent farmland and large mineral reserves make it one of the strongest new countries to emerge from the former Soviet Union. Moldova and Belarus were also part of the USSR until they became independent in 1991. Romania was a strict communist regime from 1945 until 1989.

## INDUSTRY

**In Ukraine,** most industry is based around the country's mineral reserves. The Donbass region has Europe's largest coalfield and is an important center for iron and steel production. The main industries of Belarus are chemicals, machine building, and food-processing. Romania's manufacturing industries are growing, with the help of foreign investment.

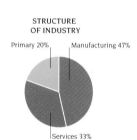

**STRUCTURE OF INDUSTRY**

Primary 20%
Manufacturing 47%
Services 33%

**INDUSTRY**

- 🚗 Car manufacturing
- 🝵 Chemicals
- ⚙ Engineering
- 🗎 Food processing
- ⛏ Iron and steel
- 👕 Textiles
- Coal
- ⛏ Mining
- Oil and gas
- 🛍 Tourism

▪ Major industrial center / area
— Major road

## FARMING AND LAND USE

**The black soils** found across much of Ukraine are very fertile and the country is a big producer of cereals, sugar beets, and sunflowers, which are grown for their oil. In Moldova and southern Romania, the warm summers are ideal for growing grapes for wine, along with sunflowers and a variety of vegetables. Cattle and pigs are farmed throughout Eastern Europe.

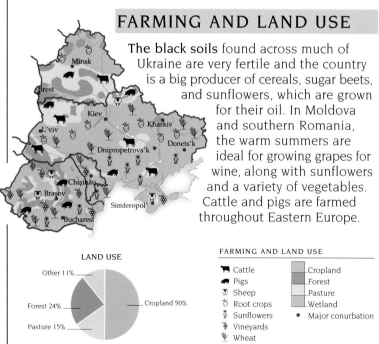

**LAND USE**

Other 11%
Forest 24%
Pasture 15%
Cropland 50%

**FARMING AND LAND USE**

- 🐄 Cattle
- 🐖 Pigs
- 🐑 Sheep
- Root crops
- Sunflowers
- Vineyards
- Wheat

Cropland
Forest
Pasture
Wetland
• Major conurbation

## POPULATION

**Most Romanians** live in Bucharest, the capital, or in other cities and towns. In Ukraine, two-thirds of the population lives in cities in the Donbass industrial area. Most people in Belarus are city dwellers. Moldova is the most rural country in Eastern Europe; half its people live in the countryside and make their living from farming.

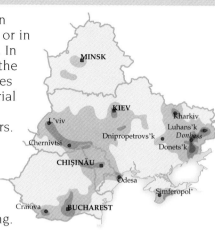

**URBAN/RURAL POPULATION DIVISION**

Bucharest 2.5%
Dnipropetrovs'k 1.3%
Kiev 3.2%
Rural population 36%
Other towns and cities 57%

**INHABITANTS PER SQ MILE**

- More than 520
- 260–520
- 130–260
- Less than 130
- ▪ Capital city
- • Major city

## THE LANDSCAPE

**Flat or rolling grasslands,** marshes, and river flood plains cover almost all of Ukraine and Belarus. The Carpathian Mountains cross the southwestern corner of Ukraine and continue in a large arc-shaped chain of high peaks at the heart of Romania. Along the southern part of this chain, the Carpathians are called the Transylvanian Alps.

**Pripet Marshes** (C 3)
The Pripet Marshes in Belarus and Ukraine form the largest area of marshland in Europe.

**The steppes**
The steppes are great, wide grasslands that are found across eastern Europe and central Asia. Over 70% of the Ukrainian landscape is steppe. Little rain falls throughout the steppes.

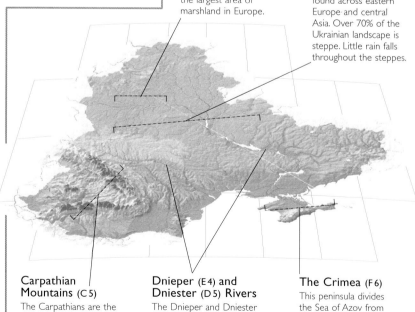

**Carpathian Mountains** (C 5)
The Carpathians are the largest mountain range in Eastern Europe. They are a rich source of timber and minerals.

**Dnieper** (E 4) **and Dniester** (D 5) **Rivers**
The Dnieper and Dniester run south and east toward the Black Sea. They flow slowly across huge areas of low-lying land.

**The Crimea** (F 6)
This peninsula divides the Sea of Azov from the Black Sea. The steep mountains of Kryms'ki Hory run along the southeastern coast of the Crimea.

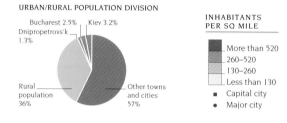

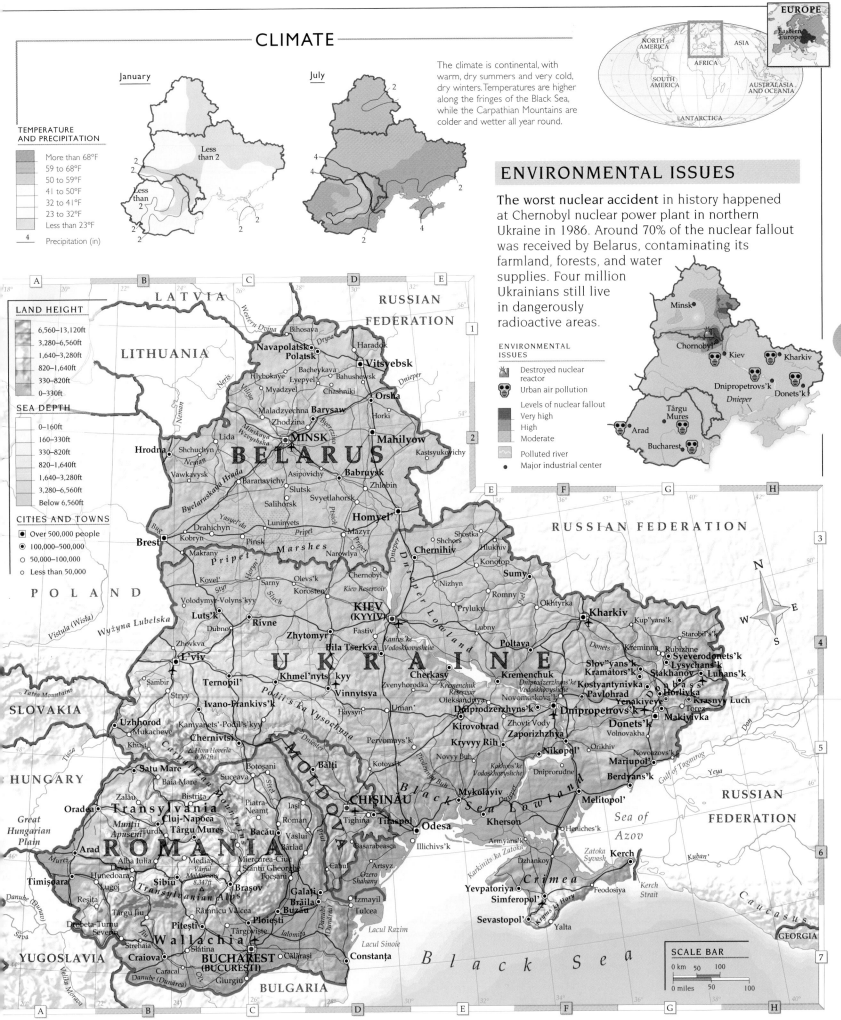

## CLIMATE

January

July

The climate is continental, with warm, dry summers and very cold, dry winters. Temperatures are higher along the fringes of the Black Sea, while the Carpathian Mountains are colder and wetter all year round.

EUROPE
Eastern Europe

NORTH AMERICA · ASIA · AFRICA · SOUTH AMERICA · AUSTRALASIA AND OCEANIA · ANTARCTICA

TEMPERATURE AND PRECIPITATION
More than 68°F
59 to 68°F
50 to 59°F
41 to 50°F
32 to 41°F
23 to 32°F
Less than 23°F
4 — Precipitation (in)

## ENVIRONMENTAL ISSUES

**The worst nuclear accident** in history happened at Chernobyl nuclear power plant in northern Ukraine in 1986. Around 70% of the nuclear fallout was received by Belarus, contaminating its farmland, forests, and water supplies. Four million Ukrainians still live in dangerously radioactive areas.

ENVIRONMENTAL ISSUES
Destroyed nuclear reactor
Urban air pollution
Levels of nuclear fallout
Very high
High
Moderate
Polluted river
● Major industrial center

Minsk · Chornobyl · Kiev · Kharkiv · Dnipropetrovs'k · Donets'k · Târgu Mures · Arad · Bucharest

LAND HEIGHT
6,560–13,120ft
3,280–6,560ft
1,640–3,280ft
820–1,640ft
330–820ft
0–330ft

SEA DEPTH
0–160ft
160–330ft
330–820ft
820–1,640ft
1,640–3,280ft
3,280–6,560ft
Below 6,560ft

CITIES AND TOWNS
● Over 500,000 people
◉ 100,000–500,000
○ 50,000–100,000
○ Less than 50,000

LATVIA
LITHUANIA
RUSSIAN FEDERATION

Bihosava · Harodok · Navapolatsk · Polatsk · Vitsyebsk · Hlybokaye · Lyepyel' · Bacheykava · Bahushewsk · Myadzyel · Chashniki · Orsha · Maladzyechna · Barysaw · Horki · Zhodzina · MINSK · Mahilyow · Lida · Maladzyechna

BELARUS

Hrodna · Shchuchyn · Asipovichy · Babruysk · Baranavichy · Slutsk · Zhlobin · Svyetlahorsk · Kastsyukovichy · Salihorsk

POLAND

Brest · Kobryn · Drahichyn · Pinsk · Luninyets · Pripet Marshes · Mazyr · Homyel' · Shchors · Hlukhiv · Chernihiv · Makrany · Narowlya · Chernobyl · Sumy

Kovel' · Sarny · Olevs'k · Korosten' · Kiev Reservoir · Nizhyn · Konotop · Shostka · Romny · Okhtyrka

Volodymyr-Volyns'kyy · Luts'k · Rivne · Dubno · Zhytomyr · KIEV (KYYIV) · Fastiv · Pryluky · Lubny · Kharkiv · Kup"yans'k · Starobil's'k

L'viv · Zhovkva · Ternopil' · Khmel'nyts'kyy · Bila Tserkva · Poltava · Donets · Kreminna · Rubizhne · Syeverodonets'k

UKRAINE

Vinnytsya · Cherkasy · Kremenchuk · Slov"yans'k · Kramators'k · Stakhanov · Lysychans'k · Luhans'k · Kostyantynivka · Horlivka · Krasnyy Luch

Sambir · Stryy · Ivano-Frankivs'k · Haysyn · Uman' · Zvenyhorodka · Oleksandriya · Novomoskovs'k · Pavlohrad · Yenakiyeve · Torez · Makiyivka

Uzhhorod · Mukacheve · Khust · Kamyanets'-Podil's'kyy · Chernivtsi · Dniprodzerzhyns'k · Kirovohrad · Zhovti Vody · Dnipropetrovs'k · Donets'k · Volnovakha

SLOVAKIA

Hora Hoverla 6,762ft · Pervomays'k · Kryvyy Rih · Zaporizhzhya · Orikhiv · Novoazovs'k

HUNGARY

Satu Mare · Botoşani · Bălţi · Kotovs'k · Novyy Buh · Nikopol' · Mariupol' · Berdyans'k · Gulf of Taganrog · Yeya

Baia Mare · Suceava · Dniprorudne · Kakhovs'ke Vodoskhovyshche

Zalău · Bistriţa · Piatra-Neamţ · Iaşi · Mykolayiv · Melitopol' · RUSSIAN FEDERATION

Oradea · Transylvania · Cluj-Napoca · Roman · CHIŞINĂU · Kherson · Heniches'k · Sea of Azov

Muntii Apuseni · Târgu Mureş · Bacău · MOLDOVA · Tighina · Tiraspol' · Odesa · Armyans'k

ROMANIA · Alba Iulia · Vaslui · Bârlad · Basarabeasch · Illichivs'k · Dzhankoy · Zatoka Syvash · Kerch · Kuban'

Arad · Mureş · Deva · Mediaş · Miercurea-Ciuc · Sfântu Gheorghe · Focşani · Artsyz · Crimea · Kerch Strait · Caucasus

Timişoara · Hunedoara · Sibiu · Vârful Moldoveanu 8,347ft · Braşov · Galaţi · Izmayil · Ozero Shahany · Yevpatoriya · Feodosiya

Lugoj · Reşiţa · Transylvanian Alps · Brăila · Buzău · Tulcea · Simferopol' · Yalta

Târgu Jiu · Râmnicu Vâlcea · Ploieşti · Târgovişte · Lacul Razim · Sevastopol'

Drobeta-Turnu Severin · Piteşti · Wallachia · Ialomiţa · Lacul Sinoie

Strehaia · Slatina · BUCHAREST (BUCUREŞTI) · Călăraşi · Constanţa

YUGOSLAVIA · Craiova · Caracal · Giurgiu · Danube (Dunărea) · BULGARIA · Black Sea · GEORGIA

Great Hungarian Plain

Tatra Mountains

Carpathian Mountains

Podil's'ka Vysochyna

Dnieper Lowland

Black Sea Lowland

SCALE BAR
0 km 50 100
0 miles 50 100

# European Russia

RUSSIAN FEDERATION

**European Russia** is separated from the Asiatic part of the Russian Federation by the Ural Mountains. It is home to two-thirds of the country's population. Russia was the largest and most powerful republic of the communist Soviet Union, which collapsed in 1991. New businesses were set up when communism ended, but many old state industries closed down, causing unemployment and further hardship for many people.

## POPULATION

**Three-quarters of** European Russia's people live in towns and cities, most in a broad band stretching south from St. Petersburg to Moscow, and eastward to the Urals. The capital, Moscow, and St. Petersburg are very crowded cities. Living conditions there are cramped, with two families often sharing one apartment. The southeast is also heavily populated. Over 12 million people live in the cities and towns that line the banks of the Volga River.

## INDUSTRY

**European Russia** is rich in natural resources. Minerals are mined on the Kola Peninsula and in the Urals, while dense forests are felled and processed in many of the larger northern cities. The Volga basin is one of Europe's largest sources of oil and gas. Moscow and the cities near the Volga are centers of skilled labor for a wide range of manufacturing industries like cars, chemicals, and heavy engineering and steel production.

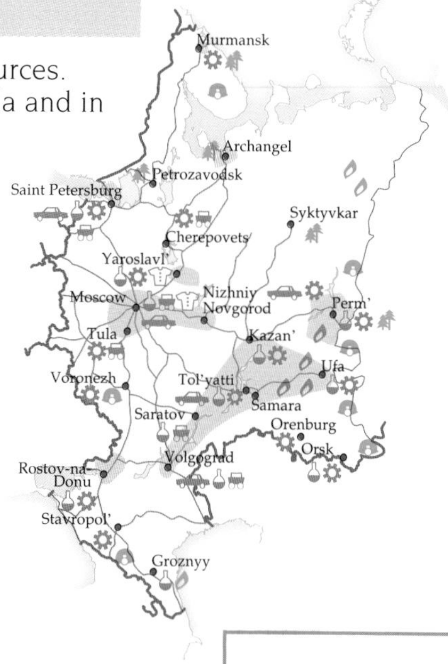


INDUSTRY

- Car manufacturing
- Chemicals
- Engineering
- Iron and steel
- Textiles
- Mining
- Oil and gas
- Timber processing
- Major industrial center/area
- Major road

## FARMING AND LAND USE

**Russia's** best farmland lies within this region. Big crops of wheat, barley and oats, potatoes and sunflowers are produced in the fertile black soil that forms a thick band across the country to the south of Moscow. The far north is cold and frozen, with bare mountains and tundra making cultivation impossible. Farther south there are extensive forests, and rough pastures that are used for herding and hunting.

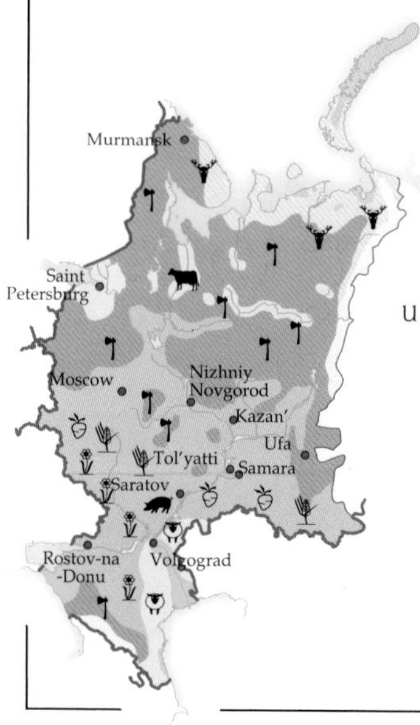


FARMING AND LAND USE

- Cattle
- Pigs
- Reindeer
- Sheep
- Cereals
- Root crops
- Sunflowers
- Timber
- Barren land
- Cropland
- Forest
- Mountain region
- Pasture
- Tundra
- Wetland
- Major conurbation

## THE LANDSCAPE

**European Russia** lies on the North European Plain, a huge, rolling lowland with wide river basins. The northern half of the plain, which was once covered by glaciers, has many lakes and swamps. The Volga River drains much of the plain as it flows south to the Caspian Sea. The Caucasus and Ural Mountains form natural boundaries in the south and east.

**Northern European Russia** (C 3)
Northern European Russia reaches into the Arctic Circle. It is a region of pine and birch forests, marshes, and tundra. There are also tens of thousands of lakes, including the biggest in Europe, Ladoga, which covers about 6,830 sq miles.

**Ural Mountains** (E 5)
The Ural Mountains run from north to south, stretching almost 2,500 miles.

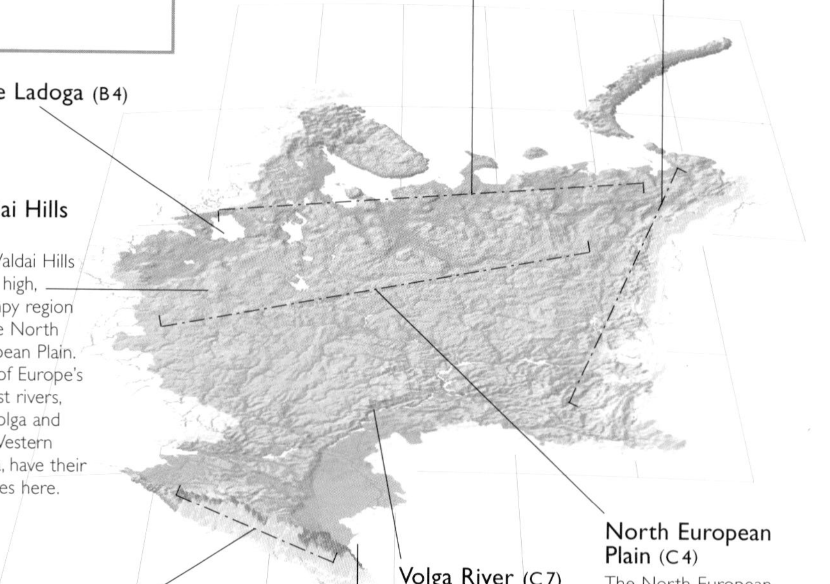

**Lake Ladoga** (B 4)

**Valdai Hills** (A 5)
The Valdai Hills are a high, swampy region of the North European Plain. Two of Europe's biggest rivers, the Volga and the Western Dvina, have their sources here.

**Caucasus** (A 9)
This massive barrier of mountains stretches from the Black Sea to the Caspian Sea. It includes El'brus, the highest peak in Europe, at 18,510 miles.

**Caspian Sea** (C 9)

**Volga River** (C 7)
The Volga River flows for 2,292 miles, making it Europe's longest river and Russia's most important inland waterway. It is used for transportation and to generate hydro-electric power.

**North European Plain** (C 4)
The North European Plain sweeps west from the Ural Mountains, all the way to the Rhine River in Germany. In European Russia it includes a number of hill ranges, such as the Volga Uplands and the Central Russian Upland.

EUROPE
European Russia

## ENVIRONMENTAL ISSUES

**The many factories** in European Russia have caused widespread pollution, and in most industrial cities air quality is poor. Several of Russia's older nuclear power plants have been declared unsafe, but are yet to be shut down. Waste from these power plants, as well as from nuclear submarines, has for many years been dumped in the Barents Sea and off Novaya Zemlya.

**ENVIRONMENTAL ISSUES**

☢ Nuclear waste dump site

⚛ Unstable nuclear reactor

☠ Urban air pollution

Polluted rivers

● Major industrial center

## CLIMATE

Winters are extremely cold and dry; temperatures plunge well below freezing in the north and east. Summer brings much warmer and wetter weather, especially in the south, while along the northern coast it remains relatively cold. Rainfall is highest in the Caucasus.

January

July

**TEMPERATURE AND PRECIPITATION**

More than 68°F
59 to 68°F
50 to 59°F
41 to 50°F
32 to 41°F
23 to 32°F
14 to 23°F
5 to 14°F
Less than 5°F

4 — Precipitation (in)

**CITIES AND TOWNS**
■ Over 500,000 people
◉ 100,000–500,000
○ 50,000–100,000
○ Less than 50,000

**LAND HEIGHT**
Above 13,120ft
6,560–13,120ft
3,280–6,560ft
1,640–3,280ft
820–1,640ft
330–820ft
0–330ft
Below sea level

**SEA DEPTH**
0–160ft
160–330ft
330–820ft
820–1,640ft
1,640–3,280ft
3,280–6,560ft
Below 6,560ft

**SCALE BAR**
0 km 100 200
0 miles 100 200

ARCTIC OCEAN
Kara Sea (Karskoye More)
Barents Sea
Norwegian Sea
Pechora Sea
Ostrov Kolguyev
Ostrov Vaygach
Kara Strait
Pomorskiy Proliv

NORWAY
SWEDEN
FINLAND
Lapland
North Cape (Nordkapp)

Nikel
Zapolyarnyy
Polyarnyy
Murmashi
Severomorsk
**Murmansk**
Monchegorsk
Olenegorsk
Apatity
Kandalaksha
Zelenoborskiy
Kola Peninsula (Kol'skiy Poluostrov)
White Sea
Kem
Belomorsk
Nadvoitsy
**Severodvinsk**
Segezha
Onega
**Archangel (Arkhangel'sk)**
Novodvinsk
Malozemel'skaya Tundra
Bol'shezemel'skaya Tundra
Nar'yan-Mar
Promyshlennyy
Severnyy
**Vorkuta**
Arctic Circle
Usinsk
Usa
Inta
Pechora
Tel'
Timan Ridge (Timanskiy Kryazh)
Mezen'
Pinega
Ukhta
Nizhniy Odes
Yarega
Severnaya Dvina
Mikun'
Yemva
Syktyvkar
Koryazhma
Kotlas
Luza
Vychegda
Ob'

Vyborg
Sortavala
Suoyarvi
Kondopoga
Medvezh'yegorsk
Savinskiy
Plesetsk
Nyandoma
Konosha
Vel'sk
Belozersk
Lake Ladoga
Lake Onega
Petrozavodsk
Olonets
Petrodvorets
**Saint Petersburg (Sankt-Peterburg)**
Gatchina
**Kolpino**
Volkhov
Tikhvin
Babayevo
Borovichi
**Cherepovets**
Sokol
Sukhona
**Vologda**
Luga
Kirishi
Novgorod
Uglovka
Valday
Rybinsk
**Yaroslavl'**
**Kostroma**
Pskov
Porkhov
Opochka
Velikiye Luki
Zapadnaya Dvina
Rzhev
Torzhok
**Tver'**
Valdai Hills
Zel. Dvina

**RUSSIAN FEDERATION**
North European Plain

Smolensk
Zelenograd
**Elektrostal'**
**MOSCOW (MOSKVA)**
Pochinok
Podol'sk
Kaluga
Aleksin
Shchëkino
Serpukhov
Kolomna
**Tula**
Novomoskovsk
Tovarkovskiy
Kirov
Kirovo-Chepetsk
Zuyevka
Kineshma
Ivanovo
**Vladimir**
Dzerzhinsk
Yaransk
Uren'
Vyatka
Glazov
Nolinsk
Krasnokamsk
Chusovoy
**Perm'**
Kungur
**Izhevsk**
Chaykovskiy
Solikamsk
**Berezniki**
Kama
Ural Mountains
Ural'skiye Gory

**Nizhniy Novgorod**
Yoshkar-Ola
Cheboksary
Novocheboksarsk
Murom
Kanash
**Kazan'**
Nizhnekamsk
**Naberezhnyye Chelny**
Birsk
Neftekamsk
Bryansk
Orel
Yefremov
Michurinsk
Saransk
Ul'yanovsk
Dimitrovgrad
Oktyabr'skiy
**Ufa**
Al'met'yevsk
Kursk
Gubkin
Lipetsk
Gryazi
**Tambov**
Penza
Kuznetsk
Kuybyshev Reservoir
**Tol'yatti**
**Samara**
Buguruslan
Sterlitamak
Beloretsk
**Voronezh**
Staryy Oskol
Liski
Borisoglebsk
Syzran'
Chapayevsk
**Salavat**
Buzuluk
Belgorod
Shebekino
Rossosh'
Balashov
Vol'sk
Sibay
Baymak
**Balakovo**
Millerovo
Kantemirovka
**Saratov**
Krasnoarmeysk
Krasnyy Kut
Kumertau
Sol'-Iletsk
Saraktash
**Orsk**
Novotroitsk
Orenburg
Kirghiz Steppe

**Novoshakhtinsk**
**Taganrog**
**Novocherkassk**
**Rostov-na-Donu**
Volgodonsk
Mikhaylovka
Ilovlya
Kamyshin
**Volzhskiy**
**Volgograd**
Akhtubinsk
Don
Donets
UKRAINE
KAZAKHSTAN
Tikhoretsk
Kropotkin
Zimovniki
Elista
Sal'sk
Svetlograd
Caspian Depression
Caspian Sea
Novorossiysk
Tuapse
**Krasnodar**
Stavropol'
Nevinnomyssk
Cherkessk
Kislovodsk
**Pyatigorsk**
Prokhladnyy
Maykop
Sochi
El'brus 18,511ft
**Nal'chik**
**Groznyy**
Khasavyurt
Nazran'
**Vladikavkaz**
Buynaksk
**Makhachkala**
Kaspiysk
Kuma
Astrakhan'
Derbent
GEORGIA
TURKEY
ARM.
AZERB.
Black Sea
Sea of Azov
Caucasus

# THE MEDITERRANEAN

The **Mediterranean Sea** separates Europe from Africa. It stretches more than 2,500 miles from east to west and is almost completely enclosed by land. Many great civilizations, including the Greek and Roman empires, grew up around the Mediterranean. It has been a crossroads of international trade routes for many centuries. More than 100 million people live in the 28 countries that border the sea, and their numbers are increased by the large crowds of tourists who regularly visit the area.

## ENVIRONMENTAL ISSUES

**Water pollution is widespread** in the Mediterranean, especially near the large coastal resorts where raw sewage and industrial effluent is pumped out to sea, and often ends up on the beaches. Oil refining and oil spills have also increased pollution.

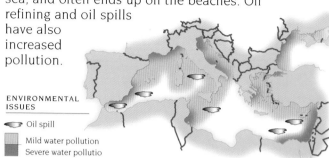

**ENVIRONMENTAL ISSUES**

🌊 Oil spill

☐ Mild water pollution

☐ Severe water pollutio

### SCALE BAR

0 km 100 200

0 miles 100 200

**LAND HEIGHT**

Above 13,120ft
6,560–13,120ft
3,280–6,560ft
1,640–3,280ft
820–1,640ft
330–820ft
0–330ft
Below sea level

**SEA DEPTH**

0–820ft
820–1,640ft
1,640–3,280ft
3,280–6,560ft
6,560–9,840ft
9,840–13,120ft
Below 13,120ft

**CITIES AND TOWNS**

■ Over 500,000 people
◉ 100,000–500,000
○ 50,000–100,000
○ Less than 50,000

## THE LANDSCAPE

The Mediterranean Sea would be an enormous lake if it were not for the Strait of Gibraltar, a narrow opening only 8 miles wide, which joins it to the Atlantic Ocean. The Mediterranean lies over the boundary of two continental plates. Where they meet, earthquakes and volcanoes are common.

**Strait of Gibraltar**

**Sandy beaches**
The Mediterranean coasts are bordered by several thousand miles of sandy beaches.

**Shallow shelves**
The area of water off the coast of Tunisia, and also the Adriatic Sea, are shallower than the rest of the Mediterranean.

**Greek islands**
Greece has thousands of islands that lie both in the Mediterranean and in the smaller Aegean Sea. Some of them are the remains of old volcanoes which have left black sand on the beaches.

**Atlas Mountains**
The rugged Atlas Mountains run through most of Morocco and Algeria. They form a barrier between the Mediterranean coast and the Sahara, which lies to the south.

**Suez Canal**
The Suez Canal links the Mediterranean to the Gulf of Suez and the Red Sea. Before it was built, ships had to sail around all of Africa to reach Asia.

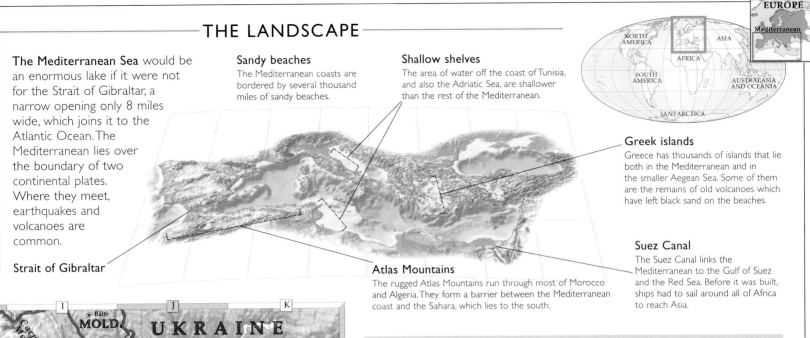

EUROPE

Mediterranean

NORTH AMERICA · ASIA · AFRICA · SOUTH AMERICA · AUSTRALASIA AND OCEANIA · ANTARCTICA

## TOURISM

The tourist industry in and around the Mediterranean is one of the most highly developed in the world. More than half the world's income from tourism is generated here. Resorts have grown up along the northwest coast of Africa, and in Egypt, southern Spain, France, Italy, Greece, and Turkey. Tourism brings huge economic benefits, but the ever-increasing number of visitors has also damaged the environment.

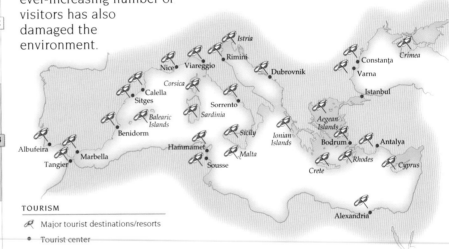

TOURISM

Major tourist destinations/resorts

Tourist center

## INDUSTRY

The Mediterranean has a large fishing industry, although most of the fishing is small-scale. Tuna and sardines are caught throughout the region, and mussels are farmed off the coast of Italy. Fish canning and packing take place at most of the larger ports. Small oil and gas reserves are extracted off the coast of North Africa and near Greece, Spain, and Italy.

INDUSTRY

Fishing ports

Oil and gas

Major city

# CONTINENTAL ASIA

**Asia is the world's largest continent**, and has the greatest range of physical extremes. Some of the highest, lowest, and coldest places on Earth are found in Asia: Mount Everest in the Himalayas is the highest, the Dead Sea in the west is the lowest, and the frozen wastes of northern Siberia are among the coldest. More people live in Asia than on any other continent – 1.2 billion of them in China, and 940 million in India.

## CROSS SECTION THROUGH ASIA

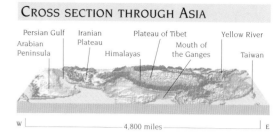

Persian Gulf / Arabian Peninsula — Iranian Plateau — Plateau of Tibet — Himalayas — Mouth of the Ganges — Yellow River — Taiwan

W ⊢——— 4,800 miles ———⊣ E

The Arabian Peninsula and the mountainous Iranian Plateau are divided by the Persian Gulf, fed by the Tigris and Euphrates Rivers. Farther east, the land begins to rise, the mountains spreading north to the Plateau of Tibet, and south to the Himalayas. The plains to the south of the Himalayas are drained by the Indus and Ganges, and to the east of the Plateau of Tibet by the Yellow River.

## PHYSICAL ASIA

**Northern Asia** is made up of old mountains and ancient, stable plateaus. The jagged Himalayan mountains dominate the central part of the continent, along with the Plateau of Tibet, which stretches north into China. In Southeast Asia, there are many islands. Volcanoes and earthquakes are common, and some of the islands are volcanically formed.

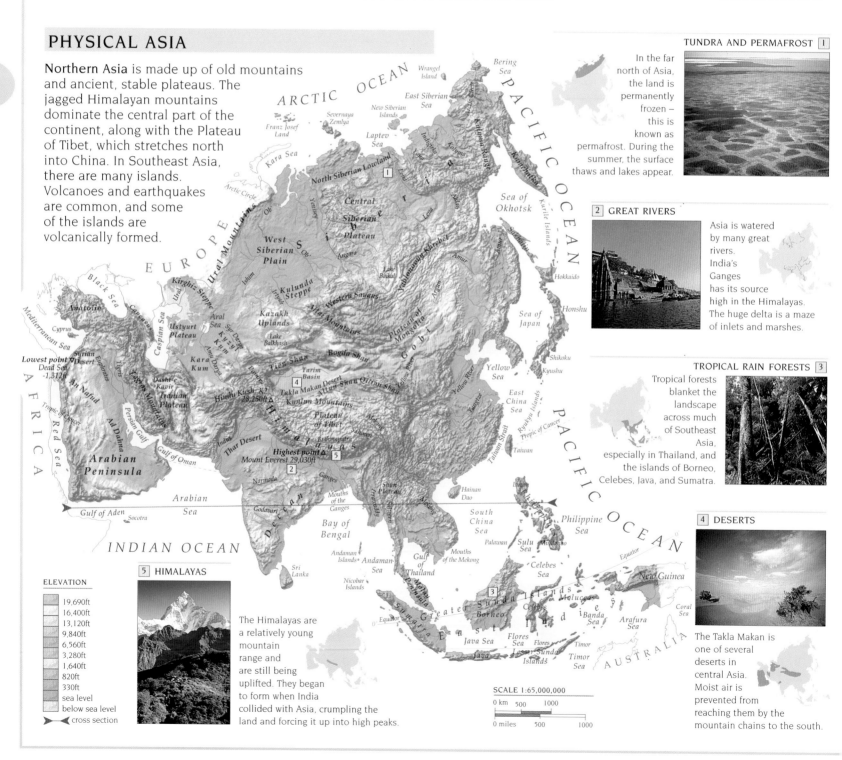

### TUNDRA AND PERMAFROST  1

In the far north of Asia, the land is permanently frozen – this is known as permafrost. During the summer, the surface thaws and lakes appear.

### 2 GREAT RIVERS

Asia is watered by many great rivers. India's Ganges has its source high in the Himalayas. The huge delta is a maze of inlets and marshes.

### TROPICAL RAIN FORESTS 3

Tropical forests blanket the landscape across much of Southeast Asia, especially in Thailand, and the islands of Borneo, Celebes, Java, and Sumatra.

### 4 DESERTS

The Takla Makan is one of several deserts in central Asia. Moist air is prevented from reaching them by the mountain chains to the south.

### 5 HIMALAYAS

The Himalayas are a relatively young mountain range and are still being uplifted. They began to form when India collided with Asia, crumpling the land and forcing it up into high peaks.

### ELEVATION

- 19,690ft
- 16,400ft
- 13,120ft
- 9,840ft
- 6,560ft
- 3,280ft
- 1,640ft
- 820ft
- 330ft
- sea level
- below sea level
- ➤◀ cross section

SCALE 1:65,000,000

0 km  500  1000

0 miles  500  1000

# POLITICAL ASIA

Asia is a continent of many contrasts: in its lands, its peoples, and its traditions. The break-up of the Soviet Union, which once stretched south from Russia to Iran, produced the new central Asian republics of Kazakhstan, Kyrgyzstan, Tajikistan, Turkmenistan, and Uzbekistan. The countries in southwest Asia are mainly Muslim, but are divided by religious differences and conflicts. India is the world's largest democracy, while China is a communist power with restricted access to the rest of the world.

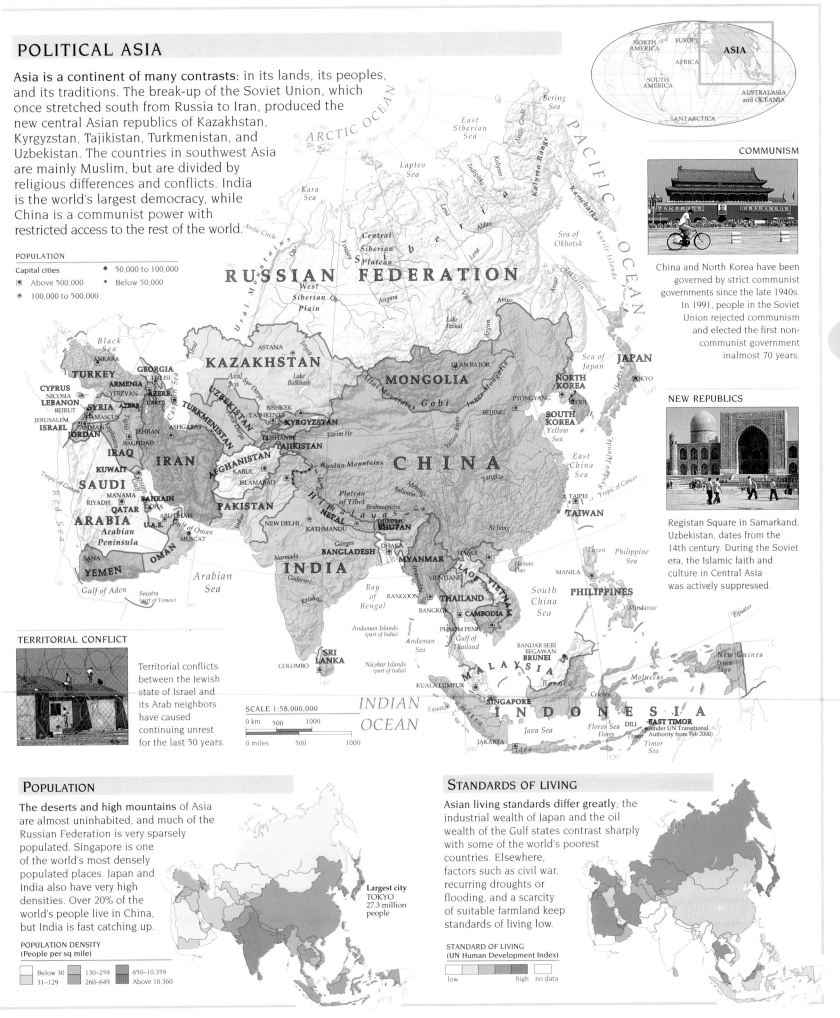

### COMMUNISM

China and North Korea have been governed by strict communist governments since the late 1940s. In 1991, people in the Soviet Union rejected communism and elected the first non-communist government in almost 70 years.

### NEW REPUBLICS

Registan Square in Samarkand, Uzbekistan, dates from the 14th century. During the Soviet era, the Islamic faith and culture in Central Asia was actively suppressed.

### TERRITORIAL CONFLICT

Territorial conflicts between the Jewish state of Israel and its Arab neighbors have caused continuing unrest for the last 50 years.

## POPULATION

The deserts and high mountains of Asia are almost uninhabited, and much of the Russian Federation is very sparsely populated. Singapore is one of the world's most densely populated places. Japan and India also have very high densities. Over 20% of the world's people live in China, but India is fast catching up.

**Largest city** TOKYO 27.3 million people

POPULATION DENSITY (People per sq mile)
Below 30 / 31–129 / 130–259 / 260–649 / 650–10,359 / Above 10,360

## STANDARDS OF LIVING

Asian living standards differ greatly; the industrial wealth of Japan and the oil wealth of the Gulf states contrast sharply with some of the world's poorest countries. Elsewhere, factors such as civil war, recurring droughts or flooding, and a scarcity of suitable farmland keep standards of living low.

STANDARD OF LIVING (UN Human Development Index)
low — high — no data

SCALE 1:58,000,000

# ASIAN GEOGRAPHY

Asia's forbidding mountain ranges, barren deserts, and fertile plains have affected the way in which people settled the continent. Intensive agriculture is found in the more fertile areas, and the largest concentrations of people grew up near fertile land and close to great rivers. Asia's mineral wealth has brought people to the more inhospitable parts of the continent: the deserts of southwest Asia for oil, and frozen Siberia for oil, gas, and minerals.

## INDUSTRY

**Many people in Asia** still rely on agriculture as a source of income, and some countries have very few industries. Heavy industry dominates eastern China and Russia, but Japan is the most industrially productive country. In recent years, booming "tiger" economies have developed in countries such as Taiwan, that border the Pacific Ocean.

## MINERAL RESOURCES

Over half of the world's oil and gas reserves are in Asia, most importantly around the Persian Gulf and in western Siberia. Coal in Siberia and China has provided power for steel industries. Metallic minerals are also abundant: tin in Southeast Asia, and platinum and nickel in Siberia.

### MINERAL RESOURCES

| | | |
|---|---|---|
| Chromium | | Oil/gas field |
| Tin | | Coal field |
| Nickel | | |
| Iron | | |
| Platinum | | |
| Gold | | |
| Lead | | |

### OIL AND GAS

The discovery of oil in the Persian Gulf has generated enormous wealth, and produced rapid industrial and social change in countries such as Saudi Arabia, U.A.E., and Kuwait that control the oil supplies.

### HIGH-TECH INDUSTRIES

Japan is a world-leading producer of electronic and high-tech goods like computers, cameras, and hi-fi equipment. Taiwan, South Korea, and Singapore also produce electronic goods.

### INDUSTRY

| | | | |
|---|---|---|---|
| ✈ | Aerospace | ⛏ | Coal |
| 🍺 | Brewing | | Electronics |
| 🚗 | Car/vehicle manufacturing | ⚙ | Engineering |
| | Cement | S | Finance |
| 🧪 | Chemicals | | Food processing |
| | | 🖥 | High-tech industry |
| | | | Iron and steel |
| | | | Mining |
| | | 🛢 | Oil and gas |
| | | | Pharmaceuticals |
| | | | Printing and publishing |
| | | | Shipbuilding |
| | | | Textiles |
| | | | Timber processing |

### FINANCE

Bombay (Mumbai) is India's leading industrial city and has a thriving stock market. Modern office blocks stand close to sprawling slums.

### INDUSTRIAL COMPLEXES

Noril'sk is one of several Soviet-era industrial complexes built in Russia, It is a processing center for the rich mineral reserves found nearby.

### GNP per capita (US$)

| | |
|---|---|
| | Below 1,999 |
| | 2,000-4,999 |
| | 5,000-9,999 |
| | 10,000-19,999 |
| | 20,000-24,999 |
| | Above 25,000 |
| • | Industrial center |

Traditional industries and methods of working are still important to less industrialized nations. Here in Vietnam, seawater has been evaporated by the sun, and the salt is collected for market.

### TRADITIONAL INDUSTRIES

# CLIMATE

**Most of Asia has a continental climate**, apart from coastal areas. Without the moderating effects of the ocean, temperatures can soar during the day and plummet at night, while rainfall is generally low – producing several large deserts. Temperatures as low as –90°F have been recorded in the frozen wastes of Siberia, while the islands in southeast Asia have tropical climates. Southern and eastern Asia are also affected by a seasonal wind called the monsoon. This originates in the Indian Ocean and brings heavy rainfall and high winds, often devastating small coastal and low-lying villages and towns.

**CLIMATE**

- Tundra
- Subarctic
- Cool continental
- Warm temperate
- Mediterranean
- Semiarid
- Arid
- Humid equatorial
- Tropical
- Hot humid

**Coldest place**
VERKHOYANSK (Russ. Fed.)
Temp -90°F

**Hottest place**
TIRAT TSVI (Israel)
Temp 129°F

**Driest place**
ADEN (Yemen)
Annual rainfall 3/16in

**Wettest place**
CHERRAPUNJI (India)
Annual rainfall 45in

**EXTREME WEATHER EVENTS**

Symbols indicate climatic extremes

**RAIN FORESTS**

The tropical climate across the islands of southeast Asia produces warm, humid conditions in which rain forests flourish. Each island provides a slightly different habitat, so the animals and plants that have evolved on one island may be very different to those on the next.

# LAND USE AND AGRICULTURE

**Large expanses of Asia are uncultivated** because the soil is too poor, or the climate is too cold or dry for crops to grow. The Plateau of Tibet, much of Siberia, and the Arabian Peninsula have limited agriculture. Some of the most fertile land is found in eastern China and India, where rice is a staple. Elsewhere, cash crops are grown for profit, such as dates in southwest Asia; rubber in Southeast Asia; tea in India, China, and Sri Lanka; and coconuts throughout the island archipelago of Southeast Asia.

**RICE**

China is the world's largest producer of rice, which is grown in muddy fields called paddy fields. Water buffaloes are used to plow the ground before planting.

**COTTON**

Uzbekistan is the world's fourth-largest producer of cotton. Water has been diverted from nearby rivers to water the crops, which has led to the drying up of the Aral Sea.

**LAND USE AND AGRICULTURE**

- 🐂 Cattle
- 🐐 Goats
- 🐖 Pigs
- 🐑 Sheep
- 🌾 Cereals
- 🥥 Coconuts
- 🌽 Corn
- Cotton
- ⊥ Dates
- Fishing
- Fruit
- Jute
- Peanuts
- Rice
- Root crops
- Rubber
- Shellfish
- Sugarcane
- Soya beans
- Tea
- Timber

- Mountains
- Cropland
- Desert
- Forest
- Pasture
- Wetland
- • Major conurbation

**DATES**

Dates have been cultivated on the Arabian Peninsula since ancient times. They are an important cash crop, grown for export in dry sandy areas where few other crops can grow.

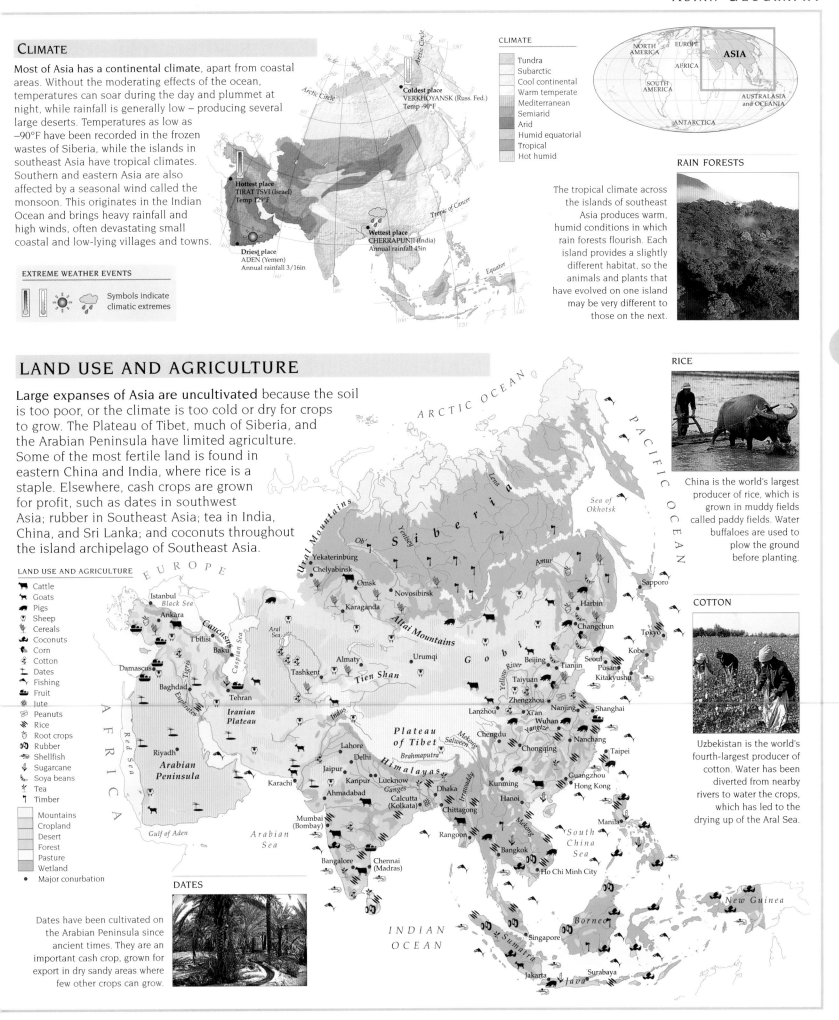

# RUSSIA AND KAZAKHSTAN

**Russia lies partly in Europe** but mostly in Asia. The land to the east of the Ural Mountains is called Siberia. This immense stretch of grasslands, thick, evergreen forest, and tundra is crossed by giant rivers. Vast areas of Siberia are almost untouched by human activity, yet in the industrial regions set up under communism (1922–1991), air, water, and soil are heavily polluted with harmful substances. Along with the former Soviet state of Kazakhstan, Siberia is rich in a huge variety of minerals.

## INDUSTRY

**The discovery of gold** in the 19th century opened Siberia up to economic and industrial development. Later, vast reserves of oil, coal, and gas were found, especially in the west, which is now the main center for oil extraction. Gold and diamonds are mined in the east. In Kazakhstan, mining and other industries are growing with the help of foreign investors.

STRUCTURE OF INDUSTRY

Primary 9%
Services 53%
Manufacturing 38%

INDUSTRY

- 🚗 Car manufacturing
- 🧪 Chemicals
- ⚙ Engineering
- 🚂 Iron and steel
- 👕 Textiles
- ⛏ Mining
- ◊ Oil and gas
- 🌲 Timber manufacturing
- ● Major industrial center / area
- — Major road

SVALBARD (Norwegian dependency)

Franz Josef Land

ARCTIC OCEAN

East Siberian Sea

Ostrov Komsomolets
October Revolution Island
Ostrov Bol'shevik
Severnaya Zemlya
New Siberian Islands
Ostrov Novaya Sibir'
Ostrov Bol'shoy Lyakhovskiy
Ostrov Kotel'nyy

Murmansk
North Cape (Nordkapp)
Kandalaksha
Kola Peninsula
Barents Sea
Novaya Zemlya
Kara Sea
Ostrov Belyy
Dikson
Ostrov Kolguyev
Nar'yan-Mar
Pechora
Ust'-Olenek
Tiksi
Kazach'ye

DENMARK
GERMANY
SWEDEN
NORWAY
Vänern
Vättern
Gulf of Bothnia
Arctic Circle
KALININGRAD (part of Russ. Fed.)
Kaliningrad
Baltic Sea
Gulf of Finland
FINLAND
Saimaa
LIT
LAT
POLAND
EST.
Saint Petersburg (Sankt-Peterburg)
Lake Ladoga
Pskov
Novgorod
Petrozavodsk
Lake Onega
Severodvinsk
Archangel
White Sea
Northern Dvina
BELARUS
Smolensk
Cherepovets
Vel'sk
Vologda
MOSCOW (MOSKVA)
Tver'
Yaroslavl'
Kineshma
Kotlas
Syktyvkar
Ukhta
Vorkuta
Salekhard
Gulf of Ob
Ob'
Nadym
Nyagan'
Igarka
Noril'sk
Talnakh
Putorana Mountains
North Siberian Lowland
Kheta
Khatanga
Poluostrov Taymyr
Ozero Taymyr
Poluostrov Yamal
Laptev Sea
Olenek
Olenëk
Lena
Vilyuy
Verkhoyanskiy Khrebet
Yana
Indigirka
Kolyma
Khrebet Cherskogo

Bryansk
Tula
Ryazan
Belgorod
Voronezh
Vladimir
Nizhniy Novgorod
Kirov
Glazov
Kazan'
Izhevsk
Perm'
Serov
Solikamsk
Ural Mountains
West Siberian Plain
Khanty-Mansiysk
Tuz
Yenisey
Central Siberian Plateau
Lower Tunguska
Nyurba
Yakutsk
Suntar
Lena
Aldan
Amga
Khrebet Dzhugdzhur
Okhotsk

UKRAINE
Mikhaylovka
Tambov
Penza
Ul'yanovsk
Tol'yatti
Naberezhnyye Chelny
Ufa
Yekaterinburg
Tyumen'
Tobol'sk
Surgut
Nizhnevartovsk
Siberian
Siberia
Mirnyy
Olëkminsk
Chunya
Angara
Rostov-na-Donu
Krasnodar
Sochi
Volgograd
Stavropol'
Samara
Sterlitamak
Ural'sk
Orenburg
Chelyabinsk
Ishim
Irtysh
RUSSIAN FEDERATION
Tömmot
Neryungri
Elbrus 18,511ft
Nal'chik
Vladikavkaz
Groznyy
Makhachkala
Astrakhan'
Atyrau
Ural
Aktyubinsk
Alga
Emba
Orsk
Magnitogorsk
Rudnyy
Kostanay
Petropavlovsk
Omsk
Novosibirsk
Tomsk
Krasnoyarsk
Kansk
Tulun
Chulym
Strelka
Ust'-Kut
Angara
Bratsk
Ust'-Ilimsk
Bodaybo
Zeya Reservoir
Tynda
Skovorodino
Svobodny
Birobidzh
GEORGIA
ARM.
AZERBAIJAN
Caspian Sea
Fort-Shevchenko
Aktau
Zhanaozen
Ustyurt Plateau
Chelkar
Emba
Aral Sea
Novokazalinsk
Aral'sk
Kokshetau
Atbasar
Shchuchinsk
Kirghiz Steppe
Kulunda Steppe
Pavlodar
Temirtau
Barnaul
Novokuznetsk
Kemerovo
Abakan
Western Sayans
Kyzyl
Eastern Sayan
Usol'ye-Sibirskoye
Angarsk
Irkutsk
Lake Baikal
Chita
Olovyannaya
Krasnokamensk
Zabaykal'sk
Blagoveshchensk
Amur
IRAN
TURKM.
KAZAKHSTAN
ASTANA
Saran'
Karaganda
Zhezkazgan
Kyzylorda
Kazakh Uplands
Semipalatinsk
Leninogorsk
Zyryanovsk
Shar
Ust'-Kamenogorsk
Gora Belukha 14,783ft
Ozero Zaysan
Selenga
Yablonovyy Khrebet
Kyakhta
Ulan-Ude
Shilda
MONGOLIA
UZBEKISTAN
Turkestan
Kentau
Karatau
Lake Balkhash
Balkhash
Ayaguz
Altai Mountains
CHINA
Arys
Shymkent
Taraz
Taldykorgan
Tekeli
Almaty (Alma-Ata)
Kyrgyz Range
Ozero Issyk-Kul'
KYRGYZSTAN
Tien Shan
TAJIKISTAN
Syr Darya
Kyzyl Kum
Dzhusaly
Kazakh Uplands
Kyzyl Kum

LAND HEIGHT
Above 13,120ft
6,560–13,120ft
3,280–6,560ft
1,640–3,280ft
820–1,640ft
330–820ft
0–330ft
Below sea level

SEA DEPTH
0–820ft
820–1,640ft
1,640–3,280ft
3,280–6,560ft
6,560–9,840ft
9,840–13,120ft
Below 13,120ft

SCALE BAR
0 km 200 400
0 miles 200 400

CITIES AND TOWNS
● Over 500,000 people
● 100,000–500,000
○ 50,000–100,000
○ Less than 50,000

# THE LANDSCAPE

**East of the Ural Mountains** lies the West Siberian Plain – the world's largest area of flat ground. The plain gradually rises to the Central Siberian Plateau and then again to highlands in the southeast. Great coniferous forests called *taiga* stretch across most of this land. The far north of Siberia extends into the Arctic Circle. Here the landscape is made up of frozen plains called tundra. Much of Kazakhstan is covered by huge rolling grasslands, or steppe. In the south are arid sandy deserts.

## Tundra and *taiga*

Stubby birch trees, dwarf bushes, moss and lichen huddle close to the ground in the frozen tundra wastes of northern Russia. They lie between the permanent ice and snow of the Arctic, and the thick *taiga* forests which cover an area greater than the Amazon rain forest.

### The Caspian Sea (A 5)
The Caspian Sea covers 143,243 sq miles and is the world's largest expanse of inland water. It is fed by the Volga and Ural Rivers, which flow in from the plains of the north.

### West Siberian Plain (D 4)
This vast, flat expanse is covered with a network of marshes and streams. The Ob' River, which winds its way north across the plains, is frozen for up to half the year.

### Lake Baikal (F 5)
Lake Baikal is the deepest lake in the world, and the largest freshwater one – it is more than 1 mile deep and covers 12,500 sq miles. It is fed by 336 rivers and contains around 20% of all the fresh water in the world.

# CLIMATE

Russia and Kazakhstan have continental climates, and their distance from seas and oceans means that temperatures fluctuate wildly, both daily and seasonally. Temperatures in eastern Siberia have been known to reach -90°F.

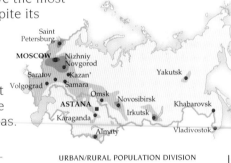

January

July

**TEMPERATURE AND PRECIPITATION**
- More than 86°F
- 77 to 86°F
- 68 to 77°F
- 59 to 68°F
- 50 to 59°F
- 41 to 50°F
- 32 to 41°F
- 23 to 32°F
- 14 to 23°F
- 5 to 14°F
- Less than 5°F

— 4 — Precipitation (mm)

# FARMING AND LAND USE

**Siberia's harsh climate** has restricted farming to the south, where there are a few areas warm enough to grow cereal crops such as wheat and oats and to raise cattle on the small pockets of pasture. The rest of the region is used for hunting, herding reindeer, and forestry – the *taiga* forests contain the world's largest timber reserves. In Kazakhstan, big herds of cattle, goats, and sheep are raised for wool and meat, and wheat is cultivated in the fertile north.

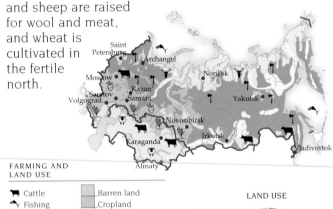

**FARMING AND LAND USE**
- Cattle
- Fishing
- Reindeer
- Sheep
- Root crops
- Timber
- Wheat
- Barren land
- Cropland
- Desert
- Forest
- Mountains
- Pasture
- Tundra
- Wetland
- • Major conurbation

**LAND USE**
- Cropland 9%
- Pasture 14%
- Forest 41%
- Other (including mountains) 36%

# POPULATION

**Siberia has** some of the world's largest areas of uninhabited land – the bitingly cold climate and harsh living conditions have kept the population small. The industrial cities in the west have the most people. Despite its huge size, Kazakhstan has only 17 million people, most of whom live in urban areas.

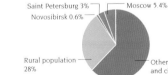

**INHABITANTS PER SQ MILE**
- More than 260
- 13–260
- 30–130
- Less than 30
- ■ Capital city
- • Major city

**URBAN/RURAL POPULATION DIVISION**
- Saint Petersburg 3%
- Moscow 5.4%
- Novosibirsk 0.6%
- Rural population 28%
- Other towns and cities 63%

# ENVIRONMENTAL ISSUES

**Decades of industrial development** during the communist regime brought new industries to undeveloped parts of the region, such as Siberia. This industrial development has led to environmental degradation on a massive scale: river, air, and land pollution in Russia is among the worst in the world.

**ENVIRONMENTAL ISSUES**
- Urban air pollution
- Polluted rivers
- • Major industrial center

# TURKEY AND THE CAUCASUS

ARMENIA, AZERBAIJAN, GEORGIA, TURKEY

**Turkey and the Caucasus** lie partly in Europe, and partly in Asia. Turkey has a long Islamic tradition, and although the country is now a secular (nonreligious) one, most Turks are Muslims. Turkey is becoming more industrialized, although half of its workforce is still employed in agriculture. The ancient countries of the Caucasus were under Russian rule for 70 years, until 1991. They are home to more than 50 different ethnic groups.

## INDUSTRY

**Turkey has a wide range** of industries and growing trade links with Europe. Azerbaijan has large oil reserves and is able to export oil. The other states use imported fuel and hydro-electric power generated by their rushing rivers. Georgia produces industrial machinery and chemicals. Armenia's economy is recovering from civil war and earthquake damage.

## FARMING AND LAND USE

**With its warm climate** and good soils, Turkey is able to produce all of its own food. Cattle and goats are kept on the central plateau. Along the Mediterranean coast, farmers grow olives, figs, grapes, and peaches. Hazelnuts are cultivated along the shores of the Black Sea. Across the Caucasus, the limited fertile land is used to grow wine grapes, tobacco, and cotton.

**FARMING AND LAND USE**

- 🐄 Livestock
- 🎣 Fishing
- Cotton
- 🍇 Fruit
- Hazelnuts
- Root crops
- Tobacco
- 🍇 Vineyards

- Pasture
- Cropland
- Forest
- • Major conurbation

**INDUSTRY**

- ⚙ Cement manufacturing
- Chemicals
- ⚙ Engineering
- Food processing
- Textiles
- Oil field
- Tourism
- Major industrial center / area
- — Major road

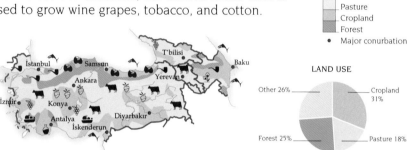

**LAND USE**

- Other 26%
- Cropland 31%
- Forest 25%
- Pasture 18%

**STRUCTURE OF INDUSTRY**

- Primary 18%
- Services 51%
- Manufacturing 31%

## THE LANDSCAPE

**A huge semiarid plateau** called Anatolia runs across the center of Turkey. It is rimmed by several mountain ranges along the Black Sea coast and the steep Taurus Mountains in the south. A narrow strip of lowland separates the Caucasus and the Lesser Caucasus mountains in the northeast.

### Anatolia

Anatolia has large areas of soft limestone rock. Over a long period of time, layers of rock have been worn away by water to produce strange landscapes with caves and tall, isolated rock pinnacles.

**Caucasus Mountains** (H1)

**Lesser Caucasus** (H2)

### Earthquakes

In 1988, 25,000 people were killed in an earthquake in the west of Armenia.

### Between two continents

The city of Istanbul (B2) in Turkey is divided in two by a narrow channel of water called the Bosporus. One part of the city is in Europe, the other in Asia. The two parts are linked by bridges.

### Taurus Mountains (D5)

The Taurus Mountains were formed around 60 to 65 million years ago. Weathering has formed caves and deep gorges.

### Lake Van (H4)

Lake Van is one of the shallow salt lakes found in Anatolia. Salt lakes develop in hot, dry areas where large quantities of water evaporate, leaving behind salty deposits.

## POPULATION

**Over 60% of Turks live** in large towns or cities, mostly in the western half of the country. The eastern and southeastern parts of Anatolia are home to the Kurdish people. The Caucasian republics became more industrialized under Russian rule, and today, over half of their people live in urban places.

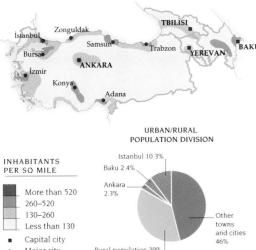

### URBAN/RURAL POPULATION DIVISION

- Istanbul 10.3%
- Baku 2.4%
- Ankara 2.3%
- Other towns and cities 46%
- Rural population 39%

**INHABITANTS PER SQ MILE**
- More than 520
- 260–520
- 130–260
- Less than 130
- ■ Capital city
- ● Major city

## ENVIRONMENTAL ISSUES

**Turkey has built** many large dams to use water from rivers – especially the Euphrates – to irrigate its farmland. Syria and Iraq, which lie downstream, have opposed the dams, because they will have less water flowing into their countries. In Armenia, a nuclear power plant that was closed after being damaged in the 1988 earthquake has reopened, although it is still unsafe.

### ENVIRONMENTAL ISSUES
- ≋ Major dam
- 🏭 Unstable nuclear power station
- 😷 Urban air pollution
- ● Major industrial center

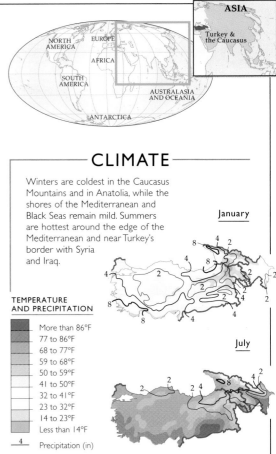

**ASIA**
Turkey & the Caucasus

## CLIMATE

Winters are coldest in the Caucasus Mountains and in Anatolia, while the shores of the Mediterranean and Black Seas remain mild. Summers are hottest around the edge of the Mediterranean and near Turkey's border with Syria and Iraq.

January

July

**TEMPERATURE AND PRECIPITATION**
- More than 86°F
- 77 to 86°F
- 68 to 77°F
- 59 to 68°F
- 50 to 59°F
- 41 to 50°F
- 32 to 41°F
- 23 to 32°F
- 14 to 23°F
- Less than 14°F
- ─4─ Precipitation (in)

**SCALE BAR**
0 km 75 150
0 miles 75 150

**CITIES AND TOWNS**
- ● Over 500,000 people
- ◉ 100,000–500,000
- ○ 50,000–100,000
- ∘ Less than 50,000

| LAND HEIGHT | SEA DEPTH |
|---|---|
| Above 13,120ft | 0–160ft |
| 6,560–13,120ft | 160–330ft |
| 3,280–6,560ft | 330–820ft |
| 1,640–3,280ft | 820–1,640ft |
| 820–1,640ft | 1,640–3,280ft |
| 330–820ft | 3,280–6,560ft |
| 0–330ft | Below 6,560ft |
| Below sea level | |

# SOUTHWEST ASIA

BAHRAIN, IRAN, IRAQ, ISRAEL, JORDAN, KUWAIT, LEBANON, OMAN, QATAR, SAUDI ARABIA, SYRIA, UNITED ARAB EMIRATES, YEMEN

**Most of southwest Asia** is barren desert, yet the world's first cities originated here over 5,000 years ago. It was the birthplace of three major religions: Islam, Judaism, and Christianity. In recent years, the discovery of oil has brought great wealth to much of the region, but it has also been torn by civil wars and conflicts between neighboring countries. Most people here are Muslims, although Israel is the world's only Jewish state.

## ENVIRONMENTAL ISSUES

**Water shortages** are common because of the hot, dry climate and the lack of rivers. Desalination plants convert seawater into freshwater, and are found along the Red Sea and Gulf coasts. Lack of water also makes the risk of desertification greater. Iran has had many catastrophic earthquakes; in 1978 an earthquake killed 25,000 people.

ENVIRONMENTAL ISSUES

- 🚰 Area with many desalination plants
- ◉ Catastrophic earthquake
- 😷 Urban air pollution
- Existing desert
- Risk of desertification
- • Major industrial center

## INDUSTRY

**Oil has made** the previously poor Arab states very wealthy. It and natural gas continue to be the main sources of income for many of the countries here. Other industries are being developed to support the region's economies when these resources run out. Iran is famous for its carpets, which are woven from wool or silk.

INDUSTRY
- 🏭 Cement manufacturing
- 🍴 Food processing
- ⚙ Iron and steel
- 🛢 Oil refining
- 👕 Textiles
- 🛢 Oil and gas
- 💲 Finance
- ▨ Major industrial center / area
- — Major road

STRUCTURE OF INDUSTRY

Primary 10%
Services 49%
Manufacturing 41%

## THE LANDSCAPE

**Great desert plateaus,** both sandy and rocky, cover much of southwest Asia. On the enormous Arabian Peninsula, which covers an area almost the size of India, narrow, sandy plains along the Red Sea and south coast rise to dry mountains. In the center is a vast, high plateau that slopes gently down to the flat shores of the Persian Gulf. The mountainous areas of Iran experience frequent earthquakes.

### Wadis
Valleys or riverbeds, called *wadis*, are found in the Saudi Arabian desert. They are usually dry, but after heavy rains, they are briefly filled by fast flowing rivers.

### Syrian Desert (B 2)
The Syrian Desert extends from the Jordan valley in the west to the fertile plains of the Tigris and Euphrates Rivers in the east. It is mainly a rocky desert, because the sand has been swept away by winds and occasional heavy rainstorms.

### Oases
Oases are areas within a desert where water is available for plants and human use. They are usually formed when a fault, or split, in the rock allows water to come to the surface. Oases can be no bigger than a few palm trees or cover several hundred sq miles.

### Dead Sea (A 2)
This large lake on the border between Israel and Jordan is the lowest point on the Earth's surface — its shores lie 1,286 ft below sea level. It is also the world's saltiest body of water, and cannot sustain any life.

### Ar Rub' al Khali (D 5)
The Ar Rub' al Khali desert, also known as the "Empty Quarter," is the largest uninterrupted stretch of sand on Earth. It covers some 250,000 sq miles and is one of the world's driest and most hostile deserts.

### Iranian Plateau (E 3)
Central Iran is taken up by a vast, semiarid plateau, that rises steeply from the coastal lowlands bordering the Persian Gulf. It is ringed by the high Zagros and Elburz mountains.

## FARMING AND LAND USE

**The best farmland** is found along the Mediterranean coast and in the fertile valleys of the Tigris, Euphrates and Jordan Rivers. Wheat is the main cereal crop, and cotton, dates, and citrus and orchard fruits are grown for export. Elsewhere, modern irrigation techniques have created patches of fertile land in the desert. Dates, wheat, and coffee are cultivated in the oases and along the Persian Gulf coast.

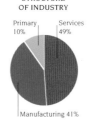

FARMING AND LAND USE
- 🐐 Goats
- 🎣 Fishing
- 🐑 Sheep
- 🍊 Citrus fruits
- ☕ Coffee
- 🌿 Cotton
- 🌴 Dates
- 🍒 Fruit
- 🌾 Wheat
- ▨ Cropland
- ▨ Desert
- ▨ Forest
- ▨ Pasture
- ▨ Wetland
- • Major conurbation

LAND USE

Forest 5%
Pasture 36%
Cropland 7%
Other (including desert) 52%

# POPULATION

Desert has kept much of the population clustered along the coastal areas and rivers or around the oases. Most people live in the cities, some of which are the fastest growing in the world. Oman and Yemen have mainly rural populations, and in Saudi Arabia, small groups of Bedouin tribespeople roam the desert with their animals.

## URBAN/RURAL POPULATION DIVISION

Baghdad 3%  Tehran 5%
Riyadh 1%
Other towns and cities 52%
Rural population 39%

### INHABITANTS PER SQ MILE

- More than 520
- 260–520
- 130–260
- Less than 130
- ■ Capital city
- ● Major city

## CLIMATE

Most of the region receives very little rain, apart from a few isolated pockets. Temperatures soar during July, but in January they are much cooler, especially in the north.

### TEMPERATURE AND PRECIPITATION

- More than 86°F
- 77 to 86°F
- 68 to 77°F
- 59 to 68°F
- 50 to 59°F
- 41 to 50°F
- 32 to 41°F
- Less than 32°F
- 4 — Precipitation (in)

ASIA
Southwest Asia

January

July

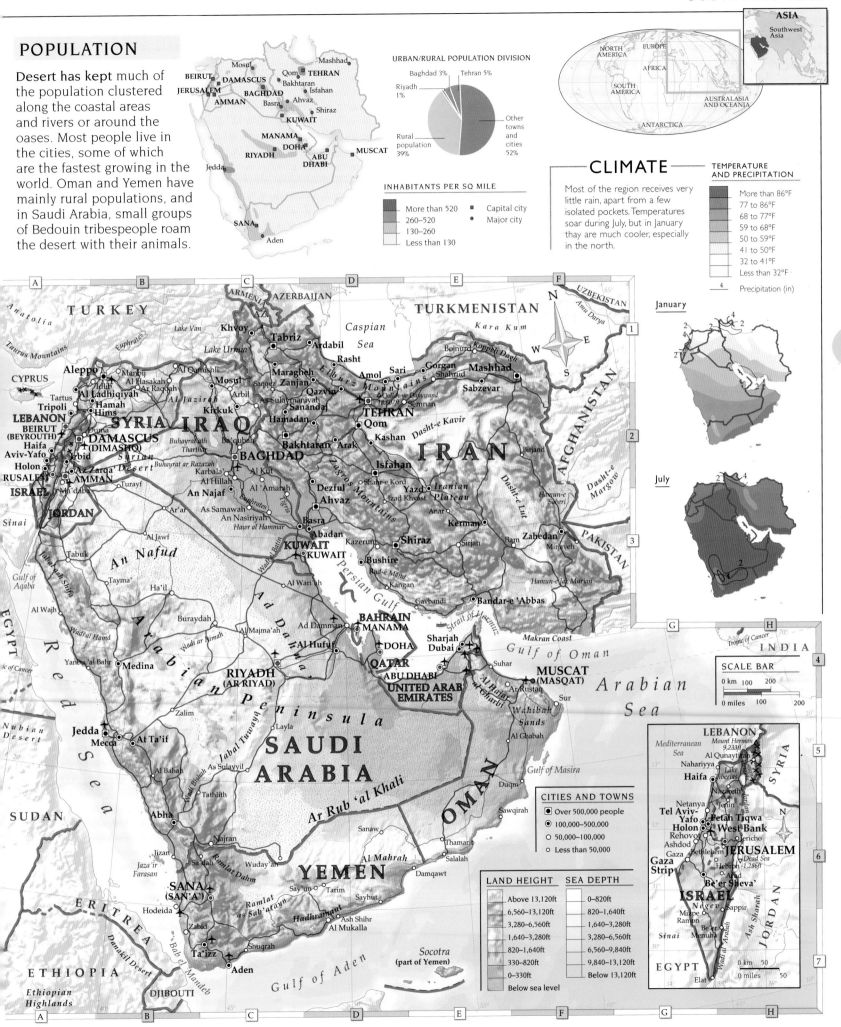

### CITIES AND TOWNS
- ◉ Over 500,000 people
- ⊙ 100,000–500,000
- ○ 50,000–100,000
- ○ Less than 50,000

### SCALE BAR
0 km 100 200
0 miles 100 200

### LAND HEIGHT
- Above 13,120ft
- 6,560–13,120ft
- 3,280–6,560ft
- 1,640–3,280ft
- 820–1,640ft
- 330–820ft
- 0–330ft
- Below sea level

### SEA DEPTH
- 0–820ft
- 820–1,640ft
- 1,640–3,280ft
- 3,280–6,560ft
- 6,560–9,840ft
- 9,840–13,120ft
- Below 13,120ft

# CENTRAL ASIA

AFGHANISTAN, KYRGYZSTAN, TAJIKISTAN, TURKMENISTAN, UZBEKISTAN

**Central Asia** is a land of hot, dry deserts and high, rugged mountains. It lies on the ancient Silk Road, an important trade route between China and Europe for over 400 years, until the 15th century. All of the countries here, except for Afghanistan, were part of the Soviet Union from the 1920s until 1991, when they gained independence. Since then, their people have reestablished their local languages and Islamic faith, which were restricted under Russian rule.

## INDUSTRY

**Fossil fuels,** especially coal, natural gas, and oil, are extracted and processed throughout Central Asia. Agriculture supplies the raw materials for many industries, including food and textile processing, and the manufacture of leather goods and clothing. The region is famous for its colorful traditional carpets, hand-woven from the wool of the Karakul sheep. The Fergana Valley, southeast of Tashkent, is the main industrial area.

INDUSTRY

- ⚗ Chemicals
- ⚙ Engineering
- 🏭 Food processing
- ⊽ Textiles
- ⛏ Mining
- ⬦ Oil and gas
- ▦ Major industrial center / area
- — Major road

STRUCTURE OF INDUSTRY

Primary 16%
Manufacturing 58%
Services 26%

## POPULATION

**The peoples of Central Asia are mostly rural farmers,** living in the river valleys and in oases. There are few large cities. A few still lead a traditional nomadic lifestyle, moving from place to place with their animals in search of new pastures. Large areas of Afghanistan, the western deserts, and the mountain regions in the east, are virtually uninhabited.

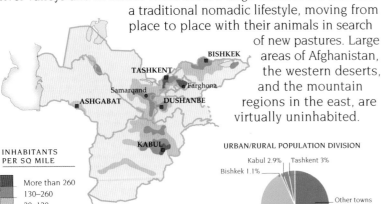

INHABITANTS PER SQ MILE

- More than 260
- 130–260
- 30–130
- Less than 30
- ▪ Capital city
- • Major city

URBAN/RURAL POPULATION DIVISION

Kabul 2.9%   Tashkent 3%
Bishkek 1.1%
Rural population 62%
Other towns and cities 31%

## FARMING AND LAND USE

**Farming is concentrated** around the fertile river valleys in the east, like the Fergana Valley. A variety of cereals and fruits – including peaches, melons, and apricots – are grown. In drier areas, animal breeding is important, with goats, sheep, and cattle supplying wool, meat, and hides. Big crops of cotton, which is a major export, are produced on land irrigated by the Amu Darya River.

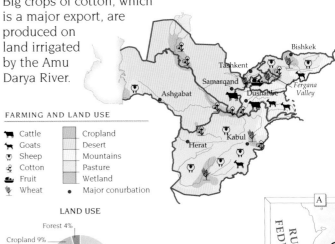

FARMING AND LAND USE

- 🐄 Cattle
- 🐐 Goats
- 🐑 Sheep
- ⚘ Cotton
- 🍇 Fruit
- 🌾 Wheat
- Cropland
- Desert
- Mountains
- Pasture
- Wetland
- • Major conurbation

LAND USE

Forest 4%
Cropland 9%
Pasture 41%
Other (including mountains and deserts) 45%

## THE LANDSCAPE

**Two of the world's great deserts,** the Kara Kum and the Kyzyl Kum, cover much of the western portion of Central Asia. In the east, a belt of high mountain ranges – the Hindu Kush, the Tien Shan, and the Pamirs – tower above the land. Few rivers cross the deserts, apart from the Amu Darya, which flows from the Pamirs to the shrinking Aral Sea.

### Aral Sea (D 1)
The Aral Sea was once the fourth largest lake in the world, but it has shrunk by 40% since 1960. Diversion of its water for irrigation has made the lake shallower, so its waters evaporate faster.

### Kara Kum (D 3)
The sandy desert of the Kara Kum occupies over 70% of Turkmenistan. Its surface consists of wind-shaped dunes and depressions. Human settlement is limited to the desert's fringes.

### Tien Shan (H 2)

### Fergana Valley (G 3)
Stresses and strains in the Earth created the Fergana Valley, a deep depression encircled by high mountains. The valley's fertile soils are irrigated by water from the Syr Darya River, and underground sources.

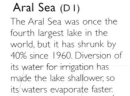

### Amu Darya River (E 3)

### Hindu Kush (G 4)

### Pamirs (G 4)
The Pamirs lie mainly in Tajikistan. Their highest point, at 24,590 ft, is Communism Peak, so named because it was the highest peak in the former Soviet Union.

# ENVIRONMENTAL ISSUES

**The Aral Sea is rapidly drying up**, because the rivers feeding it are being diverted to irrigate cottonfields. Central Asia is a very dry area, and desertification is a constant threat, especially in Afghanistan. Severe urban and industrial air pollution is a legacy from the communist era, when heavy industries were established in the countries here.

ENVIRONMENTAL
ISSUES

Urban air pollution

Existing desert
Risk of desertification
Severe risk of desertification
Polluted river

Major industrial center

# CLIMATE

Central Asia's climate is strongly inflenced by its position deep within Asia, far from the moderating effects of the oceans. Winters are cold, summers are very hot everywhere. Rainfall is virtually nonexistent all year round.

ASIA
NORTH AMERICA
EUROPE
AFRICA
SOUTH AMERICA
Central Asia
AUSTRALASIA AND OCEANIA
ANTARCTICA

January

Less than 2in precipitation

July

Less than 2in precipitation

TEMPERATURE
AND PRECIPITATION

More than 86°F
77 to 86°F
41 to 50°F
32 to 41°F
Less than 32°F

LAND HEIGHT
Above 13,120ft
6,560–3,120ft
3,280–6,560ft
1,640–3,280ft
820–1,640ft
330–820ft
0–330ft
Below sea level

SEA DEPTH
0–30ft
30–80ft
80–160ft
160–330ft
330–820ft

CITIES AND TOWNS
Over 500,000 people
100,000–500,000
50,000–100,000
Less than 50,000

SCALE BAR
0 km    100    200
0 miles    100    200

# JAPAN AND KOREA

JAPAN, NORTH KOREA, SOUTH KOREA

**Japan is a curved chain** of over 4,000 islands in the Pacific Ocean. To the west, Korea juts out from northern China. Japan has few natural resources, but it has become one of the world's most successful industrial nations, due to investment in new technology and a highly efficient workforce. North Korea is a communist state with limited contact with the outside world, while South Korea is a democracy with major international trade links.

## FARMING AND LAND USE

**Modern farming methods** allow Japan to grow much of its own food, despite a shortage of farmland. Rice is the main crop grown throughout the region. Japan has a large fishing fleet; the Japanese eat more fish than any other nation. In North Korea, farming is controlled by the government.

### FARMING AND LAND USE

- 🐂 Cattle
- ⚓ Fishing
- 🐖 Pigs
- 🍓 Fruit
- 〰 Rice
- 🌱 Soybeans
- 🌿 Tea
- Cropland
- Forest
- Pasture
- • Major conurbation

**LAND USE**

Pasture 1%
Cropland 14%
Other (including mountains) 30%
Forest 55%

## POPULATION

**Most of Japan's** 125 million people live in crowded cities on the coasts of the four main islands. The Kanto Plain around Tokyo is Japan's biggest area of flat land, and the most populous part of the country. In South Korea, a quarter of the population lives in the capital, Seoul. Most North Koreans live on the coastal plains.

**URBAN/RURAL POPULATION DIVISION**

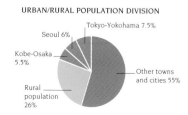

Tokyo-Yokohama 7.5%
Seoul 6%
Kobe-Osaka 5.5%
Rural population 26%
Other towns and cities 55%

**INHABITANTS PER SQ MILE**

- More than 520
- 260–520
- 130–260
- Less than 130
- ■ Capital city
- • Major city

## THE LANDSCAPE

**Most of Japan is covered** by forested mountains and hills, among which are many short, fast-flowing rivers and small lakes. Only about a quarter of the land is suitable for building and farming, and new land has been created by cutting back hillsides and reclaiming land from the sea. North and South Korea are mostly mountainous, with some coastal plains.

### Hokkaido, Honshu, Shikoku, and Kyushu
Japan's four main islands were formed when two giant plates making up the Earth's crust collided, making their edges buckle upward.

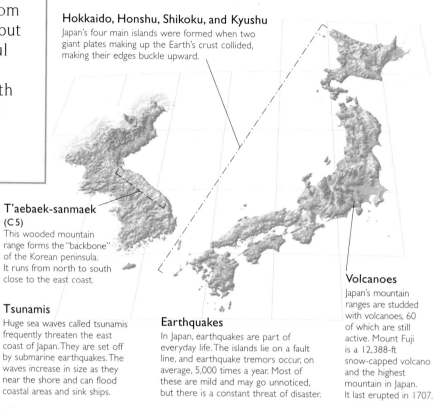

### T'aebaek-sanmaek (C 5)
This wooded mountain range forms the "backbone" of the Korean peninsula. It runs from north to south close to the east coast.

### Tsunamis
Huge sea waves called tsunamis frequently threaten the east coast of Japan. They are set off by submarine earthquakes. The waves increase in size as they near the shore and can flood coastal areas and sink ships.

### Earthquakes
In Japan, earthquakes are part of everyday life. The islands lie on a fault line, and earthquake tremors occur, on average, 5,000 times a year. Most of these are mild and may go unnoticed, but there is a constant threat of disaster.

### Volcanoes
Japan's mountain ranges are studded with volcanoes, 60 of which are still active. Mount Fuji is a 12,388-ft snow-capped volcano and the highest mountain in Japan. It last erupted in 1707.

## INDUSTRY

**Japan is a world leader in** high-tech electronic goods like computers, televisions and cameras, as well as cars. South Korea also has a thriving economy. It produces ships, cars, high-tech goods, shoes, and clothes for worldwide export. Both countries have to import most of their raw materials and energy. North Korea has little trade with other countries, but it is rich in minerals such as coal and silver.

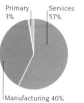

**STRUCTURE OF INDUSTRY**

Primary 3%
Services 57%
Manufacturing 40%

### INDUSTRY

- 🚗 Car manufacturing
- ⚗ Chemicals
- ⚙ Engineering
- 🍴 Food processing
- Iron and steel
- Shipbuilding
- Textiles
- $ Finance
- 💻 High-tech
- Research and Development
- • Major industrial center / area
- — Major road

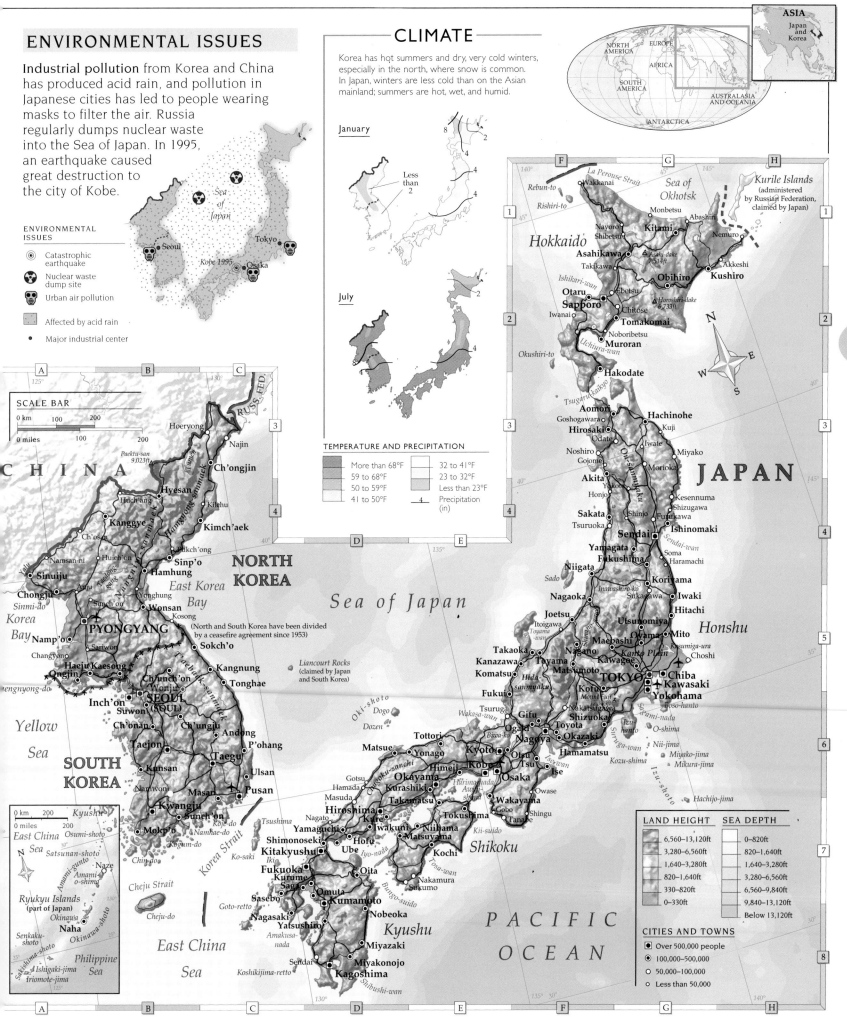

# ENVIRONMENTAL ISSUES

**Industrial pollution** from Korea and China has produced acid rain, and pollution in Japanese cities has led to people wearing masks to filter the air. Russia regularly dumps nuclear waste into the Sea of Japan. In 1995, an earthquake caused great destruction to the city of Kobe.

## CLIMATE

Korea has hot summers and dry, very cold winters, especially in the north, where snow is common. In Japan, winters are less cold than on the Asian mainland; summers are hot, wet, and humid.

# EAST ASIA

CHINA, MONGOLIA, TAIWAN

**China is the world's** third-largest country and its most populous – over one billion people live there. Under its communist government, which came to power in 1949, China has become a major industrial nation, but most of its people still live and work on the land as they have for thousands of years. Taiwan also has a booming economy and exports its products around the world. Mongolia is a vast, remote country with a small population, many of whom are nomads.

## INDUSTRY

**Chemicals,** iron and steel, engineering, and textiles are the main industries in China's east coast cities, and in industrial centers like Shenyang. Shanghai, Hong Kong, and Beijing are also important financial centers. In the interior, large deposits of coal support the heavy industries in major cities such as Chengdu and Wuhan. Taiwan specializes in textiles and shoe manufacture, along with electronic goods. Mongolia's economy is mainly agricultural.

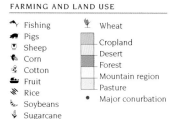

INDUSTRY

- Car manufacturing
- Chemicals
- Electronics
- Engineering
- Food processing
- Iron and steel
- Shipbuilding
- Textiles
- Coal
- Finance
- Major industrial center / area
- Major road

STRUCTURE OF INDUSTRY

Services 21%
Manufacturing 47%
Primary 32%

## POPULATION

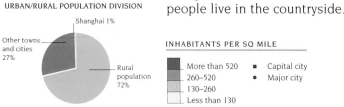

**Most of China's people** live in the eastern part of the country, where the climate, landscape and soils are most favorable. Urban areas there house more than 250 million people, but almost 75% of the population lives in villages and farms the land. Taiwan's lowlands are very densely populated. In Mongolia, about 50% of the people live in the countryside.

URBAN/RURAL POPULATION DIVISION

Shanghai 1%
Other towns and cities 27%
Rural population 72%

INHABITANTS PER SQ MILE

- More than 520
- 260–520
- 130–260
- Less than 130
- Capital city
- Major city

## FARMING AND LAND USE

**Despite its size,** about 90% of China is unsuitable for farming. Either the soils and climate are poor, or the landscape is too mountainous. In the north and west, most farmers make their living by herding animals. On the fertile eastern plains, soybeans, wheat, corn, and cotton are grown. Farther south, rice becomes the main crop, and pigs are raised in large numbers.

FARMING AND LAND USE

- Fishing
- Pigs
- Sheep
- Corn
- Cotton
- Fruit
- Rice
- Soybeans
- Sugarcane
- Wheat
- Cropland
- Desert
- Forest
- Mountain region
- Pasture
- Major conurbation

LAND USE

Cropland 7%
Pasture 42%
Other (including mountains) 24%
Forest 27%

## THE LANDSCAPE

**China's landscape is divided** into three areas. The vast Plateau of Tibet in the southwest is the highest and largest plateau on Earth. It contains both dry deserts and pockets of pasture surrounded by high mountains. Northwest China has dry highlands. The great plains of eastern China were formed from soils deposited by rivers like the Yellow River over thousands of years. Most of Mongolia is dry, grassland steppe and cold, arid desert.

### Tien Shan mountains (B 2)
The Tien Shan, or "Heavenly Mountains" reach heights of 24,393 ft. They surround fields of permanent ice and spectacular glaciers.

### Gobi (E2) and Takla Makan (B3) deserts
The arid landscapes of the Gobi and Takla Makan deserts are made up of bare rock surfaces and huge areas of shifting sand dunes. They are hot in summer, but unlike most other deserts, are extremely cold in winter.

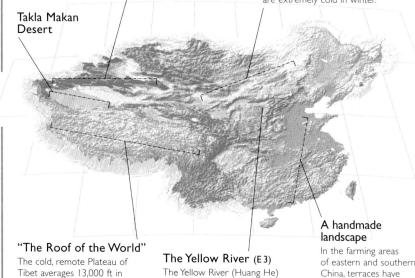
Takla Makan Desert

A handmade landscape

### "The Roof of the World"
The cold, remote Plateau of Tibet averages 13,000 ft in height. Many of China's great rivers have their sources here. The world's highest human settlement, a town called Wenquan, is found in the east of the plateau. It lies 16,729 ft above sea level.

### The Yellow River (E 3)
The Yellow River (Huang He) is the world's muddiest river, carrying hundreds of truckloads of sediment to the sea every minute. The river has burst its banks many times throughout history, causing enormous damage and claiming millions of human lives.

### A handmade landscape
In the farming areas of eastern and southern China, terraces have been carved into the hillsides to make them flat enough to grow rice and other crops. This method of farming has been used for over 7,000 years.

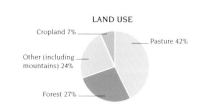

# ENVIRONMENTAL ISSUES

**The Three Gorges** hydroelectric program on the Yangtze River will be the world's largest. Nearly 350 miles of canyon will be flooded and 1.3 million people forced to move. Earthquakes are common in the area, and 100 million people downstream will be threatened if the dam breaks. In eastern China, many cities are affected by industrial pollution.

### ENVIRONMENTAL ISSUES

- Major dam
- Urban air pollution
- Industrial city

## CLIMATE

Two air masses control climate: one cold and dry from Siberia, and one moist and warm from the Pacific. Winters are long and cold away from the coast – especially on the Plateau of Tibet.

ASIA
East Asia

### TEMPERATURE AND PRECIPITATION

- More than 86°F
- 68 to 86°F
- 50 to 68°F
- 32 to 50°F
- 14° to 32°F
- -4°F to 14°F
- Less than -4°F
- Precipitation (in)

January

July

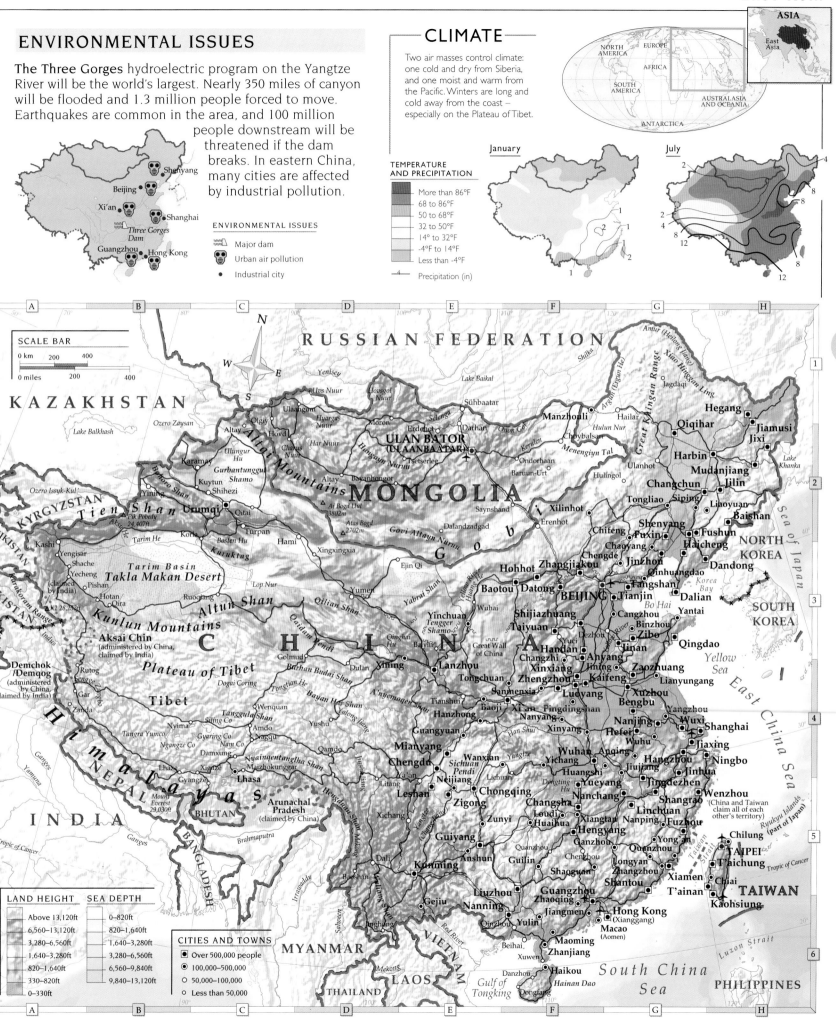

### SCALE BAR

0 km 200 400
0 miles 200 400

### LAND HEIGHT

- Above 13,120ft
- 6,560–13,120ft
- 3,280–6,560ft
- 1,640–3,280ft
- 820–1,640ft
- 330–820ft
- 0–330ft

### SEA DEPTH

- 0–820ft
- 820–1,640ft
- 1,640–3,280ft
- 3,280–6,560ft
- 6,560–9,840ft
- 9,840–13,120ft

### CITIES AND TOWNS

- Over 500,000 people
- 100,000–500,000
- 50,000–100,000
- Less than 50,000

# SOUTH ASIA

BANGLADESH, BHUTAN, INDIA, NEPAL, PAKISTAN, SRI LANKA

**South Asia** is a land of many contrasts. Its landscape ranges from the mighty peaks of the Himalayas in the north through vast plains and arid deserts, to tropical forests and palm-fringed beaches in the south. More than one-fifth of the world's people live here, and a long history of foreign invasions has left a mosaic of vastly different cultures, religions, and traditions and thousands of languages and dialects.

## INDUSTRY

Industry has expanded in India in recent years. In the cities a variety of goods are produced and processed, including cars, airplanes, chemicals, food, and drink. Service industries such as tourism and banking are also growing. Elsewhere, small-scale cottage industries serve the needs of local people, but many products, mainly silk and cotton textiles, clothing, leather, and jewelry, are also exported.

### STRUCTURE OF INDUSTRY

Primary 29%
Services 44%
Manufacturing 27%

### INDUSTRY

- ✈ Aerospace
- 🚗 Car manufacturing
- 🧪 Chemicals
- ⚡ Electronics
- ⚙ Engineering
- 🍴 Food processing
- 🏭 Iron and steel
- 👕 Textiles
- 💲 Finance
- 🛅 Tourism
- • Major industrial center / area
- — Major road

## POPULATION

Most of South Asia's people live in villages scattered across the fertile river floodplains, in mountain valleys, or along the coasts, but increasing numbers are migrating to the cities in search of work. Overcrowding is a serious problem in both rural and urban areas; in many cities, thousands of people are forced to live in slums or on the streets.

### INHABITANTS PER SQ MILE

- More than 520
- 260–520
- 130–260
- Less than 130
- ■ Capital city
- • Major city

### URBAN/RURAL POPULATION DIVISION

Calcutta 1%  Mumbai 1.2%
Karachi 0.8%
Other towns and cities 23%
Rural population 74%

## FARMING AND LAND USE

Over 60% of the population is involved in agriculture, but most farms are small and produce only enough food to feed one family. Grains are the staple food crops – rice in the wetter parts of the east and west, corn, and millet on the Deccan plateau, and wheat in the north. Peanuts are widely grown as a source of cooking oil. Cash crops include tea, which is grown on plantations, and jute.

### FARMING AND LAND USE

- 🐄 Cattle
- 🐟 Fishing
- 🐐 Goats
- 🌾 Cereals
- 🥜 Peanuts
- 🌿 Rice
- 🌱 Tea
- Cropland
- Desert
- Forest
- Pasture
- Wetland
- • Major conurbation

### LAND USE

Pasture 5%
Forest 21%
Other 24%
Cropland 50%

## THE LANDSCAPE

A massive, towering wall of snow-capped mountains stretches in an arc across the north, isolating South Asia from the rest of the continent. The huge floodplains and deltas of the Indus, Ganges, and Brahmaputra Rivers separate the mountains from the rest of the peninsula: a great rolling plateau, bordered on either side by coastal hills called the Eastern and Western Ghats.

### Himalayas (E 2)
The Himalayas are the highest mountain system in the world. They were formed about 40 million years ago when two of the Earth's plates collided, thrusting up huge masses of land.

### Mount Everest (F 3)
The northern ranges of the Himalayas average 23,000 ft in height. They include the highest point on Earth, Mount Everest on the Nepal–China border, which soars to 29,030 ft.

### Thar Desert (C 3)
The border between India and Pakistan runs through the arid, sandy Thar Desert.

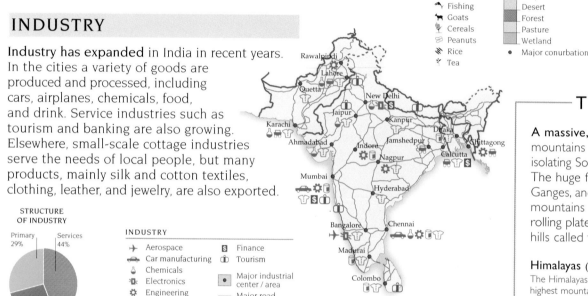

### Western Ghats (C 5)
The Western Ghats run continuously along the Arabian Sea coast. The lower Eastern Ghats are interrupted by rivers that follow the gentle slope of the Deccan plateau and flow across broad lowlands into the Bay of Bengal. This is one of the wettest regions in the world.

### Eastern Ghats (E 5)

### Deccan plateau (D 5)
This giant plateau makes up most of central and southern India. Its volcanic rock has been deeply cut by rivers such as the Krishna, creating stepped valleys called *traps*.

### Bangladesh (G 3)
Much of Bangladesh lies in an enormous delta formed by the Brahmaputra and Ganges Rivers. During the summer monsoon, the rivers become swollen by the torrential rains – and meltwater from the Himalayas – and the delta floods. Over the years, millions of people have drowned or been made homeless by heavy flooding.

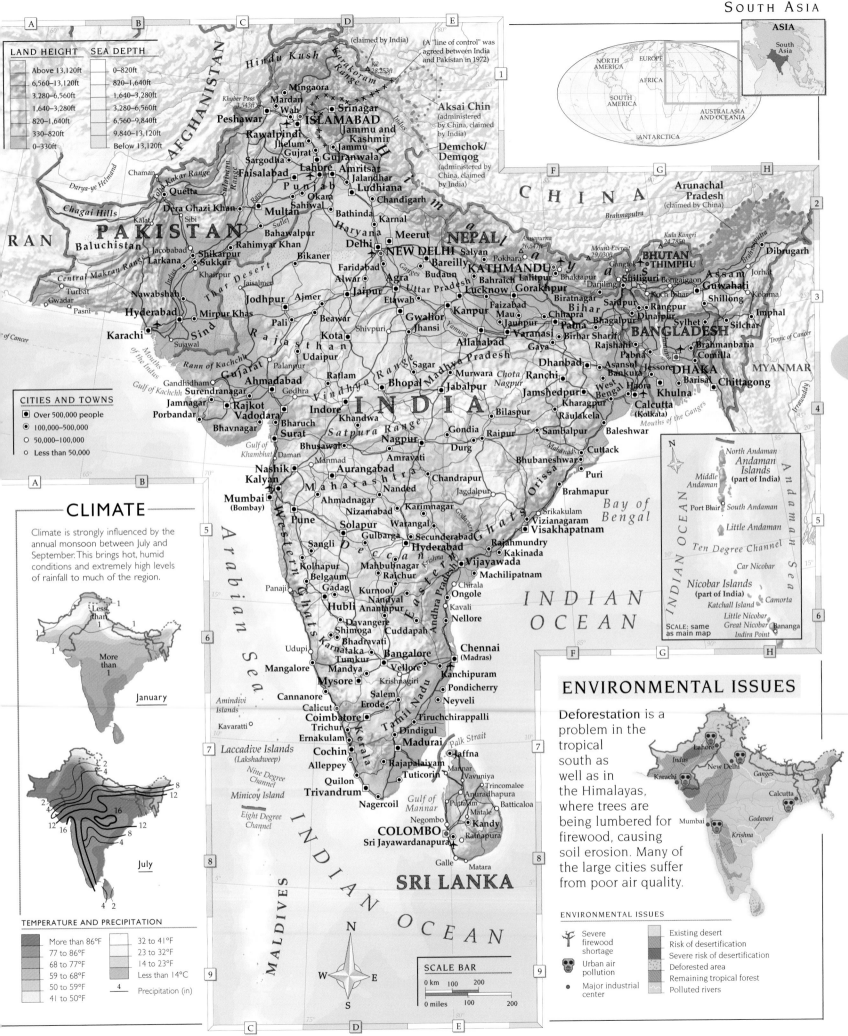

ASIA
South Asia

NORTH AMERICA
EUROPE
AFRICA
SOUTH AMERICA
AUSTRALASIA AND OCEANIA
ANTARCTICA

## LAND HEIGHT
- Above 13,120ft
- 6,560–13,120ft
- 3,280–6,560ft
- 1,640–3,280ft
- 820–1,640ft
- 330–820ft
- 0–330ft

## SEA DEPTH
- 0–820ft
- 820–1,640ft
- 1,640–3,280ft
- 3,280–6,560ft
- 6,560–9,840ft
- 9,840–13,120ft
- Below 13,120ft

(claimed by India)
(A "line of control" was agreed between India and Pakistan in 1972)

Aksai Chin (administered by China, claimed by India)

Demchok/Demqog (administered by China, claimed by India)

Arunachal Pradesh (claimed by China)

CHINA

AFGHANISTAN

Hindu Kush
Karakoram Range
Khyber Pass 3,543ft
K2 28,253ft
Mingaora
Mardan
Wah
Peshawar
Srinagar
ISLAMABAD
Jammu and Kashmir
Rawalpindi
Jhelum
Jammu
Gujrat
Sargodha
Gujranwala
Lahore
Amritsar
Faisalabad
Jalandhar
Ludhiana
Punjab
Okara
Chandigarh
Sahiwal
Bathinda
Karnal
Haryana
Meerut
Delhi
NEW DELHI
NEPAL
BHUTAN
THIMPHU
Annapurna 26,547ft
Mount Everest 29,030ft
Kula Kangri 24,780ft
Gangtok
Darjiling
Shiliguri
Bongaigaon
Dibrugarh
Assam
Jorhat

IRAN

Chaman
Toba Kakar Range
Quetta
PAKISTAN
Baluchistan
Kalat
Sibi
Darya-ye Helmand
Chagai Hills
Central Makran Range
Turbat
Gwadar
Pasni
Jacobabad
Larkana
Shikarpur
Sukkur
Khairpur
Nawabshah
Hyderabad
Mirpur Khas
Karachi
Sind
Mouths of the Indus
Gulf of Kachchh
Gandhidham
Surendranagar
Jamnagar
Rajkot
Porbandar
Bhavnagar
Gulf of Khambhat
Daman

Dera Ghazi Khan
Multan
Bahawalpur
Rahimyar Khan
Bikaner
Faridabad
Alwar
Jaipur
Jodhpur
Ajmer
Jaisalmer
Thar Desert
Pali
Beawar
Udaipur
Palanpur
Ahmadabad
Godhra
Vadodara
Bharuch
Surat

Bahraich
Lalitpur
Bhaktapur
KATHMANDU
Bareilly
Salyan
Pokhara
Lucknow
Gorakhpur
Budaun
Agra
Uttar Pradesh
Etawah
Kanpur
Faizabad
Mau
Jaunpur
Gwalior
Jhansi
Shivpuri
Kota
Ratlam
Bhopal
Indore
Khandwa
Vindhya Range
Sagar
Satpura Range
Jabalpur
Murwara
Madhya Pradesh
Allahabad
Varanasi
Birhar Sharif
Patna
Gaya
Biratnagar
Chhapra
Bihar
Bhagalpur
Dinajpur
Sajdpur
Rangpur
Koch Bihar
Guwahati
Shillong
Kohima
Imphal
Silchar
Sylhet
BANGLADESH
Brahmanbaria
Comilla
Pabna
Rajshahi
Bankura
Jessore
DHAKA
Barisal
Chittagong
MYANMAR
Asansol
Dhanbad
Ranchi
Chota Nagpur
Jamshedpur
West Bengal
Haora
Khulna
Calcutta (Kolkata)
Raulakela
Kharagpur
Baleshwar
Mouths of the Ganges

INDIA

Bhusawal
Nagpur
Amravati
Chandrapur
Gondia
Durg
Raipur
Bilaspur
Sambalpur
Bhubaneshwar
Cuttack
Puri
Orissa
Brahmapur
Bay of Bengal

Jagdalpur
Srikakulam
Vizianagaram
Visakhapatnam

Nashik
Kalyan
Mumbai (Bombay)
Manmad
Aurangabad
Nanded
Ahmadnagar
Pune
Karimnagar
Nizamabad
Warangal
Maharashtra
Solapur
Sangli
Kolhapur
Belgaum
Gulbarga
Secunderabad
Hyderabad
Raichur
Mahbubnagar
Deccan
Gadag
Kurnool
Andhra Pradesh
Rajahmundry
Kakinada
Vijayawada
Machilipatnam
Western Ghats
Eastern Ghats
Chirala
Ongole
Kavali
Nellore

Panaji
Hubli
Nandyal
Karnataka
Davangere
Shimoga
Bhadravati
Cuddapah
Udupi
Tumkur
Bangalore
Mangalore
Mandya
Mysore
Vellore
Krishnagiri
Kanchipuram
Chennai (Madras)
Cannanore
Salem
Erode
Pondicherry
Neyveli
Calicut
Trichur
Coimbatore
Tiruchchirappalli
Ernakulam
Cochin
Kerala
Dindigul
Madurai
Tamil Nadu
Alleppey
Quilon
Rajapalaiyam
Tuticorin
Nagercoil
Trivandrum
Jaffna
Palk Strait
Mannar
Vavuniya
Trincomalee
Anuradhapura
Puttalam
Batticaloa
Matale
Negombo
Kandy
COLOMBO
Sri Jayawardanapura
Ratnapura
Galle
Matara
SRI LANKA

Amindivi Islands
Kavaratti
Laccadive Islands (Lakshadweep)
Nine Degree Channel
Minicoy Island
Eight Degree Channel
MALDIVES

Arabian Sea
INDIAN OCEAN

Gulf of Mannar

## CITIES AND TOWNS
- ■ Over 500,000 people
- ◉ 100,000–500,000
- ○ 50,000–100,000
- · Less than 50,000

### Andaman Islands (part of India)
North Andaman
Middle Andaman
South Andaman
Port Blair
Little Andaman
Ten Degree Channel
Car Nicobar
Nicobar Islands (part of India)
Katchall Island
Camorta
Little Nicobar
Great Nicobar
Indira Point
Bananga
INDIAN OCEAN
Andaman Sea
SCALE: same as main map

## CLIMATE

Climate is strongly influenced by the annual monsoon between July and September. This brings hot, humid conditions and extremely high levels of rainfall to much of the region.

Less than 1
More than 1
January

July

### TEMPERATURE AND PRECIPITATION
- More than 86°F
- 77 to 86°F
- 68 to 77°F
- 59 to 68°F
- 50 to 59°F
- 41 to 50°F
- 32 to 41°F
- 23 to 32°F
- 14 to 23°F
- Less than 14°C
- 4 — Precipitation (in)

## ENVIRONMENTAL ISSUES

Deforestation is a problem in the tropical south as well as in the Himalayas, where trees are being lumbered for firewood, causing soil erosion. Many of the large cities suffer from poor air quality.

Lahore
Indus
New Delhi
Ganges
Karachi
Calcutta
Mumbai
Godavari
Krishna

### ENVIRONMENTAL ISSUES
- Severe firewood shortage
- Urban air pollution
- Major industrial center
- Existing desert
- Risk of desertification
- Severe risk of desertification
- Deforested area
- Remaining tropical forest
- Polluted rivers

## SCALE BAR
0 km 100 200
0 miles 100 200

N W E S

# SOUTHEAST ASIA

BRUNEI, CAMBODIA, INDONESIA, LAOS, MALAYSIA,
MYANMAR, PHILIPPINES, SINGAPORE, THAILAND, VIETNAM

**Southeast Asia** is made up of a mainland area
and many thousands of tropical islands. The
region has great natural wealth – from precious
stones to oil – and has recently experienced fast
industrial growth. Some countries here, especially
Singapore and Malaysia, have become prosperous,
but Laos and Cambodia remain poor and are still
recovering from years of terrible warfare.

## ENVIRONMENTAL ISSUES

In Myanmar, Malaysia, and Indonesia,
ancient rain forests are being cut down
faster than they can grow back. The
fantastic biodiversity of the forests,
with their thousands of unique
species of plants and
animals, is severely
threatened. Forest
burning has recently
caused terrible
smog in
Indonesia.

**ENVIRONMENTAL ISSUES**
- Urban air pollution
- Deforested area
  Remaining tropical forest
- Major industrial center

## POPULATION

**On the mainland,** the population is concentrated in the
river valleys, plateaus, or plains. Upland areas are
inhabited by small groups of hill peoples.
Most people still live in rural areas, but
the cities are growing fast. In Indonesia
and the Philippines, the population is
unevenly distributed. Some islands,
such as Java, are densely settled;
others are barely occupied.

**URBAN/RURAL POPULATION DIVISION**
Bangkok 1.8%
Rural population 28.2%
Other towns and cities 70%

**INHABITANTS PER SQ MILE**
- More than 520
- 260–520
- 130–260
- Less than 130
- ■ Capital city
- • Major city

## INDUSTRY

**Industries based** on the processing of raw
materials, like metallic minerals, timber, oil
and gas, and agricultural produce, are
important here, but manufacturing has grown
dramatically in recent years. Many
foreign firms, attracted by low labor
costs, have invested in the
region. Malaysia and
Singapore are
major producers
of electronic
goods like disk
drives for
computers.

**STRUCTURE OF INDUSTRY**
Primary 19%
Services 45%
Manufacturing 36%

**INDUSTRY**
- Chemicals
- Engineering
- Food processing
- Textiles
- Mining
- Oil and gas
- Timber
- High-tech
- Tourism
- ■ Major industrial center / area
- — Major road

## THE LANDSCAPE

**On the mainland,** a belt of mountain ranges,
cloaked in thick forest, runs north–south. The
mountains are cut through by the wide valleys
of five great rivers. On their way to the sea,
these rivers have deposited sediment, forming
immense, fertile flood plains and deltas. To
the southeast of the mainland lies a huge arc
of over 20,000 mountainous, volcanic islands.

### Borneo (D 7)
Borneo is the world's
third-largest island,
with a total area
of 292,298 sq miles.
Lying on the Equator
and in the path of two
monsoons, the island
is hot and one of the
wettest places on
Earth. The landscape
contains thickly forested
central highlands and
swampy lowlands.

### Mekong River (C 4)
The mighty Mekong River
flows through southern China
and Myanmar and forms
much of the border between
Laos and Thailand. It then
travels through Cambodia
before ending in a vast delta
on the southern coast of
Vietnam. This is one of the
world's most productive
rice-growing areas.

### Philippines (E 4)
The Philippines'
7,000 islands
are mountainous
and volcanic
with narrow
coastal plains.

### Irian Jaya (I 7)
Irian Jaya is a province of
Indonesia. Its dense rain
forests are some of the last
unexplored areas on Earth
and are inhabited by many
rare plant and animal species.

### Volcanoes
Indonesia is the most active volcanic region in the
world. Java alone has over 50 active volcanoes out
of the country's total of more than 220.

### Indonesia (C 7)
Indonesia is an archipelago of 13,677 islands, scattered over almost
3,110 miles. The islands lie on the boundary between two of the
Earth's tectonic plates and frequently experience earthquakes.

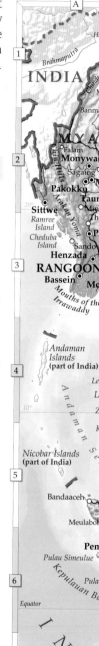

**SCALE BAR**
0 km   200   400
0 miles   200

# FARMING AND LAND USE

**The staple crop** here is rice, which grows in low-lying flooded fields called paddies, or on terraces cut into the hillsides. Sugarcane, coconuts, bananas, and pineapples are widely grown as cash crops, and Malaysia produces 25% of the world's rubber. Freshwater and marine fish are caught in large quantities; fish is one of the main foods in this region.

**FARMING AND LAND USE**

- Cattle
- Fishing
- Shellfish
- Coconuts
- Fruit
- Rice
- Rubber
- Sugarcane
- Timber
- Cropland
- Forest
- Pasture
- Wetland
- Major conurbation

**LAND USE**

- Pasture 4%
- Cropland 21%
- Other 24%
- Forest 51%

## CLIMATE

Southeast Asia's climate is strongly affected by the monsoon, which brings warm, humid air and high rainfall to mainland Southeast Asia during July and to maritime southeast Asia during January.

January

July

**TEMPERATURE AND PRECIPITATION**

- More than 86°F
- 68 to 86°F
- 50 to 68°F
- Less than 50°F
- Precipitation (in)

**ASIA**
Southeast Asia

**LAND HEIGHT**
- Above 13,120ft
- 6,560–13,120ft
- 3,280–6,560ft
- 1,640–3,280ft
- 820–1,640ft
- 330–820ft
- 0–330ft

**SEA DEPTH**
- 0–820ft
- 820–1,640ft
- 1,640–3,280ft
- 3,280–6,560ft
- 6,560–9,840ft
- 9,840–13,120ft
- Below 13,120ft

**CITIES AND TOWNS**
- Over 500,000 people
- 100,000–500,000
- 50,000–100,000
- Less than 50,000

# CONTINENTAL SOUTH AMERICA

**The towering peaks of the Andes** stand high above the western side of the South America. They act as a barrier to the sparsely inhabited interior of the continent, which includes the dense rain forest of the Amazon Basin – one of the Earth's last great wildernesses. Most people live on South America's coastal fringes. Brazil is both the largest country and the most populous. Over half of the continent's land area and half of its people are found there.

- 3,100 miles -
4,750 miles

## CROSS SECTION ACROSS SOUTH AMERICA

Andes | Amazon River | Guiana Highlands | Mouths of the Amazon | Brazilian Highlands

W ——— 3,360 miles ——— E

The high peaks of the Andes rise up from a narrow strip of land bordering the Pacific Ocean. East of the Andes, the land flattens into a broad, shallow basin into which the Amazon River flows. To the north are the older Guiana Highlands where rock has been eroded to form flat-topped "table" mountains.

## PHYSICAL SOUTH AMERICA

Ancient masses of rocks, like the Guiana and Brazilian highlands, which are known as shields, form the core of South America. The Andes are the solid backbone of the continent. They are relatively young, formed by collisions between different plates of the Earth's crust. The major rivers: the Paraná and the mighty Amazon, flow in deep depressions to the east of the mountains.

### ELEVATION

- 19,960ft
- 16,400ft
- 13,120ft
- 9,840ft
- 6,560ft
- 3,280ft
- 1,640ft
- 820ft
- 330ft
- sea level
- below sea level
- cross section

SCALE 1:40,000,000

0 km  400  800
0 miles  400  800

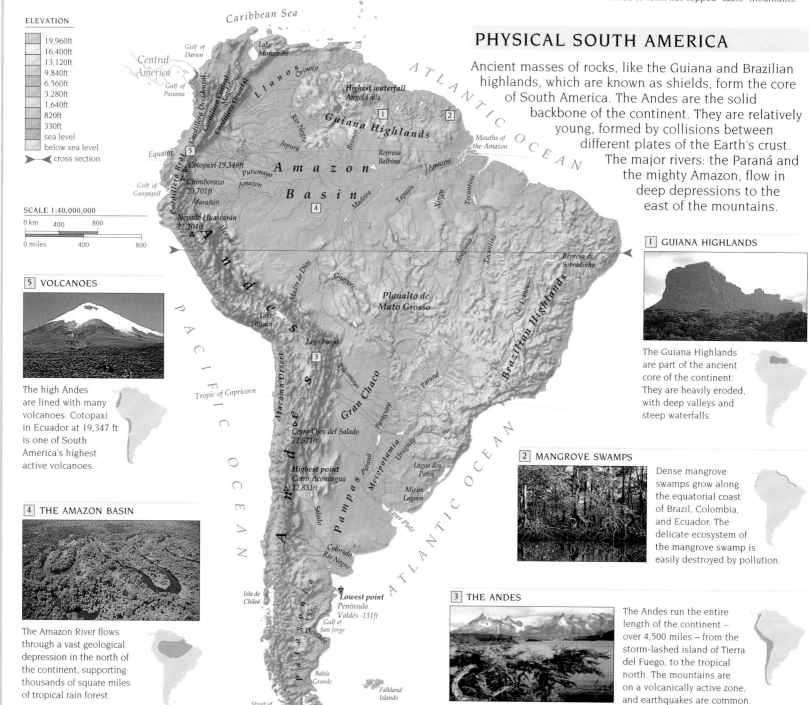

Caribbean Sea
Central America
Gulf of Darien
Gulf of Panama
Lake Maracaibo
Llanos
Orinoco
**Highest waterfall** Angel Falls
Guiana Highlands
ATLANTIC OCEAN
Mouths of the Amazon
Cordillera Occidental
Cordillera Central
Magdalena
Cordillera Oriental
Río Negro
Branco
Japurá
Represa Balbina
Amazon
Equator
Cordillera Real
Cotopaxi 19,346ft
Putumayo
Amazon
Amazon Basin
Madeira
Tapajós
Xingu
Tocantins
Chimborazo 20,701ft
Marañón
Gulf of Guayaquil
Nevado Huascarán 22,204ft
Ucayali
Andes
São Francisco
Represa de Sobradinho
Madre de Dios
Guaporé
Planalto de Mato Grosso
Araguaia
Tocantins
Brazilian Highlands
Lake Titicaca
Lago Poopó
Pilcomayo
Gran Chaco
Paraguay
Paraná
Paraná
Uruguay
Mesopotamia
Lagoa dos Patos
Atacama Desert
Tropic of Capricorn
Cerro Ojos del Salado 22,571ft
PACIFIC OCEAN
**Highest point** Cerro Aconcagua 22,831ft
Salado
Mirim Lagoon
Pampas
River Plate
ATLANTIC OCEAN
Colorado
Río Negro
Isla de Chiloé
Chico
Gulf of San Jorge
**Lowest point** Península Valdés -131ft
Patagonia
Bahía Grande
Falkland Islands
Strait of Magellan
Tierra del Fuego
Cape Horn

### 5 VOLCANOES

The high Andes are lined with many volcanoes. Cotopaxi in Ecuador at 19,347 ft is one of South America's highest active volcanoes.

### 4 THE AMAZON BASIN

The Amazon River flows through a vast geological depression in the north of the continent, supporting thousands of square miles of tropical rain forest.

### 1 GUIANA HIGHLANDS

The Guiana Highlands are part of the ancient core of the continent. They are heavily eroded, with deep valleys and steep waterfalls.

### 2 MANGROVE SWAMPS

Dense mangrove swamps grow along the equatorial coast of Brazil, Colombia, and Ecuador. The delicate ecosystem of the mangrove swamp is easily destroyed by pollution.

### 3 THE ANDES

The Andes run the entire length of the continent – over 4,500 miles – from the storm-lashed island of Tierra del Fuego, to the tropical north. The mountains are on a volcanically active zone, and earthquakes are common.

# POLITICAL SOUTH AMERICA

In the 17th century, explorers from Spain and Portugal claimed most of South America for their rulers in Europe. Their influences are still strong today: Brazilians speak Portuguese, while much of the rest of the continent is Spanish-speaking. The small nations of the north Suriname and Guyana, were Dutch and British colonies, and French Guiana is a French overseas department. The mix of peoples is mainly European, Native American, and African. Some native peoples still live in the dense Amazon rain forest.

SCALE 1:35,000,000

0 km 400 800

0 miles 400 800

## TRANSPORTATION LINKS

The Pan American Highway is a vital transportation link, running from the far south of the continent, northward along the Pacific coast. Its route takes it through sparsely populated areas like the Atacama Desert.

## POPULATION

Many South American countries have a similar pattern of population distribution. The largest concentrations of people are found near the coasts. Migration to the coastal cities has led to rocketing population figures and growing social problems. São Paulo is now the world's third-largest city after Mexico City and Tokyo; its outskirts are fringed with sprawling, shanty town suburbs, known as *favelas*.

**Largest city**
SÃO PAULO
15 million people

POPULATION DENSITY
(People per sq mile)

| | | |
|---|---|---|
| Below 13 | 30–39 | 52–77 |
| 13–29 | 40–51 | Above 78 |

## BORDER DISPUTES

Many of South America's borders have been, or remain, disputed. Bolivia is landlocked as a result of a dispute with Chile in 1883, when it lost its lands bordering the Pacific Ocean.

## URBAN GROWTH

Urban growth has transformed São Paulo into a major population and industrial center. Its rapid growth has created many problems, such as traffic congestion, overcrowding, and inadequate sewerage.

## POPULATION

**Capital cities**

◉ Above 500,000

◎ 100,000 to 500,000

● 50,000 to 100,000

• Below 50,000

**Other cities**

▣ Above 500,000

○ 50,000 to 100,000

## STANDARDS OF LIVING

There are many inequalities in living standards across South America. Argentina's wealth and strong economy means its living standards are well above those of Guyana and Bolivia, which have weak economies and are heavily reliant upon trade in raw materials. The booming black-market drugs trade increases crime and corruption.

STANDARD OF LIVING
(UN Human Development Index)

low          high     no data

# SOUTH AMERICAN GEOGRAPHY

**Agriculture is still the most** common form of employment in South America. Cattle and cash crops of coffee, cocoa, and, in some places, coca for cocaine, provide the main sources of income. Brazil has the greatest range of industries, followed by Argentina, Venezuela, and Chile. The large coastal cities such as Rio de Janeiro, Lima, and Buenos Aires are where most of the jobs are found. This encourages people to migrate from the country to the city, in search of employment.

## MINERAL RESOURCES

South America's mineral resources are highly localized. Few countries have both fossil fuels and metallic ores. The richest oilfields are in the north, especially in Venezuela. Coal, however, is scarce. When the Andes were formed, heat helped create the many metallic minerals that are mined today.

**MINERAL RESOURCES**

- Bauxite
- Copper
- Iron
- Lead
- Silver
- Tin
- Oil/Gas field
- Coal field

## INDUSTRY

**Brazil is the continent's** leading industrial producer, and São Paulo is the major industrial city. Manufactured products include iron and steel, automobiles, chemicals, textiles, and meat and leather products from the continent's vast cattle herds. In the mountains of Bolivia and Colombia, coca plants are grown to make cocaine, which has created a black market for this illegal drug.

**COPPER MINES**

Metallic mineral reserves are abundant in the Andes. Chuquicamata, northern Chile, is one of the world's largest copper mines.

### OIL AND GAS

Under the waters of Lake Maracaibo, Venezuela, lie some of South America's biggest oil reserves. Oil exploitation has brought great wealth to Venezuela. The money has helped the country to build new roads and develop other industries.

### INDUSTRIAL CENTER

São Paulo, Brazil, is the largest city in South America and a leading industrial center. A wide range of goods is manufactured here, including automobiles, chemicals, textiles, and electronic products. São Paulo is also a leading financial center. Hundreds of people flock to the city daily in search of work.

### TRADE AND EXPORTS

The Chilean port of Valparaíso ships many different products out of South America. Trade is growing with Japan and other countries around the Pacific Ocean.

**INDUSTRY**

- ✈ Aerospace
- 🍺 Brewing
- 🚗 Car/vehicle manufacturing
- ⚗ Chemicals
- 🔨 Coal
- ⚡ Electronics
- ⚙ Engineering
- Ⓢ Finance
- Fish processing
- Food processing
- High-tech industry
- Iron and steel
- △ Metal refining
- Narcotics
- Oil and gas
- Pharmaceuticals
- Printing and publishing
- Shipbuilding
- Textiles
- Timber processing
- Tobacco processing

**GNP per capita (US$)**

- Below 499
- 500–999
- 1,000–1,499
- 1,500–2,999
- 3,000–5,999
- Above 6,000
- • Industrial center

Map labels: Caribbean Sea, Barranquilla, Maracaibo, Caracas, Cartagena, Barquisimeto, Valencia, Ciudad Guayana, Central America, Medellín, VENEZUELA, Georgetown, Paramaribo, GUYANA, SURINAME, French Guiana (to France), Bogotá, COLOMBIA, Cali, Quito, ECUADOR, Guayaquil, Amazon Basin, Manaus, Belém, BRAZIL, Fortaleza, Chiclayo, Natal, Chimbote, Recife, Lima, PERU, Cusco, Maceió, BOLIVIA, Salvador, Arequipa, La Paz, Santa Cruz, Brasília, Arica, Sucre, Iquique, Chuquicamata, Belo Horizonte, Antofagasta, PARAGUAY, São Paulo, Rio de Janeiro, Asunción, Curitiba, San Miguel de Tucumán, Corrientes, Porto Alegre, Córdoba, Santa Fe, URUGUAY, Valparaíso, Mendoza, Rosario, Rio Grande, Santiago, Buenos Aires, Montevideo, Talca, Concepción, ARGENTINA, Neuquén, Bahía Blanca, Valdivia, ATLANTIC OCEAN, PACIFIC OCEAN, Comodoro Rivadavia, Falkland Islands (to UK), Punta Arenas, Cape Horn

## CLIMATE

South America has four main climatic regions: tropical, arid, temperate, and the cold climate of the far south. The Amazon Basin, covered by massive rain forests, and the Guiana Highlands have a humid, tropical climate that allows vegetation to flourish. West of the Andes the climate tends to be very dry. Moist air flowing west from the Atlantic Ocean is prevented from reaching the shores of the Pacific Ocean by the Andes, and rain falls before it can pass over the mountains. This creates arid deserts like the Atacama.

### EXTREME WEATHER EVENTS

Symbols indicate climatic extremes

Wettest place
QUIBDO (Colombia)
Annual rainfall 354in

Driest place
ARICA (Chile)
Annual rainfall 1/4in

Hottest place
RIVADAVIA (Argentina)
Temp 120°F

Coldest place
SARMIENTO (Argentina)
Temp -27°F

### CLIMATE

- Subarctic
- Cool continental
- Warm temperate
- Semiarid
- Arid
- Temperate
- Tropical
- Humid equatorial

### PATAGONIAN ICEFIELDS

Toward the south of the continent, the climate becomes very cold. Large expanses of ice, forming glaciers, are found in southern Patagonia and on islands such as Tierra del Fuego at the tip of South America.

# LAND USE AND AGRICULTURE

Many plants now found throughout the world originated in South America, like the tomato, potato, and cassava. Today, coffee, cocoa, rubber, soybeans, corn, and sugarcane are widely cultivated, and grapes are grown in sheltered valleys in the Andes. Much of the Amazon Basin is covered by dense rain forest and is unsuitable for cultivation, although some farmers practice "slash and burn" techniques to make land for crops and cattle farming, which destroy ancient forest.

### COFFEE

South America, and Brazil in particular, is a major producer of coffee. The plants thrive in the rich red soils of southern Brazil and are grown on huge plantations on the mountain slopes.

### LAND USE AND AGRICULTURE

- Cattle
- Pigs
- Sheep
- Bananas
- Corn
- Citrus fruits
- Coca
- Cocoa
- Cotton
- Coffee
- Fishing
- Oil palms
- Peanuts
- Rubber
- Shellfish
- Soybeans
- Sugarcane
- Vineyards
- Wheat

- Barren land
- Cropland
- Desert
- Forest
- Mountain region
- Pasture
- Wetland
- Major conurbation

### LOCAL MARKETS

At traditional markets such as this one in Ecuador, high in the Andes, local people trade fruit, vegetables, and goods such as clothing, rugs, and blankets. Some goods produced by Ecuadorean Indians are now exported worldwide.

### CATTLE

The vast plains of the Pampas, to the west of Buenos Aires, support large herds of cattle. Meat processing and canning is a major industry in Argentina, Paraguay, and Uruguay.

### NARCOTICS

Coca, grown in forest clearings in remote mountain areas, is used to make the drug cocaine. Government troops burn any coca plants they discover to discourage production.

# NORTHERN SOUTH AMERICA

BRAZIL, COLOMBIA, ECUADOR, GUYANA, PERU, SURINAME, VENEZUELA

**High mountains, rain forests,** and hot, grassy plains cover much of northern South America. From the 16th century, after the conquest of the Incas, the western countries were ruled by Spain. Brazil was governed by Portugal, Guyana by Britain, and Suriname by the Dutch. The more recent history of some of these countries has included periods of civil war and military rule. Most are still troubled by widespread poverty.

## INDUSTRY

**Important oil reserves** are found in Venezuela and parts of the Amazon Basin; Venezuela is one of the world's top oil producers. Brazil's cities have a wide range of industries including chemicals, clothes and shoes, and textiles. Metallic minerals, particularly iron ore, are mined throughout the area and specially built industrial centers like Ciudad Guayana have been developed to refine them.

### STRUCTURE OF INDUSTRY

Primary 11%
Services 50%
Manufacturing 39%

### INDUSTRY

- Chemicals
- Food processing
- Iron and steel
- Metal refining
- Textiles
- Mining
- Oil
- Timber processing
- Tourism
- ⊡ Major industrial center / area
- — Major road

## POPULATION

**Most of the population** lives in urban areas. Many cities are extremely overcrowded, with poor housing. São Paulo in Brazil is one of the world's fastest-growing cities. The rain forests of the interior and high Andes are sparsely populated. The few Native American peoples live in remote areas.

### INHABITANTS PER SQ MILE

- More than 520
- 260–520
- 130–260
- 30–130
- Less than 30
- ■ Capital city
- ● Major city

### URBAN/RURAL POPULATION DIVISION

Rio de Janeiro 4.6%
São Paulo 8.4%
Lima 3%
Rural population 24%
Other towns and cities 60%

## FARMING AND LAND USE

**The variety of climates** allows a wide range of crops, including sugarcane, cocoa, and bananas, to be grown for export. Coffee is the most important cash crop; Brazil is the world's leading coffee grower. Cattle are farmed on the plains of Colombia, Venezuela, and southern Brazil. Much of the good farmland is owned by a few rich landowners: many peasant farmers do not have enough land to make a living.

### FARMING AND LAND USE

- Cattle
- Fishing
- Goats
- Sheep
- Bananas
- Cocoa
- Coffee
- Rubber
- Sugarcane
- Timber
- Cropland
- Forest
- Mountain region
- Pasture
- Wetland
- ● Major conurbation

### LAND USE

- Cropland 6%
- Other (including mountains) 15%
- Forest 56%
- Pasture 23%

## THE LANDSCAPE

**The Andes run down** the western side of South America. There are many volcanoes among their peaks, and earthquakes are common. The tropical rain forests surrounding the Amazon River take up most of western Brazil. Huge, dry, flat grasslands called *llanos* cover central Venezuela and part of eastern Colombia.

### Angel Falls (D 2)
Venezuela's Angel Falls is the world's highest waterfall. Twenty times as high as Niagara Falls, it drops 3,215 ft from a spectacular plateau deep in the Guiana Highlands.

### Amazon River (D 4)
The Amazon is the longest river in South America, and the second longest in the world. It flows over 4,000 miles from the Peruvian Andes to the coast of Brazil. One-fifth of the world's freshwater is carried by the river.

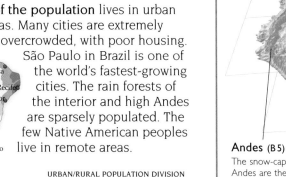

### Andes (B 5)
The snow-capped Andes are the longest mountain range on Earth. They stretch 4,500 miles down the whole length of South America.

### Lake Titicaca (C 6)
South America's largest lake is the highest navigable lake in the world at 12,500 ft above sea level. It lies across the border between Peru and Bolivia.

### Pantanal (E 6)
This is the largest area of wetlands in the world. It spreads across 50,000 sq miles of Brazil. Many hundreds of plant and animal species are found here.

### Amazon rain forest (D 4)
The enormous rain forest surrounding the Amazon River and its tributaries covers 2,510,000 sq miles, an area almost as big as Australia. It is estimated that at least half of all known living species are found in the forest.

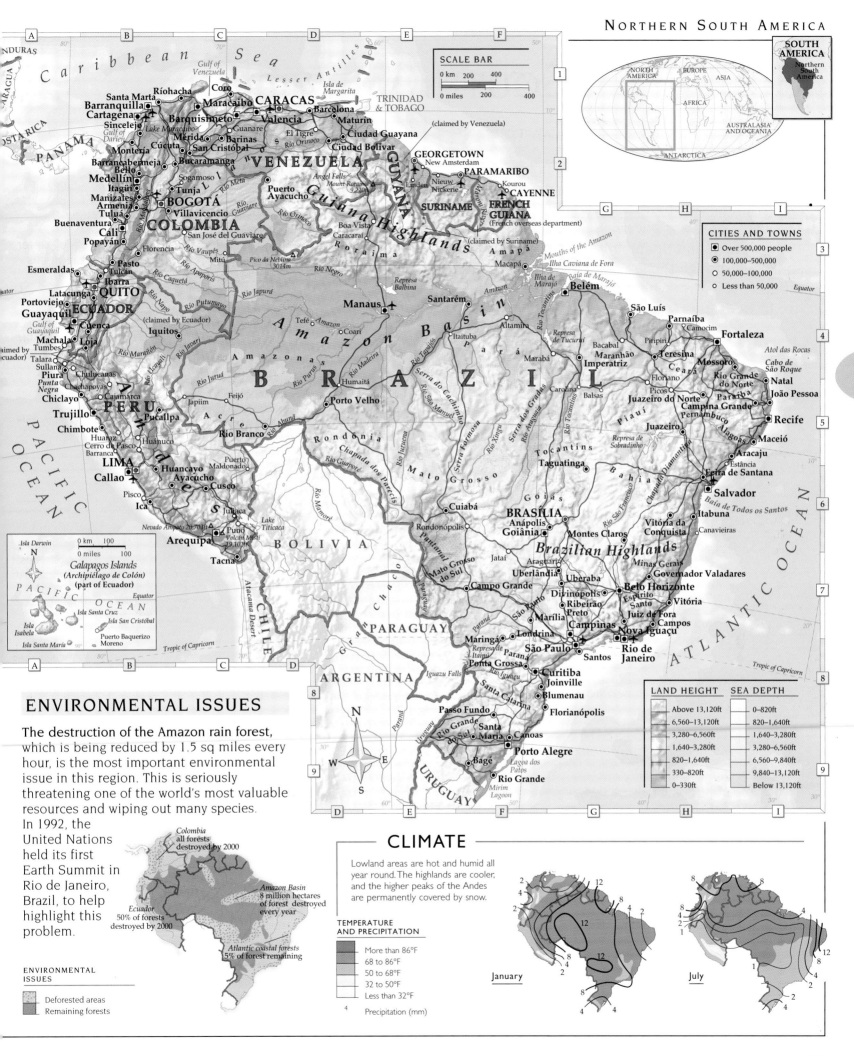

SOUTH AMERICA
Northern South America

SCALE BAR

0 km    200    400

0 miles    200    400

CITIES AND TOWNS
- ■ Over 500,000 people
- ◉ 100,000–500,000
- ◎ 50,000–100,000
- ○ Less than 50,000

Galapagos Islands
(Archipiélago de Colón)
(part of Ecuador)

0 km    100
0 miles    100

LAND HEIGHT
- Above 13,120ft
- 6,560–13,120ft
- 3,280–6,560ft
- 1,640–3,280ft
- 820–1,640ft
- 330–820ft
- 0–330ft

SEA DEPTH
- 0–820ft
- 820–1,640ft
- 1,640–3,280ft
- 3,280–6,560ft
- 6,560–9,840ft
- 9,840–13,120ft
- Below 13,120ft

# ENVIRONMENTAL ISSUES

The destruction of the Amazon rain forest, which is being reduced by 1.5 sq miles every hour, is the most important environmental issue in this region. This is seriously threatening one of the world's most valuable resources and wiping out many species. In 1992, the United Nations held its first Earth Summit in Rio de Janeiro, Brazil, to help highlight this problem.

Colombia
all forests
destroyed by 2000

Amazon Basin
8 million hectares
of forest destroyed
every year

Ecuador
50% of forests
destroyed by 2000

Atlantic coastal forests
5% of forest remaining

ENVIRONMENTAL
ISSUES
- Deforested areas
- Remaining forests

# CLIMATE

Lowland areas are hot and humid all year round. The highlands are cooler, and the higher peaks of the Andes are permanently covered by snow.

TEMPERATURE
AND PRECIPITATION
- More than 86°F
- 68 to 86°F
- 50 to 68°F
- 32 to 50°F
- Less than 32°F

4   Precipitation (mm)

January

July

115

# SOUTHERN SOUTH AMERICA

ARGENTINA, BOLIVIA, CHILE, PARAGUAY, URUGUAY

**The southern half of South America** forms a long, narrow cone, with landscapes ranging from barren desert in the west to frozen glaciers in the far south. The whole area was governed by Spain until the early 19th century, and Spanish is still the main language spoken, although the few remaining Native American groups use their own languages. Most people now live in vast cities such as Buenos Aires and Santiago.

## INDUSTRY

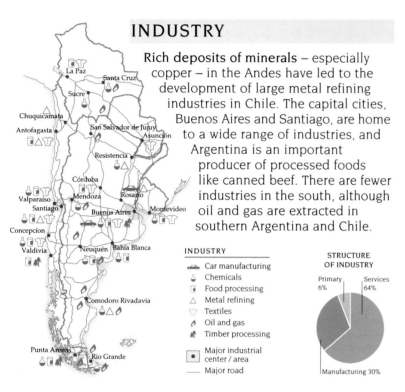

**Rich deposits of minerals** – especially copper – in the Andes have led to the development of large metal refining industries in Chile. The capital cities, Buenos Aires and Santiago, are home to a wide range of industries, and Argentina is an important producer of processed foods like canned beef. There are fewer industries in the south, although oil and gas are extracted in southern Argentina and Chile.

**INDUSTRY**

- Car manufacturing
- Chemicals
- Food processing
- Metal refining
- Textiles
- Oil and gas
- Timber processing
- Major industrial center / area
- Major road

**STRUCTURE OF INDUSTRY**

Primary 6%
Services 64%
Manufacturing 30%

## ENVIRONMENTAL ISSUES

**Many of** southern South America's rivers are polluted, particularly close to Buenos Aires. The Itaipú Dam on the Paraná River is the world's largest hydroelectric power plant. Deforestation is a persistent problem. In Bolivia, forests are being cut down at a record rate of 494,000 acres a year. Air quality in Buenos Aires and Santiago is poor, especially in Santiago, which is surrounded by mountains, making it difficult for pollution to escape.

**ENVIRONMENTAL ISSUES**

- Major dam
- Urban air pollution
- Deforested areas
- Polluted river
- Major industrial center

## POPULATION

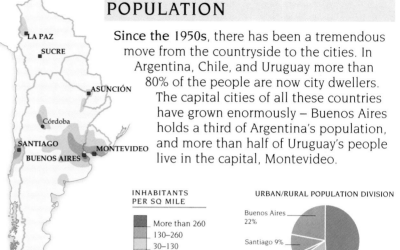

**Since the 1950s,** there has been a tremendous move from the countryside to the cities. In Argentina, Chile, and Uruguay more than 80% of the people are now city dwellers. The capital cities of all these countries have grown enormously – Buenos Aires holds a third of Argentina's population, and more than half of Uruguay's people live in the capital, Montevideo.

**INHABITANTS PER SQ MILE**

- More than 260
- 130–260
- 30–130
- Less than 30
- ■ Capital city
- ● Major city

**URBAN/RURAL POPULATION DIVISION**

- Buenos Aires 22%
- Santiago 9%
- Montevideo 2%
- Rural population 18%
- Other towns and cities 49%

## THE LANDSCAPE

**Southern South America's** landscape varies from tropical forest and dry desert in the north to subarctic conditions in the south. The towering Andes divide Chile from Argentina. East of the Andes lie forests and rolling grasslands. To the west is a thin coastal strip. The wet, windswept, freezing southern tip of the continent has volcanoes alongside glaciers and fjords.

### Gran Chaco (C3)
This huge stretch of forest and grassland runs from Bolivia, through Paraguay and into Argentina. The south and east provide grazing for cattle.

### Paraná River (C4)
South America's second-longest river is the Paraná. It stretches 2,610 miles from the Brazilian Highlands, finally flowing into the Plate River near Buenos Aires in Argentina.

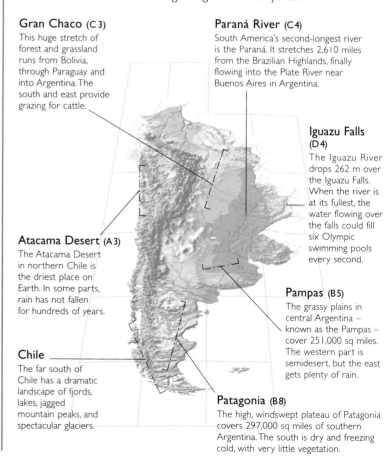

### Iguazu Falls (D4)
The Iguazu River drops 262 m over the Iguazu Falls. When the river is at its fullest, the water flowing over the falls could fill six Olympic swimming pools every second.

### Atacama Desert (A3)
The Atacama Desert in northern Chile is the driest place on Earth. In some parts, rain has not fallen for hundreds of years.

### Pampas (B5)
The grassy plains in central Argentina – known as the Pampas – cover 251,000 sq miles. The western part is semidesert, but the east gets plenty of rain.

### Chile
The far south of Chile has a dramatic landscape of fjords, lakes, jagged mountain peaks, and spectacular glaciers.

### Patagonia (B8)
The high, windswept plateau of Patagonia covers 297,000 sq miles of southern Argentina. The south is dry and freezing cold, with very little vegetation.

## CLIMATE

Temperature patterns are similar in January and July; warmer to the north and east, colder to the south and west, although January is much warmer than July. Temperatures are always low, high in the Andes.

## FARMING AND LAND USE

The enormous grasslands to the east of the Andes provide good grazing for cattle and sheep, and Argentina is one of the world's leading suppliers of meat, milk, and hides. The country is also an important grower of wheat and fruit. Chile grows grapes for its successful wine industry, and for eating; it is also the world's top producer of fishmeal. The illegal growing of coca, used to make the drug cocaine, is a major source of income in Bolivia.

# CONTINENTAL AFRICA

Africa is the second-largest continent in the world.
Its dramatic landscapes include arid deserts, humid
rain forests, and the valleys of the east African rift –
where humans may have first evolved. Today, there
are 53 separate countries in Africa, and its people
speak a rich variety of languages. The world's highest
temperatures have been recorded in Africa's deserts.

4,510 miles
4,737 miles

## CROSS SECTION THROUGH AFRICA

Niger Delta · Congo Basin · Great Rift Valley · Lake Victoria · Ethiopian Highlands · Horn of Africa

W — 3,230 miles — E

In the west, the Niger River flows into the Atlantic Ocean
through the swampy Niger Delta. Farther east is the
immense Congo Basin, where the Congo River winds its
way through thick rain forests. In the east is the Great Rift
Valley and the Ethiopian Highlands. The Horn of Africa
is Africa's most easterly point.

### 1 DESERTS

The Sahara covers
much of north
Africa. One-quarter
of the desert is sandy
dunes; the remainder
consists of bare, rocky plains and
mountainous outcrops. Other
large deserts include the Namib
and the Kalahari in the south.

### 2 GREAT RIFT VALLEY

Cracks beneath the
Earth formed this
valley, which runs
from Lake Nyasa
to the Red Sea.
It is thought that East Africa
– the Horn – will eventually
split from the rest of Africa.

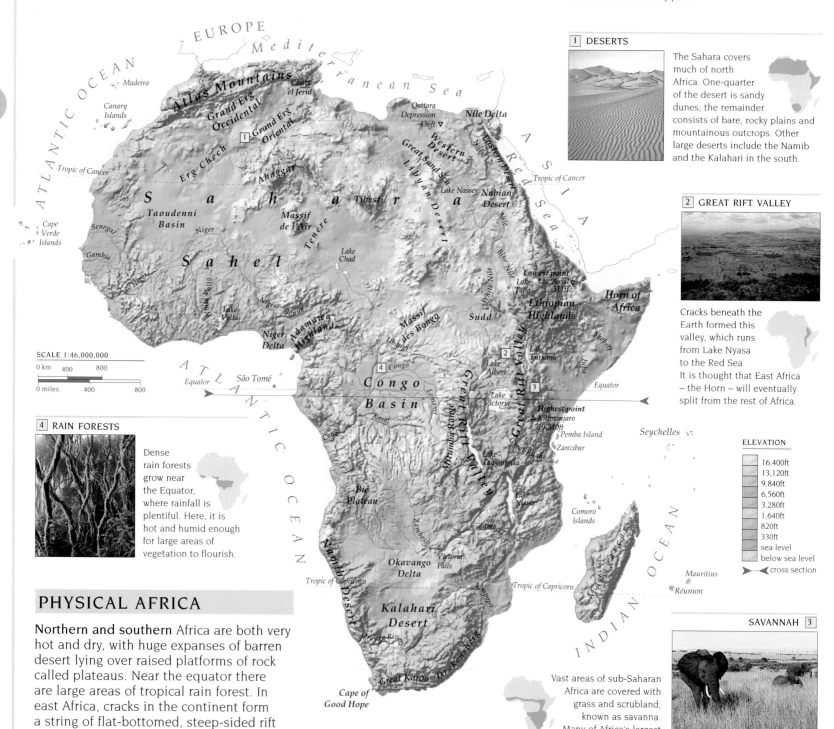

EUROPE
Mediterranean Sea
ATLANTIC OCEAN
Madeira
Canary Islands
Atlas Mountains
Grand Erg Occidental
Grand Erg Oriental
Chott el Jerid
Qattara Depression -436ft
Nile Delta
Tropic of Cancer
Erg Chech
Ahaggar
Western Desert
Great Sand Sea
Libyan Desert
Eastern Desert
Red Sea
ASIA
Cape Verde Islands
Senegal
Taoudenni Basin
Niger
Sahara
Massif de l'Air
Tibesti
Tenere
Lake Nasser
Nubian Desert
Gambia
Sahel
Lake Chad
White Volta
Niger
Benue
White Volta
Lake Volta
Niger Delta
Adamawa Highlands
Massif des Bongo
Ubangi
Sudd
Blue Nile
White Nile
Lake Tana
Lowest point Lac Assal -511ft
Ethiopian Highlands
Horn of Africa
Shebeli
Juba
SCALE 1:46,000,000
0 km 400 800
0 miles 400 800
ATLANTIC OCEAN
São Tomé
Equator
Congo
Congo Basin
Kasai
Lomami
Mitumba Range
Great Rift Valley
Lake Albert
Lake Turkana
Lake Victoria
Highest point △ Kilimanjaro 19,340ft
Great Ruaha
Pemba Island
Zanzibar
Equator
Seychelles
Bié Plateau
Zambezi
Lake Tanganyika
Lake Nyasa
Comoro Islands
Namib Desert
Okavango Delta
Victoria Falls
Zambezi
Kalahari Desert
Tropic of Capricorn
Limpopo
Tropic of Capricorn
Madagascar
Mauritius
Réunion
INDIAN OCEAN
Orange River
Great Karoo
Drakensberg
Cape of Good Hope

### 4 RAIN FORESTS

Dense
rain forests
grow near
the Equator,
where rainfall is
plentiful. Here, it is
hot and humid enough
for large areas of
vegetation to flourish.

## PHYSICAL AFRICA

**Northern and southern** Africa are both very
hot and dry, with huge expanses of barren
desert lying over raised platforms of rock
called plateaus. Near the equator there
are large areas of tropical rain forest. In
east Africa, cracks in the continent form
a string of flat-bottomed, steep-sided rift
valleys, many of which contain vast lakes.

### ELEVATION
16,400ft
13,120ft
9,840ft
6,560ft
3,280ft
1,640ft
820ft
330ft
sea level
below sea level
cross section

### SAVANNAH 3

Vast areas of sub-Saharan
Africa are covered with
grass and scrubland,
known as savanna.
Many of Africa's largest
animals, such as elephants, live here.

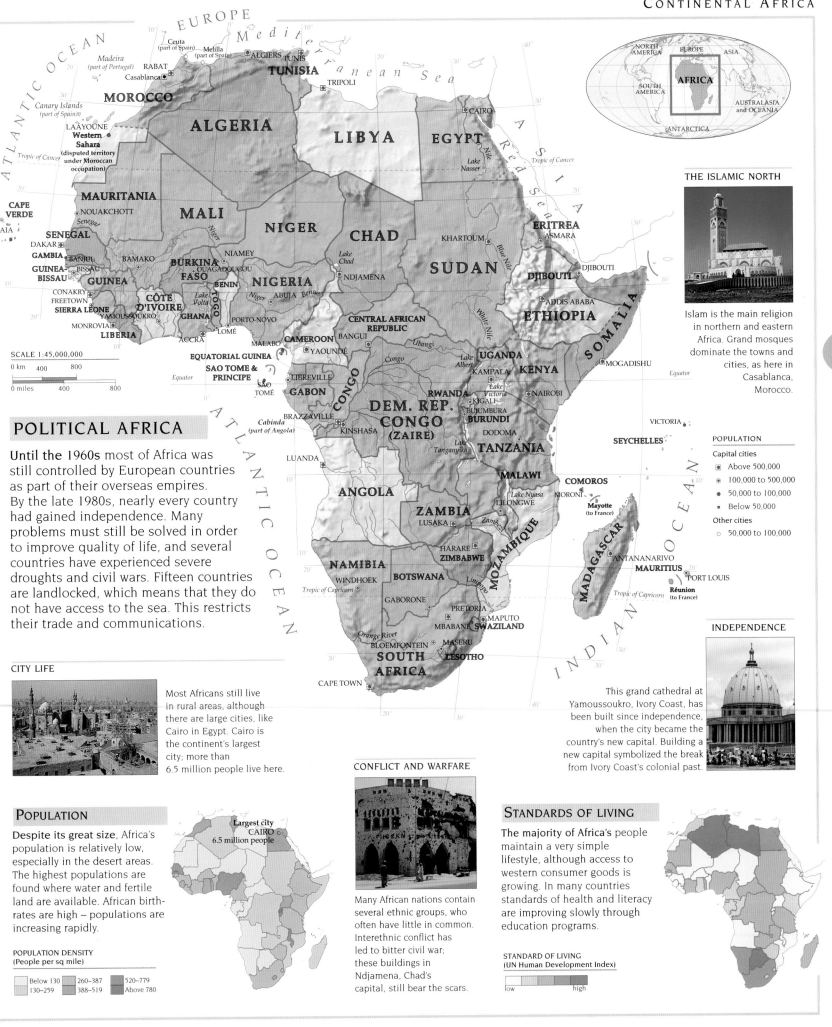

## POLITICAL AFRICA

Until the 1960s most of Africa was still controlled by European countries as part of their overseas empires. By the late 1980s, nearly every country had gained independence. Many problems must still be solved in order to improve quality of life, and several countries have experienced severe droughts and civil wars. Fifteen countries are landlocked, which means that they do not have access to the sea. This restricts their trade and communications.

### THE ISLAMIC NORTH

Islam is the main religion in northern and eastern Africa. Grand mosques dominate the towns and cities, as here in Casablanca, Morocco.

### POPULATION

**Capital cities**
- ◉ Above 500,000
- ◎ 100,000 to 500,000
- ◓ 50,000 to 100,000
- ● Below 50,000

**Other cities**
- ○ 50,000 to 100,000

### INDEPENDENCE

This grand cathedral at Yamoussoukro, Ivory Coast, has been built since independence, when the city became the country's new capital. Building a new capital symbolized the break from Ivory Coast's colonial past.

### CITY LIFE

Most Africans still live in rural areas, although there are large cities, like Cairo in Egypt. Cairo is the continent's largest city; more than 6.5 million people live here.

### CONFLICT AND WARFARE

Many African nations contain several ethnic groups, who often have little in common. Interethnic conflict has led to bitter civil war; these buildings in Ndjamena, Chad's capital, still bear the scars.

### POPULATION

Despite its great size, Africa's population is relatively low, especially in the desert areas. The highest populations are found where water and fertile land are available. African birthrates are high – populations are increasing rapidly.

**Largest city**
**CAIRO**
**6.5 million people**

**POPULATION DENSITY**
(People per sq mile)
- Below 130
- 130–259
- 260–387
- 388–519
- 520–779
- Above 780

### STANDARDS OF LIVING

The majority of Africa's people maintain a very simple lifestyle, although access to western consumer goods is growing. In many countries standards of health and literacy are improving slowly through education programs.

**STANDARD OF LIVING**
(UN Human Development Index)
low ——— high

SCALE 1:45,000,000

# AFRICAN GEOGRAPHY

Africa's massive reserves of minerals, including oil, gold, copper, and diamonds, are among the largest in the world. Mining is a very important industry for many countries and has provided money for growth and development. Many different types of crops can be grown in Africa's wide range of environments. Rubber, bananas, and oil palms are grown for export in the Tropics, and east Africa is especially famous for its tea and coffee.

## INDUSTRY

Most African industries are based on processing raw materials such as food crops or mineral ores. Some African countries depend on one product or crop for most of their income, but in many larger cities different industries are developing. Northern Africa, Nigeria, and South Africa have the widest range of industries.

## MINERAL RESOURCES

The southern countries, in particular South Africa, have large reserves of diamonds, gold, uranium, and copper. The large copper deposits in Dem. Rep. Congo (Zaire) and Zambia are known as the "copper belt." Oil and gas are extracted in Algeria, Angola, Egypt, Libya, and Nigeria.

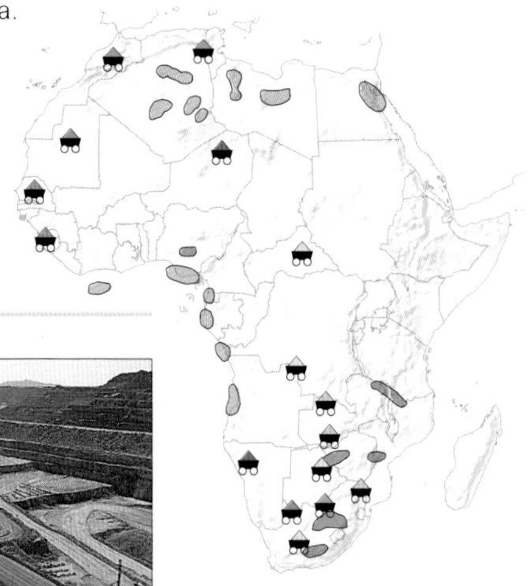

### MINING

The world's largest uranium mine is in Namibia. Uranium is used to fuel nuclear power plants, and is also mined in Niger and South Africa,

**MINERAL RESOURCES**

- Bauxite
- Copper
- Diamonds
- Iron
- Phosphates
- Gold
- Uranium
- Oil/gas field
- Coal field

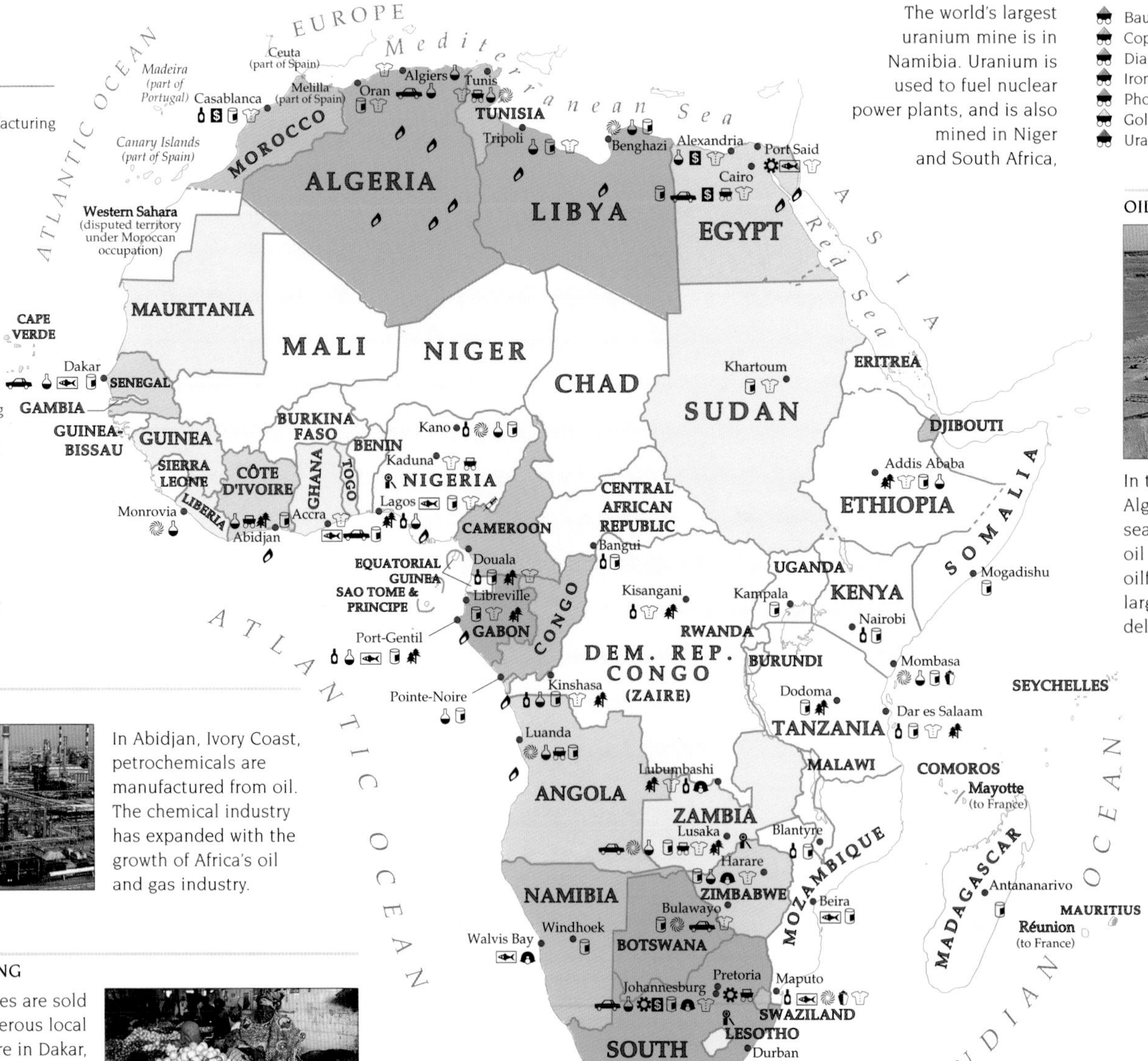

### OIL AND GAS

In the desert wastes of Algeria, a drilling rig searches for new sources of oil in the rich north African oilfields. There are several large oil fields in the Niger delta and North Africa.

**INDUSTRY**

- Brewing
- Car/vehicle manufacturing
- Cement
- Chemicals
- Coal
- Engineering
- Fish processing
- Finance
- Food processing
- Iron & steel
- Mining
- Oil & gas
- Pharmaceuticals
- Shipbuilding
- Textiles
- Timber processing

**GNP per capita (US$)**
- Below 1,999
- 2,000-4,999
- 5,000-9,999
- 10,000-19,999
- 20,000-24,999
- Above 25,000
- Industrial center

### CHEMICALS

In Abidjan, Ivory Coast, petrochemicals are manufactured from oil. The chemical industry has expanded with the growth of Africa's oil and gas industry.

### FOOD PROCESSING

Fruit and vegetables are sold in Africa's numerous local markets, as here in Dakar, Senegal. Many crops are grown especially for canning and export overseas and are known as "cash crops."

### FINANCE AND TRADE

Johannesburg, in South Africa, is home to many international banks. Wealth has been generated from the country's large mineral resources, such as diamonds.

## CLIMATE

Africa is the world's hottest continent: temperatures of more than 122°F have been recorded in the Sahara. The northern coast has a hot, dry climate with little rainfall. Farther inland, the Sahara is extremely arid, with strong, dry winds. South of the Sahara is the Sahel, where cutting down trees for fuel has turned farmland into desert. Close to the equator there is more rainfall, and huge rain forests can grow in western and central Africa. In the south, the climate is much drier, and drought is a problem.

### EXTREME WEATHER EVENTS

Symbols indicate climatic extremes

**Coldest place**
IFRANE (Morocco)
Temp. -11°F

*Tropic of Cancer*

**Hottest place**
AL 'AZÏZÏYAH (Libya)
Temp. 136°F

**Driest place**
WADI HALFA (Sudan)
Annual rainfall 1/8in

*Equator*

**Wettest place**
CAPE DEBUNDSHA (Cameroon)
Annual rainfall 405in

*Tropic of Capricorn*

### CLIMATE

- Warm temparate
- Mediterranean
- Semiarid
- Arid
- Humid equatorial
- Tropical

### THE ENCROACHING DESERT

Africa has three main desert areas: the Sahara in the north and the Namib and Kalahari deserts in the south. They are a mixture of sandy dunes and bare, rocky plateaus. At the desert's edges, low rainfall and land clearance is causing the deserts to expand into areas that were once grassland.

## LAND USE AND AGRICULTURE

The quality of land and the amount of rainfall has a great impact on the type of farming. In the mountain regions of countries such as Rwanda, Uganda, and Kenya, tea and coffee are grown. In the north, there is not enough water to produce staple crops such as wheat for all the population, but "cash crops" such as citrus fruits, dates, and olives are grown for export. Subtropical west Africa grows peanuts, cocoa, and coffee. In the southern part of the continent, South Africa grows many different crops: citrus fruits are grown for export, as well as grapes, which are used to make wine.

### PASTORALISM

At the southern edge of the Sahara is a fragile region known as the Sahel. In this area shifting cultivation and nomadic herding are widely practiced.

### LAND USE AND AGRICULTURE

| | |
|---|---|
| Cattle | Rice |
| Goats | Rubber |
| Sheep | Shellfish |
| Bananas | Sugarcane |
| Cereals | Tea |
| Citrus fruits | Tobacco |
| Cocoa | Vineyards |
| Cotton | |
| Coffee | Cropland |
| Dates | Desert |
| Fishing | Forest |
| Oil palms | Pasture |
| Olives | Wetland |
| Peanuts | • Major conurbation |

### SUBSISTENCE AGRICULTURE

Although African countries produce a wide range of crops, in many cases people rely on a few basic crops, like cassava and yams, as a staple. The yam is a starchy root that is ground to make flour.

### CASH CROPS

Kenya, Malawi, Tanzania, and Zimbabwe are renowned for their teas. The leaves are picked by hand and dried. When mixed with boiling water, tea is enjoyed by over half the world's population.

# NORTH AFRICA

ALGERIA, EGYPT, LIBYA, MOROCCO, TUNISIA.

**Sandwiched between** the Mediterranean and the Sahara, North Africa has a history dating back to the dawn of civilization. About 6,000 years ago, settlements were established along the banks of the Nile River. Since then, waves of settlers, including Romans, Arabs, and Turks, have brought a mix of different cultures to the area. In the 19th century, Spain, France, and Britain claimed colonies in the region, but today North Africa is independent, although Western Sahara is occupied by Morocco.

## FARMING AND LAND USE

**FARMING AND LAND USE**
- Fishing
- Goats
- Sheep
- Cork
- Cotton
- Dates
- Olives
- Vineyards
- Cropland
- Desert
- Forest
- Pasture
- Major conurbation

Most farming in North Africa is restricted to the fertile Mediterranean coastal strip, and the banks of the Nile where it relies heavily on irrigation. In spite of these seemingly inhospitable conditions, the region is a major producer of dates, which grow in desert oases, and of cork, made from the bark of the cork oak tree. A wide variety of other crops is also grown, including grapes, olives, and cotton.

### CLIMATE

Most of north Africa is desert, and the climate is harsh. Rainfall is scarce, and drought is common. Temperatures are freezing at night, scorching by day and have been known to climb to over 120°F.

January

July

whole area has below 1in rainfall

**LAND USE**

Forest 3%
Pasture 9%
Cropland 12%
Other (including desert) 76%

**TEMPERATURE AND PRECIPITATION**
- More than 95°F
- 86 to 95°F
- 77 to 86°F
- 68 to 77°F
- 59 to 68°F
- 50 to 59°F
- 41 to 50°F
- Less than 41°F
- 4 — Precipitation (in)

**LAND HEIGHT**
- Above 13,120ft
- 6,560–13,120ft
- 3,280–6,560ft
- 1,640–3,280ft
- 820–1,640ft
- 330–820ft
- 0–330ft
- Below sea level

**SEA DEPTH**
- 0–820ft
- 820–1,640ft
- 1,640–3,280ft
- 3,280–6,560ft
- 6,560–9,840ft
- 9,840–13,120ft
- Below 13,120ft

**CITIES AND TOWNS**
- Over 500,000 people
- 100,000–500,000
- 50,000–100,000
- Less than 50,000

**SCALE BAR**
0 km   200   400
0 miles   200   400

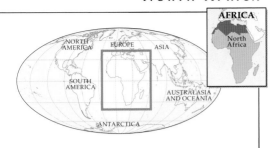

## POPULATION

The majority of the population, and all of the big towns and cities, are found on the coastal plains, or along the banks of the Nile – about 99% of Egyptians live along the river. Egypt's capital, Cairo, is Africa's largest city, with over six million people. Western Sahara and the southern portions of Egypt, Algeria, and Libya are sparsely populated by Taureg nomads who roam the desert.

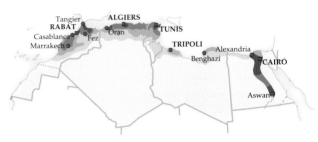

INHABITANTS
PER SQ MILE

- More than 520
- 260–520
- 130–260
- 30–130
- Less than 30
- ■ Capital city
- ● Major city

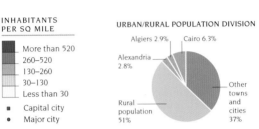

URBAN/RURAL POPULATION DIVISION

Algiers 2.9%  Cairo 6.3%
Alexandria 2.8%
Other towns and cities 37%
Rural population 51%

## THE LANDSCAPE

**The parched rocks** and endless sandy expanses of the Sahara occupy much of North Africa. The only major river here is the Nile, with a delta that extends into the Mediterranean Sea. The old, eroded Atlas Mountains are the highest mountain range.

**Sand dunes**
Winds blowing across the Sahara cause the sand to build up into dunes which can reach heights of up to 1,411 ft.

**Nile Delta (I2)**
As the Nile River nears the Mediterranean, it separates into many small streams, which flow over a fertile triangle of land. Mud and rock carried by the river and deposited in the delta have formed new land.

**Red Sea (J3)**
The Red Sea gets its name from red algae that live on the sea floor and make the water appear red.

**Atlas Mountains (C 2)**
The Atlas Mountains are made up of a number of different ranges – the Anti-Atlas, High Atlas, Middle Atlas, Tell Atlas, and Saharan Atlas. They stretch some 1,400 miles from the north of Tunisia to the Atlantic coast of Morocco.

**Qattara Depression (I3)**
In the northwest of Egypt is a huge desert depression 200 miles long and 75 miles wide. Its floor, part of which is 440 ft below sea level, is covered with sand, brackish ponds and salt marshes.

**Nile River (I3)**
The world's longest river flows 4,160 miles to the Mediterranean Sea. The system of rivers and lakes that flow into the Nile drain some 1,100,000 sq miles – about 10% of the entire African continent.

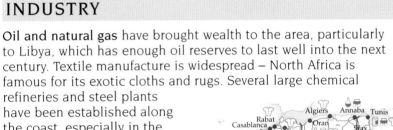

## INDUSTRY

**Oil and natural gas** have brought wealth to the area, particularly to Libya, which has enough oil reserves to last well into the next century. Textile manufacture is widespread – North Africa is famous for its exotic cloths and rugs. Several large chemical refineries and steel plants have been established along the coast, especially in the major industrial cities like Alexandria and Cairo in Egypt.

INDUSTRY
- Chemicals
- Food processing
- Iron and steel
- Textiles
- Oil and gas
- Tourism
- Major industrial center / area
- Major road

STRUCTURE OF INDUSTRY

Primary 16%
Services 49%
Manufacturing 35%

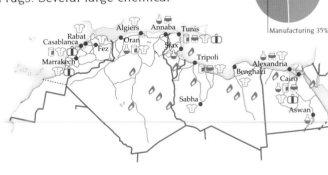

## ENVIRONMENTAL ISSUES

**Droughts, overgrazing, and the stripping** of vegetation for firewood and animal food have caused the Sahara to expand northward. This has reduced the already limited amount of land available for farming. The risk of desertification is acute in many coastal areas. North Africa is very dry, and there are severe droughts periodically. Many of the larger cities like Alexandria and Cairo have very poor air quality.

ENVIRONMENTAL ISSUES
- Drought
- Urban air pollution
- Existing desert
- Risk of desertification
- Severe risk of desertification
- Unaffected area
- ● Major industrial center

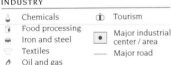

# WEST AFRICA

BENIN, BURKINA FASO, CAMEROON, CENTRAL AFRICAN REPUBLIC, CHAD, CÔTE D'IVOIRE, EQUATORIAL GUINEA, GAMBIA, GHANA, GUINEA, GUINEA-BISSAU, LIBERIA, MALI, MAURITANIA, NIGER, NIGERIA, SAO TOME & PRINCIPE, SENEGAL, SIERRA LEONE, TOGO

West Africa's varied climate and agricultural and mineral wealth have provided the foundation for some of Africa's greatest civilizations, like those of the Malinke and Asante people. The area remains ethnically and culturally diverse today as well as densely populated. Nigeria is the most populous country in Africa. Since independence from European colonial powers in the 1960s, political instability has been a reality for many countries here.

## INDUSTRY

Agricultural products still form the basis of most economies in West Africa. Food processing is widespread – oil palms and peanuts are processed for their valuable vegetable oils. Oil and gas are found off the coast of Côte D'Ivoire and around the Niger delta, where a large chemical industry has developed.

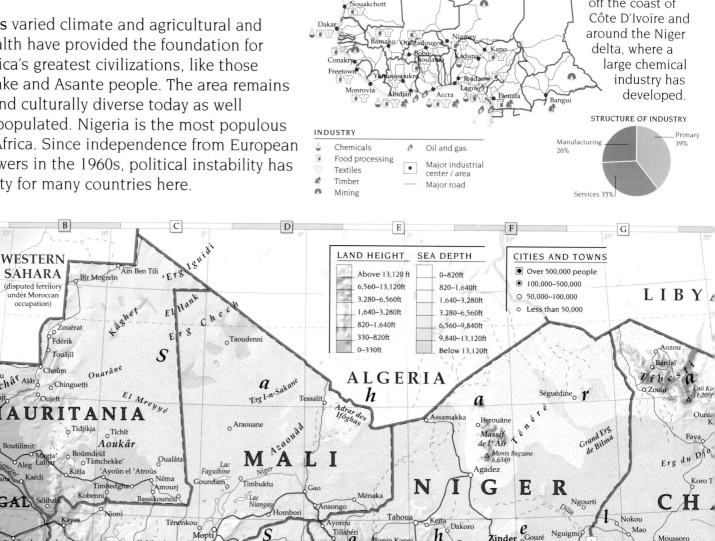

INDUSTRY

- ⚗ Chemicals
- 🏭 Food processing
- 👕 Textiles
- 🌲 Timber
- ⛰ Mining
- ◊ Oil and gas
- ◼ Major industrial center / area
- — Major road

STRUCTURE OF INDUSTRY

Manufacturing 26%
Primary 39%
Services 35%

LAND HEIGHT
- Above 13,120 ft
- 6,560–13,120ft
- 3,280–6,560ft
- 1,640–3,280ft
- 820–1,640ft
- 330–820ft
- 0–330ft

SEA DEPTH
- 0–820ft
- 820–1,640ft
- 1,640–3,280ft
- 3,280–6,560ft
- 6,560–9,840ft
- 9,840–13,120ft
- Below 13,120ft

CITIES AND TOWNS
- ◼ Over 500,000 people
- ● 100,000–500,000
- ○ 50,000–100,000
- ○ Less than 50,000

# FARMING AND LAND USE

**Plentiful rainfall** along the coast allows a wide variety of crops to be grown, including cocoa and oil palms, both of which provide important cash crops. In the drier north, goats and sheep are grazed and subsistence crops such as yams, millet, and cassava are grown.

**FARMING AND LAND USE**

- 🐐 Goats
- 🐑 Sheep
- 🦪 Shellfish
- 🌿 Cocoa
- 🌾 Cotton
- 🌴 Oil palms
- 🥜 Peanuts
- ▨ Cropland
- Desert
- Forest
- Pasture
- Wetland
- ● Major conurbation

**LAND USE**

- Cropland 10%
- Pasture 23%
- Forest 27 %
- Other (including desert) 40%

# CLIMATE

The climate differs immensely from the hot desert north to the tropical rainforest south. July is the wet season, and rainfall is heavy in the south. The desert areas remain dry throughout the year.

AFRICA
West Africa

*January*

*July*

**TEMPERATURE AND PRECIPITATION**

- More than 95°F
- 86 to 95°F
- 77 to 86°F
- 68 to 77°F
- Less than 68°F
- ―4― Precipitation (in)

# ENVIRONMENTAL ISSUES

**Persistent droughts** are the main concerns in the north of the region. The problem is made worse by a shortage of wood needed for fuel, which leads to the cutting down of any available trees. In the tropical south, the timber industry is destroying much of the ancient forest.

*1968–1977 1982–1985*

*1968–1977 1982–1985*

*1973–1974*  *1971–1974*  *1967–1974*  *1971–1974*

**ENVIRONMENTAL ISSUES**

- 🐂 Drought
- 🌳 Severe fuelwood shortage
- Existing desert
- Risk of desertification
- Severe risk of desertification
- Deforested area

# POPULATION

**Most of the population** lives in the southern coastal regions. In the drier north, settlement is sparser, and nomadic tribespeople are best suited to live in the desert north. Nigeria is the most populated country in Africa and Lagos is one of the continent's larger cities, although West Africa's population remains mainly rural.

**INHABITANTS PER SQ MILE**

- More than 520
- 260–520
- 130–260
- 30–130
- Less than 30
- ■ Capital city
- ● Major city

**URBAN/RURAL POPULATION DIVISION**

- Abidjan 1%
- Lagos 2%
- Dakar 1%
- Other towns and cities 31%
- Rural population 65%

# THE LANDSCAPE

**Major differences** in rainfall from north to south have led to a varied landscape. The wet coastal regions contain tropical rain forests. To the north, savanna grasslands, arid Sahel scrubland, and barren desert lie in successive bands. The Niger is one of the larger rivers and is unusual because it has two deltas: one at the sea and one inland.

### Sahel (E 3)
The band of semidesert stretching from Senegal to Sudan along the southern boundary of the Sahara is called the Sahel. Frequent droughts in recent years and excessive cutting of trees have meant that much of the Sahel is turning to desert.

### Tibesti mountains (G 2)
These mountains in north-western Chad are a chain of extinct volcanoes that now form solitary peaks in the midst of the Sahara.

### Niger River (D 3)
The Niger River is West Africa's longest river. When it reaches the sea, it flows through a vast delta of mudflats and mangrove swamps. Great oil deposits have been found here.

### Adamawa Highlands (G 5)
This mountainous spine separates West Africa from the vast Congo Basin to the southeast.

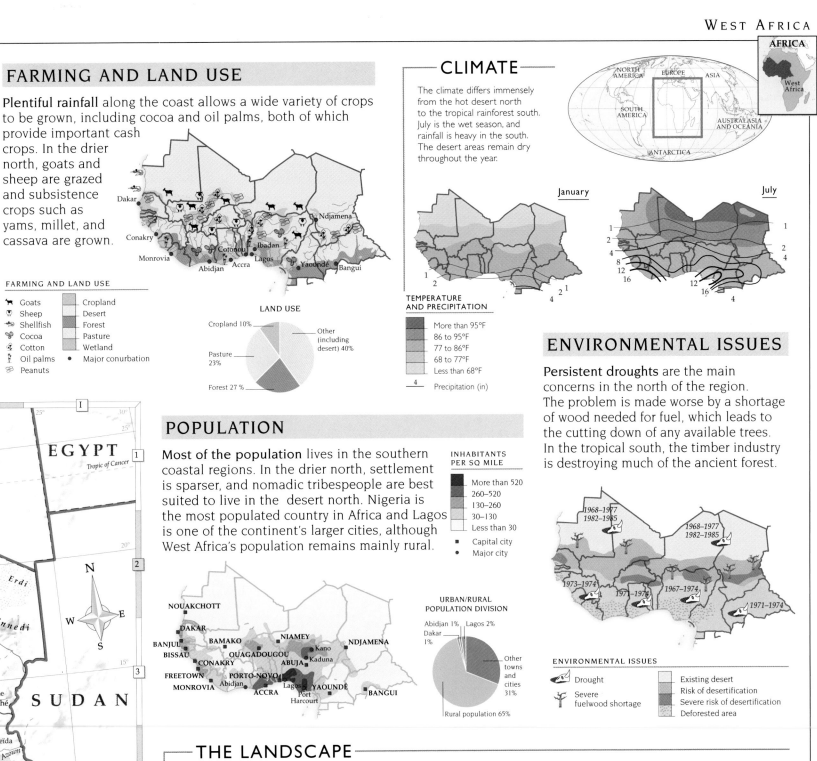

SCALE BAR

0 km   200   400

0 miles   200   400

EGYPT
Tropic of Cancer

SUDAN

CENTRAL AFRICAN REPUBLIC

Ippy  Bria  Djéma
Bambari  Dembia  Obo
Alindao  Bomu
Mobaye

DEM. REP. CONGO (ZAIRE)
Equator

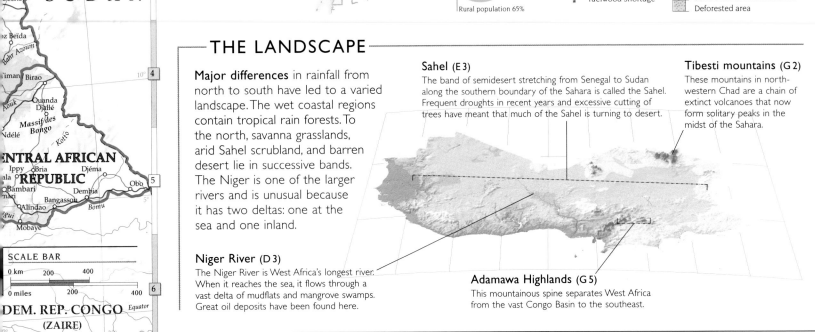

# EAST AFRICA

BURUNDI, DJIBOUTI, ERITREA, ETHIOPIA, KENYA, RWANDA, SOMALIA, SUDAN, TANZANIA, UGANDA

**Much of East Africa** is covered by long grass, scrub, and scattered trees, called savanna. This land is grazed by both domestic animals and a great variety of wild animals including lions, giraffes and elephants. The east of the region is known as the Horn of Africa, because it is shaped like an animal horn. Sudan, and the other countries there have recently been devastated by civil wars, and periods of drought and famine. In contrast, Kenya in the south is one of Africa's more stable and wealthy countries.

## FARMING AND LAND USE

**Much of the north** and east is too dry for farming, but in Sudan, cotton is grown on land irrigated by the Nile River. The Lake Victoria basin and rich volcanic soils of the highlands in Kenya, Uganda, and Tanzania support staple food crops, and those grown for export, such as tea and coffee. Kenya also grows high-quality vegetables, like mangetout, and exports them by air to supermarkets abroad. Sheep, goats, and cattle are herded on the savanna.

### LAND USE

- Cropland 9%
- Pasture 40%
- Other 26%
- Forest 25%

### FARMING AND LAND USE

- Cattle
- Goats
- Sheep
- Coffee
- Cotton
- Dates
- Market gardening
- Sugarcane
- Sisal
- Tea
- Cropland
- Desert
- Forest
- Pasture
- Wetland
- Major conurbation

## INDUSTRY

**East Africa** has few mineral resources, and industry is mainly based on processing raw materials. Coffee, tea, sugarcane, and sisal, are harvested and processed before being exported. Textile production is widespread, but is only on a small scale. Tourism is increasingly important in Kenya and Tanzania; each year, many thousands of people visit the wildlife reserves there.

### INDUSTRY

- Cement manufacturing
- Chemicals
- Food processing
- Textiles
- Tourism
- Major industrial center / area
- Major road

### STRUCTURE OF INDUSTRY

- Primary 15%
- Services 46%
- Manufacturing 39%

## THE LANDSCAPE

**The south of East Africa** is savanna grassland, broken by the rugged mountains – some of them active volcanoes – and large fresh and saltwater lakes that make up part of the Great Rift Valley. The Nile River has its source here, flowing through Lakes Victoria, Kyoga, and Albert as it takes much-needed water to the arid desert areas in the north.

### Great Rift Valley (D 6) (D 4)
The Great Rift Valley is like a deep scar running 4,300 miles from north to south through East Africa. It has been formed by the movements of two of the Earth's plates over millions of years. If these movements continue, East Africa may eventually become an island, separated by the ocean from the rest of the continent.

### Sudd (B 4)
The north of Sudan is rocky desert, but in the south, the waters of the White Nile run into a swampy area called the Sudd where much of its water disperses and evaporates.

### Juba River (E 5)
This river rises in the highlands of Ethiopia and flows some 750 miles southwards to the Indian Ocean. It, and the Shebeli River, which joins it about 19 miles from the coast, are the only permanent rivers in Somalia.

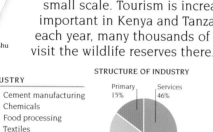

### Lake Victoria (C 5)
Lake Victoria is Africa's largest lake and the second largest freshwater lake in the world. It lies on the equator, between Kenya, Tanzania and Uganda, and covers 26,800 sq miles. Its only outlet is the Nile River in the north.

### Kilimanjaro (D 6)
This old volcano, made up of alternating layers of lava and ash, is Africa's highest mountain, rising to 19,341 ft. Although it lies only three degrees from the Equator, its peak is permanently covered with snow.

## ENVIRONMENTAL ISSUES

**Rapid population growth** has created a need for increasing amounts of land for farming. This, in addition to the need for firewood, has led to tree cover being stripped, allowing the soil to be washed or blown away. Over the past 25 years, East Africa has been stricken by many catastrophic droughts that have made desertification worse, and brought much human suffering.

1973
1980
1985–1986
1989

1973–1975
1980
1985
1989

1973–1975
1980
1986–1987
1989

1986

1972–1974
1973–1974

1973–1975
1980
1985
1987
1989

### ENVIRONMENTAL ISSUES

- Drought
- Severe firewood shortage
- Existing desert
- Risk of desertification
- Severe risk of desertification

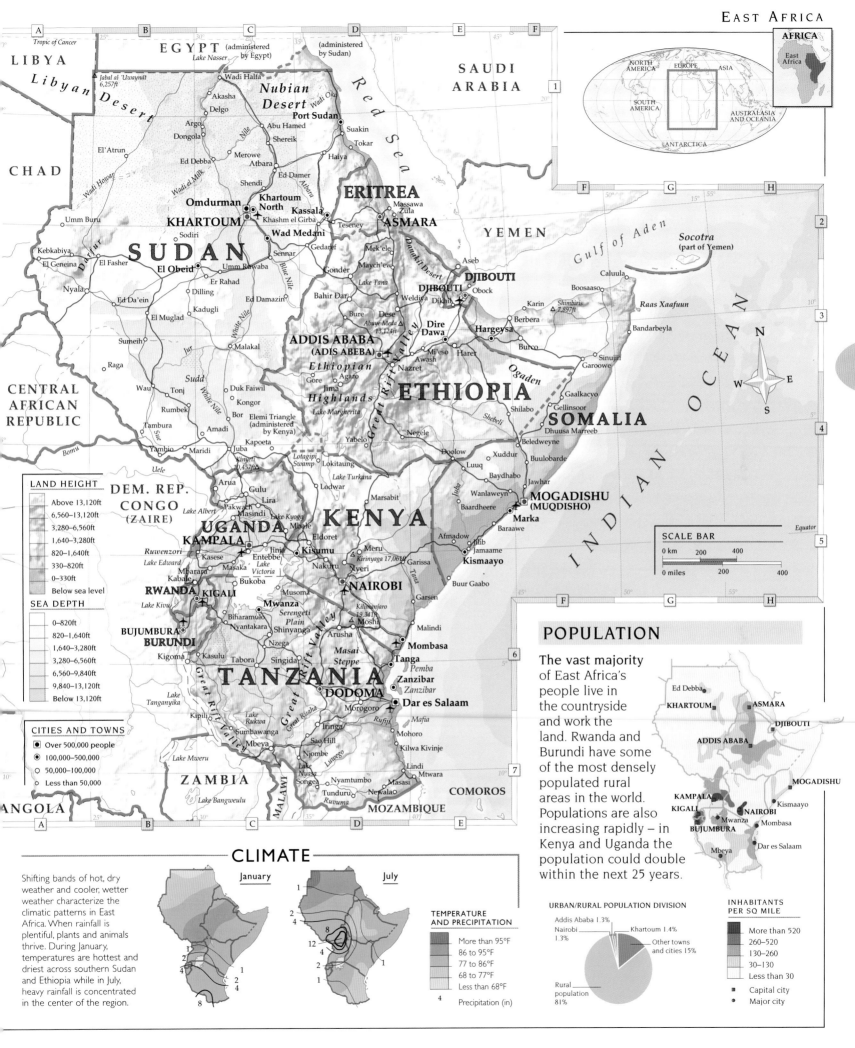

AFRICA
East Africa

LAND HEIGHT
Above 13,120ft
6,560–13,120ft
3,280–6,560ft
1,640–3,280ft
820–1,640ft
330–820ft
0–330ft
Below sea level

SEA DEPTH
0–820ft
820–1,640ft
1,640–3,280ft
3,280–6,560ft
6,560–9,840ft
9,840–13,120ft
Below 13,120ft

CITIES AND TOWNS
● Over 500,000 people
◉ 100,000–500,000
○ 50,000–100,000
○ Less than 50,000

SCALE BAR
0 km    200    400
0 miles    200    400
Equator

## POPULATION

The vast majority of East Africa's people live in the countryside and work the land. Rwanda and Burundi have some of the most densely populated rural areas in the world. Populations are also increasing rapidly – in Kenya and Uganda the population could double within the next 25 years.

URBAN/RURAL POPULATION DIVISION
Addis Ababa 1.3%
Nairobi 1.3%
Khartoum 1.4%
Other towns and cities 15%
Rural population 81%

INHABITANTS PER SQ MILE
More than 520
260–520
130–260
30–130
Less than 30
■ Capital city
● Major city

## CLIMATE

Shifting bands of hot, dry weather and cooler, wetter weather characterize the climatic patterns in East Africa. When rainfall is plentiful, plants and animals thrive. During January, temperatures are hottest and driest across southern Sudan and Ethiopia while in July, heavy rainfall is concentrated in the center of the region.

January

July

TEMPERATURE AND PRECIPITATION
More than 95°F
86 to 95°F
77 to 86°F
68 to 77°F
Less than 68°F
4    Precipitation (in)

# SOUTHERN AFRICA

ANGOLA, BOTSWANA, COMOROS, CONGO, DEM. REP. CONGO (ZAIRE), GABON, LESOTHO, MADAGASCAR, MALAWI, MOZAMBIQUE, NAMIBIA, SOUTH AFRICA, SWAZILAND, ZAMBIA, ZIMBABWE

**Southern Africa** contains the richest deposits of valuable minerals on the continent. South Africa is the wealthiest and most industrialized country in the region. Most of the surrounding countries rely on it for trade and work. Racial segregation under apartheid operated from 1948 until 1994, when South Africa held its first multiracial elections.

## FARMING AND LAND USE

Most of **southern Africa's** farmers grow just enough food to feed their families, although much of the farmland is in the hands of a few wealthy landowners. In the tropical north, oil palms and rubber are grown on large commercial plantations. Fruits are cultivated in the south, and tea and coffee are important in the east. Cattle farming is widespread across the dry grasslands.

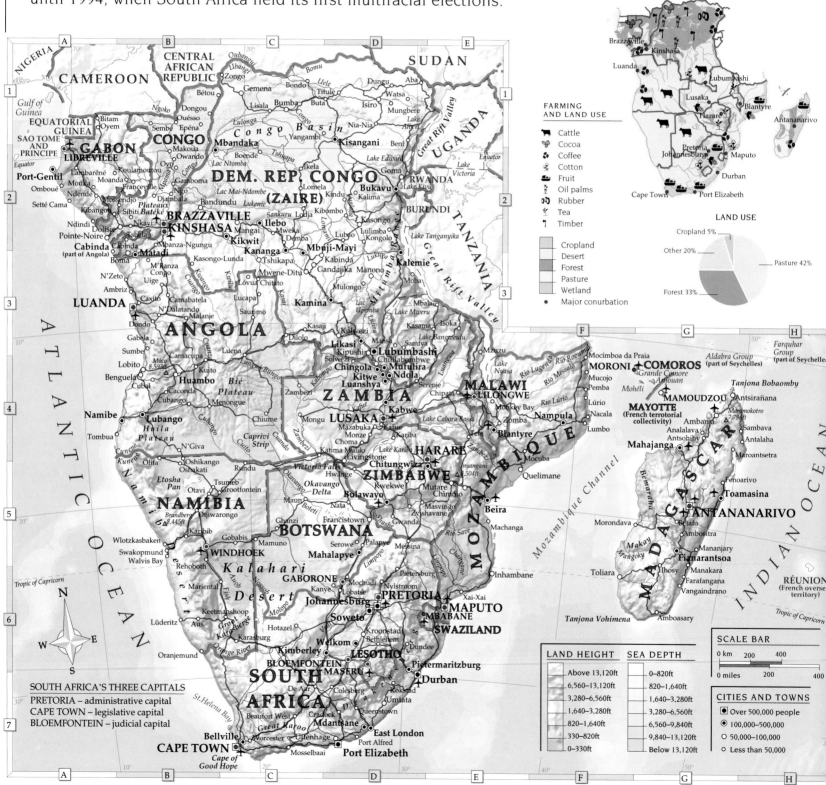

**FARMING AND LAND USE**

- 🐂 Cattle
- Cocoa
- Coffee
- Cotton
- Fruit
- Oil palms
- Rubber
- Tea
- Timber

**LAND USE**
- Cropland
- Desert
- Forest
- Pasture
- Wetland
- ● Major conurbation

**LAND USE**
- Cropland 5%
- Other 20%
- Pasture 42%
- Forest 33%

**SCALE BAR**

| LAND HEIGHT | SEA DEPTH |
|---|---|
| Above 13,120ft | 0–820ft |
| 6,560–13,120ft | 820–1,640ft |
| 3,280–6,560ft | 1,640–3,280ft |
| 1,640–3,280ft | 3,280–6,560ft |
| 820–1,640ft | 6,560–9,840ft |
| 330–820ft | 9,840–13,120ft |
| 0–330ft | Below 13,120ft |

**CITIES AND TOWNS**
- ■ Over 500,000 people
- ◉ 100,000–500,000
- ○ 50,000–100,000
- ○ Less than 50,000

SOUTH AFRICA'S THREE CAPITALS
PRETORIA – administrative capital
CAPE TOWN – legislative capital
BLOEMFONTEIN – judicial capital

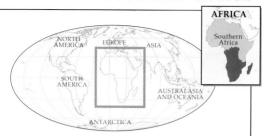

## CLIMATE

During January, temperatures are highest in the Kalahari Desert and rainfall is plentiful in the center of southern Africa. July is cooler and drier, with rainfall concentrated in the north of Dem. Rep. Congo (Zaire). The Atlantic coast of Namibia receives little rain all year round.

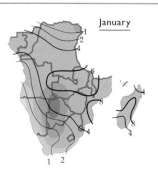

January    July

**TEMPERATURE AND PRECIPITATION**

- More than 95°F
- 86 to 95°F
- 77 to 86°F
- 68 to 77°F
- 59 to 68°F
- Less than 59°F
- 4 — Precipitation (in)

## ENVIRONMENTAL ISSUES

The immense rain forests of the Congo Basin in the north remain relatively untouched, but deforestation is beginning to occur at its edges, with much more forest due to be cleared in the future. Large parts of Madagascar have also been deforested. Farther south, occasional drought and the clearing of bushlands for firewood can cause soil loss.

Congo Basin

1971–1974
1979–1985
1982–1984
1983–1985
1983
1985

**ENVIRONMENTAL ISSUES**

- Drought
- Severe firewood shortage
- Existing desert
- Risk of desertification
- Severe risk of desertification
- Deforested area
- Remaining tropical forest

## INDUSTRY

Southern Africa has extraordinary mineral resources. Angola has large deposits of oil, and diamonds are found in Angola, Botswana, Namibia, and South Africa. Copper is mined in the region known as the "copper belt," that runs from Dem. Rep. Congo (Zaire) into Zambia. South Africa produces 40% of the world's gold. Manufacturing, such as fruit canning and steel production, is most developed in South Africa.

Libreville, Kisangani, Brazzaville, Bukavu, Kinshasa, Luanda, Kolwezi, Lubumbashi, Ndola, Lusaka, Blantyre, Harare, Antananarivo, Bulawayo, Beira, Pretoria, Johannesburg, Maputo, Durban, Cape Town, Port Elizabeth

**INDUSTRY**

- Car manufacturing
- Chemicals
- Engineering
- Food processing
- Iron and steel
- Metal refining
- Textiles
- Oil and gas
- Mining
- Timber processing
- Tourism
- Major industrial center / area
- Major road

**STRUCTURE OF INDUSTRY**

Primary 10%
Services 59%
Manufacturing 31%

## THE LANDSCAPE

Southern Africa stretches from just north of the equator down to the southern tip of the continent. It is an area with an extremely varied climate and geography. In the north are the tropical rain forests of the Congo Basin, while arid desert covers much of the southwest. The eastern regions are mostly grasslands, with lush vegetation found on the tropical coast of Mozambique.

### Congo Basin (C 1)

The Congo River is Africa's second longest river, flowing in an arc through the dense tropical forests of the Congo Basin before emptying into the Atlantic Ocean.

### Namib Desert (B 5)

The Namib is one of the world's driest deserts. The only water it receives is from mists that roll in from the sea. Where the desert meets the coast is known as the Skeleton Coast because of sailors who were shipwrecked and died there.

### Victoria Falls (D 5)

On its way to the Indian Ocean, the Zambezi River plunges over a 420-ft cliff, into a narrow chasm. The resultant spray rises up to 1,600 ft, and the thunder of the water can be heard up to 25 miles away.

### Madagascar (G 5)

The world's fourth largest island lies in isolation 155 miles off the east coast of southern Africa. It became separated from the African continent 135 million years ago, and its plant and animal life are unique. The rich biodiversity of the rain forests is being threatened by uncontrolled lumbering.

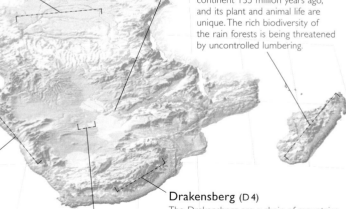

### Okavango Delta (C 5)

The Okavango River terminates in the Kalahari Desert, forming a vast, swampy inland delta.

### Drakensberg (D 4)

The Drakensberg are a chain of mountains that lie at the edge of a broad plateau that has tilted because of the movement of the Earth's plates. Rivers have carved through the high mountains, creating dramatic gorges and waterfalls.

## POPULATION

Although the population is still mostly rural, southern Africa has some of the continent's most urbanized nations. Dense tropical rain forest in the north and arid desert in the southwest have kept habitation to a bare minimum. Malawi is the most densely populated country in the region.

LIBREVILLE, Kisangani, BRAZZAVILLE, Bukavu, KINSHASA, LUANDA, Lobito, Lubumbashi, LUSAKA, LILONGWE, Blantyre, HARARE, WINDHOEK, Bulawayo, ANTANANARIVO, GABORONE, PRETORIA, MAPUTO, Johannesburg, MBANE, BLOEMFONTEIN, MASERU, Durban, CAPE TOWN, Port Elizabeth

**URBAN/RURAL POPULATION DIVISION**

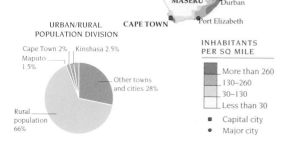

Cape Town 2%
Kinshasa 2.5%
Maputo 1.5%
Other towns and cities 28%
Rural population 66%

**INHABITANTS PER SQ MILE**

- More than 260
- 130–260
- 30–130
- Less than 30
- ■ Capital city
- • Major city

# AUSTRALASIA & OCEANIA

**Australasia and Oceania** encompasses the ancient landmass of Australia, the islands of New Zealand, and the scattering of thousands of small islands that stretch out into the Pacific Ocean. Indigenous peoples of the South Pacific, such as the Aborigines, Maoris, Polynesians, Micronesians, and Melanesians, inhabit the region. In Australia and New Zealand, they live alongside people of European origin who settled in the 18th century, and more recent arrivals from East and Southeast Asia.

**PACIFIC ISLANDS**

Micronesia is one of the Pacific's island nations, consisting of a group of volcanic islands, low-lying coral reefs, and lagoons. Many of the smaller Pacific islands are only a few feet above sea level.

## LAND USE AND AGRICULTURE

**Much of the center of Australia** is a dry, barren desert and unsuitable for agriculture. At its fringes, sheep farming is practiced, and both Australia and New Zealand are massive producers of wool and lamb. The Pacific islands export many exotic fruits and crops – especially oil palms and coconut palms. Oil from the palms is processed and sold as well as the fruits themselves. Small-scale fishing is common, but larger operations are run by foreign fishing fleets, especially the Japanese, who fish for tuna in the deeper waters of the Pacific.

**SHEEP FARMING**

New Zealand and Australia are the world's biggest producers of wool. In New Zealand, sheep outnumber people by 20:1.

**POPULATION**

Capital cities
- ◉ Above 500,000
- ◉ 100,000 to 500,000
- ● 50,000 to 100,000
- • Below 50,000

State capitals
- ◉ Above 500,000
- ◉ 100,000 to 500,000
- ○ 50,000 to 100,000

**BORDERS**

- full international border
- indication of maritime country extent
- indication of maritime dependent territory extent
- state border

SCALE 1:37,250,000

0 km 300 600

0 miles 300 600

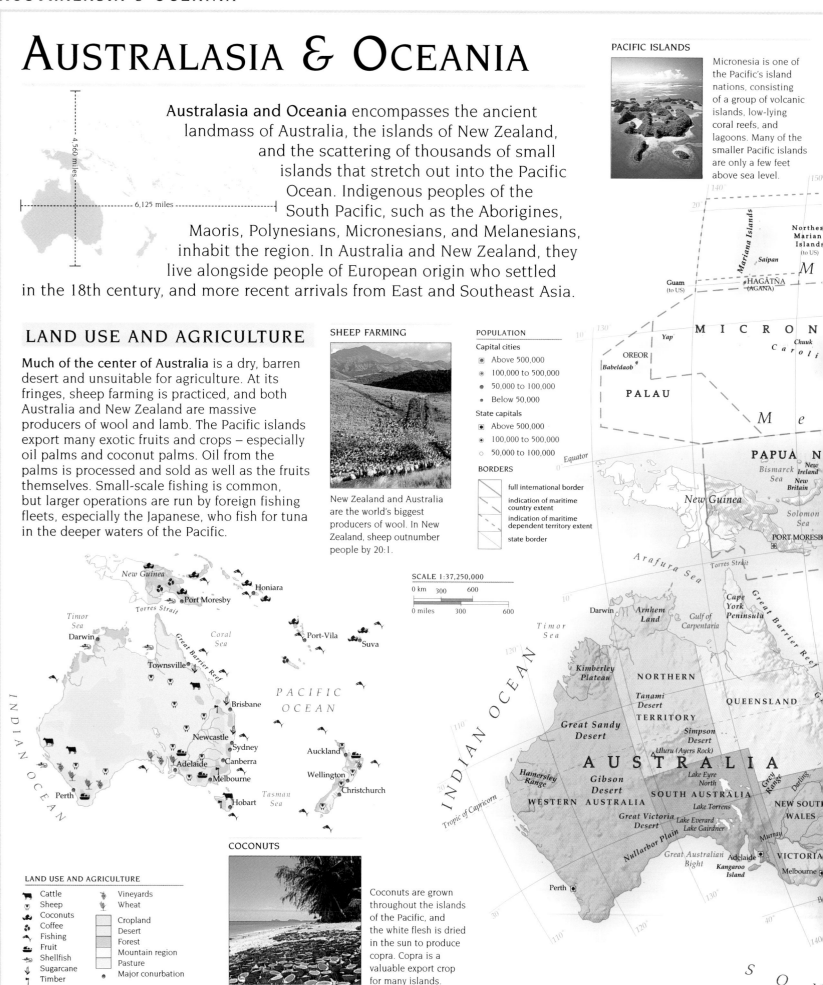

**COCONUTS**

Coconuts are grown throughout the islands of the Pacific, and the white flesh is dried in the sun to produce copra. Copra is a valuable export crop for many islands.

**LAND USE AND AGRICULTURE**

- Cattle
- Sheep
- Coconuts
- Coffee
- Fishing
- Fruit
- Shellfish
- Sugarcane
- Timber
- Vineyards
- Wheat
- Cropland
- Desert
- Forest
- Mountain region
- Pasture
- Major conurbation

## MINERAL RESOURCES

Mineral resources are not widespread, but where they are found, they are in great abundance. Most of the small Pacific islands have no mineral resources, but Australia has enormous reserves of bauxite and iron ore, and also sizable reserves of gold and zinc. Copper is found in Papua New Guinea, and New Caledonia has large nickel reserves. There are ample supplies of fossil fuels, and although coal is plentiful in eastern Australia, oil and gas are found only in isolated pockets around Australia's coast.

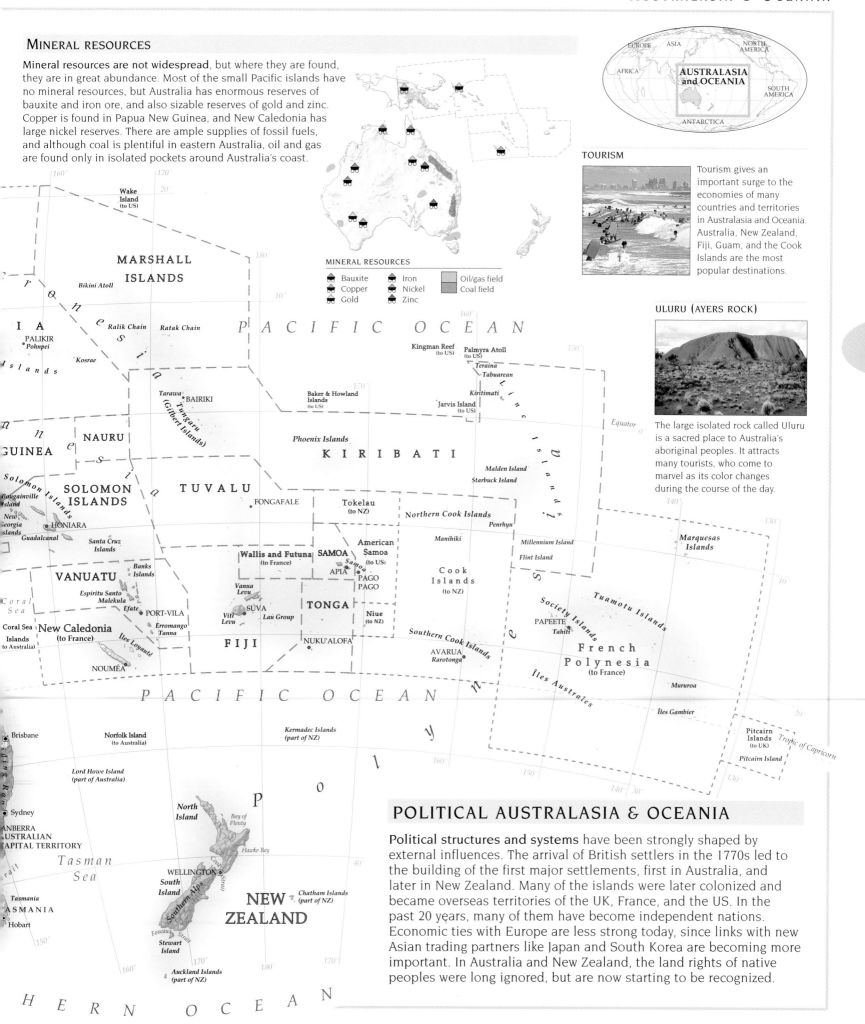

**AUSTRALASIA and OCEANIA**

### MINERAL RESOURCES

| | | |
|---|---|---|
| Bauxite | Iron | Oil/gas field |
| Copper | Nickel | Coal field |
| Gold | Zinc | |

### TOURISM

Tourism gives an important surge to the economies of many countries and territories in Australasia and Oceania. Australia, New Zealand, Fiji, Guam, and the Cook Islands are the most popular destinations.

### ULURU (AYERS ROCK)

The large isolated rock called Uluru is a sacred place to Australia's aboriginal peoples. It attracts many tourists, who come to marvel as its color changes during the course of the day.

## POLITICAL AUSTRALASIA & OCEANIA

**Political structures and systems** have been strongly shaped by external influences. The arrival of British settlers in the 1770s led to the building of the first major settlements, first in Australia, and later in New Zealand. Many of the islands were later colonized and became overseas territories of the UK, France, and the US. In the past 20 years, many of them have become independent nations. Economic ties with Europe are less strong today, since links with new Asian trading partners like Japan and South Korea are becoming more important. In Australia and New Zealand, the land rights of native peoples were long ignored, but are now starting to be recognized.

# AUSTRALIA

**Australia is the world's** sixth-largest country, and also the smallest, flattest continent, with the lowest rainfall. Most Australians are of European, mainly British, origin but in the past 50 years almost five million settlers from more than 200 countries have made Australia their home. The Aboriginal people, now only a tiny minority, were the first inhabitants. Recently, there have been several moves to restore their ancient lands.

## INDUSTRY

**Australia has one of** the world's biggest mining industries. Bauxite, coal, copper, gold, and iron ore are mined and exported, especially to Japan. In the cities, service industries, particularly tourism, are growing fast; Australia's sunshine and dramatic scenery are attracting an increasing number of overseas visitors.

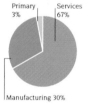

### STRUCTURE OF INDUSTRY

Primary 3%
Services 67%
Manufacturing 30%

**INDUSTRY**

- Brewing
- Car manufacturing
- Chemicals
- Electronics
- Engineering
- Food processing
- Coal
- Mining
- Oil and gas
- Tourism
- Major industrial center / area
- Major road

## POPULATION

**Despite its vast size,** Australia is sparsely populated. The desert outback, which covers most of the interior, is too dry and barren to support many people. About 70% of the population live in the cities and towns on the east and southeast coasts, and around Perth in the west.

### INHABITANTS PER SQ MILE

- More than 130
- 30–130
- 3–30
- Less than 3
- ■ Capital city
- ● Major city

### URBAN/RURAL POPULATION DIVISION

Sydney 22%
Melbourne 18%
Brisbane 8%
Other towns and cities 37%
Rural population 15%

## FARMING AND LAND USE

**Away from the coasts,** much of the land is too dry for agriculture. Fields of sugarcane grow close the east coast, and grapes for the thriving wine industry are cultivated in the south and west, along with wheat. Vast numbers of cattle and sheep are raised for their meat and wool – both of which are major exports. They are grazed in the desert, on huge farms called "stations," and in more fertile areas.

**FARMING AND LAND USE**

- Cattle
- Sheep
- Wheat
- Sugarcane
- Timber
- Vineyards
- Cropland
- Desert
- Forest
- Pasture
- ● Major conurbation

**LAND USE**

Cropland 6%
Other (including desert) 21%
Forest 19%
Pasture 54%

## THE LANDSCAPE

**Most of Australia** is dry, flat, and barren; all of the wetter, fertile land is found along its coastline. Huge sun-baked deserts, fringed by semiarid plains of scrub and grassland cover most of the west and center of the country. In the east, the land rises to the highlands of the Great Dividing Range, which run the whole length of the east coast. The tropical north coast has rainforests and mangrove swamps.

### Blue Mountains (G 6)
The Blue Mountains lie toward the southern end of the Great Dividing Range. They get their name from the blue haze of oil droplets given off by the eucalyptus trees covering their slopes.

### Great Barrier Reef (G 2)
This spectacular coral reef, which stretches for over 1,200 miles off the coast of Queensland, is the largest living structure on Earth. The reef has built up over millions of years and its waters are home to thousands of different species of coral and marine animals.

### Uluru (Ayers Rock) (D 4)
Uluru is an enormous block of red sandstone, standing almost in the middle of Australia. It is the world's biggest free-standing rock – 5.8 miles around the base, and 2,844 ft high. It is the summit of a sandstone hill that is buried beneath the sands of the desert.

### Simpson Desert (E 4)
The Simpson Desert covers around 50,000 sq miles. It contains long, parallel lines of sand dunes and is scattered with large salt pans and salt lakes, which were created when old rivers evaporated. They are now fed by the seasonal rains.

### Murray River (F 5)
Together with its tributaries, the Murray River is Australia's main river system. It winds slowly westward for more than 1,562 miles from the Great Dividing Range to the Indian Ocean. It is fed by snow from mountains in the far southeast.

### Great Dividing Range (H 5)
These highlands separate the desert regions from the fertile eastern plains. Rivers and streams have eroded them, creating deep valleys and gorges.

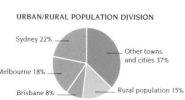

# ENVIRONMENTAL ISSUES

**Australia's dry climate** and low rainfall make it susceptible to desertification. Around the edges of the large deserts – especially in the north and southeast – cattle grazing and the removal of natural vegetation are destroying the natural habitat, allowing the desert areas to spread. During the dry season, vegetation becomes tinder-dry, and bush fires are common, burning huge tracts of land.

## CLIMATE

Much of Australia's climate is continental, and temperatures soar during the day and fall rapidly at night. The climate is also arid and very little rain falls, apart from in the summer months when the north is affected by tropical storms.

January

July

AUSTRALASIA AND OCEANIA

Australia

**TEMPERATURE AND PRECIPITATION**

- More than 95°F
- 86 to 95°F
- 77 to 86°F
- 68 to 77°F
- 59 to 68°F
- 50 to 59°F
- 41 to 50°C
- Less than 41°F

4 Precipitation (in.)

**ENVIRONMENTAL ISSUES**

- ✕ Area at risk from bushfires
- Existing desert
- Risk of desertification
- Severe risk of desertification

**LAND HEIGHT / SEA DEPTH**

| LAND HEIGHT | SEA DEPTH |
|---|---|
| 6,560–13,120ft | 0–820ft |
| 3,280–6,560ft | 820–1,640ft |
| 1,640–3,280ft | 1,640–3,280ft |
| 820–1,640ft | 3,280–6,560ft |
| 330–820ft | 6,560–9,840ft |
| 0–330ft | 9,840–13,120ft |
| Below sea level | Below 13,120ft |

**CITIES AND TOWNS**
- ▣ Over 500,000 people
- ◉ 100,000–500,000
- ◎ 50,000–100,000
- ○ Less than 50,000

**SCALE BAR**
0 km 100 200
0 miles 100 200

# NEW ZEALAND

New Zealand is one of the most remote populated places in the world, and was one of the last places on Earth to be inhabited by people. The first people to settle on the islands were the Maori, a Polynesian people. When European settlers arrived during the 19th century, the Maori became a minority and today make up only about 9% of the population. With few people and rich natural resources, New Zealand's inhabitants have high living standards.

## INDUSTRY

High-tech industries such as electronics and computing are growing in the major cities of Auckland and Wellington. Agricultural products such as meat, wool, and milk are still among New Zealand's major exports, and large pine forests supply wood for paper pulp and timber. The magnificent scenery and varied climate draw tourists from all over the world, especially for hiking and other special vacations.

STRUCTURE OF INDUSTRY

Primary 5%
Services 68%
Manufacturing 27%

INDUSTRY
- Chemicals
- Electronics
- Engineering
- Fish processing
- Food processing
- Iron and steel
- Textiles
- Timber
- Tourism
- Major industrial center / area
- Major road

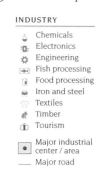

## POPULATION

Most of the population is descended from European settlers, although immigrants from Asia and the Pacific islands are increasing. More than one-third of New Zealand's 3.5 million people live in Auckland on North Island, which also has the largest Polynesian population of any city in the Pacific. Elsewhere, the population is clustered along the coasts, where the land is lower.

URBAN/RURAL POPULATION DIVISION

Auckland 27.2%
Other towns and cities 38%
Wellington 9.5%
Christchurch 9.3%
Rural population 16%

INHABITANTS PER SQ MILE
- More than 130
- 30–130
- 3–30
- Less than 3
- Capital city
- Major city

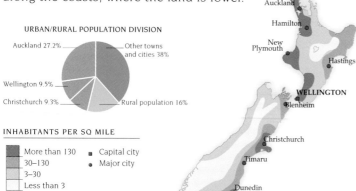

## ENVIRONMENTAL ISSUES

New Zealand is one of the world's least polluted countries, largely due to its small population and lack of heavy industries. Air quality is occasionally poor in Auckland and Christchurch. Environment-friendly geothermal energy is tapped to make electricity in the volcanic region of North Island. Recently, logging companies have begun to exploit the rich forest reserves, although this has been widely opposed.

ENVIRONMENTAL ISSUES
- Geothermal power generation
- Logging activity
- Urban air pollution
- Major industrial center

## THE LANDSCAPE

Two large, mountainous islands form New Zealand's main land areas. A large crack or fault – the Alpine Fault, in the west of South Island – is the boundary between two plates in the Earth's crust. Land on either side of the fault tends to move, causing earthquakes. Volcanoes, many of them still active, are also found on both islands. South Island has many high peaks, several more than 10,000 ft high.

### Geysers and boiling mud
Geysers occur when hot volcanic rocks come into contact with underground water. The water boils and turns to steam, forcing the water above it to burst through the Earth's surface into the air. There are many geysers and boiling mud pools in the areas around Rotorua and Taupo.

**Northland (C 1)**
This is a tropical region in the far northwest. Many of the inlets are fringed by mangrove swamps.

**Mount Taranaki (C 4)**
The dormant volcano of Mount Taranaki lies on New Zealand's North Island. It rises to a height of 8,261 ft.

**Probable location of Alpine Fault**

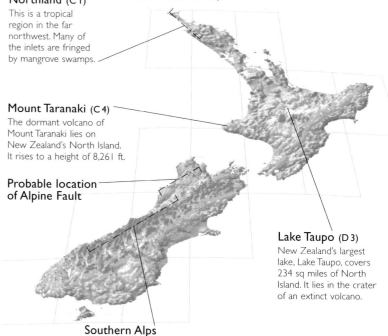

**Lake Taupo (D 3)**
New Zealand's largest lake, Lake Taupo, covers 234 sq miles of North Island. It lies in the crater of an extinct volcano.

**Southern Alps**
New Zealand's Southern Alps stretch more than 300 miles down the backbone of South Island. They were formed by the collision of the Indo-Australian and Pacific plates. Heavy snowfalls here, brought by westerly winds, feed the Fox Glacier, which moves at a speed of 1.5–15 ft a day.

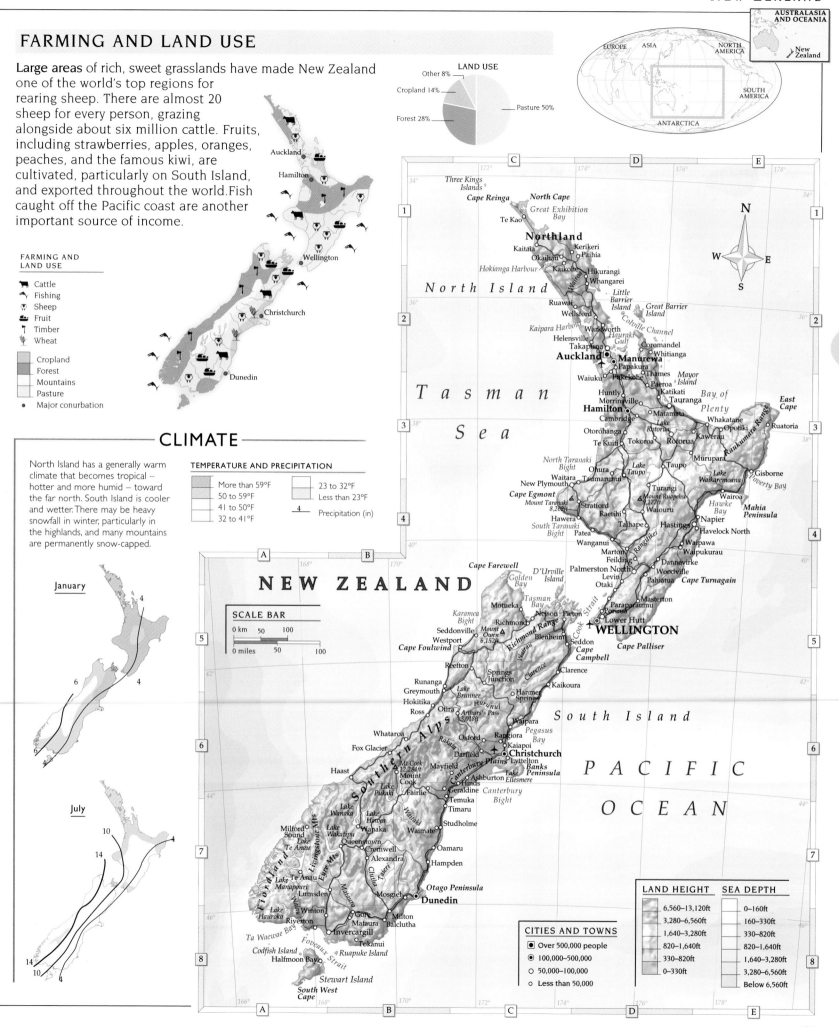

# FARMING AND LAND USE

**Large areas** of rich, sweet grasslands have made New Zealand one of the world's top regions for rearing sheep. There are almost 20 sheep for every person, grazing alongside about six million cattle. Fruits, including strawberries, apples, oranges, peaches, and the famous kiwi, are cultivated, particularly on South Island, and exported throughout the world. Fish caught off the Pacific coast are another important source of income.

### LAND USE

- Other 8%
- Cropland 14%
- Forest 28%
- Pasture 50%

### FARMING AND LAND USE

- Cattle
- Fishing
- Sheep
- Fruit
- Timber
- Wheat

- Cropland
- Forest
- Mountains
- Pasture
- ● Major conurbation

## CLIMATE

North Island has a generally warm climate that becomes tropical – hotter and more humid – toward the far north. South Island is cooler and wetter. There may be heavy snowfall in winter, particularly in the highlands, and many mountains are permanently snow-capped.

### TEMPERATURE AND PRECIPITATION

- More than 59°F
- 50 to 59°F
- 41 to 50°F
- 32 to 41°F
- 23 to 32°F
- Less than 23°F
- 4 — Precipitation (in)

January

July

## NEW ZEALAND

### SCALE BAR

0 km 50 100

0 miles 50 100

### CITIES AND TOWNS

- ■ Over 500,000 people
- ◉ 100,000–500,000
- ○ 50,000–100,000
- ○ Less than 50,000

### LAND HEIGHT

- 6,560–13,120ft
- 3,280–6,560ft
- 1,640–3,280ft
- 820–1,640ft
- 330–820ft
- 0–330ft

### SEA DEPTH

- 0–160ft
- 160–330ft
- 330–820ft
- 820–1,640ft
- 1,640–3,280ft
- 3,280–6,560ft
- Below 6,560ft

### AUSTRALASIA AND OCEANIA

EUROPE ASIA NORTH AMERICA
SOUTH AMERICA
ANTARCTICA
New Zealand

*Three Kings Islands*
Cape Reinga
*North Cape*
Te Kao
*Great Exhibition Bay*
**Northland**
Kaitaia
Kerikeri
Okaihau Paihia
*Hokianga Harbour* Kaikohe Hikurangi
Whangarei
*North Island*
Ruawai
*Little Barrier Island*
Wellsford
*Great Barrier Island*
*Kaipara Harbour* *Colville Channel*
Helensville *Hauraki Gulf*
Takapuna Coromandel
**Auckland** **Manurewa** Whitianga
Papakura *Mayor Island*
Waiuku Pukekohe Thames
Huntly Paeroa Katikati
Morrinsville Tauranga
**Hamilton** Matamata *Bay of Plenty*
Cambridge Whakatane *East Cape*
Otorohanga *Lake Rotorua* Opotiki Ruatoria
Te Kuiti Rotorua Kawerau
Tokoroa Murupara
*North Taranaki Bight*
Ohura *Lake Taupo* Taupo
New Plymouth Waitara Taumarunui *Lake Waikaremoana*
Turangi *Poverty Bay*
*Cape Egmont* Gisborne
*Mount Taranaki* ▲ Mount Ruapehu Wairoa
*8,261ft* *3,177ft* *Hawke Bay*
Stratford Waiouru *Mahia Peninsula*
Hawera Raetihi Waiouru
*South Taranaki Bight* Taihape Napier
Patea Hastings
Wanganui Havelock North
Marton Waipawa
*Cape Farewell* Feilding Waipukurau
*D'Urville Island* Palmerston North Dannevirke
*Golden Bay* Woodville
*Tasman Bay* Levin Pahiatua *Cape Turnagain*
Motueka Otaki
Nelson Masterton
Picton Paraparaumu
Richmond *Cook Strait* Porirua
Seddonville *Richmond Range* Blenheim Lower Hutt
Westport Mount Owen **WELLINGTON**
*Cape Foulwind* *6,152ft* Seddon
*Cape Campbell* *Cape Palliser*
Reefton *Wairau*
Runanga Springs Junction *Clarence*
Greymouth Clarence
Hokitika *Lake Brunner* Hanmer Springs Kaikoura
Ross Otira *Hurunui*
Arthur's Pass *South Island*
*3,018ft* Waipara
Whataroa Oxford Rangiora *Pegasus Bay*
Fox Glacier *Southern Alps* Darfield Kaiapoi
*Rakaia* **Christchurch**
Haast *Mt Cook* Mayfield Lyttelton
*12,284ft* Mount *Banks Peninsula*
Cook Ashburton *Canterbury Plains*
*Lake* Hinds *Lake Ellesmere*
*Pukaki* Fairlie Geraldine
Temuka *Canterbury Bight*
*Lake* Timaru
*Lake* *Hawea*
*Wanaka* Wanaka Waimate
Milford *Lake Wakatipu* Studholme
Sound *Fiordland* Queenstown Waimate
*Lake Te Anau* Cromwell Oamaru
*Eyre Mts* Alexandra
*Lake Te Anau* Hampden
*Lake Manapouri* *Clutha* Mosgiel *Otago Peninsula*
Lumsden *Taieri* **Dunedin**
*Lake Hauroko* Winton Milton
Riverton Gore Balclutha
*Ta Waewae Bay* Mataura
Invercargill
*Codfish Island* Tokanui
Halfmoon Bay *Ruapuke Island*
*Foveaux Strait*
*Stewart Island*
*South West Cape*

*Tasman Sea*

*PACIFIC OCEAN*

# SOUTHWEST PACIFIC

**The many thousands** of islands in the Pacific Ocean are scattered across an enormous area. The original inhabitants, the Polynesians, Melanesians, and Micronesians, settled the islands following the last Ice Age. In the 1700s Europeans arrived. They colonized all of the Pacific islands, introducing their culture, languages, and religion. Today many, though not all, of the islands have become independent. Their economies are simple, based largely on fishing and agriculture. Many are increasingly relying on their beautiful scenery and tropical climates to attract tourists and give a valuable boost to their economies.

## LANDSCAPE

**Most of the Pacific islands** are extremely small, the largest landmass is the half of the island of New Guinea occupied by Papua New Guinea. The edges of the Indo-Australian and Pacific plates meet on the western edge of the area, leading to much volcanic and earthquake activity. Many of the islands are coral atolls, originally formed by volcanic activity, and some are no more than a few feet above sea level.

### New Guinea (A 2)
A mountainous spine runs through the center of the island, separating the northern coast from the dense forests and mangroves found in the south.

### Pacific Ocean
The Pacific Ocean is the Earth's oldest and deepest. Its name means peaceful, though it is far from being so; the highest wave ever recorded in open ocean – 112 ft – occurred during a hurricane in the Pacific.

### Kavachi
Kavachi is an underwater volcano lying off the coast of New Georgia, in the Solomon Islands. It still erupts every few years.

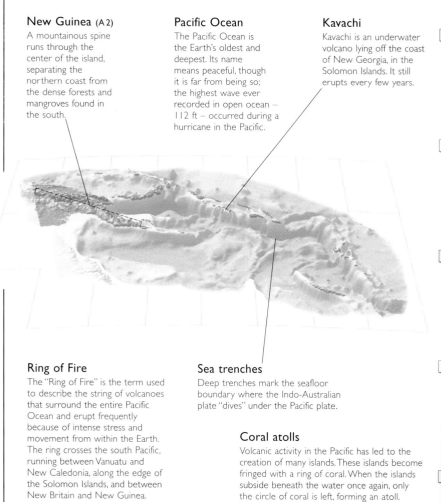

### Ring of Fire
The "Ring of Fire" is the term used to describe the string of volcanoes that surround the entire Pacific Ocean and erupt frequently because of intense stress and movement from within the Earth. The ring crosses the south Pacific, running between Vanuatu and New Caledonia, along the edge of the Solomon Islands, and between New Britain and New Guinea.

### Sea trenches
Deep trenches mark the seafloor boundary where the Indo-Australian plate "dives" under the Pacific plate.

### Coral atolls
Volcanic activity in the Pacific has led to the creation of many islands. These islands become fringed with a ring of coral. When the islands subside beneath the water once again, only the circle of coral is left, forming an atoll.

## INDUSTRY

Today, **the main industry** for many of the Pacific islands is tourism. Food processing and small-scale textile industries are also common on many islands.

**INDUSTRY**
- Brewing
- Food processing
- Textiles
- Timber processing
- Mining
- Tourism
- Major industrial center
- Major road

Mount Hagen, Madang, Rabaul, Lae, Port Moresby, Honiara, Port-Vila, Suva, Nouméa

*(Map: Papua New Guinea and surrounding islands — places labeled: Ninigo Group, Hermit Islands, Admiralty Islands, St. Matthias Group, Manus Island, Lotengau, New Hanover, Kavieng, Lihir Group, Vanimo, Bismarck Archipelago, New Ireland, Lumi, Wewak, Bismarck Sea, Green River, Angoram, Bogia, Karkar Island, Witu Islands, Rabaul, Tar, Sepik, Madang, Gloucester, Torin, Telbubil, Mount Wilhelm 14,794ft, Vitiaz Strait, Pomio, New Britain, Mount Hagen, Anepmete, Kimbe, Kiunga, Mendi, Mount Giluwe 14,332ft, Gordka, Sialum, Gasmata, Solomon Sea, Lake Murray, Huon Gulf, Finschhafen, Fly, Emeti, PAPUA NEW GUINEA, Kiriwina Islands, Woodlark Island, Gulf of Papua, Kerema, Manau, Popondetta, Tufi, D'Entrecasteaux Islands, Guasopa, Weam, Oriomo, Kiwai Island, Hisiu, Mount Suckling 12,061ft, Mari, Daru, PORT MORESBY, Kupiano, Magarida, Alotau, Louisiade Archipelago, Torres Strait, Cape York, Great Barrier Range, Owen Stanley Range, Arafura Sea, Cape York Peninsula, Great Barrier Reef, AUSTRALIA, Coral Sea)*

**SAMOA** — Fagamalo, Falealupo, Savai'i, Silisili 6,096ft, Salelologa, Apolima Strait, APIA, Upolu, Matautu, Fito 3,652ft, Ti'avea, PACIFIC OCEAN
0 km 50 / 0 miles 50

**CORAL SEA ISLANDS**
(Australian external territory)

**Tahiti (FRENCH POLYNESIA)**
(French overseas territory)
Moorea, PAPEETE, Afareaitu, Faaa, Tahiti, Tiarei, Mont Orohena 7,353ft, Maraa, Taravao, Tautira, Presqu'île de Taiarapu, Teahupoo, Îles du Vent, PACIFIC OCEAN
0 km 30 / 0 miles 30

**Easter Island (Isla de Pascua)** (to Chile)
Maunga Terevaka 1,660ft, Punta Rosalia, Maunga Pukao 1,214ft, Mataveri, Maunga Tangaroa 886ft, Punta Baja, Motu Nui, Cabo Sur, PACIFIC OCEAN
0 km 10 / 0 miles

# FARMING AND LAND USE

**Most farming** that takes place on the Pacific islands is at a subsistence level, and many people keep pigs and chickens. A few crops are grown for export, especially oil palms, and coconuts, which are dried in the sun to produce copra. Many islanders make their living from the rich fishing grounds of the Pacific. The thick forests of Papua New Guinea are increasingly cut down for timber.

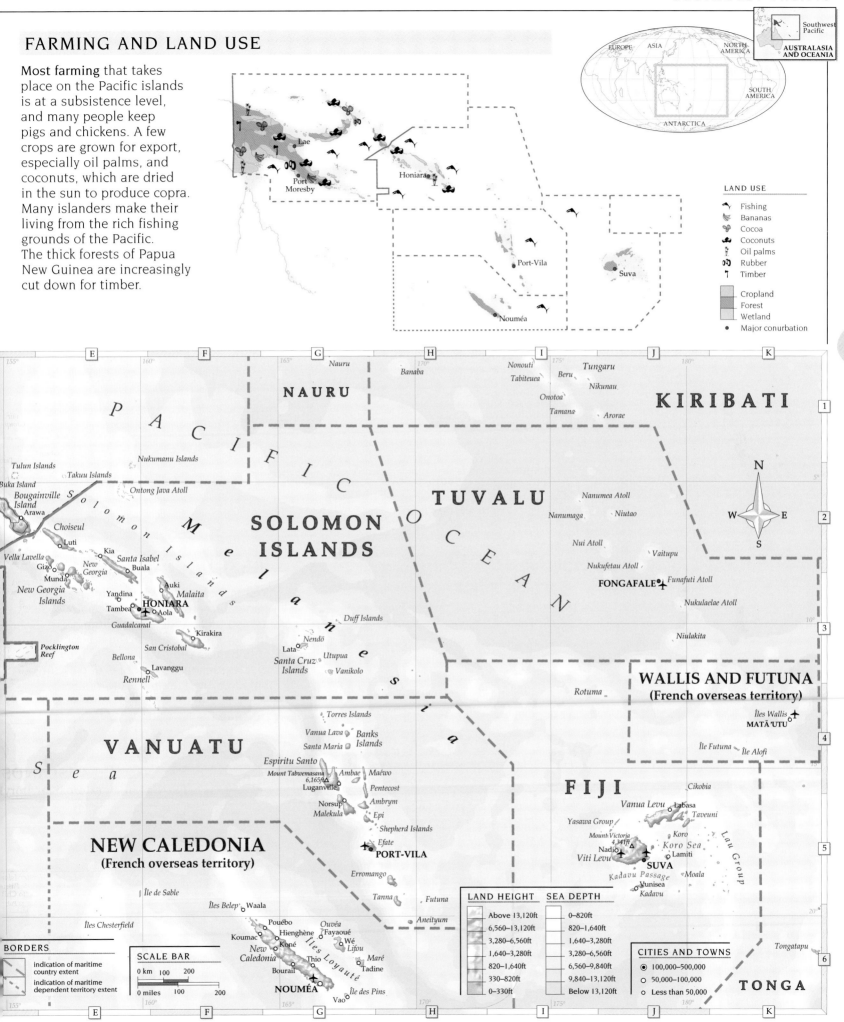

EUROPE  ASIA  NORTH AMERICA
SOUTH AMERICA
ANTARCTICA

Southwest Pacific

**AUSTRALASIA AND OCEANIA**

Lae
Port Moresby
Honiara
Port-Vila
Suva
Nouméa

**LAND USE**

- Fishing
- Bananas
- Cocoa
- Coconuts
- Oil palms
- Rubber
- Timber

Cropland
Forest
Wetland
• Major conurbation

## Map

155°  160°  165°  170°  175°  180°
E  F  G  H  I  J  K

Nauru
Banaba
Nonouti  Tungaru
Tabiteuea  Beru
**NAURU**  Onotoa  Nikunau
Tamana  Arorae
**KIRIBATI**  1

Tulun Islands
Nukumanu Islands
Takuu Islands
Buka Island
Bougainville Island
Arawa
Ontong Java Atoll
**TUVALU**
Nanumea Atoll
Nanumaga  Niutao
Nui Atoll
Vaitupu
Nukufetau Atoll
FONGAFALE  Funafuti Atoll
Nukulaelae Atoll
2

Choiseul
Luti
Vella Lavella  Kia  Santa Isabel
Gizo  New  Buala
Munda  Georgia
New Georgia Islands  Yandina
Tambea  Malaita
HONIARA  Auki
Aola
**SOLOMON ISLANDS**
Duff Islands
Niulakita
3

Guadalcanal  Kirakira
Pocklington Reef
Bellona  San Cristobal
Rennell  Lavanggu
Lata  Nendö
Santa Cruz Islands  Utupua
Vanikolo
**WALLIS AND FUTUNA**
(French overseas territory)
Îles Wallis
MATĀ'UTU
4

Torres Islands
Vanua Lava  Banks Islands
Santa Maria
**VANUATU**
Espiritu Santo
Mount Tabwemasana 6,165ft  Ambae  Maéwo
Luganville  Pentecost
Norsup  Ambrym
Malekula  Epi
Shepherd Islands
Efate
PORT-VILA
Erromango
Tanna  Futuna
Aneityum
Rotuma
**FIJI**
Cikobia
Vanua Levu  Labasa
Taveuni
Yasawa Group  Koro
Mount Victoria 4,341ft  Koro Sea  Lamiti
Nadi  Viti Levu  Moala
SUVA
Kadavu Passage  Vunisea
Kadavu
Lau Group
5

**NEW CALEDONIA**
(French overseas territory)
Île de Sable
Îles Belep  Waala
Îles Chesterfield
Pouébo  Ouvéa
Koumac  Hienghène  Fayaoué
Koné  Wé
New Caledonia  Lifou
Thio  Maré
Bourail  Tadine
NOUMÉA
Îles Loyauté
Île des Pins
Vao
Tongatapu
**TONGA**
6

### LAND HEIGHT

- Above 13,120ft
- 6,560–13,120ft
- 3,280–6,560ft
- 1,640–3,280ft
- 820–1,640ft
- 330–820ft
- 0–330ft

### SEA DEPTH

- 0–820ft
- 820–1,640ft
- 1,640–3,280ft
- 3,280–6,560ft
- 6,560–9,840ft
- 9,840–13,120ft
- Below 13,120ft

### CITIES AND TOWNS

- ⊙ 100,000–500,000
- ◎ 50,000–100,000
- ○ Less than 50,000

### BORDERS

- indication of maritime country extent
- indication of maritime dependent territory extent

### SCALE BAR

0 km  100  200
0 miles  100  200

# ANTARCTICA

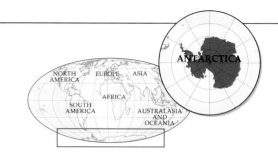

The continent of Antarctica has no permanent human population and very few animals can survive on the frozen land, although the surrounding waters teem with fish and mammals. Even in the summer, the temperature is rarely above freezing and the sea-ice only partly melts; in winter, temperatures plummet to –112°F. The only people who live in Antarctica are teams of scientists who study the wildlife and monitor the ice for changes in the Earth's atmosphere.

## THE LANDSCAPE

### Frozen seas
During the cold winter months, the water surrounding Antarctica freezes, almost doubling the size of the continent.

**Antarctica is the world's** most southerly continent. It is also the world's coldest continent and its highest, mainly due to the great ice sheet – up to 1.25 miles thick in parts – that lies over the mountains of the Antarctic Peninsula and the plateau of Greater Antarctica.

### Lambert Glacier (E4)
The Lambert Glacier is the world's largest series of glaciers. It is 50 miles wide at the coast and reaches more than 180 miles inland.

### Transantarctic Mountains (C5)
The Transantarctic Mountains run across the continent, splitting it into Greater and Lesser Antarctica.

### Ice sheet
A massive sheet of ice, about 15,700 ft thick at its deepest point, covers almost the entire area of Antarctica. It contains most of the freshwater on Earth. The weight of the ice pushes the land down below sea level.

### The Ross Ice Shelf (C5)
The Ross Sea is part of the Pacific Ocean. This deep bay is covered with a thick sheet of ice that floats on the ocean.

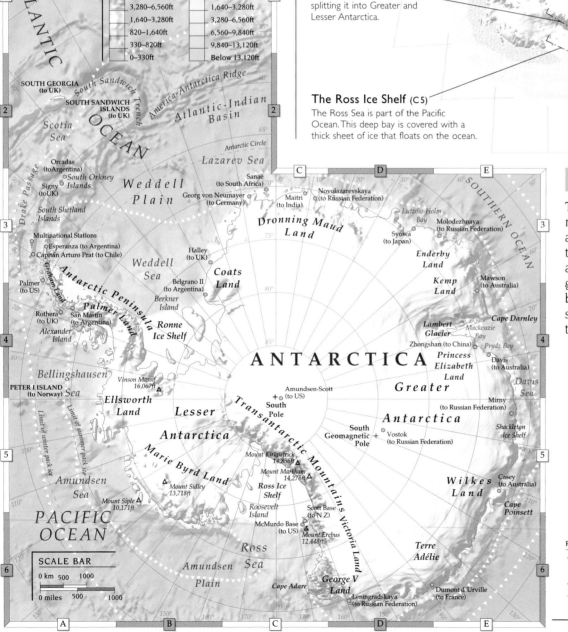

## RESOURCES

The mountains of Antarctica have rich mineral reserves. Gold, iron, and coal are found, and there is natural gas in the surrounding water. The unique and abundant marine wildlife is Antarctica's greatest resource. Colonies of penguins breed on the ice sheet, and whales, seals, and many bird and fish species thrive in the icy waters.

RESOURCES (including wildlife)

- Fish
- Penguins
- Seals
- Whales
- Coal
- Minerals
- Gas

# THE ARCTIC

THE ARCTIC

The ice-covered Arctic Ocean is encircled by the most northerly parts of Europe, North America, and Asia. Very few people live in the often-freezing conditions. Those who do, including the Sami of northern Scandinavia, the Siberian Yugyt and Nenet people, and the Canadian Inuit, were nomads who lived by hunting and herding. Some live like this today, but many have now settled in small towns.

## THE LANDSCAPE

The Arctic Ocean is the smallest ocean in the world, covering a total area of 5,440,000 sq miles. The ocean is divided into two large basins, divided by three great underwater mountain ranges including the Lomonosov Ridge which is more than 9,842 ft high on average.

### Lomonosov Ridge (C 4)

### Arctic islands (A 4)
In the far north of Canada, there are many thousands of islands including Baffin Island and Victoria Island. Many of them are almost entirely surrounded by pack ice.

### Pack ice
Much of the Arctic Ocean is permanently covered by pack ice. When the ice breaks up, it forms enormous floating ice masses called icebergs.

### Greenland (A 3)
Greenland is the world's largest island. It is covered by a huge ice sheet, more than 649,960 sq miles across. The weight of the ice has pushed most of the land below sea level.

### Sastrugi
Snow, blown by strong winds, can scratch deep patterns in the snow. These patterns are known as sastrugi and line up with the direction of the wind.

## RESOURCES

Coal, oil, and gas are found beneath the Arctic Ocean and in Canada, Alaska, and Russia. Fears about damage to the environment and the cost of extracting these resources have restricted the quantities removed. Overfishing has reduced fish stocks to very low levels. Quotas have been put in place to allow them to revive.

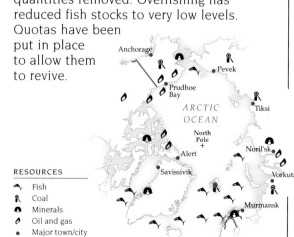

**RESOURCES**
- ↞ Fish
- ⚒ Coal
- ⬗ Minerals
- ◗ Oil and gas
- ● Major town/city

---

### Map

**SCALE BAR**
0 km  250  500
0 miles  250  500

**CITIES AND TOWNS**
- ◉ 100,000–500,000
- ○ Less than 50,000

**SEA DEPTH**
- 0–820ft
- 820–1,640ft
- 1,640–3,280ft
- 3,280–6,560ft
- 6,560–9,840ft
- 9,840–13,120ft
- Below 13,120ft

Anchorage

ALASKA (part of US)

NORTH AMERICA

Saint Lawrence Island
Bering Sea
Provideniya
Nome
Norton Sound
Bering Strait
Chukchi Sea
Pevek
Wrangel Island
Barrow
Prudhoe Bay
Inuvik
Tuktoyaktuk
Northwind Plain
Chukchi Plain
East Siberian Sea
RUSSIAN FEDERATION
ASIA
Beaufort Sea
Chukchi Plateau
Canada Basin
New Siberian Islands
Tiksi
Mendeleyev Ridge
Wrangel Plain
Laptev Sea
Victoria Island
ARCTIC
Alpha Cordillera
Makarov Basin
Lomonosov Ridge
North Pole
Fram Basin
Nansen Cordillera
Nansen Basin
Queen Elizabeth Islands
North Geomagnetic Pole
OCEAN
Khatanga
Severnaya Zemlya
CANADA
Lancaster Sound
Ellesmere Island
Alert
Lincoln Sea
Nares Strait
Pond Inlet
Knud Rasmussen Land
Savissivik
Kap Morris Jesup
Wandel Sea
Svyataya Anna Trough
Franz Josef Land
Ostrov Belyy
Kara Sea
Noril'sk
Dikson
East Novaya Zemlya Trough
Baffin Bay
Kong Frederik VIII Land
Novaya Zemlya
Vorkuta
GREENLAND (Danish external territory)
SVALBARD (to Norway)
Spitsbergen
Longyearbyen
Bjørnøya (part of Norway)
Ostrov Kotel'nyy
Cheshskaya Guba
Limit of winter pack ice
Daneborg
Greenland Sea
JAN MAYEN (to Norway)
Barents Sea
Arctic Circle
Sisimiut
Limit of summer pack ice
Gunnbjørn Fjeld 12,140ft△
Ammassalik
Denmark Strait
Iceland Plateau
North Cape
Norwegian Sea
Murmansk
Kola Peninsula
Archangel
White Sea
ATLANTIC OCEAN
NORWAY
SWEDEN
FINLAND
EUROPE

# GLOSSARY

This glossary defines certain geographical and technical terms used in this Atlas.

**Acid rain** Rain, sleet, snow or mist that has absorbed waste gases from fossil-fueled power stations and vehicle exhausts, becoming acidic and poisonous.

**Alluvium** Material deposited by a river, such as silt, sand, and mud

**Archipelago** A group, or chain, of islands.

**Atoll** A circular or horseshoe-shaped coral reef enclosing a shallow area of water (lagoon).

**Aquifer** A body of rock that can absorb water. It may be a source of water for wells or springs.

**Bar, coastal** An offshore strip of sand or shingle, either above or below the water.

**Biodiversity** The quantity of different animal or plant species in a given area.

**Birthrate** The number of live births per 1,000 individuals annually within a population.

**Cash crop** Agricultural produce grown for sale, often for foreign export, rather than to be consumed by the country or area where it was grown.

**Climate** The long term trends in weather conditions for an area.

**Coniferous forest** A type of forest containing trees or shrubs, like pines and firs, that have needles instead of leaves. They are found in temperate zones.

**Continental plates** The huge interlocking plates that make up the Earth's surface. A plate boundary is an area where two plates meet, and is the point at which earthquakes occur most frequently.

**Conurbation** A large urban area created by the merging of several towns.

**Coral reef** An underwater barrier created by colonies of coral polyps. The polyps secrete a protective skeleton of calcium carbonate, and reefs develop as live polyps build on the skeletons of dead generations.

**Core** The layers of liquid rock and solid iron at the center of the Earth.

**Crust** The hard, thin outer shell of the Earth. The crust floats on the mantle, which is softer, but more dense.

**Deciduous forest** A type of broadleaf forest found in temperate regions.

**Deforestation** Cutting down trees or forest for timber or farmland. It can lead to soil erosion, flooding, and landslides.

**Delta** A low-lying, fan-shaped area at a river mouth, formed by the deposition of successive layers of sediment. Slowing as it enters the sea, a river deposits sediment and may, as a result, split into many smaller channels called distributaries.

**Deposition** The laying down of material broken down by erosion or weathering and transported by the wind, water, or gravity.

**Desertification** The spread of desert conditions into a region that was not previously a desert.

**Drainage basin** The land drained by a river and its tributaries.

**Drought** A long period of continuously low rainfall.

**Earthquake** A trembling or shaking of the ground caused by the sudden movement of rocks in the Earth's crust – and sometimes deeper than the crust. Earthquakes occur most frequently along continental plate boundaries.

**Economy** The organization of a country's finances, exports, imports, industry, agriculture, and services.

**Ecosytem** A community of species dependent on each other and on the habitat in which they live.

**Equator** The 0° line of latitude. Equatorial climates are hot and there is plenty of rain.

**Erosion** The wearing down of the land surface by running water, waves, moving ice, wind, and weather.

**Estuary** The mouth of a river, where the saltwater from the sea meets the freshwater of the river.

**Fault** A crack or fracture in the Earth along which there has been movement of the rock masses relative to one another.

**Fjord** A coastal valley that was sculpted by glacial action.

**Flood plain** The broad, flat part of a river valley, next to the river itself, formed by sediment deposited during flooding.

**Geyser** A fountain of hot water or steam that erupts periodically as a result of underground streams coming into contact with hot rocks.

**GDP** Gross Domestic Product. The total value of goods and services produced by a country, excluding income from foreign countries.

**GIS** Geographic Information System. A computerized system for the collection, storage, and retrieval of geographic data.

**Glacier** A huge mass of ice made up of compacted and frozen snow, that moves slowly, eroding and depositing rock.

**Glaciation** The molding of the land by a glacier or ice sheet.

**GNP** Gross National Product. The total value of goods and services produced by a country.

**Groundwater** Water that has seeped into the pores, cavities, and cracks of rocks or into soil and water held in an aquifer or permeable rock.

**Gully** A deep, narrow chasm eroded in the landscape by a fast-flowing stream.

**Heavy industry** Industry that uses large amounts of energy and raw materials to produce heavy goods, such as machinery, ships, or locomotives.

**Humidity** The moisture content of the air.

**Hurricane** Violent tropical storms, also known as cyclones in the Indian Ocean and typhoons in the Pacific Ocean.

**Hydroelectric power** Energy produced by harnessing the rapid movement of water down steep mountain slopes to drive turbines to generate electricity.

**Ice Age** Periods of time in the past when much of the Earth's surface was covered by massive ice sheets. The most recent Ice Age began two million years ago and ended 10,000 years ago.

**Iceberg** A floating mass of ice that has broken off from a glacier or ice sheet.

**Ice sheet** A massive area of ice, thousands of feet thick.

**Irrigation** The artificial supply of water to dry areas – mainly for agricultural use. Water is carried or pumped to the area through pipes or ditches.

**Lagoon** A shallow stretch of coastal saltwater behind a partial barrier such as a sandbank or coral reef.

**Latitude** The distance north or south of the equator, measured in degrees, and shown on a globe as imaginary circles running around the Earth parallel to the equator.

**Lava** The molten rock, magma, that erupts onto the Earth's surface through a volcano, or through a fault or crack in the Earth's crust. Lava refers to the rock both in its liquid and its later, solidified form.

**Load** The material that is carried by a river or stream.

**Longitude** The distance, measured in degrees, east or west of the Prime Meridian.

**Limestone** A type of rock, formed by sediment, through which water can pass.

**Magma** Underground, molten rock, that is very hot and highly charged with gas. It originates in the Earth's lower crust or mantle.

**Mantle** The layer of the Earth's interior between the crust and the core. It is about 1,800 miles thick.

**Map projection** A mathematical formula that is used to show the curved surface of the Earth on a flat map.

**Market gardening** The intensive growing of fruit and vegetables close to large local markets.

**Meander** A looplike bend in a river. As a river nears the sea, it tends to wind more and more. The bigger the river and the shallower its slope, the more likely it is that meanders will form.

**Mediterranean climate** A temperate climate of hot, dry summers and warm, damp winters.

**Meltwater** Water that has melted from glaciers or ice sheets.

**Mestizo** A person of mixed native American and European origin.

**Mineral** A chemical compound that occurs naturally in the Earth.

**Monsoon** Winds that change direction according to the seasons. They are most common in South and East Asia, where they blow from the southwest in summer, bringing heavy rainfall, and the northeast in winter.

**Moraine** Sand and gravel that have been deposited by a glacier or ice sheet.

**Nomads (nomadic)** Wandering communities who move around in search of suitable pasture for their herds of animals.

**Oasis** A fertile area in a desert, usually watered by an underground aquifer.

**Pack ice** Ice masses more than 10 ft thick that form on the sea surface and are not attached to a landmass.

**Pacific Rim** The name given to the economically dynamic countries bordering the Pacific Ocean.

**Peat** Decomposed vegetation found in bogs. It can be dried and used as fuel.

**Per capita** A latin term meaning "for each person."

**Plantation** A large farm on which only one crop is usually grown, e.g. bananas or coffee.

**Plain** A flat, level region of land, often relatively low-lying.

**Plateau** A large area of high, flat land. When surrounded by steep slopes it is called a tableland.

**Peninsula** A thin strip of land surrounded on three of its sides by water. Large examples include Italy, Florida, and Korea.

**Permafrost** Permanently frozen ground, in which temperatures have remained below 32°F for more than two years.

**Precipitation** The fall of moisture from the atmosphere onto the surface of the Earth, as dew, hail, rain, sleet, or snow.

**Prairie** A Spanish-American term for grassy plains, with few or no trees.

**Prime Meridian** 0° longitude. Also known as the Greenwich Meridian because it runs through Greenwich in England.

**Rain forest** Dense forests in tropical zones with high rainfall, temperature and humidity.

**Rain shadow** An area downwind from high terrain that has little or no rainfall because it has fallen upon the high relief.

**Remote-sensing** A way of obtaining information about the environment by using unmanned equipment, such as a satellite, that relays the information to a point where it is collected.

**Ria** A flooded V-shaped river valley or estuary flooded by a rise in sea level or sinking land.

**Rift valley** A long, narrow depression in the Earth's crust, formed by the sinking of rocks between two faults.

**Savanna** Open grassland, where an annual dry season prevents the growth of most trees. They lie between the tropical rain forest and hot desert regions.

**Scale** The relationship between distance on a map and on the Earth's surface

**Sediment** Grains of rock transported and deposited by rivers, sea, ice, or wind.

**Semiarid** Areas between deserts and better-watered areas, where there is sufficient moisture to support a little more vegetation than in a true desert.

**Service industry** An industry that supplies services, such as banking, rather than producing manufactured goods.

**Shanty town** An area in or around a city where people live in temporary shacks, usually without basic facilities such as running water.

**Silt** Small particles, finer than sand, often carried by water and deposited on riverbanks, at river mouths, and harbors.

**Soil** A thin layer of rock particles mixed with the remains of dead organisms. Soil occurs naturally on the surface of the Earth and provides a medium for plants to grow.

**Soil erosion** The wearing away of soil more quickly than it is replaced by natural processes. Over-grazing and the clearing of land for farming, speeds up the process.

**Sorghum** A type of grass found in South America, similar to sugarcane.

**Spit** A narrow bank of pebbles or sand extending out from the seashore. Spits are made out of material transported along the coast by currents, wind, and waves.

**Staple crop** The main food crop grown in a region, for example, rice in Southeast Asia.

**Steppe** Large areas of dry grassland in the Northern Hemisphere – particularly found in southeast Europe and central Asia.

**Subsistence farming** A method of farming in which enough food is produced to feed farmers and their families but not providing any extra to generate an income.

**Taiga** A Russian name given to the belt of coniferous forest found in Russia, that borders tundra in the north and mixed forests and grasslands in the south.

**Temperate** The mild, variable climate found in areas between the tropics and cold polar regions.

**Terrace** Steps cut into steep slopes to create flat surfaces for cultivating crops.

**Tropics** An area between the equator and the Tropic of Cancer and Tropic of Capricorn that has heavy rainfall, high temperatures, and lacks any clear seasonal variation.

**Tundra** The land area lying in the very cold northern regions of Europe, Asia, and Canada, where winters are long and cold and the ground beneath the surface is permanently frozen.

**U-shaped valley** A river valley that has been deepened and widened by a glacier. They are flat-bottomed and steep-sided, and usually much deeper than river valleys.

**V-shaped valley** A typical valley eroded by a river in its upper course.

**Volcano** An opening or vent in the Earth's crust where magma erupts. Volcanos are caused by the movement of the Earth's plates. When the plates collide or spread apart, magma is forced to the surface, at or near the place where the plates meet.

**Watershed** The dividing line between one drainage basin and another.

# INDEX

**Armagnac** 73 C6 *Cultural region,* S France
**Armenia** 115 B2 W Colombia
**Armenia** 97 H2 ◆ *Republic,* SW Asia
**Armidale** 133 H5 NSW, SE Australia
**Armstrong** 35 B4 Ontario, S Canada
**Armyans'k** 85 F6 S Ukraine
**Arnedo** 75 E2 N Spain
**Arnhem** 68 E4 SE Netherlands
**Arnhem Land** 133 E1 *Physical region,* Northern Territory, N Australia
**Arno** 79 C3 ♒ C Italy
**Arnold** 53 C6 California, USA
**Arnold** 47 B5 Missouri, USA
**Arorae** 137 J1 *Atoll, Tungaru,* W Kiribati
**Arran, Isle of** 71 C5 *Island,* SW Scotland, UK
**Ar Raqqah** 97 B2 N Syria
**Arras** 73 D1 N France
**Arriaga** 57 G5 SE Mexico
**Ar Riyad** *see* Riyadh
**Ar Rub 'al Khali** 99 D6 *Desert,* SW Asia
**Ar Rustaq** 99 F4 N Oman
**Árta** 83 D5 W Greece
**Artashat** 97 H3 S Armenia
**Artemisa** 61 B2 W Cuba
**Artesia** 48 E2 New Mexico, USA
**Arthurs's Pass** 135 C6 *Pass,* South Island, NZ
**Artigas** 117 C5 N Uruguay
**Art'ik** 97 H2 W Armenia
**Artois** 73 D1 *Cultural region,* N France
**Artsyz** 85 D6 SW Ukraine
**Artvin** 97 G2 NE Turkey
**Arua** 127 C5 NW Uganda
**Aruba** 61 G7 *Dutch* ◇ S West Indies
**Aru, Kepulauan** 109 H7 *Island group,* E Indonesia
**Arunachal Pradesh** 107 F2 *Cultural region,* NE India
**Arusha** 127 D6 N Tanzania
**Arviat** 33 H5 Nunavut, C Canada
**Arvidsjaur** 67 D3 N Sweden
**Arys'** 94 C6 S Kazakhstan
**Asadabad** 101 G5 E Afghanistan
**Asahi-dake** 103 G1 ▲ N Japan
**Asahikawa** 103 F1 N Japan
**Asamankese** 124 E5 SE Ghana
**Asansol** 107 F4 NE India
**Ascension Island** 26 *Saint Helena* ◇, C Atlantic Ocean
**Ascoli Piceno** 79 D4 C Italy
**Aseb** 127 E3 SE Eritrea
**Ashburton** 135 C6 South Island, NZ
**Ashburton River** 133 B4 ♒ W Australia
**Ashdod** 99 G6 W Israel
**Asheville** 43 F3 North Carolina, USA
**Ashgabat** 101 C3 ● C Turkmenistan
**Ashland** 53 B4 Oregon, USA
**Ashland** 44 B2 Wisconsin, USA
**Ash Sharah** 99 H7 ▲ W Jordan
**Ash Shihr** 99 D7 SE Yemen
**Ashtabula** 44 F5 Ohio, USA
**Asia** 90 *Continent*
**Asinara** 79 A5 *Island,* W Italy
**Asipovichy** 85 D2 C Belarus
**Aşkale** 97 F3 NE Turkey
**Askersund** 67 C6 S Sweden
**Asmara** 127 D3 ● C Eritrea
**Aspermont** 48 F3 Texas, USA
**Assad, Lake** 97 E5 ⊠ N Syria
**Assam** 107 G3 *Cultural region,* NE India
**Assamakka** 124 E2 NW Niger
**As Samawah** 99 C3 S Iraq
**Assen** 68 F2 NE Netherlands
**Assenede** 68 B5 NW Belgium
**As Sulaymaniyah** 99 C2 NE Iraq
**As Sulayyil** 99 C5 S Saudi Arabia
**Astana** 94 C5 ● E Kazakhstan
**Asti** 79 B2 NW Italy
**Astorga** 75 C2 N Spain
**Astrakhan'** 87 B8 SW Russ. Fed.
**Asturias** 75 C1 *Cultural region,* NW Spain
**Astypálaia** 83 F6 *Island,* Cyclades, Greece
**Asunción** 117 C6 ● S Paraguay
**Aswan** 122 J4 SE Egypt
**Asyut** 122 I3 C Egypt
**Atacama Desert** 117 A3 *Desert,* N Chile
**Atâr** 124 B2 W Mauritania
**Atas Bogd** 105 D2 ▲ SW Mongolia
**Atascadero** 53 B8 California, USA
**Atatürk Baraji** 97 F4 ⊠ S Turkey
**Atbara** 127 C2 NE Sudan
**Atbara** 127 D2 ♒ Eritrea/Sudan
**Atbasar** 94 C5 N Kazakhstan
**Atchison** 47 E6 Kansas, USA
**Ath** 68 B7 SW Belgium
**Athabasca** 33 G6 Alberta, SW Canada
**Athabasca** 33 F6 ♒ Alberta, SW Canada
**Athabasca, Lake** 33 G5 ⊠ Alberta/Saskatchewan, SW Canada
**Athens** 83 E5 ● C Greece

**Athens** 43 F4 Georgia, USA
**Athens** 44 F7 Ohio, USA
**Athens** 48 H3 Texas, USA
**Athina** *see* Athens
**Athlone** 71 B6 C Ireland
**Ati** 124 H3 C Chad
**Atikokan** 35 A4 Ontario, S Canada
**Atka** 94 H3 E Russ. Fed.
**Atka** 54 B2 Atka Island, Alaska, USA
**Atlanta** 43 E4 Georgia, USA
**Atlanta** 48 I3 Texas, USA
**Atlantic** 43 I3 North Carolina, USA
**Atlantic City** 41 D6 New Jersey, USA
**Atlantic Ocean** 14 *Ocean*
**Atlas Mountains** 122 C2 ▲ NW Africa
**Atlasovo** 94 I3 E Russ. Fed.
**Atlin** 33 E5 British Columbia, W Canada
**Atrak** 101 B3 ♒ Iran/Turkmenistan
**At Ta'if** 99 B5 W Saudi Arabia
**Attawapiskat** 35 C3 Ontario, C Canada
**Attawapiskat** 35 C3 ♒ Ontario, S Canada
**Attu Island** 54 A1 *Island* Aleutian Islands, Alaska, USA
**Atyrau** 94 B4 W Kazakhstan
**Aubagne** 73 E7 SE France
**Aubange** 68 E9 SE Belgium
**Auburn** 41 D3 New York, USA
**Auburn** 53 B2 Washington, USA
**Auch** 73 C6 S France
**Auckland** 135 D2 North Island, NZ
**Audincourt** 73 F3 E France
**Augathella** 133 G4 Queensland, E Australia
**Augsburg** 77 C7 S Germany
**Augusta** 133 B6 W Australia
**Augusta** 43 F4 Georgia, USA
**Augusta** 41 G3 Maine, USA
**Augustów** 81 G2 NE Poland
**Auki** 137 F3 Malaita, N Solomon Islands
**Aunu'u Island** 55 *Island* W American Samoa
**Auob** 128 C6 ♒ Namibia/ South Africa
**Aurangabad** 107 D5 C India
**Auray** 73 B3 NW France
**Aurillac** 73 D5 C France
**Aurora** 51 F5 Colorado, USA
**Aurora** 44 C5 Illinois, USA
**Aurora** 47 E7 Missouri, USA
**Aus** 128 B6 SW Namibia
**Austin** 47 B4 Minnesota, USA
**Austin** 51 B5 Nevada, USA
**Austin** 48 G4 Texas, USA
**Australes, Îles** 131 *Island group,* SW French Polynesia
**Australia** 133 D3 ◆ *Commonwealth Republic*
**Australian Alps** 133 G6 ▲ SE Australia
**Australian Capital Territory** 133 G6 *Territory,* SE Australia
**Austria** 77 E8 ◆ *Republic,* C Europe
**Auvergne** 73 D5 *Cultural region,* C France
**Auxerre** 73 D3 C France
**Avarua** 131 ● Rarotonga, S Cook Islands
**Aveiro** 75 B3 W Portugal
**Avellino** 79 D6 S Italy
**Avesta** 67 C5 C Sweden
**Aveyron** 73 D6 ♒ S France
**Avezzano** 79 D5 C Italy
**Aviemore** 71 D3 N Scotland, UK
**Avignon** 73 E6 SE France
**Ávila** 75 D3 C Spain
**Avilés** 75 C1 N Spain
**Avranches** 73 B2 N France
**Awaji-shima** 103 E6 *Island,* SW Japan
**Awash** 127 E3 C Ethiopia
**Awbari** 122 F3 SW Libya
**Axel** 68 B6 SW Netherlands
**Axel Heiberg Island** 33 G1 *Island,* Nunavut, N Canada
**Ayacucho** 115 C6 S Peru
**Ayaguz** 94 D6 E Kazakhstan
**Ayamonte** 75 B5 S Spain
**Aydarkul** 101 F3 ⊡ C Uzbekistan
**Aydın** 97 A4 SW Turkey
**Ayorou** 124 E4 W Niger
**'Ayoûn el 'Atroûs** 124 B3 SE Mauritania
**Ayr** 71 C5 W Scotland, UK
**Aytos** 83 F3 E Bulgaria
**Ayvalık** 97 A3 W Turkey
**Azahar, Costa del** 75 F4 *Coastal region,* E Spain
**Azaouâd** 124 D2 *Desert,* C Mali
**Azerbaijan** 97 I2 ◆ *Republic,* SE Asia
**Azoum, Bahr** 124 H4 *Seasonal river,* SE Chad
**Azov** 94 A4 SW Russ. Fed.
**Azov, Sea of** 85 F6 *Sea,* NE Black Sea
**Aztec** 48 C1 New Mexico, USA
**Azuaga** 75 C4 W Spain

**Azuero, Península de** 59 G7 *Peninsula,* S Panama
**Azul** 117 C6 E Argentina
**Az Zarqa'** 99 A2 NW Jordan
**Az Zawiyah** 122 F2 NW Libya

# B

**Baardheere** 127 E5 SW Somalia
**Baarle-Hertog** 68 D5 N Belgium
**Baarn** 68 D4 C Netherlands
**Babayevo** 87 B4 NW Russ. Fed.
**Babeldaob** 109 H5 *Island,* N Palau
**Bab el Mandeb** 99 B7 *Strait,* Gulf of Aden/Red Sea
**Babruysk** 85 D3 E Belarus
**Bacabal** 115 G4 E Brazil
**Bacău** 85 C6 NE Romania
**Bacheykava** 85 D2 N Belarus
**Back** 33 G4 ♒ Nunavut, N Canada
**Badajoz** 75 B4 W Spain
**Baden-Baden** 77 B6 SW Germany
**Bad Freienwalde** 77 E7 NE Germany
**Badgastein** 77 D8 NW Austria
**Bad Hersfeld** 77 C5 C Germany
**Bad Homburg vor der Höhe** 77 B5 W Germany
**Bad Ischl** 77 E7 N Austria
**Bad Krozingen** 77 B7 SW Germany
**Badlands** 47 A4 *Physical region,* North Dakota, USA
**Badlands** 47 A2 *Physical region,* South Dakota, USA
**Badu Island** 133 F1 *Island,* Queensland, NE Australia
**Badwater Basin** 53 D7 *Depression,* California, USA
**Bafatá** 124 A4 C Guinea-Bissau
**Baffin Bay** 33 I2 *Bay,* Canada/Greenland
**Baffin Island** 33 I3 *Island,* Nunavut, NE Canada
**Bafing** 124 B4 ♒ W Africa
**Bafoussam** 124 F5 W Cameroon
**Bafra** 97 D2 N Turkey
**Bagaces** 59 E5 NW Costa Rica
**Bagé** 115 F9 S Brazil
**Baghdad** 99 C2 ● C Iraq
**Baghlan** 101 F4 NE Afghanistan
**Baghran** 101 E5 S Afghanistan
**Bagoé** 124 C4 ♒ Côte d'Ivoire/Mali
**Baguio** 109 F3 Luzon, N Philippines
**Bagzane, Monts** 124 F3 ▲ N Niger
**Bahamas** 61 D2 ◆ *Commonwealth Republic,* N West Indies
**Bahawalpur** 107 C2 E Pakistan
**Bahia** 115 G5 ◇ *State,* E Brazil
**Bahía Blanca** 117 B6 E Argentina
**Bahir Dar** 127 D3 NW Ethiopia
**Bahraich** 107 E3 N India
**Bahrain** 99 D4 ◆ *Monarchy,* SW Asia
**Bahushewsk** 85 D2 NE Belarus
**Baia Mare** 85 B5 NW Romania
**Baïbokoum** 124 G5 SW Chad
**Baie-Comeau** 35 F4 Quebec, SE Canada
**Baikal, Lake** 94 F5 ⊡ S Russ. Fed.
**Bailén** 75 D5 S Spain
**Ba Illi** 124 G4 SW Chad
**Bainbridge** 43 E6 Georgia, USA
**Bairiki** 137 ● Tarawa, NW Kiribati
**Bairnsdale** 133 G6 Victoria, SE Australia
**Baishan** 105 H2 NE China
**Baiyin** 105 E3 N China
**Baja** 81 E8 S Hungary
**Baja, Punta** 137 C6 *Headland,* Easter Island, Chile
**Bajram Curri** 83 D3 N Albania
**Bakala** 124 H5 C CAR
**Baker** 53 C3 Oregon, USA
**Baker & Howland Islands** 131 *US* ◇ C Pacific Ocean
**Baker Lake** 33 H4 Nunavut, N Canada
**Bakersfield** 53 C8 California, USA
**Bakharden** 101 C3 C Turkmenistan
**Bakhtaran** 99 C2 W Iran
**Baki** *see* Baku
**Bakony** 81 D8 ▲ W Hungary
**Baku** 97 J2 ● E Azerbaijan
**Balabac Strait** 109 E5 *Strait,* Malaysia/Philippines
**Balaguer** 75 G2 NE Spain
**Balaitous** 73 B7 ▲ France/Spain
**Balakovo** 87 C7 W Russ. Fed.
**Bala Morghab** 101 E4 NW Afghanistan
**Balashov** 87 B6 W Russ. Fed.
**Balaton, Lake** 81 D8 ⊡ Hungary
**Balbina, Represa** 115 E3 ⊠ NW Brazil
**Balboa** 59 H6 C Panama
**Balcarce** 117 C6 E Argentina
**Balclutha** 135 B8 South Island, NZ
**Baldy Mountain** 51 D1 ▲ Montana, USA
**Baldy Peak** 48 C3 ▲ Arizona, USA
**Baleares, Islas** *see* Balearic Islands
**Balearic Islands** 75 G4 *Island group,* Spain
**Baleine, Rivière à la** 35 E2 ♒ Quebec, E Canada
**Balen** 68 D6 N Belgium

**Baleshwar** 107 F4 E India
**Bali** 109 E8 *Island,* C Indonesia
**Balıkesir** 97 A3 W Turkey
**Balikpapan** 109 E7 C Indonesia
**Balkan Mountains** 83 E3 ▲ Bulgaria/Yugoslavia
**Balkh** 101 F4 N Afghanistan
**Balkhash** 94 C6 SE Kazakhstan
**Balkhash, Lake** 94 C6 ⊡ SE Kazakhstan
**Balladonia** 133 C5 W Australia
**Ballarat** 133 F7 Victoria, SE Australia
**Ballinger** 48 G4 Texas, USA
**Balsas** 115 G4 E Brazil
**Balsas, Río** 57 E5 ♒ S Mexico
**Bălţi** 85 D5 N Moldova
**Baltic Sea** 67 D7 *Sea,* N Europe
**Baltimore** 41 A5 Maryland, USA
**Baluchistan** 107 A3 *Cultural region,* SW Pakistan
**Balykchy** 101 H2 NE Kyrgyzstan
**Bam** 99 F3 SE Iran
**Bamako** 124 C4 ● SW Mali
**Bambari** 124 H5 C CAR
**Bamberg** 77 C5 SE Germany
**Bamenda** 124 F5 W Cameroon
**Banaba** 137 H1 *Island,* W Kiribati
**Bananga** 107 H6 Nicobar Islands, India
**Bandaaceh** 109 A5 Sumatra, W Indonesia
**Bandama** 124 C5 ♒ S Côte d'Ivoire
**Bandarbeyla** 127 G3 NE Somalia
**Bandar-e 'Abbas** 99 E4 S Iran
**Bandarlampung** 109 B7 Sumatra, W Indonesia
**Bandar Seri Begawan** 109 D5 ● N Brunei
**Banda Sea** 109 G7 *Sea,* E Indonesia
**Bandırma** 97 A2 NW Turkey
**Bandundu** 128 B2 W Dem. Rep. Congo (Zaire)
**Bandung** 109 C8 Java, C Indonesia
**Bangalore** 107 D6 S India
**Bangassou** 124 I5 SE CAR
**Banggai, Kepulauan** 109 F6 *Island group,* C Indonesia
**Banghazi** *see* Benghazi
**Bangka, Pulau** 109 C7 *Island,* W Indonesia
**Bangkok** 109 B4 ● C Thailand
**Bangladesh** 107 G3 ◆ *Republic,* S Asia
**Bangor** 71 C5 E Northern Ireland, UK
**Bangor** 71 D6 NW Wales, UK
**Bangor** 41 G2 Maine, USA
**Bangui** 124 H5 ● SW CAR
**Bangweulu, Lake** 128 D3 ⊡ N Zambia
**Bani** 124 C4 ♒ S Mali
**Banja Luka** 83 C2 NW Bosnia and Herzegovina
**Banjarmasin** 109 C4 NW Cambodia
**Banjul** 124 A3 ● W Gambia
**Banks Island** 33 F3 *Island,* NW Terr., NW Canada
**Banks Islands** 137 G4 *Island group,* N Vanuatu
**Banks Lake** 53 C2 ⊡ Washington, USA
**Banks Peninsula** 135 C6 *Peninsula,* South Island, NZ
**Banks Strait** 133 G7 *Strait,* SW Tasman Sea
**Bankura** 107 F4 NE India
**Banmauk** 109 A2 N Myanmar
**Ban Nadou** 109 C3 S Laos
**Banská Bystrica** 81 E6 C Slovakia
**Bantry Bay** 71 A7 *Bay,* SW Ireland
**Banyak, Kepulauan** 109 A6 *Island group,* NW Indonesia
**Banyo** 124 F5 NW Cameroon
**Banyoles** 75 H2 NE Spain
**Baoji** 105 E4 C China
**Baoro** 124 G5 W CAR
**Baoshan** 105 D6 SW China
**Baotou** 105 F3 N China
**Ba'qubah** 99 C2 C Iraq
**Baraawe** 127 E5 S Somalia
**Baranavichy** 85 C3 SW Belarus
**Barbados** 61 K6 ◆ *Commonwealth Republic,* SE West Indies
**Barbastro** 75 F2 NE Spain
**Barbate de Franco** 75 C6 S Spain
**Barbuda** 61 J4 *Island,* N Antigua and Barbuda
**Barcaldine** 133 G3 Queensland, E Australia
**Barcelona** 75 G2 E Spain
**Barcelona** 115 D1 NE Venezuela
**Barcs** 81 D9 SW Hungary
**Bardaï** 124 G2 N Chad
**Bardejov** 81 F6 NE Slovakia
**Bareilly** 107 E3 N India
**Barendrecht** 68 C4 SW Netherlands
**Barentin** 73 C2 N France
**Barents Sea** 87 C2 *Sea,* Arctic Ocean
**Bar Harbor** 41 G2 Mount Desert Island, Maine, USA
**Bari** 79 E6 SE Italy
**Barikowt** 101 G4 NE Afghanistan
**Barillas** 59 A2 NW Guatemala
**Barinas** 115 C2 W Venezuela
**Barisal** 107 G4 S Bangladesh
**Barisan, Pegunungan** 109 B7 ▲ Sumatra, W Indonesia
**Barito, Sungai** 109 E7 ♒ Borneo, C Indonesia
**Barkly Tableland** 133 E2 *Plateau,* Northern Territory/Queensland, N Australia

**Bârlad** 85 C6 E Romania
**Bar-le-Duc** 73 E2 NE France
**Barlee, Lake** 133 B5 ⊡ W Australia
**Barlee Range** 133 B4 ▲ W Australia
**Barletta** 79 E5 SE Italy
**Barlinek** 81 C3 W Poland
**Barmouth** 71 D7 NW Wales, UK
**Barnaul** 94 D5 C Russ. Fed.
**Barnstaple** 71 D8 SW England, UK
**Baroghil Pass** 101 G4 *Pass,* Afghanistan/Pakistan
**Barquisimeto** 115 C1 NW Venezuela
**Barra de Río Grande** 59 E4 E Nicaragua
**Barranca** 115 B5 W Peru
**Barrancabermeja** 115 B2 N Colombia
**Barranquilla** 115 B1 N Colombia
**Barreiro** 75 A4 W Portugal
**Barrier Range** 133 F5 *Hill range,* NSW, SE Australia
**Barrier Reef** 59 C1 *Reef,* E Belize
**Barrow** 54 E1 Alaska, USA
**Barrow** 71 B7 ♒ S Ireland
**Barrow-in-Furness** 71 D6 NW England, UK
**Barrow Island** 133 A3 *Island,* W Australia
**Barstow** 53 D8 California, USA
**Bartang** 101 G4 ♒ SE Tajikistan
**Bartın** 97 C2 N Turkey
**Bartlesville** 47 D7 Oklahoma, USA
**Bartoszyce** 81 E2 N Poland
**Baruun-Urt** 105 F2 E Mongolia
**Barú, Volcán** 59 F6 ▲ W Panama
**Barva, Volcán** 59 E6 ♒ NW Costa Rica
**Barwon River** 133 G5 ♒ NSW, SE Australia
**Barysaw** 85 D2 NE Belarus
**Basarabeasca** 85 D6 SE Moldova
**Basel** 77 B7 NW Switzerland
**Basilan** 109 F5 *Island,* SW Philippines
**Basingstoke** 71 E8 S England, UK
**Basque Country, The** 75 E1 *Cultural region,* N Spain
**Basra** 99 D3 SE Iraq
**Bassano del Grappa** 79 C2 NE Italy
**Bassein** 109 A3 SW Myanmar
**Basse-Terre** 61 J5 ○ Basse Terre, SW Guadeloupe
**Basseterre** 61 J4 ● Saint Kitts, Saint Kitts and Nevis
**Bassett** 47 C4 Nebraska, USA
**Bassikounou** 124 C3 SE Mauritania
**Bass Strait** 133 F7 *Strait,* SE Australia
**Bassum** 77 B3 NW Germany
**Bastia** 73 G5 Corsica, France
**Bastogne** 68 E8 SE Belgium
**Bata** 124 F6 NW Equatorial Guinea
**Batangas** 109 F4 Luzon, N Philippines
**Batdambang** 109 C4 NW Cambodia
**Batéké, Plateaux** 128 B2 *Plateau,* S Congo
**Bath** 71 D8 SW England, UK
**Bath** 41 G3 Maine, USA
**Bathinda** 107 D2 NW India
**Bathurst** 133 G5 NSW, SE Australia
**Bathurst** 35 F4 New Brunswick, SE Canada
**Bathurst Island** 133 C1 *Island,* Northern Territory, N Australia
**Bathurst Island** 33 H2 *Island,* Parry Islands, Nunavut, N Canada
**Batin, Wadi al** 99 C3 *Dry watercourse,* SW Asia
**Batman** 97 G4 SE Turkey
**Batna** 122 E1 NE Algeria
**Baton Rouge** 43 C6 Louisiana, USA
**Batticaloa** 107 E8 E Sri Lanka
**Battipaglia** 79 D6 S Italy
**Battle Mountain** 51 B5 Nevada, USA
**Bat'umi** 97 G2 W Georgia
**Batu Pahat** 109 C6 Peninsular Malaysia
**Bauchi** 124 F4 NE Nigeria
**Bautzen** 77 E4 E Germany
**Bavaria** 77 C7 *Cultural region,* SE Germany
**Bavarian Alps** 77 C7 ▲ Austria/Germany
**Bavispe, Río** 57 C2 ♒ NW Mexico
**Bawiti** 122 I3 N Egypt
**Bawku** 124 D4 N Ghana
**Bayamo** 61 D3 E Cuba
**Bayamón** 55 E Puerto Rico
**Bayan Har Shan** 105 D4 ▲ C China
**Bayanhongor** 105 D2 C Mongolia
**Bayano, Lago** 59 H6 ⊡ E Panama
**Bayard** 48 C3 New Mexico, USA
**Bay City** 44 E4 Michigan, USA
**Bay City** 48 H5 Texas, USA
**Baydhabo** 127 E5 SW Somalia
**Baydaratskaya** *?*
**Bayern** *see* Bavaria
**Bayeux** 73 C2 N France
**Bay Islands** 59 D2 *Island group,* N Honduras
**Baymak** 87 D7 W Russ. Fed.
**Bayonne** 73 B6 SW France
**Bayramaly** 101 D4 S Turkmenistan
**Bayreuth** 77 C5 SE Germany
**Baytown** 48 I4 Texas, USA
**Baza** 75 E5 S Spain
**Beacon** 41 E4 New York, USA
**Beagle Channel** 117 B9 *Channel,* Argentina/Chile
**Bear Lake** 51 D4 ⊡ NW USA
**Beas de Segura** 75 E5 S Spain
**Beata, Isla** 61 F5 *Island,* SW Dominican Republic

**Beatrice** 47 D5 Nebraska, USA
**Beatty** 51 B6 Nevada, USA
**Beaufort Sea** 54 F1 *Sea* Arctic Ocean
**Beaufort West** 128 C7 SW South Africa
**Beaumont** 48 I4 Texas, USA
**Beaune** 73 E4 C France
**Beauvais** 73 D2 N France
**Beaver Falls** 41 A5 Pennsylvania, USA
**Beaver Island** 44 C3 *Island,* Michigan, USA
**Beaver River** 47 B7 ♒ Oklahoma, USA
**Beaverton** 53 B3 Oregon, USA
**Beawar** 107 D3 N India
**Béchar** 122 D2 W Algeria
**Beckley** 43 G2 West Virginia, USA
**Bedford** 71 E7 E England, UK
**Bedford** 44 D7 Indiana, USA
**Bedum** 68 F2 NE Netherlands
**Be'er Menuha** 99 H7 S Israel
**Beernem** 68 B6 NW Belgium
**Be'er Sheva'** 99 G6 S Israel
**Beesel** 68 E6 SE Netherlands
**Beeville** 48 G5 Texas, USA
**Bega** 133 G6 NSW, SE Australia
**Beihai** 105 F6 S China
**Beijing** 105 F3 ● E China
**Beilen** 68 E3 NE Netherlands
**Beira** 128 E5 C Mozambique
**Beirut** 99 A2 ● W Lebanon
**Beja** 75 B5 SE Portugal
**Béjar** 75 C3 W Spain
**Békéscsaba** 81 F8 SE Hungary
**Bekobod** 101 F3 E Uzbekistan
**Belarus** 85 C2 ◆ *Republic,* E Europe
**Bełchatów** 81 E4 C Poland
**Belcher Islands** 35 C2 *Island group,* Nunavut, SE Canada
**Beledweyne** 127 F4 C Somalia
**Belém** 115 G3 N Brazil
**Belén** 59 B2 SW Nicaragua
**Belen** 48 C2 New Mexico, USA
**Belep, Îles** 137 F6 *Island group,* W New Caledonia
**Belfast** 71 C5 *Political division capital,* E Northern Ireland, UK
**Belfield** 47 A2 North Dakota, USA
**Belfort** 73 F3 E France
**Belgaum** 107 D6 W India
**Belgium** 68 B7 ◆ *Monarchy,* NW Europe
**Belgorod** 87 A6 W Russ. Fed.
**Belgrade** 83 D2 ● N Yugoslavia
**Belgrano II** 138 B4 *Argentinian research station,* Antarctica
**Belitung, Pulau** 109 C7 *Island,* W Indonesia
**Belize** 59 B2 ◆ *Commonwealth Republic,* Central America
**Belize** 59 B2 ♒ Belize/Guatemala
**Belize City** 59 C1 NE Belize
**Belkofski** 54 C3 Alaska, USA
**Belle Île** 73 A4 *Island,* NW France
**Belle Isle, Strait of** 35 G2 *Strait,* Newfoundland, E Canada
**Belleville** 44 B7 Illinois, USA
**Bellevue** 47 D5 Nebraska, USA
**Bellevue** 53 B2 Washington, USA
**Bellingham** 53 B1 Washington, USA
**Bellingshausen Sea** 138 A4 *Sea,* Antarctica
**Bellinzona** 77 B8 S Switzerland
**Bello** 115 B2 W Colombia
**Bellona** 137 E3 *Island,* S Solomon Islands
**Bellville** 128 C7 SW South Africa
**Belmopan** 59 B2 ● C Belize
**Belo Horizonte** 115 G7 SE Brazil
**Belomorsk** 87 B3 NW Russ. Fed.
**Beloretsk** 87 D6 W Russ. Fed.
**Belorussia** *see* Belarus
**Belozersk** 87 B4 NW Russ. Fed.
**Belton** 48 H4 Texas, USA
**Belukha, Gora** 94 D5 ▲ Kazakhstan/Russ. Fed.
**Belyy, Ostrov** 94 D2 *Island,* N Russ. Fed.
**Bemaraha** 128 G5 ▲ W Madagascar
**Bemidji** 47 E2 Minnesota, USA
**Bemmel** 68 E4 SE Netherlands
**Benavente** 75 C2 N Spain
**Bend** 53 B4 Oregon, USA
**Bendigo** 133 F6 Victoria, SE Australia
**Benešov** 81 B5 N Czech Republic
**Benevento** 79 D6 S Italy
**Bengbu** 105 G4 E China
**Benghazi** 122 G2 NE Libya
**Bengkulu** 109 B7 Sumatra, W Indonesia
**Benguela** 128 B4 W Angola
**Ben Hope** 71 I3 ▲ N Scotland, UK
**Beni** 128 D1 NE Dem. Rep. Congo (Zaire)
**Benidorm** 75 F4 SE Spain
**Beni-Mellal** 122 C2 C Morocco
**Benin** 124 D4 ◆ *Republic,* W Africa
**Benin, Bight of** 124 E5 *Gulf,* W Africa
**Beni, Río** 117 A2 N Bolivia
**Benin City** 124 E5 SW Nigeria
**Beni Suef** 122 I3 N Egypt
**Ben Nevis** 71 C4 ▲ N Scotland, UK
**Benson** 48 C3 Arizona, USA
**Benton** 43 B4 Arkansas, USA
**Benton Harbor** 44 D7 Michigan, USA
**Benue** 124 F5 ♒ Cameroon/Nigeria
**Beograd** *see* Belgrade
**Berat** 83 D4 C Albania
**Berau, Teluk** 109 H7 *Bay,* E Indonesia

# INDEX

◆ Administrative region　● Country　● Country capital　◇ Dependent territory　○ Dependent territory capital　▲ Mountain range　▲ Mountain　☒ Volcano　⚲ River　⚲ Lake　☒ Reservoir

141

**Armagnac** 73 C6 *Cultural region,* S France
**Armenia** 115 B2 W Colombia
**Armenia** 97 H2 ◆ *Republic,* SW Asia
**Armidale** 133 H5 NSW, SE Australia
**Armstrong** 35 B4 Ontario, S Canada
**Armyans'k** 85 F6 S Ukraine
**Arnedo** 75 E2 N Spain
**Arnhem** 68 E4 SE Netherlands
**Arnhem Land** 133 E1 *Physical region,* Northern Territory, N Australia
**Arno** 79 C3 ↝ C Italy
**Arnold** 53 C6 California, USA
**Arnold** 47 G6 Missouri, USA
**Arorae** 137 J1 *Atoll,* Tungaru, W Kiribati
**Arran, Isle of** 71 C5 *Island,* SW Scotland, UK
**Ar Raqqah** 99 B2 N Syria
**Arras** 73 D1 N France
**Arriaga** 57 G5 SE Mexico
**Ar Riyad** *see* Riyadh
**Ar Rub 'al Khali** 99 D6 *Desert,* SW Asia
**Ar Rustaq** 99 F4 N Oman
**Árta** 83 D5 W Greece
**Artashat** 97 H3 S Armenia
**Artemisa** 61 B2 W Cuba
**Artesia** 48 E3 New Mexico, USA
**Arthurs's Pass** 135 C6 *Pass,* South Island, NZ
**Artigas** 117 C5 N Uruguay
**Art'ik** 97 H2 W Armenia
**Artois** 73 D1 *Cultural region,* N France
**Artsyz** 85 D6 SW Ukraine
**Artvin** 97 G2 NE Turkey
**Arua** 127 C5 NW Uganda
**Aruba** 61 G7 *Dutch* ◊ S West Indies
**Aru, Kepulauan** 109 H7 *Island group,* E Indonesia
**Arunachal Pradesh** 107 F2 *Cultural region,* NE India
**Arusha** 127 D6 N Tanzania
**Arviat** 33 H5 Nunavut, C Canada
**Arvidsjaur** 67 D3 N Sweden
**Arys'** 94 C6 S Kazakhstan
**Asadabad** 101 G5 E Afghanistan
**Asahi-dake** 103 G1 ▲ N Japan
**Asahikawa** 103 F1 N Japan
**Asamankese** 124 D5 SE Ghana
**Asansol** 107 F4 NE India
**Ascension Island** 26 *Saint Helena* ◊, C Atlantic Ocean
**Ascoli Piceno** 79 D4 C Italy
**Aseb** 127 E3 SE Eritrea
**Ashburton** 135 C6 South Island, NZ
**Ashburton River** 133 B4 ↝ W Australia
**Ashdod** 99 G6 W Israel
**Asheville** 43 F3 North Carolina, USA
**Ashgabat** 101 C3 ● C Turkmenistan
**Ashland** 53 B4 Oregon, USA
**Ashland** 44 B2 Wisconsin, USA
**Ash Sharah** 99 H7 ▲ W Jordan
**Ash Shihr** 99 D7 SE Yemen
**Ashtabula** 44 F5 Ohio, USA
**Asia** 90 *Continent*
**Asinara** 79 A5 *Island,* W Italy
**Asipovichy** 85 D2 C Belarus
**Aşkale** 97 F3 NE Turkey
**Askersund** 67 C6 S Sweden
**Asmar** 101 G5 E Afghanistan
**Asmara** 127 D2 ● C Eritrea
**Aspermont** 48 F3 Texas, USA
**Assad, Lake** 97 E5 S Syria
**Assam** 107 G3 *Cultural region,* NE India
**Assamakka** 124 E2 NW Niger
**As Samawah** 99 C3 S Iraq
**Assen** 68 E2 NE Netherlands
**Assenede** 68 B6 NW Belgium
**As Sulaymaniyah** 99 C2 NE Iraq
**As Sulayyil** 99 C5 S Saudi Arabia
**Astana** 94 C5 ● E Kazakhstan
**Asti** 79 B2 NW Italy
**Astorga** 75 C5 N Spain
**Astrakhan'** 87 B8 SW Russ. Fed.
**Astypálaia** 83 F6 *Island,* Cyclades, Greece
**Asunción** 117 C4 ● S Paraguay
**Aswan** 122 J4 SE Egypt
**Asyut** 122 I3 C Egypt
**Atacama Desert** 117 A3 *Desert,* N Chile
**Atâr** 124 B2 W Mauritania
**Atas Bogd** 105 D2 ▲ SW Mongolia
**Atascadero** 53 B8 California, USA
**Atatürk Baraji** 97 F4 ⊞ S Turkey
**Atbara** 127 C2 NE Sudan
**Atbara** 127 D2 ↝ Eritrea/Sudan
**Atbasar** 94 C5 N Kazakhstan
**Atchison** 47 E6 Kansas, USA
**Ath** 68 B7 SW Belgium
**Athabasca** 33 G6 Alberta, SW Canada
**Athabasca** 33 F6 ↝ Alberta, SW Canada
**Athabasca, Lake** 33 G5 ⊜ Alberta/Saskatchewan, SW Canada
**Athens** 83 E5 ● C Greece

**Athens** 43 F4 Georgia, USA
**Athens** 41 F7 Ohio, USA
**Athens** 48 H3 Texas, USA
**Atherton** 133 G2 Queensland, NE Australia
**Athina** *see* Athens
**Athlone** 71 B6 C Ireland
**Ati** 124 H3 C Chad
**Atikokan** 35 A4 Ontario, S Canada
**Atka** 94 H3 E Russ. Fed.
**Atka** 54 B2 Atka Island, Alaska, USA
**Atlanta** 43 E4 Georgia, USA
**Atlanta** 48 I3 Texas, USA
**Atlantic** 43 I3 North Carolina, USA
**Atlantic City** 41 D6 New Jersey, USA
**Atlantic Ocean** 14 *Ocean*
**Atlas Mountains** 122 C2 ▲ NW Africa
**Atlasovo** 94 I3 E Russ. Fed.
**Atlin** 33 E5 British Columbia, W Canada
**Atrak** 101 B3 ↝ Iran/Turkmenistan
**At Ta'if** 99 B5 W Saudi Arabia
**Attawapiskat** 35 C3 Ontario, C Canada
**Attawapiskat** 35 C3 ↝ Ontario, S Canada
**Attu Island** 54 A1 *Island* Aleutian Islands, Alaska, USA
**Atyrau** 94 B4 W Kazakhstan
**Aubagne** 73 E7 SE France
**Aubange** 68 E9 SE Belgium
**Auburn** 41 D3 New York, USA
**Auburn** 53 B2 Washington, USA
**Auch** 73 C6 S France
**Auckland** 135 D2 North Island, NZ
**Audincourt** 73 F3 E France
**Augathella** 133 G4 Queensland, E Australia
**Augsburg** 77 C7 S Germany
**Augusta** 133 B6 W Australia
**Augusta** 43 F4 Georgia, USA
**Augusta** 41 G3 Maine, USA
**Augustów** 81 G2 NE Poland
**Auki** 137 F3 Malaita, N Solomon Islands
**Aunu'u Island** 55 *Island* W American Samoa
**Auob** 128 C6 ↝ Namibia/ South Africa
**Aurangabad** 107 D5 C India
**Auray** 73 B3 NW France
**Aurès, Massif de l'** 88 D4 ▲ NE Algeria
**Aurillac** 73 D5 C France
**Aurora** 51 F5 Colorado, USA
**Aurora** 44 C5 Illinois, USA
**Aurora** 47 E7 Missouri, USA
**Aus** 128 B6 SW Namibia
**Austin** 47 E4 Minnesota, USA
**Austin** 51 B5 Nevada, USA
**Austin** 48 G4 Texas, USA
**Australes, Îles** 131 *Island group,* SW French Polynesia
**Australia** 133 ◆ *Commonwealth Republic*
**Australian Alps** 133 G6 ▲ SE Australia
**Australian Capital Territory** 133 G6 *Territory,* SE Australia
**Austria** 77 E8 ◆ *Republic,* C Europe
**Auvergne** 73 D5 *Cultural region,* C France
**Auxerre** 73 D3 C France
**Avarua** 131 ○ Rarotonga, S Cook Islands
**Aveiro** 75 B3 W Portugal
**Avellino** 79 D6 S Italy
**Avesta** 67 C5 C Sweden
**Aveyron** 73 C6 ↝ S France
**Avezzano** 79 D5 C Italy
**Aviemore** 71 D3 N Scotland, UK
**Avignon** 73 E6 SE France
**Ávila** 75 D3 C Spain
**Avilés** 75 C1 NW Spain
**Avranches** 73 B2 N France
**Awaji-shima** 103 E6 *Island,* SW Japan
**Awash** 127 E3 C Ethiopia
**Awbari** 122 F3 SW Libya
**Axel** 68 B6 SW Netherlands
**Axel Heiberg Island** 33 G1 *Island,* Nunavut, N Canada
**Ayacucho** 115 D5 S Peru
**Ayamonte** 75 B5 S Spain
**Ayaguz** 94 D6 E Kazakhstan
**Aydarkul** 101 F3 ◊ C Uzbekistan
**Aydın** 97 A4 SW Turkey
**Ayers Rock** *see* Uluru
**Ayorou** 124 D3 W Niger
**'Ayoûn el 'Atroûs** 124 B3 SE Mauritania
**Ayr** 71 C5 W Scotland, UK
**Aytos** 83 F3 E Bulgaria
**Ayvalık** 97 A3 W Turkey
**Azahar, Costa del** 75 F4 *Coastal region,* E Spain
**Azaouâd** 124 D2 *Desert,* C Mali
**Azerbaijan** 97 I2 ◆ *Republic,* SE Asia
**Azoum, Bahr** 124 H4 *Seasonal river,* SE Chad
**Azov** 94 A4 SW Russ. Fed.
**Azov, Sea of** 85 F6 *Sea,* NE Black Sea
**Aztec** 48 C1 New Mexico, USA
**Azuaga** 75 C5 W Spain

**Azuero, Península de** 59 G7 *Peninsula,* S Panama
**Azul** 117 C6 E Argentina
**Az Zarqa'** 99 A2 NW Jordan
**Az Zawiyah** 122 F2 NW Libya

# B

**Baardheere** 127 E5 SW Somalia
**Baarle-Hertog** 68 D5 N Belgium
**Baarn** 68 D4 C Netherlands
**Babeldaob** 109 H5 *Island,* N Palau
**Babayevo** 87 B4 NW Russ. Fed.
**Bab el Mandeb** 99 B7 *Strait,* Gulf of Aden/Red Sea
**Babruysk** 85 D3 E Belarus
**Babuyan Channel** 109 F3 *Channel,* N Philippines
**Babuyan Island** 109 F3 *Island,* N Philippines
**Bacabal** 115 G4 E Brazil
**Bacău** 85 C6 NE Romania
**Bacheykava** 85 D2 N Belarus
**Back** 33 G4 ↝ Nunavut, N Canada
**Badajoz** 75 B4 W Spain
**Baden-Baden** 77 B6 SW Germany
**Bad Freienwalde** 77 E3 NE Germany
**Badgastein** 77 D8 NW Austria
**Bad Hersfeld** 77 C5 C Germany
**Bad Homburg vor der Höhe** 77 B5 W Germany
**Bad Ischl** 77 E7 N Austria
**Bad Krozingen** 77 B7 SW Germany
**Badlands** 47 A5 *Physical region,* North Dakota, USA
**Badlands** 47 A2 *Physical region,* South Dakota, USA
**Badu Island** 133 F1 *Island,* Queensland, NE Australia
**Bad Vöslau** 77 F7 NE Austria
**Badwater Basin** 53 D7 *Depression,* California, USA
**Bafatá** 124 A4 C Guinea-Bissau
**Baffin Bay** 33 I2 *Bay,* Canada/Greenland
**Baffin Island** 33 I3 *Island,* Nunavut, NE Canada
**Bafing** 124 B4 ↝ W Africa
**Bafoussam** 124 F5 W Cameroon
**Bafra** 97 D2 N Turkey
**Bagaces** 59 E5 NW Costa Rica
**Bagé** 115 F9 S Brazil
**Baghdad** 99 C2 ● C Iraq
**Baghlan** 101 E5 N Afghanistan
**Baghran** 101 E5 S Afghanistan
**Bagoé** 124 C4 ↝ Côte d'Ivoire/Mali
**Baguio** 109 F3 Luzon, N Philippines
**Bagzane, Monts** 124 F3 ▲ N Niger
**Bahamas** 61 C2 ◆ *Commonwealth Republic,* N West Indies
**Bahawalpur** 107 C2 E Pakistan
**Bahia** 115 G5 ◆ *State,* E Brazil
**Bahía Blanca** 117 B6 E Argentina
**Bahir Dar** 127 D3 NW Ethiopia
**Bahraich** 107 E3 N India
**Bahrain** 99 D4 ◆ *Monarchy,* SW Asia
**Bahushewsk** 85 D2 NE Belarus
**Baia Mare** 85 B5 NW Romania
**Baïbokoum** 124 G5 SW Chad
**Baie-Comeau** 35 F4 Quebec, SE Canada
**Baikal, Lake** 94 F5 ⊜ S Russ. Fed.
**Bailén** 75 D5 S Spain
**Ba Illi** 124 G4 SW Chad
**Bainbridge** 43 E6 Georgia, USA
**Bairiki** 131 ● Tarawa, NW Kiribati
**Bairnsdale** 133 G6 Victoria, SE Australia
**Baishan** 105 H2 NE China
**Baiyin** 105 E3 N China
**Baja** 81 E8 S Hungary
**Baja, Punta** 137 C6 *Headland,* Easter Island, Chile
**Bajram Curri** 83 D3 N Albania
**Bakala** 124 H5 C CAR
**Baker** 53 C3 Oregon, USA
**Bakersfield** 53 C8 California, USA
**Bakharden** 101 C3 C Turkmenistan
**Bakhtaran** 99 C2 W Iran
**Baki** *see* Baku
**Bakony** 81 D8 ▲ W Hungary
**Baku** 97 J2 ● E Azerbaijan
**Balabac Strait** 109 E5 *Strait,* Malaysia/Philippines
**Balaguer** 75 E2 NE Spain
**Balaitous** 73 B7 ▲ France/Spain
**Balakovo** 87 C7 W Russ. Fed.
**Bala Morghab** 101 E4 NW Afghanistan
**Balashov** 87 B6 W Russ. Fed.
**Balaton, Lake** 81 D8 ⊜ Hungary
**Balbina, Represa** 115 E3 ⊞ NW Brazil
**Balboa** 59 H6 C Panama
**Balcarce** 117 C6 E Argentina
**Balclutha** 135 B8 South Island, NZ
**Baldy Mountain** 51 D1 ▲ Montana, USA
**Baldy Peak** 48 C3 ▲ Arizona, USA
**Baleares, Islas** *see* Balearic Islands
**Balearic Islands** 75 G4 *Island group,* Spain
**Baleine, Rivière à la** 35 E2 ↝ Quebec, E Canada
**Balen** 68 D6 N Belgium

**Baleshwar** 107 F4 E India
**Bali** 109 E8 *Island,* C Indonesia
**Balıkesir** 97 A3 W Turkey
**Balikpapan** 109 E7 C Indonesia
**Balkan Mountains** 83 E3 ▲ Bulgaria/Yugoslavia
**Balkh** 101 D7 N Afghanistan
**Balkhash** 94 C6 SE Kazakhstan
**Balkhash, Lake** 94 C6 ⊜ SE Kazakhstan
**Balladonia** 133 C5 W Australia
**Ballarat** 133 F6 Victoria, SE Australia
**Ballinger** 48 G4 Texas, USA
**Balsas** 115 G4 E Brazil
**Balsas, Río** 57 E5 ↝ S Mexico
**Bâlti** 85 D5 N Moldova
**Baltic Sea** 67 D7 *Sea,* N Europe
**Baltimore** 43 H1 Maryland, USA
**Baluchistan** 107 B3 *Cultural region,* SW Pakistan
**Balykchy** 101 H2 NE Kyrgyzstan
**Bam** 99 F3 SE Iran
**Bamako** 124 C4 ● SW Mali
**Bambari** 124 H5 C CAR
**Bamberg** 77 C5 SE Germany
**Bamenda** 124 F5 W Cameroon
**Banaba** 137 H1 *Island,* W Kiribati
**Bananga** 107 H6 Nicobar Islands, India
**Bandaaceh** 109 A5 Sumatra, W Indonesia
**Bandama** 124 C5 ↝ S Côte d'Ivoire
**Bandarbeyla** 127 F4 NE Somalia
**Bandar-e 'Abbas** 99 E4 S Iran
**Bandarlampung** 109 B7 Sumatra, W Indonesia
**Bandar Seri Begawan** 109 D5 ● N Brunei
**Banda Sea** 109 G7 *Sea,* E Indonesia
**Bandırma** 97 A2 NW Turkey
**Bandundu** 128 B2 W Dem. Rep. Congo (Zaire)
**Bandung** 109 C8 Java, C Indonesia
**Banff** 33 F6 Alberta, SW Canada
**Banfora** 124 D4 SW Burkina
**Bangalore** 107 D6 S India
**Bangassou** 124 I5 SE CAR
**Banggai, Kepulauan** 109 F6 *Island group,* C Indonesia
**Banghazi** *see* Benghazi
**Bangka, Pulau** 109 C7 *Island,* W Indonesia
**Bangkok** 109 B4 ● C Thailand
**Bangladesh** 107 G3 ◆ *Republic,* S Asia
**Bangor** 71 C5 E Northern Ireland, UK
**Bangor** 71 D6 NW Wales, UK
**Bangor** 41 G2 Maine, USA
**Bangui** 124 H5 ● SW CAR
**Bangweulu, Lake** 128 D3 ⊜ N Zambia
**Banja Luka** 83 C2 NW Bosnia and Herzegovina
**Banjarmasin** 109 E7 C Indonesia
**Banjul** 124 A3 ● W Gambia
**Banks Island** 33 F3 *Island,* NW Terr., NW Canada
**Banks Islands** 137 G4 *Island group,* N Vanuatu
**Banks Lake** 53 C2 ⊞ Washington, USA
**Banks Peninsula** 135 C6 *Peninsula,* South Island, NZ
**Banks Strait** 133 G7 *Strait,* SW Tasman Sea
**Bankura** 107 F4 NE India
**Banmauk** 109 A2 N Myanmar
**Ban Nadou** 109 C3 S Laos
**Banská Bystrica** 81 E6 C Slovakia
**Bantry Bay** 71 A7 *Bay,* SW Ireland
**Banyak, Kepulauan** 109 A6 *Island group,* NW Indonesia
**Banyo** 124 F5 NW Cameroon
**Banyoles** 75 H2 NE Spain
**Baoji** 105 E4 C China
**Baoshan** 105 D5 SW China
**Baotou** 105 F3 N China
**Ba'qubah** 99 C2 C Iraq
**Baraawe** 127 E5 S Somalia
**Baranavichy** 85 C3 SW Belarus
**Barbados** 61 K6 ◆ *Commonwealth Republic,* SE West Indies
**Barbastro** 75 F2 NE Spain
**Barbate de Franco** 75 C6 S Spain
**Barbuda** 61 J4 *Island,* N Antigua and Barbuda
**Barcaldine** 133 G3 Queensland, E Australia
**Barcelona** 75 G2 E Spain
**Barcelona** 115 D1 NE Venezuela
**Barcs** 81 D9 SW Hungary
**Bardaï** 124 G2 N Chad
**Bardejov** 81 F6 NE Slovakia
**Bareilly** 107 E3 N India
**Barendrecht** 68 C4 SW Netherlands
**Barentin** 73 C2 N France
**Barents Sea** 87 C2 *Sea,* Arctic Ocean
**Bar Harbor** 41 G2 Mount Desert Island, Maine, USA
**Bari** 79 E6 SE Italy
**Barikowt** 101 G4 NE Afghanistan
**Barillas** 59 A2 NW Guatemala
**Barinas** 115 C2 W Venezuela
**Barisal** 107 G4 S Bangladesh
**Barisan, Pegunungan** 109 B7 ▲ Sumatra, W Indonesia
**Barito, Sungai** 109 E7 ↝ Borneo, C Indonesia
**Barkly Tableland** 133 E2 *Plateau,* Northern Territory/Queensland, N Australia

**Bârlad** 85 C6 E Romania
**Bar-le-Duc** 73 E2 NE France
**Barlee, Lake** 133 B5 ⊜ W Australia
**Barlee Range** 133 B4 ▲ W Australia
**Barletta** 79 E5 SE Italy
**Barlinek** 81 C3 W Poland
**Barmouth** 71 D7 NW Wales, UK
**Barnaul** 94 D5 C Russ. Fed.
**Barnstaple** 71 D8 SW England, UK
**Baroghil Pass** 101 G4 *Pass,* Afghanistan/Pakistan
**Barquisimeto** 115 D1 NW Venezuela
**Barra de Río Grande** 59 E4 E Nicaragua
**Barranca** 115 B5 W Peru
**Barrancabermeja** 115 B2 N Colombia
**Barranquilla** 115 B1 N Colombia
**Barreiro** 75 A4 W Portugal
**Barrier Range** 133 F5 *Hill range,* NSW, SE Australia
**Barrier Reef** 59 C1 *Reef,* E Belize
**Barrow** 54 E1 Alaska, USA
**Barrow** 71 B7 ↝ SE Ireland
**Barrow-in-Furness** 71 D6 NW England, UK
**Barrow Island** 133 A3 *Island,* W Australia
**Barstow** 53 D8 California, USA
**Bartang** 101 G4 ↝ SE Tajikistan
**Bartın** 97 C2 N Turkey
**Bartlesville** 47 D7 Oklahoma, USA
**Bartoszyce** 81 E2 N Poland
**Barú, Volcán** 59 F6 ▲ W Panama
**Barva, Volcán** 59 E6 ▲ NW Costa Rica
**Barwon River** 133 G5 ↝ NSW, SE Australia
**Barysaw** 85 D2 N Belarus
**Basarabeasca** 85 D6 SE Moldova
**Basel** 77 B7 NW Switzerland
**Basilan** 109 F5 *Island,* SW Philippines
**Basingstoke** 71 E8 S England, UK
**Basque Country, The** 75 E1 *Cultural region,* N Spain
**Basra** 99 D3 SE Iraq
**Bassano del Grappa** 79 C2 NE Italy
**Bassein** 109 A3 SW Myanmar
**Basse-Terre** 61 J5 ○ Basse Terre, SW Guadeloupe
**Basseterre** 61 J4 ● Saint Kitts, Saint Kitts and Nevis
**Bassett** 47 C4 Nebraska, USA
**Bassikounou** 124 C3 SE Mauritania
**Bass Strait** 133 F7 *Strait,* SE Australia
**Bassum** 77 B3 NW Germany
**Bastia** 73 G5 Corsica, France
**Bastogne** 68 E8 SE Belgium
**Bata** 124 F6 NW Equatorial Guinea
**Batangas** 109 F4 Luzon, N Philippines
**Batdambang** 109 C4 NW Cambodia
**Batéké, Plateaux** 128 B2 *Plateau,* S Congo
**Bath** 71 D8 SW England, UK
**Bath** 41 G3 Maine, USA
**Bathinda** 107 D2 NW India
**Bathurst** 133 G6 NSW, SE Australia
**Bathurst** 35 F4 New Brunswick, SE Canada
**Bathurst Island** 133 C1 *Island,* Northern Territory, N Australia
**Bathurst Island** 33 G2 *Island,* Parry Islands, Nunavut, N Canada
**Batin, Wadi al** 99 C3 *Dry watercourse,* SW Asia
**Batman** 97 E4 SE Turkey
**Batna** 122 E1 NE Algeria
**Baton Rouge** 43 C6 Louisiana, USA
**Batticaloa** 107 E8 SE Sri Lanka
**Battipaglia** 79 D6 S Italy
**Battle Mountain** 51 B5 Nevada, USA
**Bat'umi** 97 F2 W Georgia
**Batu Pahat** 109 C6 Peninsular Malaysia
**Bauchi** 124 F4 NE Nigeria
**Bautzen** 77 E5 E Germany
**Bavaria** 77 C7 *Cultural region,* SE Germany
**Bavarian Alps** 77 C7 ▲ Austria/Germany
**Bavispe, Río** 57 C2 ↝ NW Mexico
**Bawiti** 122 I3 N Egypt
**Bawku** 124 D4 N Ghana
**Bayamo** 61 D3 E Cuba
**Bayamón** 55 E Puerto Rico
**Bayan Har Shan** 105 D4 ▲ C China
**Bayanhongor** 105 D2 C Mongolia
**Bayano, Lago** 59 H6 ⊜ E Panama
**Bayard** 48 C3 New Mexico, USA
**Bay City** 44 E4 Michigan, USA
**Bay City** 48 H5 Texas, USA
**Baydhabo** 127 E5 SW Somalia
**Bayern** *see* Bavaria
**Baymak** 87 D7 W Russ. Fed.
**Bayonne** 73 B6 SW France
**Bayramaly** 101 D4 S Turkmenistan
**Bayreuth** 77 C5 SE Germany
**Baytown** 48 I4 Texas, USA
**Baza** 75 E5 S Spain
**Beacon** 41 E4 New York, USA
**Beagle Channel** 117 B9 *Channel,* Argentina/Chile
**Bear Lake** 51 D4 ⊜ NW USA
**Beas de Segura** 75 E5 S Spain
**Beata, Isla** 61 F5 *Island,* SW Dominican Republic

**Beatrice** 47 D5 Nebraska, USA
**Beatty** 51 H6 Nevada, USA
**Beaufort Sea** 54 F1 *Sea* Arctic Ocean
**Beaufort West** 128 C7 SW South Africa
**Beaumont** 48 I4 Texas, USA
**Beaune** 73 E4 C France
**Beauvais** 73 D2 N France
**Beaver Falls** 41 A5 Pennsylvania, USA
**Beaver Island** 44 C3 *Island,* Michigan, USA
**Beaver River** 47 B7 ↝ Oklahoma, USA
**Beaverton** 53 B3 Oregon, USA
**Beawar** 107 D3 N India
**Béchar** 122 D2 W Algeria
**Beckley** 43 G2 West Virginia, USA
**Bedford** 71 E7 E England, UK
**Bedford** 44 D7 Indiana, USA
**Bedum** 68 F2 NE Netherlands
**Be'er Menuha** 99 H7 S Israel
**Beernem** 68 B6 NW Belgium
**Be'er Sheva'** 99 G6 S Israel
**Beesel** 68 E6 SE Netherlands
**Beeville** 48 G5 Texas, USA
**Bega** 133 G6 NSW, SE Australia
**Beihai** 105 F6 S China
**Beijing** 105 F3 ● E China
**Beilen** 68 E3 NE Netherlands
**Beira** 128 E5 C Mozambique
**Beirut** 99 A2 ● W Lebanon
**Beja** 75 B5 SE Portugal
**Béjar** 75 D3 W Spain
**Békéscsaba** 81 F8 SE Hungary
**Bekobod** 101 F3 E Uzbekistan
**Belarus** 85 C2 ◆ *Republic,* E Europe
**Belchatów** 81 E4 C Poland
**Belcher Islands** 35 C2 *Island group,* Nunavut, SE Canada
**Beledweyne** 127 F4 C Somalia
**Belém** 115 G3 N Brazil
**Belén** 59 D5 SW Nicaragua
**Belen** 48 D2 New Mexico, USA
**Belep, Îles** 137 F6 *Island group,* W New Caledonia
**Belfast** 71 C5 *Political division capital,* E Northern Ireland, UK
**Belfield** 47 A2 North Dakota, USA
**Belfort** 73 F3 E France
**Belgaum** 107 D6 W India
**Belgium** 68 B7 ◆ *Monarchy,* NW Europe
**Belgorod** 87 A6 W Russ. Fed.
**Belgrade** 83 D2 ● N Yugoslavia
**Belgrano II** 138 B4 *Argentinian research station,* Antarctica
**Belitung, Pulau** 109 C7 *Island,* W Indonesia
**Belize** 59 B2 ◆ *Commonwealth Republic,* Central America
**Belize** 59 B2 *River* Belize/Guatemala
**Belize City** 59 C1 NE Belize
**Belkofski** 54 C3 Alaska, USA
**Belle Île** 73 A3 *Island,* NW France
**Belle Isle, Strait of** 35 G3 *Strait,* Newfoundland, E Canada
**Belleville** 44 B7 Illinois, USA
**Bellevue** 47 D5 Nebraska, USA
**Bellevue** 53 B2 Washington, USA
**Bellingham** 53 B1 Washington, USA
**Bellingshausen Sea** 138 A4 *Sea,* Antarctica
**Bellinzona** 77 B8 S Switzerland
**Bello** 115 B2 W Colombia
**Bellona** 137 E3 *Island,* S Solomon Islands
**Bellville** 128 C7 SW South Africa
**Belmopan** 59 B2 ● C Belize
**Belo Horizonte** 115 G7 SE Brazil
**Belomorsk** 87 B3 NW Russ. Fed.
**Beloretsk** 87 D6 W Russ. Fed.
**Belorussia** *see* Belarus
**Belozersk** 87 B4 NW Russ. Fed.
**Belton** 48 H4 Texas, USA
**Belukha, Gora** 94 D5 ▲ Kazakhstan/Russ. Fed.
**Belyy, Ostrov** 94 D2 *Island,* N Russ. Fed.
**Bemaraha** 128 G5 ▲ W Madagascar
**Bemidji** 47 E2 Minnesota, USA
**Bemmel** 68 E4 SE Netherlands
**Benavente** 75 C2 N Spain
**Bend** 53 B4 Oregon, USA
**Bendigo** 133 F6 Victoria, SE Australia
**Benešov** 81 B5 W Czech Republic
**Benevento** 79 D6 S Italy
**Bengbu** 105 F4 E China
**Benghazi** 122 G2 NE Libya
**Bengkulu** 109 B7 Sumatra, W Indonesia
**Benguela** 128 B4 W Angola
**Ben Hope** 71 C3 N Scotland, UK
**Beni** 128 D1 NE Dem. Rep. Congo (Zaire)
**Benidorm** 75 F4 SE Spain
**Beni-Mellal** 122 C2 C Morocco
**Benin** 124 D4 ◆ *Republic,* W Africa
**Benin, Bight of** 124 E5 *Gulf,* W Africa
**Beni, Río** 117 A2 ↝ N Bolivia
**Benin City** 124 E5 SW Nigeria
**Beni Suef** 122 I3 N Egypt
**Ben Nevis** 71 C4 ▲ N Scotland, UK
**Benson** 48 C3 Arizona, USA
**Benton** 43 B4 Arkansas, USA
**Benton Harbor** 44 D5 Michigan, USA
**Benue** 124 F5 ↝ Cameroon/Nigeria
**Beograd** *see* Belgrade
**Berat** 83 D4 C Albania
**Berau, Teluk** 109 H7 *Bay,* E Indonesia

◈ Administrative region   ◆ Country   ● Country capital   ◊ Dependent territory   ○ Dependent territory capital   ▲ Mountain range   ▲ Mountain   ▲ Volcano   ↝ River   ⊜ Lake   ⊞ Reservoir

CAMBRIDGE


Berbera 127 F3 NW Somalia
Berbérati 124 G5 SW CAR
Berck-Plage 73 D1 N France
Berdyans'k 85 G6 SE Ukraine
Berettyó 81 F8 ≈ Hungary/Romania
Berettyóújfalu 81 F7 E Hungary
Berezniki 87 D5 NW Russ. Fed.
Berga 75 G2 NE Spain
Bergamo 79 B2 N Italy
Bergen 77 D2 NE Germany
Bergen 68 C3 NW Netherlands
Bergen 67 A5 S Norway
Bergerac 73 C5 SW France
Bergeyk 68 D6 S Netherlands
Bergse Maas 68 D5 ≈ S Netherlands
Beringen 68 D6 NE Belgium
Bering Sea 54 B1 *Sea* N Pacific Ocean
Bering Strait 54 D1 *Strait* Bering Sea/Chukchi Sea
Berja 75 E6 S Spain
Berkeley 53 B7 California, USA
Berkner Island 138 B4 *Island,* Antarctica
Berlin 77 D3 ● NE Germany
Berlin 41 F3 New Hampshire, USA
Bermejo, Río 117 B3 ≈ N Argentina
Bermuda 26 *UK* ◈ N Atlantic Ocean
Bermeo 75 E1 N Spain
Bern 77 A8 ● W Switzerland
Bernau 77 D3 NE Germany
Bernburg 77 D4 C Germany
Berner Alpen 77 A8 ▲▲ SW Switzerland
Bernier Island 133 A4 *Island,* W Australia
Berry 73 D3 *Cultural region,* C France
Berry Islands 61 C1 *Island group,* N Bahamas
Bertoua 124 G5 E Cameroon
Berwick-upon-Tweed 71 D4 N England, UK
Besançon 73 E4 E France
Betafo 128 G5 C Madagascar
Betanzos 75 B1 NW Spain
Bethlehem 128 D6 C South Africa
Bethlehem 41 D5 Pennsylvania, USA
Bethlehem 99 H6 C West Bank
Béticos, Sistemas 75 D5 ▲▲ S Spain
Bétou 128 C1 N Congo
Bette, Pic 122 G4 ▲ S Libya
Beulah 44 D3 Michigan, USA
Beveren 68 C6 N Belgium
Beverley 71 E6 E England, UK
Beyla 124 C4 SE Guinea
Beyrouth *see* Beirut
Beyşehir Gölü 97 B4 ◎ C Turkey
Béziers 73 D6 S France
Bhadravati 107 D6 SW India
Bhagalpur 107 F3 NE India
Bhaktapur 107 F3 C Nepal
Bharuch 107 C4 W India
Bhavnagar 107 C4 W India
Bhopal 107 D4 C India
Bhubaneshwar 107 F4 E India
Bhusawal 107 D4 C India
Bhutan 107 G3 ◆ *Monarchy,* S Asia
Biak, Pulau 109 H6 *Island,* E Indonesia
Biała Podlaska 81 G3 E Poland
Białogard 81 C2 NW Poland
Białystok 81 G2 E Poland
Biarritz 73 B6 SW France
Biddeford 41 F3 Maine, USA
Bideford 71 D8 SW England, UK
Biel 77 A8 W Switzerland
Bielefeld 77 B4 NW Germany
Bielsko-Biała 81 E5 S Poland
Bielsk Podlaski 81 G3 E Poland
Biên Hoa 109 C4 S Vietnam
Bienville, Lac 35 D3 ◎ Quebec, C Canada
Bié Plateau 128 C4 *Plateau,* C Angola
Big Bend National Park 48 E5 *National park,* Texas, USA
Big Cypress Swamp 43 G8 *Wetland,* SE USA
Bighorn Mountains 51 E3 ▲▲ Wyoming, USA
Bighorn River 51 E3 ≈ NW USA
Big Sioux River 47 D4 ≈ N USA
Big Smoky Valley 51 B6 *Valley,* Nevada, USA
Big Spring 48 F3 Texas, USA
Bihać 83 B2 NW Bosnia and Herzegovina
Bihar 107 F3 *Cultural region,* N India
Biharamulo 127 C6 NW Tanzania
Bihosava 85 C1 NW Belarus
Bijelo Polje 83 D3 SW Yugoslavia
Bikaner 107 D3 NW India
Bikin 94 H5 SE Russ. Fed.
Bilaspur 107 E4 C India
Biläsuvar 97 I3 SE Azerbaijan
Bila Tserkva 85 D4 N Ukraine
Bilauktaung Range 109 B4 ▲▲ Myanmar/Thailand
Bilbao 75 E1 N Spain
Bilecik 97 B3 NW Turkey
Billings 51 E2 Montana, USA
Bilma, Grand Erg de 124 G2 *Desert,* NE Niger
Biloela 133 H4 Queensland, E Australia
Biloxi 43 C6 Mississippi, USA
Biltine 124 H3 E Chad
Bilzen 68 D6 NE Belgium
Bimini Islands 61 C1 *Island group,* W Bahamas
Binche 68 C7 S Belgium
Binghamton 41 D4 New York, USA
Bingöl 97 F3 E Turkey
Bintulu 109 D6 East Malaysia
Binzhou 105 G3 E China
Bío Bío, Río 117 A6 ≈ C Chile
Bioco, Isla de 124 F6 *Island,* NW Equatorial Guinea
Birak 122 F3 C Libya
Birao 124 I4 NE CAR
Biratnagar 107 F3 SE Nepal
Birhar Sharif 107 F3 N India
Birjand 99 F2 E Iran
Birkenfeld 77 A6 SW Germany
Birkenhead 71 D6 NW England, UK
Birmingham 71 E7 C England, UK
Birmingham 43 D4 Alabama, USA
Bîr Mogreïn 124 B1 N Mauritania
Birnin Kebbi 124 E4 NW Nigeria
Birnin Konni 124 E3 SW Niger
Birobidzhan 94 H5 SE Russ. Fed.
Birsk 87 D6 W Russ. Fed.
Birżebbuġa 88 B6 SE Malta
Bisbee 48 C4 Arizona, USA
Biscay, Bay of 73 B4 *Bay,* France/Spain
Bishah, Wadi 99 B5 *Dry watercourse,* C Saudi Arabia
Bishkek 101 H2 ● N Kyrgyzstan
Bishop 53 C7 California, USA
Biskra 122 E1 NE Algeria
Biskupiec 81 F2 N Poland
Bislig 109 G5 S Philippines
Bismarck 47 B2 North Dakota, USA
Bismarck Archipelago 137 B1 *Island group,* NE PNG
Bismarck Sea 137 B1 *Sea,* W Pacific Ocean
Bissau 124 A4 ● W Guinea-Bissau
Bistriţa 85 B6 N Romania
Bitam 128 A1 N Gabon
Bitburg 77 A5 SW Germany
Bitlis 97 G4 SE Turkey
Bitola 83 D4 S FYR Macedonia
Bitonto 79 E6 SE Italy
Bitterfeld 77 D4 E Germany
Bitterroot Range 51 C2 ▲▲ NW USA
Biu 124 G4 E Nigeria
Biwa-ko 103 E6 ◎ Honshu, SW Japan
Bizerte 122 F1 N Tunisia
Bjørnøya 139 D5 *Island,* N Norway
Blackall 133 G4 Queensland, E Australia
Black Drin 83 D3 ≈ Albania/FYR Macedonia
Blackfoot 51 D4 Idaho, USA
Black Forest 77 B7 ▲▲ SW Germany
Black Hills 47 A4 ▲▲ N USA
Black Mountain 51 D5 ▲ Colorado, USA
Blackpool 71 D6 NW England, UK
Black Range 48 D3 ▲▲ New Mexico, USA
Black River 109 B2 ≈ China/Vietnam
Black Rock Desert 51 A4 *Desert,* Nevada, USA
Black Sea 62 *Sea,* Asia/Europe
Black Sea Lowland 85 E6 *Depression,* SE Europe
Black Volta 124 D4 ≈ W Africa
Blackwater 71 B7 ≈ S Ireland
Blagoevgrad 83 E3 W Bulgaria
Blagoveshchensk 94 H5 SE Russ. Fed.
Blanca, Bahía 117 B6 *Bay,* E Argentina
Blanca, Costa 75 F5 *Physical region,* SE Spain
Blanche, Lake 133 F4 ◎ S Australia
Blanc, Mont 73 F5 ▲ France/Italy
Blanco, Cape 53 A4 *Headland,* Oregon, USA
Blanes 75 H2 NE Spain
Blankenberge 68 B5 NW Belgium
Blankenheim 77 A5 W Germany
Blanquilla, Isla 61 I7 *Island,* N Venezuela
Blantyre 128 E4 S Malawi
Blaricum 68 D4 C Netherlands
Blenheim 135 C5 South Island, NZ
Blida 122 D1 N Algeria
Bloemfontein 128 D6 ● C South Africa
Blois 73 C3 C France
Bloomfield 48 C1 New Mexico, USA
Bloomington 44 B6 Illinois, USA
Bloomington 44 D7 Indiana, USA
Bloomington 47 E3 Minnesota, USA
Bloomsburg 41 D5 Pennsylvania, USA
Bloomsbury 133 G3 Queensland, NE Australia
Bluefield 43 G2 West Virginia, USA
Bluefields 59 E4 SE Nicaragua
Blue Mountains 133 G6 ▲▲ NSW, SE Australia
Blue Mountains 53 C3 ▲▲ NW USA
Blue Nile 127 C3 ≈ Ethiopia/Sudan
Bluff 51 D6 Utah, USA
Blumenau 115 F8 S Brazil
Blythe 53 E9 California, USA
Blytheville 43 C3 Arkansas, USA
Bo 124 B5 S Sierra Leone
Boaco 59 D4 S Nicaragua
Boa Vista 115 E3 NW Brazil
Bobaomby, Tanjona 128 G4 *Headland,* N Madagascar
Bobo-Dioulasso 124 C4 SW Burkina Faso
Boca Raton 43 G8 Florida, USA
Bocay 59 D3 N Nicaragua
Bocholt 77 A4 W Germany
Bochum 77 A4 W Germany
Bodaybo 94 F4 E Russ. Fed.
Boden 67 D3 N Sweden
Bodmin 71 C8 SW England, UK
Bodø 67 C2 C Norway
Bodrum 97 A4 SW Turkey
Boende 128 C2 C Dem. Rep. Congo (Zaire)
Bogalusa 43 C6 Louisiana, USA
Bogatynia 81 B4 SW Poland
Boğazlıyan 97 D3 C Turkey
Bogia 137 B1 N PNG
Bogor 109 C8 Java, C Indonesia
Bogotá 115 B2 ● C Colombia
Bo Hai 105 G3 *Gulf,* NE China
Bohemia 81 B6 *Cultural region,* W Czech Republic
Bohemian Forest 77 D6 ▲▲ C Europe
Bohol Sea 109 F5 *Sea,* S Philippines
Bohoro Shan 105 B2 ▲▲ NW China
Boise 51 B3 Idaho, USA
Boise City 47 A7 Oklahoma, USA
Boizenburg 77 C3 N Germany
Bojnūrd 99 E1 N Iran
Boké 124 A4 W Guinea
Boknafjorden 67 A5 *Fjord,* S Norway
Bol 124 G3 W Chad
Bolesławiec 81 C4 SW Poland
Bolgatanga 124 D4 N Ghana
Bolivia 117 A2 ◆ *Republic,* W South America
Bollene 73 E6 SE France
Bollnäs 67 C5 C Sweden
Bollon 133 G4 Queensland, C Australia
Bologna 79 C3 N Italy
Bol'shevik, Ostrov 94 F2 *Island,* Severnaya Zemlya, N Russ. Fed.
Bol'shezemel'skaya Tundra 87 E3 *Physical region,* NW Russ. Fed.
Bol'shoy Lyakhovskiy, Ostrov 94 G2 *Island,* NE Russ. Fed.
Bolton 71 D6 NW England, UK
Bolu 97 C2 NW Turkey
Bolungarvík 67 A1 NW Iceland
Bolzano 79 C1 N Italy
Boma 128 B3 W Dem. Rep. Congo (Zaire)
Bombay *see* Mumbai
Bomu 128 C1 ≈ CAR/Dem. Rep. Congo (Zaire)
Bonaire 61 H7 *Island,* E Netherlands Antilles
Bonanza 59 E3 NE Nicaragua
Bonaparte Archipelago 133 B2 *Island group,* W Australia
Bon, Cap 88 E4 *Headland,* N Tunisia
Bondo 128 C1 N Dem. Rep. Congo (Zaire)
Bondoukou 124 D5 E Côte d'Ivoire
Bone, Teluk 109 F7 *Bay,* Celebes, C Indonesia
Bongaigaon 107 G3 NE India
Bongo, Massif des 124 H4 ▲▲ NE CAR
Bongor 124 G4 SW Chad
Bonifacio 73 G6 Corsica, France
Bonifacio, Strait of 79 A5 *Strait,* C Mediterranean Sea
Bonin Trench 15 *Undersea feature,* NW Pacific Ocean
Bonn 77 A5 W Germany
Boonville 41 D3 New York, USA
Boosaaso 127 F3 N Somalia
Boothia, Gulf of 33 H3 *Gulf,* Nunavut, NE Canada
Boothia Peninsula 33 H3 *Peninsula,* Nunavut, NE Canada
Boppard 77 B5 W Germany
Boquete 59 F6 W Panama
Boquillas 57 D2 NE Mexico
Bor 127 C4 S Sudan
Bor 83 D2 E Yugoslavia
Borah Peak 51 B3 ▲ Idaho, USA
Borås 67 C6 S Sweden
Bordeaux 73 B5 SW France
Bordj Omar Driss 122 E3 E Algeria
Børgefjellet 67 C3 ▲ C Norway
Borger 68 F2 NE Netherlands
Borger 48 F2 Texas, USA
Borgholm 67 C6 S Sweden
Borisoglebsk 87 B6 W Russ. Fed.
Borlänge 67 C5 C Sweden
Borne 68 F4 E Netherlands
Borneo 109 D7 *Island,* Brunei/Indonesia/Malaysia
Bornholm 67 C7 *Island,* E Denmark
Borovichi 87 A4 W Russ. Fed.
Bosanski Novi 83 B1 NW Bosnia and Herzegovina
Boskovice 81 C6 SE Czech Republic
Bosna 83 C2 ≈ N Bosnia and Herzegovina
Bosna i Hercegovina, Federacija 65 ◈ *Republic,* Bosnia and Herzegovina
Bosnia and Herzegovina 83 C2 ◆ *Republic,* SE Europe
Boso-hanto 103 G6 *Peninsula,* Honshu, S Japan
Bosporus 96 B2 *Strait,* NW Turkey
Bossangoa 124 H5 C CAR
Bossembélé 124 H5 C CAR
Bossier City 43 B5 Louisiana, USA
Bosten Hu 105 C3 ◎ NW China
Boston 71 E6 E England, UK
Boston 41 F4 Massachusetts, USA
Boston Mountains 43 B3 ▲▲ Arkansas, USA
Botany Bay 133 H6 *Inlet,* NSW, SE Australia
Boteti 128 C5 ≈ N Botswana
Bothnia, Gulf of 67 D4 *Gulf,* N Baltic Sea
Botoşani 85 C5 NE Romania
Botrange 68 E7 ▲ E Belgium
Botswana 128 C5 ◆ *Republic,* S Africa
Bouar 124 G5 W CAR
Bou Craa 122 B3 NW Western Sahara
Bougainville Island 137 D2 *Island,* NE PNG
Bougaroun, Cap 88 D4 *Headland,* NE Algeria
Bougouni 124 C4 SW Mali
Boujdour 122 A3 W Western Sahara
Boulder 51 F5 Colorado, USA
Boulder 51 D2 Montana, USA
Boulogne-sur-Mer 73 D1 N France
Boûmdeïd 124 B3 S Mauritania
Boundiali 124 C4 N Côte d'Ivoire
Bountiful 51 D5 Utah, USA
Bourail 137 G6 C New Caledonia
Bourbonnais 73 D4 *Cultural region,* C France
Bourg-en-Bresse 73 E4 E France
Bourges 73 D4 C France
Bourgogne *see* Burgundy
Bourke 133 G5 NSW, SE Australia
Bournemouth 71 E8 S England, UK
Boutilimit 124 A3 SW Mauritania
Bowen 133 G3 Queensland, NE Australia
Bowling Green 43 E3 Kentucky, USA
Bowling Green 44 E5 Ohio, USA
Bowman 47 A2 North Dakota, USA
Boxmeer 68 E5 SE Netherlands
Boysun 101 F3 S Uzbekistan
Bozeman 51 D3 Montana, USA
Bozüyük 97 B3 NW Turkey
Brač 83 B3 *Island,* S Croatia
Bradford 71 E6 N England, UK
Bradford 41 B4 Pennsylvania, USA
Brady 48 G4 Texas, USA
Braga 75 B2 NW Portugal
Bragança 75 C2 NE Portugal
Brahmanbaria 107 G3 E Bangladesh
Brahmapur 107 F5 E India
Brahmaputra 107 H3 ≈ S Asia
Brăila 85 D7 E Romania
Braine-le-Comte 68 C7 SW Belgium
Brainerd 47 E2 Minnesota, USA
Brampton 35 D6 Ontario, S Canada
Brandberg 128 B5 ▲ NW Namibia
Brandenburg 77 D3 NE Germany
Brandon 33 H7 Manitoba, S Canada
Braniewo 81 E2 N Poland
Brasília 115 G6 ● C Brazil
Braşov 85 C6 C Romania
Bratislava 81 D7 ● SW Slovakia
Bratsk 94 F5 C Russ. Fed.
Braunschweig 77 C4 N Germany
Brava, Costa 75 H2 *Coastal region,* NE Spain
Bravo, Río 57 D2 ≈ Mexico/USA
Brawley 53 D9 California, USA
Brazil 115 C4 ◆ *Federal Republic,* South America
Brazil Basin 14 *Undersea feature,* W Atlantic Ocean
Brazilian Highlands 115 G6 ▲▲ E Brazil
Brazos River 48 H4 ≈ Texas, USA
Brazzaville 128 B2 ● S Congo
Brecht 68 C5 N Belgium
Breda 68 D5 S Netherlands
Bree 68 D6 NE Belgium
Bregalnica 83 E3 ≈ E FYR Macedonia
Bremen 77 B3 NW Germany
Bremerhaven 77 B3 NW Germany
Bremerton 53 B2 Washington, USA
Brenham 48 H4 Texas, USA
Brenner Pass 77 C8 *Pass,* Austria/Italy
Brescia 79 C2 N Italy
Bressanone 79 C1 N Italy
Brest 85 B3 SW Belarus
Brest 73 A2 NW France
Bretagne *see* Brittany
Brewton 43 D6 Alabama, USA
Bria 124 H5 C CAR
Briançon 73 F5 SE France
Bridgeport 53 C6 California, USA
Bridgeport 41 E5 Connecticut, USA
Bridgetown 61 K6 ● SW Barbados
Bridlington 71 E6 E England, UK
Bridport 71 D8 S England, UK
Brig 77 B8 SW Switzerland
Brigham City 51 D4 Utah, USA
Brighton 71 E8 SE England, UK
Brighton 51 F5 Colorado, USA
Brindisi 79 F6 SE Italy
Brisbane 133 H4 Queensland, E Australia
Bristol 71 D7 SW England, UK
Bristol 41 E4 Connecticut, USA
Bristol 43 F3 Virginia, USA
Bristol Bay 54 C2 *Bay,* Alaska, USA
Bristol Channel 71 D8 *Inlet,* England/Wales, UK
British Columbia 33 E5 ◈ *Province,* SW Canada
British Indian Ocean Territory 27 *UK* ◈ C Indian Ocean
British Isles 62 *Island group,* Ireland/United Kingdom
British Virgin Islands 61 I4 *UK* ◈ E West Indies
Brittany 73 B2 *Cultural region,* NW France
Brive-la-Gaillarde 73 C5 C France
Brno 81 C6 SE Czech Republic
Brockton 41 F4 Massachusetts, USA
Brodeur Peninsula 33 H3 *Peninsula,* Baffin Island, Nunavut, NE Canada
Brodnica 81 E2 N Poland
Broek-in-Waterland 68 D3 C Netherlands
Broken Hill 133 F5 NSW, SE Australia
Brookhaven 43 C5 Mississippi, USA
Brookings 47 D3 South Dakota, USA
Brooks Range 54 E2 *Mountain range* Alaska, USA
Brookton 133 B5 W Australia
Broome 133 C2 W Australia
Broomfield 51 F5 Colorado, USA
Brownfield 48 F3 Texas, USA
Brownsville 48 H6 Texas, USA
Brownwood 48 G4 Texas, USA
Bruges 68 B6 NW Belgium
Brugge *see* Bruges
Brummen 68 E4 E Netherlands
Brunei 109 D5 ◆ *Monarchy,* SE Asia
Brunner, Lake 135 C6 ◎ South Island, NZ
Brunswick 43 G6 Georgia, USA
Brunswick 41 G3 Maine, USA
Brus Laguna 59 E2 E Honduras
Brussel *see* Brussels
Brussels 68 C6 ● C Belgium
Bruxelles *see* Brussels
Bryan 48 H4 Texas, USA
Bryansk 87 A6 W Russ. Fed.
Brzeg 81 D4 SW Poland
Buala 137 E2 E Solomon Islands
Bucaramanga 115 C2 N Colombia
Buchanan 124 B5 SW Liberia
Buchanan, Lake 48 G4 ▨ Texas, USA
Bucharest 85 C7 ● S Romania
Bucureşti *see* Bucharest
Bucyrus 44 E6 Ohio, USA
Budapest 81 E7 ● N Hungary
Budaun 107 E3 N India
Buenaventura 115 B3 W Colombia
Buena Vista 117 B2 C Bolivia
Buenos Aires 117 C5 ● E Argentina
Buenos Aires 59 F6 SE Costa Rica
Buenos Aires, Lago 117 A8 ◎ Argentina/Chile
Buffalo 41 B3 New York, USA
Buffalo 47 A3 South Dakota, USA
Buffalo 48 H4 Texas, USA
Buffalo Narrows 33 G6 Saskatchewan, C Canada
Bug 85 B3 ≈ E Europe
Buguruslan 87 D6 W Russ. Fed.
Bujalance 75 D5 S Spain
Bujanovac 83 D3 SE Yugoslavia
Bujumbura 127 B6 ● W Burundi
Buka Island 137 D2 *Island,* NE PNG
Bukavu 128 D2 E Dem. Rep. Congo (Zaire)
Bukhoro 101 E3 C Uzbekistan
Bukoba 127 C5 NW Tanzania
Bülach 77 B7 NW Switzerland
Bulawayo 128 D5 SW Zimbabwe
Bulgaria 83 E3 ◆ *Republic,* SE Europe
Bullhead City 48 A2 Arizona, USA
Bull Shoals Lake 47 F7 ▨ C USA
Bulukumba 109 E7 Celebes, C Indonesia
Bumba 128 C1 N Dem. Rep. Congo (Zaire)
Bunbury 133 B6 W Australia
Bundaberg 133 H4 Queensland, E Australia
Bungo-suido 103 D7 *Strait,* SW Japan
Bünyan 97 D3 C Turkey
Buon Ma Thuot 109 C4 S Vietnam
Buraydah 99 C4 N Saudi Arabia
Burco 127 F3 NW Somalia
Burdur 97 B4 SW Turkey
Burdur Gölü 97 B4 *Salt lake,* SW Turkey
Bure 127 D3 NW Ethiopia
Burgas 83 G3 E Bulgaria
Burgaski Zaliv 97 A1 *Gulf,* E Bulgaria
Burgos 75 D2 N Spain
Burgundy 73 E4 *Cultural region,* E France
Burhan Budai Shan 105 D4 ▲▲ C China
Burjassot 75 F4 E Spain
Burkburnett 48 G2 Texas, USA
Burketown 133 F2 Queensland, NE Australia
Burkina Faso 124 C4 ◆ *Republic,* W Africa
Burkina *see* Burkina Faso
Burley 51 C4 Idaho, USA
Burlington 51 G5 Colorado, USA
Burlington 47 F5 Iowa, USA
Burlington 41 E3 Vermont, USA
Burma *see* Myanmar
Burnie 133 F7 Tasmania, SE Australia
Burns 53 C4 Oregon, USA
Burnside 33 G4 ≈ Nunavut, NW Canada
Burns Junction 53 C4 Oregon, USA
Burnsville 47 E3 Minnesota, USA
Burriana 75 F3 E Spain
Bursa 97 B3 NW Turkey
Burundi 127 B6 ◆ *Republic,* C Africa
Buru, Pulau 109 F7 *Island,* E Indonesia
Bushire 99 D3 S Iran
Busselton 133 B6 W Australia
Buta 128 D1 N Dem. Rep. Congo (Zaire)
Butler 41 B5 Pennsylvania, USA
Buton, Pulau 109 F7 *Island,* C Indonesia
Butte 51 C2 Montana, USA
Button Islands 35 E1 *Island group,* Quebec, NE Canada
Butuan 109 F5 S Philippines
Buulobarde 127 F4 C Somalia
Buur Gaabo 127 E5 S Somalia
Buynaksk 87 B9 SW Russ. Fed.
Büyükmenderes Nehri 97 A4 ≈ SW Turkey
Buzău 85 C7 SE Romania
Buzuluk 87 C6 W Russ. Fed.
Bydgoszcz 81 D3 W Poland
Byelaruskaya Hrada 85 C3 *Ridge,* N Belarus
Byerezino 85 D2 ≈ C Belarus
Bytča 81 D6 NW Slovakia
Bytów 81 D2 NW Poland
Byuzmeyin 101 C3 C Turkmenistan


## C


Caazapá 117 C4 S Paraguay
Caballo Reservoir 48 D3 ▨ New Mexico, USA
Cabañaquinta 75 C1 N Spain
Cabanatuan 109 F3 N Philippines
Cabinda 128 B2 NW Angola
Cabinda 128 B3 *Province,* NW Angola
Cabora Bassa, Lake 128 E4 ▨ NW Mozambique
Caborca 57 B2 NW Mexico
Cabo Rojo 55 Puerto Rico, North America
Cabot Strait 35 G4 *Strait,* E Canada
Cabras Island 55 *Island* W Guam
Cabrera 75 G4 *Island,* Balearic Islands, Spain
Cáceres 75 C4 W Spain
Cachimbo, Serra do 115 E4 ▲▲ C Brazil
Caconda 128 B4 C Angola
Čadca 81 D6 N Slovakia
Cadillac 44 D4 Michigan, USA
Cadiz 109 F4 C Philippines
Cádiz 75 C6 SW Spain
Cádiz, Golfo de *see* Cadiz, Gulf of
Cadiz, Gulf of 75 B6 *Gulf,* Portugal/Spain
Caen 73 C2 N France
Cafayate 117 B4 N Argentina
Cagayan de Oro 109 F5 Mindanao, S Philippines
Cagliari 79 A6 Sardinia, Italy
Caguas 61 I4 E Puerto Rico
Cahors 73 C6 S France
Cahul 85 D6 S Moldova
Caicos Passage 61 F3 *Strait,* Bahamas/Turks and Caicos Islands
Cairns 133 G2 Queensland, NE Australia
Cairo 122 I2 ● N Egypt
Cajamarca 115 B5 NW Peru
Calabar 124 F5 S Nigeria
Calahorra 75 E2 N Spain
Calais 73 D1 N France
Calais 41 H2 Maine, USA
Calama 117 A3 N Chile
Călăraşi 85 C7 SE Romania
Calatayud 75 E3 NE Spain
Calbayog 109 F4 Samar, C Philippines
Calcasieu Lake 43 B6 ◎ Louisiana, USA
Calcutta 107 G4 NE India
Caldas da Rainha 75 A4 W Portugal
Caldera 117 A4 N Chile
Caldwell 51 B3 Idaho, USA
Caledonia 59 C1 N Belize
Caleta Olivia 117 B8 SE Argentina
Calgary 33 G7 Alberta, SW Canada
Cali 115 B3 W Colombia
Calicut 107 D7 SW India
Caliente 51 C6 Nevada, USA
California 53 C8 ◈ *State,* W USA
California, Gulf of 57 B2 *Gulf,* NE Mexico
Callabonna, Lake 133 F5 ◎ S Australia
Callao 115 B5 W Peru
Callosa de Segura 75 F5 E Spain
Caloundra 133 H4 Queensland, E Australia
Caltanissetta 79 D8 Sicily, Italy
Caluula 127 G3 NE Somalia
Camabatela 128 B3 NW Angola
Camacupa 128 B4 C Angola
Camagüey 61 D3 C Cuba
Camagüey, Archipiélago de 61 D3 *Island group,* C Cuba
Camargue 73 E6 *Physical region,* SE France
Ca Mau 109 C5 S Vietnam
Cambodia 109 C4 ◆ *Republic,* SE Asia
Cambrai 73 D1 N France
Cambridge 135 D3 North Island, NZ
Cambridge 71 F7 E England, UK


**CAR** Central African Republic **FYR** Former Yugoslavian Rebublic **NSW** New South Wales **NZ** New Zealand **PNG** Papua New Guinea **Russ. Fed.** Russian Federation **UAE** United Arab Emirates **UK** United Kingdom **USA** United States of America 143

HAREN


Haren 68 F2 NE Netherlands
Harer 127 E3 E Ethiopia
Hargeysa 127 E3 NW Somalia
Harima-nada 103 E6 Sea, S Japan
Harirud 101 E5 ≈ Afghanistan/Iran
Harlan 47 D5 Iowa, USA
Harlingen 68 D2 N Netherlands
Harlingen 48 H6 Texas, USA
Harlow 71 F7 E England, UK
Harney Basin 53 C4 Basin, Oregon, USA
Härnösand 67 D4 C Sweden
Har Nuur 105 D2 ◎ NW Mongolia
Harper 124 C5 NE Liberia
Harricana 35 D4 ≈ Quebec, SE Canada
Harrisburg 44 C8 Illinois, USA
Harrisburg 41 C5 Pennsylvania, USA
Harrisonburg 43 H2 Virginia, USA
Harrison, Cape 35 G2 Headland, Newfoundland, E Canada
Harrogate 71 E6 N England, UK
Harstad 67 C2 N Norway
Hartford 41 E4 Connecticut, USA
Hartlepool 71 E5 N England, UK
Hartwell Lake 43 F4 ⊡ SE USA
Harvey 47 C2 North Dakota, USA
Harwich 71 F7 E England, UK
Haryana 107 D2 Cultural region, N India
Harz 77 C4 ⛰ C Germany
Hasselt 68 D6 NE Belgium
Hastings 135 E4 North Island, NZ
Hastings 71 F8 SE England, UK
Hastings 47 C5 Nebraska, USA
Hatch 48 D3 New Mexico, USA
Hattem 68 E3 E Netherlands
Hatteras, Cape 43 I3 Headland, North Carolina, USA
Hattiesburg 43 C6 Mississippi, USA
Hat Yai 109 B5 SW Thailand
Haugesund 67 A5 S Norway
Haukeligrend 67 B5 S Norway
Haukivesi 67 F4 ◎ SE Finland
Hauraki Gulf 135 D2 Gulf, North Island, N NZ
Hauroko, Lake 135 A8 ◎ South Island, NZ
Hautes Fagnes 68 E7 ⛰ E Belgium
Hauts Plateaux 122 D2 Plateau, Algeria/Morocco
Hauzenberg 77 E6 SE Germany
Havana 61 B2 ● W Cuba
Havant 71 E8 S England, UK
Havelock 43 H4 North Carolina, USA
Havelock North 135 E4 North Island, NZ
Haverfordwest 71 C7 SW Wales, UK
Havířov 81 D5 E Czech Republic
Havre 51 D1 Montana, USA
Havre-St-Pierre 35 F4 Quebec, E Canada
Hawaii 55 C1 ◐ State, USA, C Pacific Ocean
Hawaii 55 D3 Island, Hawaii, USA
Hawea, Lake 135 B7 ◎ South Island, NZ
Hawera 135 D4 North Island, NZ
Hawi 55 D2 Hawaii, USA
Hawick 71 D5 SE Scotland, UK
Hawke Bay 135 E4 Bay, North Island, NZ
Hawthorne 51 A6 Nevada, USA
Hay 133 F6 NSW, SE Australia
Hayden 48 B3 Arizona, USA
Hayes 35 A2 ≈ Manitoba, C Canada
Hay River 33 G5 NW Terr., W Canada
Hays 47 C6 Kansas, USA
Haysyn 85 D5 C Ukraine
Hearne 48 H4 Texas, USA
Hearst 35 C4 Ontario, S Canada
Hebbronville 48 G6 Texas, USA
Hebron 99 H6 S West Bank
Heemskerk 68 C3 W Netherlands
Heerde 68 E3 E Netherlands
Heerenveen 68 E2 N Netherlands
Heerhugowaard 68 D3 NW Netherlands
Heerlen 68 D6 SE Netherlands
Hefei 105 G4 E China
Hegang 105 H1 NE China
Heide 77 B2 N Germany
Heidelberg 77 B6 SW Germany
Heidenheim an der Brenz 77 C6 S Germany
Heilbronn 77 B6 SW Germany
Heilong Jiang see Amur
Heiloo 68 C3 NW Netherlands
Heimdal 67 B4 S Norway
Hekimhan 97 E3 C Turkey
Helena 51 D2 Montana, USA
Helensville 135 D2 North Island, NZ
Helgoländer Bucht 77 B2 Bay, NW Germany
Hellevoetsluis 68 C5 SW Netherlands
Hellín 75 E4 C Spain
Hells Canyon 53 D3 Valley, NW USA
Helmand, Darya-ye 101 D6 ≈ Afghanistan/Iran
Helmond 68 E5 S Netherlands
Helsingborg 67 C7 S Sweden
Helsinki 67 E5 ● S Finland
Henderson 51 C7 Nevada, USA
Henderson 48 H3 Texas, USA
Hengduan Shan 105 D5 ⛰ SW China
Hengelo 68 F4 E Netherlands
Hengyang 105 F5 S China
Heniches'k 85 F6 S Ukraine
Hennebont 73 B3 NW France
Henzada 109 A3 SW Myanmar
Herat 101 D5 W Afghanistan
Heredia 59 E6 C Costa Rica
Hereford 48 F2 Texas, USA
Herford 77 B4 NW Germany
Herk-de-Stad 68 D6 NE Belgium
Hermansverk 67 B5 S Norway
Hermiston 53 C3 Oregon, USA
Hermit Islands 137 B1 Island group, N PNG
Hermon, Mount 99 H5 ▲ S Syria
Hermosillo 57 B2 NW Mexico
Herrera del Duque 75 C4 W Spain
Herselt 68 D6 C Belgium
Herstal 68 E7 E Belgium
Hessen 77 C5 Cultural region, C Germany
Hettinger 47 B3 North Dakota, USA
Hidalgo del Parral 57 D3 N Mexico
Hida-sanmyaku 103 E5 ⛰ Honshu, S Japan
Hienghène 137 G6 C New Caledonia
High Atlas 122 C2 ⛰ C Morocco
High Point 43 G3 North Carolina, USA
Higüero, Punta 55 Headland W Puerto Rico
Hiiumaa 67 D6 Island, W Estonia
Hikurangi 135 D2 North Island, NZ
Hildesheim 77 C4 N Germany
Hill Bank 59 B1 N Belize
Hillegom 68 C4 W Netherlands
Hilo 55 D3 Hawaii, USA
Hilversum 68 D4 C Netherlands
Himalayas 107 E2 ⛰ S Asia
Himeji 103 E6 SW Japan
Hims 99 B2 C Syria
Hinchinbrook Island 133 G2 Island, Queensland, NE Australia
Hinds 135 C6 South Island, NZ
Hindu Kush 101 F4 ⛰ Afghanistan/Pakistan
Hinesville 43 G5 Georgia, USA
Hinnøya 67 C2 Island, C Norway
Hirfanli Baraji 97 C3 ⊡ C Turkey
Hirosaki 103 F3 C Japan
Hiroshima 103 D7 SW Japan
Hirson 73 E2 N France
Hisiu 137 B3 SW PNG
Hispaniola 61 F4 Island, Dominion Republic/Haiti
Hitachi 103 G5 S Japan
Hitra 67 B4 Island, S Norway
Hjälmaren 67 C6 ◎ C Sweden
Hjørring 67 B6 N Denmark
Hkakabo Razi 109 A1 ▲ Myanmar/China
Hlukhiv 85 E3 NE Ukraine
Hlybokaye 85 C2 N Belarus
Hoang Lien Son 109 C2 ⛰ N Vietnam
Hobart 133 G7 Tasmania, SE Australia
Hobbs 48 F3 New Mexico, USA
Hobro 67 B6 N Denmark
Ho Chi Minh 109 C4 S Vietnam
Hocking River 44 F7 ≈ Ohio, USA
Hodeida 99 B6 W Yemen
Hódmezővásárhely 81 E8 SE Hungary
Hodna, Chott El 88 D4 Salt lake, N Algeria
Hodonín 81 D6 SE Czech Republic
Hoeryong 103 C3 NE North Korea
Hof 77 D5 SE Germany
Hofu 103 D7 SW Japan
Hohenems 77 C7 W Austria
Hohe Tauern 77 D8 ⛰ W Austria
Hohhot 105 F3 N China
Hokianga Harbour 135 C2 Inlet, SE Tasman Sea
Hokitika 135 B6 South Island, NZ
Hokkaido 103 F1 Island, NE Japan
Holbrook 48 C2 Arizona, USA
Holden 51 D5 Utah, USA
Holguín 61 D3 SE Cuba
Hollabrunn 77 F6 NE Austria
Holland see Netherlands
Holly Springs 43 C4 Mississippi, USA
Hollywood 43 G8 Florida, USA
Holman 33 G3 Victoria Island, NW Terr., N Canada
Holmsund 67 D4 N Sweden
Holon 99 G6 C Israel
Holstebro 67 B6 W Denmark
Holyhead 71 C6 NW Wales, UK
Holyoke 41 E4 Massachusetts, USA
Hombori 124 D3 S Mali
Homyel' 85 D3 SE Belarus
Hondo 48 G5 Texas, USA
Hondo 59 B1 ≈ Central America
Honduras 59 C3 ◆ Republic, Central America
Honduras, Gulf of 59 C2 Gulf, W Caribbean Sea
Hønefoss 67 B5 S Norway
Honey Lake 53 B6 ◎ California, USA
Hong Gai 109 C2 N Vietnam
Hong Kong (Xianggang) 105 H6 Special Administrative Region of China, Former UK dependency, S China
Honiara 137 E3 ● C Solomon Islands
Honjo 103 F4 C Japan
Honolulu 55 B1 Oahu, Hawaii, USA
Honshu 103 G5 Island, SW Japan
Hoogeveen 68 E3 NE Netherlands
Hoogezand-Sappemeer 68 F2 NE Netherlands
Hoorn 68 D3 NW Netherlands
Hoover Dam 51 C7 Dam, W USA
Hopa 97 G2 NE Turkey
Hope 33 D4 British Columbia, SW Canada
Hope 54 E3 Alaska, USA
Hopedale 35 F2 Newfoundland, NE Canada
Hopkinsville 43 D3 Kentucky, USA
Horasan 97 G3 NE Turkey
Horki 85 D2 E Belarus
Horlivka 85 G5 E Ukraine
Hormuz, Strait of 99 E4 Strait, Iran/Oman
Horn, Cape 117 B9 Headland, S Chile
Horoshiri-dake 103 G2 ▲ N Japan
Horsham 133 F6 Victoria, SE Australia
Horst 68 E5 SE Netherlands
Horten 67 B5 S Norway
Horyn' 85 C4 ≈ NW Ukraine
Hosingen 68 E8 NE Luxembourg
Hotan 105 B3 NW China
Hotazel 128 C6 N South Africa
Hoting 67 C4 C Sweden
Hot Springs 43 B4 Arkansas, USA
Houayxay 109 B2 N Laos
Houghton 44 C2 Michigan, USA
Houghton Lake 44 D4 Michigan, USA
Houilles 73 C6 N France
Houlton 41 G1 Maine, USA
Houma 43 C6 Louisiana, USA
Houston 48 H4 Texas, USA
Hovd 105 C2 W Mongolia
Hove 71 E8 SE England, UK
Hoverla, Hora 85 B5 ▲ W Ukraine
Hövsgöl Nuur 105 D1 ◎ N Mongolia
Howar, Wadi 127 B2 ≈ Chad/Sudan
Hoy 71 D2 Island, N Scotland, UK
Hoyerswerda 77 E4 E Germany
Hradec Králové 81 C5 NE Czech Republic
Hranice 81 D6 E Czech Republic
Hrodna 85 B2 W Belarus
Huaihua 105 F5 S China
Huajuapan 57 F5 SE Mexico
Hualapai Peak 48 A2 ▲ Arizona, USA
Huambo 128 B4 C Angola
Huancayo 115 B5 C Peru
Huangshi 105 G4 C China
Huánuco 115 B5 C Peru
Huanuni 117 A2 W Bolivia
Huaraz 115 B5 W Peru
Huatabampo 57 C3 NW Mexico
Hubli 107 D6 SW India
Huch'ang 103 B4 N North Korea
Huddersfield 71 E6 N England, UK
Hudiksvall 67 D4 C Sweden
Hudson Bay 35 B2 Bay, NE Canada
Hudson River 41 E4 ≈ NE USA
Hudson Strait 33 J4 Strait, Nunavut/Quebec, NE Canada
Hue 109 C3 C Vietnam
Huehuetenango 59 A3 W Guatemala
Huelva 75 B5 SW Spain
Huesca 75 F2 NE Spain
Huéscar 75 E5 S Spain
Hughenden 133 G3 Queensland, NE Australia
Hugo 47 D9 Oklahoma, USA
Huich'on 103 B4 C North Korea
Huíla Plateau 128 B4 Plateau, S Angola
Huixtla 57 H6 SE Mexico
Hulingol 105 G2 N China
Hull 35 D5 Quebec, SE Canada
Hulst 68 C6 SW Netherlands
Hulun Nur 105 F2 ◎ NE China
Humacao 55 E Puerto Rico
Humaitá 115 D4 N Brazil
Humboldt River 51 B5 ≈ Nevada, USA
Humphreys Peak 48 A2 ▲ Arizona, USA
Humpolec 81 C6 C Czech Republic
Hunedoara 85 B6 SW Romania
Hünfeld 77 C5 C Germany
Hungary 81 D8 ◆ Republic, C Europe
Hunter Island 133 F7 Island, Tasmania, SE Australia
Huntington 43 F2 West Virginia, USA
Huntington Beach 53 C9 California, USA
Huntly 135 D3 North Island, NZ
Huntsville 43 E4 Alabama, USA
Huntsville 48 H4 Texas, USA
Huon Gulf 137 B2 Gulf, E PNG
Hurghada 122 J3 E Egypt
Huron 47 C3 South Dakota, USA
Huron, Lake 44 E3 ◎ Canada/USA
Hurunui 135 C6 ≈ South Island, NZ
Húsavík 67 A1 NE Iceland
Husum 77 B2 N Germany
Hutchinson 47 C6 Kansas, USA
Huy 68 D7 E Belgium
Hvannadalshnúkur 67 B1 ※ S Iceland
Hvar 83 B3 Island, S Croatia
Hwange 128 D5 W Zimbabwe
Hyargas Nuur 105 D2 ◎ NW Mongolia
Hyderabad 107 E5 C India
Hyderabad 107 B3 SE Pakistan
Hyères 73 E7 SE France
Hyères, Îles d' 73 E7 Island group, S France
Hyesan 103 B4 NE North Korea
Hyvinkää 67 E5 S Finland


# I


Ialomița 85 C7 ≈ SE Romania
Iași 85 C6 NE Romania
Ibadan 124 E5 SW Nigeria
Ibar 83 D2 ≈ C Yugoslavia
Ibarra 115 B3 N Ecuador
Iberian Peninsula 62 Physical region, Portugal/Spain
Ibérico, Sistema 75 E2 ⛰ NE Spain
Ibiza 75 G4 Island, Balearic Islands, Spain
Ica 115 B6 SW Peru
Iceland 67 A1 ◆ Republic, N Atlantic Ocean
Iceland Plateau 139 B6 Undersea feature, S Greenland Sea
Idabel 47 E9 Oklahoma, USA
Idaho 53 D3 ◐ State, NW USA
Idaho Falls 51 D3 Idaho, USA
Idfu 122 J3 SE Egypt
Idîni 124 A2 W Mauritania
Idlib 99 B2 NW Syria
Idre 67 C4 C Sweden
Ieper 68 A6 W Belgium
Iferouâne 124 F2 N Niger
Ifôghas, Adrar des 124 E2 ⛰ NE Mali
Igarka 94 E3 N Russ. Fed.
Iglesias 79 A6 Sardinia, Italy
Igloolik 33 I3 Nunavut, N Canada
Igoumenítsa 83 D5 W Greece
Iguaçu, Rio 115 F8 ≈ Argentina/Brazil
Iguala 57 F5 S Mexico
Iguazu Falls 117 D4 Waterfall, Argentina/Brazil
Iguidi, 'Erg 122 C3 Desert, Algeria/Mauritania
Ihosy 128 G5 S Madagascar
Iisalmi 67 E4 C Finland
IJssel 68 E4 ≈ Netherlands
IJsselmeer 68 D3 ◎ N Netherlands
IJsselmuiden 68 E3 E Netherlands
Ijzer 68 A6 ≈ W Belgium
Ikaría 83 F6 Island, Dodecanese, Greece
Ikela 128 C2 C Dem. Rep. Congo (Zaire)
Iki 103 C7 Island, SW Japan
Ilagan 109 F3 Luzon, N Philippines
Iława 81 E2 N Poland
Ilebo 128 C2 W Dem. Rep. Congo (Zaire)
Île-de-France 73 D3 Cultural region, N France
Ilfracombe 71 D8 SW England, UK
Ílhavo 75 B3 N Portugal
Ili 101 H1 ≈ China/Kazakhstan
Iliamna Lake 54 D2 lake Alaska, USA
Iligan 109 F5 Mindanao, S Philippines
Illapel 117 A5 C Chile
Illichivs'k 85 E6 SW Ukraine
Illinois 44 B7 ◐ State, C USA
Illinois River 44 B6 ≈ Illinois, USA
Iloilo 109 F4 Panay Island, C Philippines
Ilorin 124 E4 W Nigeria
Ilovlya 87 B7 SW Russ. Fed.
Il'yaly 101 D2 N Turkmenistan
Imatra 67 F4 SE Finland
Imisli 97 I2 C Azerbaijan
Imola 79 C3 N Italy
Imperatriz 115 G4 NE Brazil
Imperia 79 A3 NW Italy
Imphal 107 H3 NE India
Inarajan 55 SE Guam
Inarijärvi 67 E1 ◎ N Finland
Inawashiro-ko 103 F5 ◎ Honshu, C Japan
İncesu 97 D4 C Turkey
Inch'on 103 B5 NW South Korea
Independence 47 E6 Missouri, USA
Independence Mountains 51 B4 ⛰ Nevada, USA
India 107 D4 ◆ Republic, S Asia
Indiana 41 B5 Pennsylvania, USA
Indiana 44 C6 ◐ State, N USA
Indianapolis 44 D7 Indiana, USA
Indian Church 59 B1 N Belize
Indian Ocean 15 Ocean
Indianola 47 E5 Iowa, USA
Indigirka 94 G2 ≈ NE Russ. Fed.
Indira Point 107 H6 Headland, Andaman and Nicobar Islands, India
Indonesia 109 C7 ◆ Republic, SE Asia
Indore 107 D4 C India
Indus 107 B3 ≈ S Asia
Indus, Mouths of the 107 B3 Delta, S Pakistan
İnebolu 97 D2 N Turkey
Infiernillo, Presa del 57 E5 S Mexico
Ingolstadt 77 C6 S Germany
Inhambane 128 E6 SE Mozambique
Inn 77 D7 ≈ C Europe
Inner Hebrides 71 B4 Island group, W Scotland, UK
Innisfail 133 G2 Queensland, NE Australia
Innsbruck 77 C7 W Austria
Inowrocław 81 D3 C Poland
I-n-Sakane, 'Erg 124 D2 Desert, N Mali
I-n-Salah 122 D3 C Algeria
Inta 87 E3 NW Russ. Fed.
Interlaken 77 B8 SW Switzerland
International Falls 47 E1 Minnesota, USA
Inukjuak 35 D2 Quebec, NE Canada
Inuvik 33 F4 NW Terr., NW Canada
Invercargill 135 B8 South Island, NZ
Inverness 71 D3 N Scotland, UK
Investigator Strait 133 E6 Strait, S Australia
Inyangani 128 E5 ▲ NE Zimbabwe
Ioánnina 83 D5 W Greece
Iola 47 E7 Kansas, USA
Iónia Nisiá see Ionian Islands
Ionian Islands 83 D5 Island group, W Greece
Ionian Sea 88 G3 Sea, C Mediterranean Sea
Íos 83 F6 Island, Cyclades, Greece
Iowa 47 E5 State, C USA
Iowa City 47 F5 Iowa, USA
Iowa Falls 47 E4 Iowa, USA
Iowa River 44 A5 ≈ Iowa, USA
Ipel' 81 E7 ≈ Hungary/Slovakia
Ipoh 109 B5 Peninsular Malaysia
Ippy 124 H5 C CAR
Ipswich 133 H5 Queensland, E Australia
Ipswich 71 F7 E England, UK
Iqaluit 33 J3 Baffin Island, Nunavut, NE Canada
Iquique 117 A3 N Chile
Iquitos 115 C4 N Peru
Irákleio 83 F7 Crete, Greece
Iran 99 E2 ◆ Republic, SW Asia
Iranian Plateau 99 E3 Plateau, N Iran
Irapuato 57 E4 C Mexico
Iraq 99 B2 ◆ Republic, SW Asia
Irbid 99 A2 N Jordan
Ireland, Republic of 71 A6 ◆ Republic, NW Europe
Irian Jaya 109 I7 Province, E Indonesia
Iringa 127 D7 C Tanzania
Iriomote-jima 103 A8 Island, Sakishima-shoto, SW Japan
Iriona 59 D2 NE Honduras
Irish Sea 71 C6 Sea, C British Isles
Irkutsk 94 F5 S Russ. Fed.
Iroise 73 A2 Sea, NW France
Iron Mountain 44 C3 Michigan, USA
Ironwood 44 B2 Michigan, USA
Irrawaddy 109 A2 ≈ W Myanmar
Irrawaddy, Mouths of the 109 A3 Delta, SW Myanmar
Irtysh 94 D4 ≈ C Asia
Irún 75 E1 N Spain
Iruña see Pamplona
Isabela, Isla 115 A7 Island, Galapagos Islands, Ecuador
Isabella, Cordillera 59 D4 ⛰ NW Nicaragua
Isachsen 33 G2 Ellef Ringnes Island, Nunavut, N Canada
Ísafjördhur 67 A1 NW Iceland
Ise 103 F6 SW Japan
Isère 73 E5 ≈ E France
Isernia 79 D5 C Italy
Ise-wan 103 F6 Bay, S Japan
Isfahan 99 D2 C Iran
Ishigaki-jima 103 A8 Island, Sakishima-shoto, SW Japan
Ishikari-wan 103 F2 Bay, NE Japan
Ishim 94 C4 C Russ. Fed.
Ishim 94 D4 ≈ Kazakhstan/Russ. Fed.
Ishinomaki 103 G4 C Japan
Ishkoshim 101 G4 S Tajikistan
Isiro 128 D1 NE Dem. Rep. Congo (Zaire)
İskenderun 97 E5 S Turkey
Iskur 83 E3 ≈ NW Bulgaria
Iskur, Yazovir 83 E3 ⊡ W Bulgaria
Isla Cristina 75 B5 S Spain
Islamabad 107 D1 ● NE Pakistan
Islay 71 B4 Island, SW Scotland, UK
Isle 73 C5 ≈ W France
Isle of Man 71 C6 UK ◇ NW Europe
Isle of Wight 71 E8 Unitary auth., S England, UK
Ismâ'ilîya 122 I2 N Egypt
Isna 122 J3 SE Egypt
Isoka 128 E3 NE Zambia
Isparta 97 B4 Isparta, SW Turkey
İspir 97 F2 NE Turkey
Israel 99 G6 ◆ Republic, SW Asia
Issoire 73 D5 C France
Issyk-Kul', Ozero 101 H2 ◎ E Kyrgyzstan
Istanbul 97 B2 NW Turkey
Istra 83 A1 Cultural region, Croatia/Slovenia
Itabuna 115 H6 E Brazil
Itagüí 115 B2 W Colombia
Itaipú Dam 117 C4 Dam, Brazil/Paraguay
Itaipú, Represa de 115 F7 ⊡ Brazil/Paraguay
Itaituba 115 F4 NE Brazil
Italy 79 C4 ◆ Republic, S Europe
Ithaca 41 D4 New York, USA
Itoigawa 103 F5 C Japan
Iturup, Ostrov 94 I5 Island, Kurile Islands, SE Russ. Fed.
Itzehoe 77 C2 N Germany
Ivalo 67 E2 N Finland
Ivanhoe 133 F5 NSW, SE Australia
Ivano-Frankivs'k 85 B5 W Ukraine
Ivanovo 87 B5 W Russ. Fed.
Ivoire, Côte d' 124 C5 ◆ Republic, W Africa
Ivory Coast see Ivoire, Côte d'
Ivujivik 35 D1 Quebec, NE Canada
Iwaki 103 G5 N Japan
Iwakuni 103 D7 SW Japan
Iwanai 103 F2 NE Japan
Iwate 103 G3 N Japan
Ixtapa 57 E5 S Mexico
Ixtepec 57 G5 SE Mexico
Iyo-nada 103 D7 Sea, S Japan
Izabal, Lago de 59 B3 ◎ E Guatemala
Izad Khvast 99 D3 C Iran
Izegem 68 B6 W Belgium
Izhevsk 87 D6 NW Russ. Fed.
Izmayil 85 D7 SW Ukraine
İzmir 97 A4 W Turkey
İzmit 97 B2 NW Turkey
İznik Gölü 97 B2 ◎ NW Turkey
Izu-hanto 103 G6 Peninsula, Honshu, S Japan
Izu-shoto 103 G6 Island group, S Japan


# J


Jabal ash Shifa 99 A3 Desert, NW Saudi Arabia
Jabalpur 107 E4 C India
Jaca 75 F2 NE Spain
Jacaltenango 59 A3 W Guatemala
Jackman 41 F2 Maine, USA
Jackpot 51 C4 Nevada, USA
Jackson 43 C5 Mississippi, USA
Jackson 47 G7 Missouri, USA
Jackson 43 D3 Tennessee, USA
Jacksonville 43 G6 Florida, USA
Jacksonville 44 B6 Illinois, USA
Jacksonville 43 H4 North Carolina, USA
Jacksonville 48 H3 Texas, USA
Jacmel 61 F4 S Haiti
Jacobabad 107 C3 SE Pakistan
Jaén 75 D5 SW Spain
Jaffna 107 E7 N Sri Lanka
Jagdalpur 107 E5 C India
Jagdaqi 105 G1 N China
Jaipur 107 D3 N India
Jaisalmer 107 C3 NW India
Jakarta 109 C7 ● Java, C Indonesia
Jakobstad 67 E4 W Finland
Jalalabad 101 G5 E Afghanistan
Jalandhar 107 D2 N India
Jalapa 59 D3 NW Nicaragua
Jalpa 57 E4 C Mexico
Jalu 122 H3 NE Libya
Jamaame 127 E5 S Somalia
Jamaica 61 C5 ◆ Commonwealth Republic, W West Indies
Jamaica Channel 61 E4 Channel, Haiti/Jamaica
Jambi 109 C7 Sumatra, W Indonesia
James Bay 35 C3 Bay, Ontario/Quebec, E Canada
James River 47 C4 ≈ N USA
James River 43 H2 ≈ Virginia, USA
Jamestown 41 B4 New York, USA
Jamestown 47 C2 North Dakota, USA
Jammu 107 D2 NW India
Jammu and Kashmir 107 D2 disputed region, India/Pakistan
Jamnagar 107 C4 W India
Jamshedpur 107 F4 NE India
Jamuna 107 G4 ≈ Bangladesh
Janesville 44 B5 Wisconsin, USA
Jan Mayen 139 C6 Norwegian ◇ N Atlantic Ocean
Jánoshalma 81 E8 S Hungary
Japan 103 G4 ◆ Monarchy, E Asia
Japan, Sea of 103 D5 Sea, NW Pacific Ocean
Japiim 115 C5 W Brazil
Japurá, Rio 115 C3 ≈ Brazil/Colombia
Jaqué 59 I7 SE Panama
Jardines de la Reina, Archipiélago de los 61 C3 Island group, C Cuba
Jarocin 81 D4 C Poland
Jarosław 81 G5 SE Poland
Jarqurghon 101 F4 S Uzbekistan
Jarvis Island 131 US ◇, C Pacific Ocean
Jasło 81 F5 SE Poland
Jastrzębie-Zdrój 81 D5 S Poland
Jataí 115 F6 C Brazil
Jaunpur 107 F3 N India
Java 109 C8 Island, C Indonesia
Javalambre 75 E3 ▲ E Spain
Javari, Rio 115 C4 ≈ Brazil/Peru
Java Sea 109 D7 Sea, W Indonesia
Jawhar 127 F5 S Somalia
Jaya, Puncak 109 H7 ▲ E Indonesia
Jayapura 109 I7 E Indonesia
Jaz Murian, Hamun-e 99 F3 ◎ SE Iran
Jebba 124 E4 W Nigeria
Jedda 99 B5 W Saudi Arabia
Jędrzejów 81 E5 S Poland
Jefferson City 47 F6 Missouri, USA
Jefferson, Mount 51 B6 ▲ Nevada, USA
Jelenia Góra 81 C4 SW Poland
Jelgava 67 E6 C Latvia
Jemappes 68 B7 S Belgium
Jember 109 D8 Java, C Indonesia
Jena 77 C5 C Germany
Jenin 99 H6 N West Bank
Jérémie 61 E4 SW Haiti




◐ Administrative region ◆ Country ● Country capital ◇ Dependent territory ○ Dependent territory capital ⛰ Mountain range ▲ Mountain ※ Volcano ≈ River ◎ Lake ⊡ Reservoir

MATTHEW TOWN


**Matthew Town 61 E3** S Bahamas
**Maturín 115 D1** NE Venezuela
**Mau 107 E3** N India
**Maui 55 D2** *Island,* Hawaii, USA
**Maun 128 C5** C Botswana
**Mauna Loa 55 D3** ⛰ Hawaii, Moloka'i, USA
**Mauritania 124 A2** ◆ *Republic,* W Africa
**Mauritius 118** ◆ *Republic,* W Indian Ocean
**Mawson 138 E4** *Australian research station,* Antarctica
**Maya 59 B2** ≈ E Russ. Fed.
**Mayaguana 61 F3** *Island,* SE Bahamas
**Mayaguana Passage 61 E3** *Passage,* SE Bahamas
**Mayagüez 61 H4** W Puerto Rico
**Maych'ew 127 D3** N Ethiopia
**Maydan Shahr 101 F5** E Afghanistan
**Mayfield 135 C6** South Island, NZ
**Maykop 87 A8** SW Russ. Fed.
**Maymyo 109 A2** C Myanmar
**Mayor Island 135 D3** *Island,* NE NZ
**Mayotte 128 G4** *French* ◇ E Africa
**Mazabuka 128 D4** S Zambia
**Mazar-e Sharif 101 F4** N Afghanistan
**Mazatlán 57 D4** C Mexico
**Mazury 81 F2** *Physical region,* NE Poland
**Mazyr 85 D3** SE Belarus
**Mbabane 128 E6** ● NW Swaziland
**Mbala 128 E3** NE Zambia
**Mbale 127 C5** E Uganda
**Mbandaka 128 C2** NW Dem. Rep. Congo (Zaire)
**M'Banza Congo 128 B3** NW Angola
**Mbanza-Ngungu 128 B2** W Dem. Rep. Congo (Zaire)
**Mbarara 127 C5** SW Uganda
**Mbé 124 G5** N Cameroon
**Mbeya 127 C7** Mbeya, SW Tanzania
**Mbuji-Mayi 128 C3** S Dem. Rep. Congo (Zaire)
**McAlester 47 D8** Oklahoma, USA
**McAllen 48 G6** Texas, USA
**McCamey 48 F4** Texas, USA
**McCammon 51 D4** Idaho, USA
**McClintock Channel 33 G3** *Channel,* Nunavut, N Canada
**McComb 43 C6** Mississippi, USA
**McCook 47 B5** Nebraska, USA
**McDermitt 51 B4** Nevada, USA
**McKinley, Mount 54 D2** ▲ Alaska, USA
**McKinley Park 54 E2** Alaska, USA
**McLaughlin 47 B3** South Dakota, USA
**McMinnville 53 B3** Oregon, USA
**McMurdo Base 138 C6** *US research station,* Antarctica
**McNary 48 D4** Texas, USA
**McPherson 47 D6** Kansas, USA
**Mdantsane 128 D7** SE South Africa
**Mead, Lake 51 C7** ⊡ Arizona/Nevada, USA
**Meadville 41 B4** Pennsylvania, USA
**Mecca 99 B5** W Saudi Arabia
**Mechelen 68 C6** C Belgium
**Mecklenburger Bucht 77 C2** *Bay,* N Germany
**Mecsek 81 D8** ⛰ SW Hungary
**Medan 109 B6** Sumatra, E Indonesia
**Medellín 115 B2** NW Colombia
**Médenine 122 F2** SE Tunisia
**Medford 53 B4** Oregon, USA
**Mediaş 85 B6** C Romania
**Medicine Hat 33 G7** Alberta, SW Canada
**Medina 99 B4** W Saudi Arabia
**Medinaceli 75 E3** N Spain
**Medina del Campo 75 D3** N Spain
**Mediterranean Sea 88 D4** *Sea,* Africa/Asia/Europe
**Médoc 73 B5** *Cultural region,* SW France
**Medvezh'yegorsk 87 B3** NW Russ. Fed.
**Meekatharra 133 B4** W Australia
**Meerssen 68 E6** SE Netherlands
**Meerut 107 D2** N India
**Mehtarlam 101 G5** E Afghanistan
**Mejillones 117 A3** N Chile
**Mek'ele 127 D2** N Ethiopia
**Meknès 122 C1** N Morocco
**Mekong 109 C4** ≈ SE Asia
**Mekong, Mouths of the 109 C5** *Delta,* S Vietnam
**Melaka 109 B6** Peninsular Malaysia
**Melanesia 137 G3** *Island group,* W Pacific Ocean
**Melbourne 133 F6** Victoria, SE Australia
**Melbourne 43 G7** Florida, USA
**Melghir, Chott 122 E2** *Salt lake,* E Algeria
**Melilla 121 D1** Spain, N Africa
**Melita 33 H7** Manitoba, S Canada
**Melitopol' 85 F6** SE Ukraine
**Melle 68 B6** NW Belgium
**Mellerud 67 C6** S Sweden
**Mellieha 88 B6** E Malta
**Mellizo Sur, Cerro 117 A8** ▲ S Chile
**Melo 117 D5** NE Uruguay
**Melsungen 77 C5** C Germany
**Melun 73 D3** N France
**Melville Island 133 D1** *Island,* Northern Territory, N Australia
**Melville Island 33 G2** *Island,* Parry Islands, NW Terr/Nunavut, NW Canada
**Melville, Lake 35 G3** ◎ Newfoundland, E Canada
**Melville Peninsula 33 H3** *Peninsula,* Nunavut, NE Canada
**Memmingen 77 C7** S Germany
**Memphis 43 C3** Tennessee, USA
**Ménaka 124 E3** E Mali
**Menaldum 68 D2** N Netherlands
**Mende 73 D6** S France
**Mendeleyev Ridge 139 C3** *Undersea feature,* Arctic Ocean
**Mendi 137 B2** W PNG
**Mendocino, Cape 53 A5** *Headland,* California, USA
**Mendoza 117 A5** W Argentina
**Menemen 97 A3** W Turkey
**Menengiyn Tal 105 F2** *Plain,* E Mongolia
**Menongue 128 B4** C Angola
**Menorca** *see* Minorca
**Mentawai, Kepulauan 109 B7** *Island group,* W Indonesia
**Meppel 68 E3** NE Netherlands
**Merano 79 C1** N Italy
**Mercedes 117 C4** NE Argentina
**Mercedes 48 G6** Texas, USA
**Meredith, Lake 48 E2** ⊡ Texas, USA
**Mergui 109 B4** S Myanmar
**Mérida 57 H4** SW Mexico
**Mérida 75 C4** W Spain
**Mérida 115 C2** W Venezuela
**Meridian 43 D5** Mississippi, USA
**Mérignac 73 B5** SW France
**Merizo 55** SW Guam
**Merowe 127 C2** *Desert,* W Sudan Africa
**Merredin 133 B5** W Australia
**Merrimack River 41 F4** ≈ NE USA
**Mersey 71 D6** ≈ NW England, UK
**Mersin 97 D5** S Turkey
**Meru 127 D5** C Kenya
**Merzifon 97 D2** N Turkey
**Merzig 77 A6** SW Germany
**Mesa 48 B3** Arizona, USA
**Messalo, Rio 128 F4** ≈ NE Mozambique
**Messina 79 D8** Sicily, Italy
**Messina 128 D5** NE South Africa
**Messina, Strait of 79 E8** *Strait,* C Mediterranean Sea
**Mestia 97 G1** N Georgia
**Mestre 79 D2** NE Italy
**Metairie 43 C6** Louisiana, USA
**Metán 117 B4** N Argentina
**Metapán 59 B3** NW El Salvador
**Meta, Río 115 C2** ≈ Colombia/Venezuela
**Métsovo 83 D4** C Greece
**Metz 73 F2** NE France
**Meulaboh 109 A6** Sumatra, W Indonesia
**Meuse 73 E2** ≈ W Europe
**Mexicali 57 A1** NW Mexico
**Mexico 47 F6** Missouri, USA
**Mexico 57 D3** ◆ *Federal Republic,* N Central America
**Mexico City 57 E5** ● C Mexico
**Mexico, Gulf of 28 G3** *Gulf,* W Atlantic Ocean
**Meymaneh 101 E4** NW Afghanistan
**Mezen' 87 C3** ≈ NW Russ. Fed.
**Mezőtúr 81 F8** E Hungary
**Mġarr 88 A6** N Malta
**Miahuatlán 57 G6** SE Mexico
**Miami 43 G9** Florida, USA
**Miami 47 E7** Oklahoma, USA
**Miami Beach 43 G8** Florida, USA
**Mianyang 105 E4** C China
**Miastko 81 C2** NW Poland
**Michalovce 81 F6** E Slovakia
**Michigan 44 D4** ◐ *State,* N USA
**Michigan, Lake 44 C4** ◎ N USA
**Michurinsk 87 B6** W Russ. Fed.
**Micronesia 131** ◆ *Federation,* W Pacific Ocean
**Mid-Indian Ridge 15** *Undersea feature,* C Indian Ocean
**Mid-Atlantic Ridge 14** *Undersea feature,* Atlantic Ocean
**Middelburg 68 B5** SW Netherlands
**Middelharnis 68 C5** SW Netherlands
**Middelkerke 68 A6** W Belgium
**Middle Andaman 107 H5** *Island,* Andaman Islands, India
**Middlesboro 43 F3** Kentucky, USA
**Middlesbrough 71 E5** N England, UK
**Middletown 41 D6** Delaware, USA
**Middletown 41 E5** New Jersey, USA
**Middletown 41 E4** New York, USA
**Midland 35 D5** Ontario, S Canada
**Midland 44 E4** Michigan, USA
**Midland 47 B4** South Dakota, USA
**Midland 48 F3** Texas, USA
**Mid-Pacific Mountains 15** *Undersea feature,* NW Pacific Ocean
**Midway Islands 27** *US* ◇ C Pacific Ocean
**Miechów 81 E5** S Poland
**Międzyrzecz 81 C3** W Poland
**Międzyrzecz Podlaski 81 G3** E Poland
**Mielec 81 F5** SE Poland
**Miercurea-Ciuc 85 C6** C Romania
**Mieres del Camino 75 C1** NW Spain
**Mi'eso 127 E3** C Ethiopia
**Miguel Asua 57 D3** C Mexico
**Mijdrecht 68 D4** C Netherlands
**Mikhaylovka 87 B7** SW Russ. Fed.
**Mikun' 87 D4** NW Russ. Fed.
**Mikura-jima 103 G6** *Island,* E Japan
**Milan 79 B2** N Italy
**Milano** *see* Milan
**Milas 97 A4** SW Turkey
**Mildura 133 F5** Victoria, SE Australia
**Miles 133 G4** Queensland, E Australia
**Miles City 51 F2** Montana, USA
**Milford Haven 71 C7** SW Wales, UK
**Milford Sound 135 A7** South Island, NZ
**Mil'kovo 94 I3** E Russ. Fed.
**Milk River 33 G7** Alberta, SW Canada
**Milk River 51 E1** ≈ Montana, USA
**Milk, Wadi el 127 B2** ≈ C Sudan
**Milledgeville 43 F5** Georgia, USA
**Mille Lacs Lake 47 E2** ◎ Minnesota, USA
**Millerovo 87 A7** SW Russ. Fed.
**Millville 41 D6** New Jersey, USA
**Mílos 83 F6** *Island,* Cyclades, Greece
**Milton 135 B8** South Island, NZ
**Milton Keynes 71 E7** SE England, UK
**Milwaukee 44 C4** Wisconsin, USA
**Minas Gerais 115 H7** ◐ *State,* E Brazil
**Minatitlán 57 G5** E Mexico
**Minbu 109 A2** W Myanmar
**Minch, The 71 C3** *Strait,* NW Scotland, UK
**Mindanao 109 G5** *Island,* S Philippines
**Mindelheim 77 C7** S Germany
**Minden 77 B4** NW Germany
**Mindoro 109 F4** *Island,* N Philippines
**Mindoro Strait 109 E4** *Strait,* W Philippines
**Mineral Wells 48 G3** Texas, USA
**Mingäçevir 97 I2** C Azerbaijan
**Mingaora 107 C1** N Pakistan
**Minho 75 B2** ≈ Portugal/Spain
**Minicoy Island 107 C7** *Island,* SW India
**Minna 124 E4** Niger, C Nigeria
**Minneapolis 47 E3** Minnesota, USA
**Minnesota 47 D3** ◐ *State,* N USA
**Miño 75 B2** ≈ Portugal/Spain
**Minorca 75 H3** *Island,* Balearic Islands, Spain
**Minot 47 B1** North Dakota, USA
**Minsk 85 C2** ● C Belarus
**Minskaya Wzvyshsha 85 C2** ⛰ C Belarus
**Minto, Lac 35 D2** ◎ Quebec, C Canada
**Miraflores 57 C4** W Mexico
**Miranda de Ebro 75 E2** N Spain
**Miri 109 D5** East Malaysia
**Mirim Lagoon 117 D5** *Lagoon,* Brazil/Uruguay
**Mirjaveh 99 F3** SE Iran
**Mirny 138 D5** *Russian research station,* Antarctica
**Mirnyy 94 F4** NE Russ. Fed.
**Mirpur Khas 107 C3** SE Pakistan
**Mirtoan Sea 83 E6** *Sea,* S Greece
**Miskitos, Cayos 59 F3** *Island group,* NE Nicaragua
**Miskolc 81 F7** NE Hungary
**Misool, Pulau 109 G7** *Island,* Maluku, E Indonesia
**Misratah 122 F2** NW Libya
**Mission 47 B4** South Dakota, USA
**Mississippi 43 C5** ◐ *State,* SE USA
**Mississippi Delta 43 C7** *Delta,* Louisiana, USA
**Mississippi River 43 C4** ≈ C USA
**Missoula 51 C2** Montana, USA
**Missouri 47 E6** ◐ *State,* C USA
**Missouri River 47 C4** ≈ C USA
**Mistassini, Lac 35 D4** ◎ Quebec, SE Canada
**Mistelbach an der Zaya 77 F6** NE Austria
**Misti, Volcán 115 C6** Ѫ S Peru
**Mitchell 133 G4** Queensland, E Australia
**Mitchell 53 C3** Oregon, USA
**Mitchell 47 C4** South Dakota, USA
**Mitchell, Mount 43 F3** ▲ North Carolina, USA
**Mitchell River 133 F2** ≈ Queensland, NE Australia
**Mito 103 G5** S Japan
**Mitú 115 C3** SE Colombia
**Mitumba Range 128 D3** ⛰ E Dem. Rep. Congo (Zaire)
**Miyako 103 G3** C Japan
**Miyako-jima 103 G6** *Island,* SW Japan
**Miyakonojō 103 D8** SW Japan
**Miyazaki 103 D8** SW Japan
**Mizpe Ramon 99 G7** S Israel
**Mjøsa 67 B5** ◎ S Norway
**Mława 81 E3** C Poland
**Mljet 83 C3** *Island,* S Croatia
**Moab 51 D6** Utah, USA
**Moa Island 133 F1** *Island,* Queensland, NE Australia
**Moala 137 J5** *Island,* S Fiji
**Moanda 128 B2** SE Gabon
**Moba 128 D3** E Dem. Rep. Congo (Zaire)
**Mobaye 124 H5** S CAR
**Moberly 47 F6** Missouri, USA
**Mobile 43 D6** Alabama, USA
**Mochudi 128 D6** SE Botswana
**Mocímboa da Praia 128 F3** N Mozambique
**Môco 128 B4** ▲ W Angola
**Mocuba 128 F4** NE Mozambique
**Modena 79 C3** N Italy
**Modesto 53 B7** California, USA
**Modica 79 D8** Sicily, Italy
**Moe 133 F6** Victoria, SE Australia
**Mogadishu 127 F5** ● S Somalia
**Mogilno 81 D3** C Poland
**Mogollon Rim 48 B2** *Cliff,* Arizona, USA
**Mohammedia 122 C1** NW Morocco
**Mohawk River 41 D4** ≈ New York, USA
**Mohéli 128 F4** *Island,* S Comoros
**Mohoro 127 D7** E Tanzania
**Moi 67 A6** S Norway
**Mo i Rana 67 C3** C Norway
**Mõisaküla 67 E6** S Estonia
**Moissac 73 C6** S France
**Mojácar 75 E5** S Spain
**Mojave 53 C8** California, USA
**Mojave Desert 53 D8** *Plain,* California, USA
**Mokp'o 103 B7** SW South Korea
**Mol 68 D6** N Belgium
**Moldavia** *see* Moldova
**Molde 67 B4** S Norway
**Moldo-Too, Khrebet 101 H2** ⛰ C Kyrgyzstan
**Moldova 85 C5** ◆ *Republic,* SE Europe
**Molfetta 79 E6** SE Italy
**Mölndal 67 B6** S Sweden
**Molodezhnaya 138 E3** *Russian research station,* Antarctica
**Molokai 55 C1** *Island* Hawaii, USA
**Molopo 128 C6** *Seasonal river,* Botswana/South Africa
**Moluccas 109 G7** *Island group,* Indonesia
**Molucca Sea 109 F6** *Sea,* E Indonesia
**Mombacho, Volcán 59 D5** Ѫ SW Nicaragua
**Mombasa 127 E6** SE Kenya
**Møn 67 B7** *Island,* SE Denmark
**Monaco 73 F6** ● S Monaco
**Monaco 73 F6** ◆ *Monarchy,* W Europe
**Monahans 48 E4** Texas, USA
**Mona, Isla 61 H4** *Island,* W Puerto Rico
**Mona Passage 61 H4** *Channel,* Dominican Republic/Puerto Rico
**Monbetsu 103 G1** NE Japan
**Moncalieri 79 A2** NW Italy
**Monchegorsk 87 B2** NW Russ. Fed.
**Monclova 57 E3** NE Mexico
**Moncton 35 F5** New Brunswick, SE Canada
**Mondovì 79 A3** NW Italy
**Monfalcone 79 D2** NE Italy
**Monforte 75 B2** NW Spain
**Mongo 124 H4** C Chad
**Mongolia 105 D2** ◆ *Republic,* E Asia
**Mongu 128 C4** W Zambia
**Monkey Bay 128 E4** SE Malawi
**Monkey River Town 59 C2** SE Belize
**Mono Lake 53 C7** ◎ California, USA
**Monovar 75 F5** E Spain
**Monroe 43 B5** Louisiana, USA
**Monrovia 124 B5** ● W Liberia
**Mons 68 C7** S Belgium
**Monselice 79 C2** NE Italy
**Montana 83 E2** NW Bulgaria
**Montana 51 D2** ◐ *State,* NW USA
**Montargis 73 D3** C France
**Montauban 73 C6** S France
**Montbéliard 73 F3** E France
**Mont Cenis, Col du 73 F5** *Pass,* E France
**Mont-de-Marsan 73 B6** SW France
**Monteagudo 117 B3** S Bolivia
**Monte Caseros 117 C5** NE Argentina
**Monte Cristi 61 F4** NW Dominican Republic
**Montego Bay 61 D4** W Jamaica
**Montélimar 73 E6** E France
**Montemorelos 57 E3** NE Mexico
**Montenegro 83 C3** ◐ *Republic,* SW Yugoslavia
**Monte Patria 117 A5** N Chile
**Monterey 53 B7** California, USA
**Monterey Bay 53 B7** *Bay,* California, USA
**Montería 115 B2** NW Colombia
**Montero 117 B2** C Bolivia
**Monterrey 57 E3** NE Mexico
**Montes Claros 115 G6** SE Brazil
**Montevideo 47 D3** Minnesota, USA
**Montevideo 117 C6** ● S Uruguay
**Montgenèvre, Col de 73 F5** *Pass,* France/Italy
**Montgomery 43 E5** Alabama, USA
**Monthey 77 A8** SW Switzerland
**Monticello 41 D4** New York, USA
**Monticello 51 E6** Utah, USA
**Montluçon 73 D4** C France
**Montoro 75 D5** S Spain
**Montpelier 51 D4** Idaho, USA
**Montpelier 41 E3** Vermont, USA
**Montpellier 73 D6** S France
**Montréal 35 E5** Quebec, SE Canada
**Montrose 71 D4** E Scotland, UK
**Montrose 51 E6** Colorado, USA
**Montserrat 61 J5** *UK* ◇ E West Indies
**Monywa 109 A2** C Myanmar
**Monza 79 B2** N Italy
**Monze 128 D4** S Zambia
**Monzón 75 F2** NE Spain
**Moonie 133 G4** Queensland, E Australia
**Moora 133 B5** W Australia
**Moore 47 D8** Oklahoma, USA
**Moorea 137 A5** *Island,* Îles du Vent, W French Polynesia
**Moore, Lake 133 B5** ◎ W Australia
**Moorhead 47 D2** Minnesota, USA
**Moose 51 D3** Wyoming, USA
**Moose 35 C4** ≈ Ontario, S Canada
**Moosehead Lake 41 F1** ◎ Maine, USA
**Moosonee 35 C4** Ontario, SE Canada
**Mopti 124 C3** C Mali
**Mora 67 C5** C Sweden
**Morales 59 B3** E Guatemala
**Moratalla 75 E5** SE Spain
**Morava 81 D6** ≈ C Europe
**Moravia 81 D6** *Cultural region,* E Czech Republic
**Moray Firth 71 D3** *Inlet,* N Scotland, UK
**Moreau River 47 B3** ≈ South Dakota, USA
**Moree 133 G5** NSW, SE Australia
**Morelia 57 E5** S Mexico
**Morena, Sierra 75 C5** ⛰ S Spain
**Morfou 88 C6** W Cyprus
**Morgan City 43 B6** Louisiana, USA
**Morghab, Darya-ye 101 E4** ≈ Afghanistan/Turkmenistan
**Moriarty 48 D2** New Mexico, USA
**Morioka 103 G3** C Japan
**Morlaix 73 A2** NW France
**Morocco 122 B2** ◆ *Monarchy,* N Africa
**Morogoro 127 D6** E Tanzania
**Moro Gulf 109 F5** *Gulf,* S Philippines
**Morón 61 D3** C Cuba
**Mörön 105 D1** N Mongolia
**Morondava 128 G5** W Madagascar
**Moroni 128 F4** ● Grande Comore, NW Comoros
**Morotai, Pulau 109 G6** *Island,* Moluccas, E Indonesia
**Morrinsville 135 D3** North Island, NZ
**Morris 47 D3** Minnesota, USA
**Morris Jesup, Kap 139 C4** *Headland,* N Greenland
**Morvan 73 E4** *Physical region,* C France
**Moscow 87 B5** ● Russ. Fed.
**Moscow 51 B2** Idaho, USA
**Mosel 73 F2** ≈ W Europe
**Moselle 73 F3** ≈ W Europe
**Mosgiel 135 B7** South Island, NZ
**Moshi 127 D6** NE Tanzania
**Mosjøen 67 C3** C Norway
**Moskva 101 F4** SW Tajikistan
**Moskva** *see* Moscow
**Mosonmagyaróvár 81 D7** NW Hungary
**Mosquito Coast 59 E4** *Physical region,* Nicaragua
**Mosquito Gulf 59 G6** *Gulf,* N Panama
**Moss 67 B5** S Norway
**Mosselbaai 128 C7** SW South Africa
**Mossendjo 128 B2** SW Congo
**Mossoró 115 I4** NE Brazil
**Most 81 B5** NW Czech Republic
**Mosta 88 B6** C Malta
**Mostaganem 122 D1** NW Algeria
**Mostar 83 C2** S Bosnia and Herzegovina
**Mosul 99 C2** N Iraq
**Mota del Cuervo 75 E4** C Spain
**Motagua, Río 59 B3** ≈ Guatemala/Honduras
**Motril 75 D6** S Spain
**Motueka 135 C5** South Island, NZ
**Motul 57 H4** SE Mexico
**Motu Nui 137 C6** *Island,* Easter Island, Chile
**Mouila 128 A2** C Gabon
**Mould Bay 33 G2** Prince Patrick Island, NW Terr., N Canada
**Moulins 73 D4** C France
**Moulmein 109 B3** S Myanmar
**Moundou 124 G4** SW Chad
**Mountain Home 43 B3** Arkansas, USA
**Mountain Home 51 B4** Idaho, USA
**Mount Cook 135 B6** South Island, NZ
**Mount Desert Island 41 G3** *Island,* Maine, USA
**Mount Gambier 133 F6** S Australia
**Mount Hagen 137 B2** C PNG
**Mount Isa 133 F3** Queensland, C Australia
**Mount Magnet 133 B4** W Australia
**Mount Pleasant 47 F5** Iowa, USA
**Mount Pleasant 44 D4** Michigan, N USA
**Mount Vernon 44 B7** Illinois, USA
**Mount Vernon 53 B1** Washington, USA
**Mouscron 68 B7** W Belgium
**Moussoro 124 G3** W Chad
**Moyen Atlas 122 C2** ⛰ N Morocco
**Moyynkum, Peski 101 G1** *Desert,* S Kazakhstan
**Mozambique 128 E5** ◆ *Republic,* S Africa
**Mozambique Channel 128 F5** *Strait,* W Indian Ocean
**Mpama 128 B2** ≈ C Congo
**Mragowo 81 F2** NE Poland
**Mtwara 127 E7** SE Tanzania
**Muar 109 B6** Peninsular Malaysia
**Mucojo 128 F4** N Mozambique
**Mudanjiang 105 H2** NE China
**Muddy Gap 51 E4** Wyoming, USA
**Mufulira 128 D4** C Zambia
**Muğla 97 A4** SW Turkey
**Mukacheve 85 B5** W Ukraine
**Mula 75 E5** SE Spain
**Muleshoe 48 E2** Texas, USA
**Mulhacén 75 D5** ▲ S Spain
**Mulhouse 73 F3** NE France
**Muller, Pegunungan 109 D6** ⛰ C Indonesia
**Müllheim 77 B7** SW Germany
**Mull, Isle of 71 B4** *Island,* W Scotland, UK
**Mulongo 128 D3** SE Dem. Rep. Congo (Zaire)
**Multan 107 C2** E Pakistan
**Mumbai 107 C5** W India
**Münchberg 77 D5** E Germany
**München** *see* Munich
**Muncie 44 D6** Indiana, USA
**Munda 137 E2** NW Solomon Islands
**Mungbere 128 D1** NE Dem. Rep. Congo (Zaire)
**Munich 77 D7** SE Germany
**Munster 77 B4** NW Germany
**Munster 71 A7** *Cultural region,* S Ireland
**Muonio 67 E2** N Finland
**Muonioälv 67 D2** Finland/Sweden
**Muqdisho** *see* Mogadishu
**Mur 77 F8** ≈ C Europe
**Muradiye 97 H3** E Turkey
**Murchison River 133 B4** ≈ W Australia
**Murcia 75 F5** SE Spain
**Murcia 75 E5** *Cultural region,* SE Spain
**Mureş 85 A6** ≈ Hungary/Romania
**Murfreesboro 43 E3** Tennessee, USA
**Murgab 101 D4** S Turkmenistan
**Murgab 101 D4** ≈ SE Tajikistan
**Murghob 101 H3** SE Tajikistan
**Murgon 133 H4** Queensland, E Australia
**Müritz 77 D3** ◎ NE Germany
**Murmansk 87 C2** NW Russ. Fed.
**Murmashi 87 B2** NW Russ. Fed.
**Murom 87 B5** W Russ. Fed.
**Muroran 103 F2** NE Japan
**Muros 75 A1** NW Spain
**Murray, Lake 137 A2** ◎ SW PNG
**Murray River 133 F5** ≈ SE Australia
**Murrumbidgee River 133 F6** ≈ NSW, SE Australia
**Murska Sobota 77 F8** NE Slovenia
**Murupara 135 E3** North Island, NZ
**Mururoa 131** *Atoll,* Îles Tuamotu, SE French Polynesia
**Murwara 107 E4** N India
**Murwillumbah 133 H5** NSW, SE Australia
**Murzuq, Idhan 122 F4** *Desert,* SW Libya
**Mürzzuschlag 77 F7** E Austria
**Muş 97 G3** E Turkey
**Musa, Gebel 122 I3** ▲ NE Egypt
**Musala 83 E3** ▲ W Bulgaria
**Muscat 99 F4** ● NE Oman
**Muscatine 47 F5** Iowa, USA
**Musgrave Ranges 133 D4** ⛰ S Australia
**Muskegon 44 D4** Michigan, USA
**Muskegon River 44 D4** ≈ Michigan, USA
**Muskogee 47 E8** Oklahoma, USA
**Musoma 127 C5** N Tanzania
**Musselshell River 51 E2** ≈ Montana, USA
**Musters, Lago 117 A7** ◎ S Argentina
**Muswellbrook 133 G5** NSW, SE Australia
**Mut 97 C5** S Turkey
**Mutare 128 E5** E Zimbabwe
**Muy Muy 59 D4** C Nicaragua
**Muynoq 101 D1** NW Uzbekistan
**Mwanza 127 C6** NW Tanzania
**Mweka 128 C2** C Dem. Rep. Congo (Zaire)
**Mwene-Ditu 128 C3** S Dem. Rep. Congo (Zaire)
**Mweru, Lake 128 D3** ◎ Dem. Rep. Congo (Zaire)/Zambia
**Myadzyel 85 C2** N Belarus
**Myanmar 109 A2** ◆ *military dictatorship,* SE Asia
**Myingyan 109 A2** C Myanmar
**Myitkyina 109 B1** N Myanmar
**Mykolayiv 85 E6** S Ukraine
**Mykonos 83 F6** *Island,* Cyclades, Greece
**Myrina 83 F4** Límnos, SE Greece
**Myrtle Beach 43 H4** South Carolina, USA
**Myślibórz 81 B3** W Poland
**Mysore 107 D6** W India
**My Tho 109 C4** S Vietnam
**Mytilíni 83 F5** Lesbos, E Greece
**Mzuzu 128 E3** N Malawi

# N

**Naalehu 55 D3** Hawaii, USA
**Naberezhnyye Chelny 87 D6** W Russ. Fed.
**Nacala 128 F4** NE Mozambique
**Nacogdoches 48 I3** Texas, USA
**Nadi 137 J5** Viti Levu, W Fiji
**Nadur 88 A6** N Malta
**Nadvoitsy 87 B3** NW Russ. Fed.




◐ Administrative region ◆ Country ● Country capital ◇ Dependent territory ○ Dependent territory capital ⛰ Mountain range ▲ Mountain Ѫ Volcano ≈ River ◎ Lake ⊡ Reservoir

OLENEGORSK

**Nadym** 94 D3 N Russ. Fed.
**Náfpaktos** 83 D5 C Greece
**Náfplio** 83 E6 S Greece
**Naga** 109 F4 N Philippines
**Nagano** 103 F5 S Japan
**Nagaoka** 103 F5 C Japan
**Nagasaki** 103 C8 SW Japan
**Nagato** 103 D7 Honshu, SW Japan
**Nagercoil** 107 D7 SE India
**Nagornyy Karabakh** 97 H2 *Former autonomous region*, SW Azerbaijan
**Nagoya** 103 F6 SW Japan
**Nagpur** 107 E4 C India
**Nagqu** 105 C4 W China
**Nagykálló** 81 F7 E Hungary
**Nagykanizsa** 81 C8 SW Hungary
**Nagykörös** 81 E8 C Hungary
**Naha** 103 A8 Okinawa, SW Japan
**Nahariyya** 99 H5 N Israel
**Nahuel Huapi, Lago** 117 A7 ◎ W Argentina
**Nain** 35 F2 Newfoundland, NE Canada
**Nairobi** 127 D5 ● S Kenya
**Naitogi** 55 W American Samoa
**Najin** 103 C3 NE North Korea
**Najran** 99 C6 S Saudi Arabia
**Nakamura** 103 E7 Shikoku, SW Japan
**Nakatsugawa** 103 F6 SW Japan
**Nakhodka** 94 H6 SE Russ. Fed.
**Nakhon Ratchasima** 109 B3 E Thailand
**Nakhon Sawan** 109 B3 W Thailand
**Nakhon Si Thammarat** 109 B5 SW Thailand
**Nakuru** 127 D5 SW Kenya
**Nal'chik** 87 A8 SW Russ. Fed.
**Nalut** 122 F2 NW Libya
**Namangan** 101 G3 E Uzbekistan
**Nam Co** 105 C4 ◎ W China
**Nam Dinh** 109 C2 N Vietnam
**Namhae-do** 103 B7 *Island*, S South Korea
**Namib Desert** 128 B5 *Desert*, W Namibia
**Namibe** 128 B4 SW Angola
**Namibia** 128 B5 ◆ *Republic*, S Africa
**Nam Ou** 109 B2 ≈ N Laos
**Nampa** 51 B3 Idaho, USA
**Namp'o** 103 A5 SW North Korea
**Nampula** 128 F4 NE Mozambique
**Namsan-ni** 103 A4 NW North Korea
**Namsos** 67 C3 C Norway
**Namur** 68 D7 SE Belgium
**Namwon** 103 B6 S South Korea
**Nanaimo** 33 E7 Vancouver Island, British Columbia, SW Canada
**Nanchang** 105 F5 S China
**Nancy** 73 F3 NE France
**Nandaime** 59 D5 SW Nicaragua
**Nanded** 107 D5 C India
**Nandyal** 107 E6 E India
**Nangnim-sanmaek** 103 B4 ⛰ C North Korea
**Nanjing** 105 G4 E China
**Nanning** 105 F6 S China
**Nanping** 105 G5 SE China
**Nansen Basin** 139 D4 *Undersea feature*, Arctic Ocean
**Nansen Cordillera** 139 C4 *Undersea feature*, Arctic Ocean
**Nanterre** 73 D2 N France
**Nantes** 73 B3 NW France
**Nantucket Island** 41 G4 *Island*, Massachusetts, USA
**Nanumaga** 137 I2 *Atoll*, NW Tuvalu
**Nanumea Atoll** 137 I2 *Atoll*, NW Tuvalu
**Nanyang** 105 F4 C China
**Napa** 53 B6 California, USA
**Napier** 135 E4 North Island, NZ
**Naples** 79 D6 S Italy
**Naples** 43 G8 Florida, USA
**Napoli** *see* Naples
**Napo, Río** 115 B3 ≈ Ecuador/Peru
**Naracoorte** 133 F6 S Australia
**Nara Visa** 48 E2 New Mexico, USA
**Narbonne** 73 D7 S France
**Nares Strait** 33 H1 *Strait*, Canada/Greenland
**Narew** 81 F3 ≈ E Poland
**Narowlya** 85 D3 SE Belarus
**Närpes** 67 D4 W Finland
**Närpiö** *see* Närpes
**Narrabri** 133 G5 NSW, SE Australia
**Narrogin** 133 B5 W Australia
**Narva** 67 F5 NE Estonia
**Narvik** 67 D2 C Norway
**Nar'yan-Mar** 87 D3 NW Russ. Fed.
**Naryn** 101 H2 C Kyrgyzstan
**Nashik** 107 D5 W India
**Nashua** 41 F4 New Hampshire, USA
**Nashville** 43 D3 Tennessee, USA
**Näsijärvi** 67 E4 ◎ SW Finland
**Nassau** 61 D2 ● New Providence, N Bahamas
**Nasser, Lake** 122 J4 ◎ Egypt/Sudan
**Nata** 128 D5 NE Botswana
**Natal** 115 I4 E Brazil
**Natchez** 43 B5 Mississippi, USA
**Natchitoches** 43 B5 Louisiana, USA
**Natitingou** 124 D4 NW Benin
**Natuna, Kepulauan** 109 C6 *Island group*, W Indonesia
**Nauru** 137 G1 ◆ *Republic*, W Pacific Ocean
**Navapolatsk** 85 D1 N Belarus
**Navarra** 75 E2 *Cultural region*, N Spain
**Navassa Island** 61 D4 *US* ◇ C West Indies
**Navojoa** 57 C3 NW Mexico
**Navolato** 57 C3 C Mexico
**Nawabshah** 107 B3 S Pakistan
**Nawoiy** 101 E3 C Uzbekistan
**Naxcivan** 97 H3 SW Azerbaijan
**Náxos** 83 F6 *Island*, Cyclades, Greece
**Nayoro** 103 G1 NE Japan
**Nazareth** 99 H5 N Israel
**Nazca Ridge** 14 *Undersea feature*, E Pacific Ocean
**Naze** 103 B7 SW Japan
**Nazilli** 97 A4 SW Turkey
**Nazret** 127 D3 C Ethiopia
**N'Dalatando** 128 B3 NW Angola
**Ndélé** 124 H4 N CAR
**Ndendé** 128 A2 S Gabon
**Ndindi** 128 A2 S Gabon
**Ndjamena** 124 G4 ● W Chad
**Ndola** 128 D4 C Zambia
**Neagh, Lough** 71 B5 ◎ E Northern Ireland, UK
**Neápoli** 83 E6 S Greece
**Neápoli** 83 D4 N Greece
**Near Islands** 54 A1 *Island group*, Aleutian Islands, Alaska, USA
**Nebaj** 59 A3 W Guatemala
**Nebitdag** 101 B3 W Turkmenistan
**Neblina, Pico da** 115 C3 ▲ NW Brazil
**Nebraska** 47 D5 ⬖ *State*, C USA
**Nebraska City** 47 D5 Nebraska, USA
**Neches River** 48 I4 ≈ Texas, USA
**Neckar** 77 B6 ≈ SW Germany
**Necochea** 117 C6 E Argentina
**Neder Rijn** 68 D4 ≈ C Netherlands
**Nederweert** 68 E6 SE Netherlands
**Neede** 68 F4 E Netherlands
**Needles** 53 E8 California, USA
**Neerpelt** 68 D6 NE Belgium
**Neftekamsk** 87 D6 W Russ. Fed.
**Negele** 127 E4 S Ethiopia
**Negev** 99 G6 *Desert*, S Israel
**Negombo** 107 E8 SW Sri Lanka
**Negotin** 83 D2 E Yugoslavia
**Negra, Punta** 115 A4 *Headland*, NW Peru
**Negro, Río** 117 B6 ≈ E Argentina
**Negro, Río** 115 D3 ≈ N South America
**Negros** 109 F5 *Island*, C Philippines
**Neijiang** 105 E5 C China
**Nellore** 107 E6 E India
**Nelson** 135 C5 South Island, NZ
**Nelson** 33 H6 ≈ Manitoba, C Canada
**Néma** 124 C3 SE Mauritania
**Neman** 67 E7 ≈ NE Europe
**Nemours** 73 D3 N France
**Nemuro** 103 H1 NE Japan
**Nendö** 137 G3 *Island*, Santa Cruz Islands, E Solomon Islands
**Nepal** 107 E3 ◆ *Monarchy*, S Asia
**Nepean** 35 D5 Ontario, SE Canada
**Neretva** 83 C2 ≈ Bosnia and Herzegovina/Croatia
**Neringa** 67 E7 SW Lithuania
**Neris** 85 C2 ≈ Belarus/Lithuania
**Nerva** 75 C5 S Spain
**Neryungri** 94 G4 NE Russ. Fed.
**Neskaupstadhur** 67 B1 E Iceland
**Ness, Loch** 71 C3 ◎ N Scotland, UK
**Néstos** 83 E4 ≈ Bulgaria/Greece
**Netanya** 99 G6 C Israel
**Netherlands** 68 D3 ◆ *Monarchy*, NW Europe
**Netherlands Antilles** 61 G7 *Dutch* ◇ S Caribbean Sea
**Nettilling Lake** 33 I3 ◎ Baffin Island, Nunavut, N Canada
**Neubrandenburg** 77 D3 NE Germany
**Neuchâtel** 77 A8 W Switzerland
**Neuchâtel, Lac de** 77 A8 ◎ W Switzerland
**Neufchâteau** 68 D8 SE Belgium
**Neumünster** 77 C2 N Germany
**Neunkirchen** 77 A6 SW Germany
**Neuquén** 117 A6 SE Argentina
**Neuruppin** 77 D3 NE Germany
**Neusiedler See** 77 F7 ◎ Austria/Hungary
**Neustadt an der Weinstrasse** 77 A6 SW Germany
**Neustrelitz** 77 D3 NE Germany
**Neu-Ulm** 77 C7 S Germany
**Neuwied** 77 B5 W Germany
**Nevada** 51 B5 ⬖ *State*, W USA
**Nevers** 73 D4 C France
**Nevinnomyssk** 87 A8 SW Russ. Fed.
**Nevşehir** 97 D4 C Turkey
**Newala** 127 D7 SE Tanzania
**New Albany** 44 D7 Indiana, USA
**New Amsterdam** 115 E2 E Guyana
**Newark** 41 E5 New Jersey, USA
**New Bedford** 41 F4 Massachusetts, USA
**New Bern** 43 H3 North Carolina, USA
**New Braunfels** 48 G4 Texas, USA
**Newbridge** 71 B6 C Ireland
**New Britain** 137 C2 *Island*, E PNG
**New Brunswick** 35 F5 ⬖ *Province*, SE Canada
**New Caledonia** 137 D5 *French* ◇ SW Pacific Ocean
**New Castle** 41 B5 Pennsylvania, USA
**Newcastle** 133 G5 NSW, SE Australia
**Newcastle** 51 F3 Wyoming, USA
**Newcastle upon Tyne** 71 E5 NE England, UK
**New Delhi** 107 D3 ● N India
**New England** 41 F3 *Cultural region*, NE USA
**Newfoundland** 35 G4 *Island*, Newfoundland, SE Canada
**Newfoundland** 35 G3 ⬖ *Province*, E Canada
**New Georgia** 137 E2 *Island*, New Georgia Islands, NW Solomon Islands
**New Georgia Islands** 137 D3 *Island group*, NW Solomon Islands
**New Glasgow** 35 G5 Nova Scotia, SE Canada
**New Guinea** 137 A2 *Island*, Indonesia/PNG
**New Hampshire** 41 E2 ⬖ *State*, NE USA
**New Hanover** 137 C1 *Island*, NE PNG
**New Haven** 41 E5 Connecticut, USA
**New Iberia** 43 B6 Louisiana, USA
**New Ireland** 137 C1 *Island*, NE PNG
**New Jersey** 41 E5 ⬖ *State*, NE USA
**Newman** 133 B3 W Australia
**Newmarket** 71 F7 E England, UK
**New Mexico** 48 D2 ⬖ *State*, SW USA
**New Orleans** 43 C6 Louisiana, USA
**New Plymouth** 135 D4 North Island, NZ
**Newport** 71 E8 S England, UK
**Newport** 71 D7 SE Wales, UK
**Newport** 43 E1 Kentucky, USA
**Newport** 41 F4 Rhode Island, USA
**Newport** 41 F2 Vermont, USA
**Newport News** 43 I2 Virginia, USA
**New Providence** 61 D1 *Island*, N Bahamas
**Newquay** 71 C8 SW England, UK
**Newry** 71 C6 SE Northern Ireland, UK
**New Siberian Islands** 94 F2 *Island group*, N Russ. Fed.
**New South Wales** 133 F5 ⬖ *State*, SE Australia
**Newton** 47 E5 Iowa, USA
**Newton** 47 D7 Kansas, USA
**Newtownabbey** 71 C5 E Northern Ireland, UK
**New Ulm** 47 E3 Minnesota, USA
**New York** 41 E5 New York, USA
**New York** 41 C4 ⬖ *State*, NE USA
**New Zealand** 135 A5 ◆ *Commonwealth Republic*, SW Pacific Ocean
**Neyveli** 107 E7 SE India
**Ngangze Co** 105 B4 ◎ W China
**Ngaoundéré** 124 G5 N Cameroon
**N'Giva** 128 B4 S Angola
**Ngo** 128 B2 SE Congo
**Ngoko** 124 G6 ≈ Cameroon/Congo
**Ngourti** 124 G3 E Niger
**Nguigmi** 124 G3 SE Niger
**Nguru** 124 F4 NE Nigeria
**Nha Trang** 109 D4 S Vietnam
**Nhulunbuy** 133 E1 Northern Territory, N Australia
**Niagara Falls** 35 D6 Ontario, S Canada
**Niagara Falls** 41 B3 New York, USA
**Niagara Falls** 41 B3 *Waterfall*, Canada/USA
**Niamey** 124 E3 ● SW Niger
**Niangay, Lac** 124 D3 ◎ E Mali
**Nia-Nia** 128 D1 NE Dem. Rep. Congo (Zaire)
**Nias, Pulau** 109 A6 *Island*, W Indonesia
**Nicaragua** 59 D4 ◆ *republic*, Central America
**Nicaragua, Lake** 59 E5 ◎ S Nicaragua
**Nice** 73 F6 SE France
**Nicholls Town** 61 D1 NW Bahamas
**Nicobar Islands** 107 H6 *Island group*, India, E Indian Ocean
**Nicosia** 88 C6 ● C Cyprus
**Nicoya** 59 D6 W Costa Rica
**Nicoya, Golfo de** 59 E6 *Gulf*, W Costa Rica
**Nicoya, Península de** 59 D6 *Peninsula*, NW Costa Rica
**Nidzica** 81 E2 N Poland
**Nieuw-Bergen** 68 E5 SE Netherlands
**Nieuwegein** 68 D4 C Netherlands
**Nieuw Nickerie** 115 E2 NW Suriname
**Niğde** 97 D4 C Turkey
**Niger** 124 E3 ◆ *Republic*, W Africa
**Niger** 124 E4 ≈ W Africa
**Niger Delta** 118 *Delta*, S Nigeria
**Nigeria** 124 E4 ◆ *Federal Republic*, W Africa
**Niger, Mouths of the** 124 E5 *Delta*, S Nigeria
**Niigata** 103 F4 C Japan
**Niihama** 103 E7 Shikoku, SW Japan
**Niihau** 55 A1 *Island* Hawaii, USA
**Nii-jima** 103 G6 *Island*, E Japan
**Nijkerk** 68 D4 C Netherlands
**Nijlen** 68 C6 N Belgium
**Nijmegen** 68 E4 SE Netherlands
**Nikel'** 87 B2 NW Russ. Fed.
**Nikiniki** 109 F8 S Indonesia
**Nikopol'** 85 F5 SE Ukraine
**Nikšić** 83 C3 SW Yugoslavia
**Nile** 122 I3 ≈ N Africa
**Nile Delta** 122 I2 *Delta*, N Egypt
**Nimes** 73 E6 S France
**Nine Degree Channel** 107 C7 *Channel*, India/Maldives
**Ninetyeast Ridge** 15 *Undersea feature*, E Indian Ocean
**Ningbo** 105 G4 SE China
**Ninigo Group** 137 A1 *Island group*, N PNG
**Niobrara River** 47 C4 ≈ C USA
**Nioro** 124 B3 W Mali
**Niort** 73 C4 W France
**Nipigon** 35 B4 Ontario, S Canada
**Nipigon, Lake** 35 B4 ◎ Ontario, S Canada
**Niš** 83 D2 SE Yugoslavia
**Nisko** 81 F5 SE Poland
**Nísyros** 83 G6 *Island*, Dodecanese, Greece
**Nitra** 81 D7 SW Slovakia
**Nitra** 81 D7 ≈ W Slovakia
**Niue** 131 *NZ* ◇ S Pacific Ocean
**Niulakita** 137 J3 *Atoll*, S Tuvalu
**Niutao** 137 J2 *Atoll*, NW Tuvalu
**Nivernais** 73 D4 *Cultural region*, C France
**Nizamabad** 107 D5 C India
**Nizhnekamsk** 87 C6 W Russ. Fed.
**Nizhnevartovsk** 94 D4 C Russ. Fed.
**Nizhniy Novgorod** 87 B5 W Russ. Fed.
**Nizhniy Odes** 87 D4 NW Russ. Fed.
**Nizhyn** 85 E4 NE Ukraine
**Njombe** 127 D7 S Tanzania
**Nkayi** 128 B2 S Congo
**Nkongsamba** 124 F5 W Cameroon
**Nmai Hka** 109 B1 ≈ N Myanmar
**Nobeoka** 103 D8 SW Japan
**Noboribetsu** 103 F2 NE Japan
**Nogales** 57 B2 NW Mexico
**Nogales** 48 B4 Arizona, USA
**Nokia** 67 E5 SW Finland
**Nokou** 124 G3 W Chad
**Nola** 124 G5 SW CAR
**Nolinsk** 87 C5 NW Russ. Fed.
**Nome** 139 B1 Alaska, USA
**Noord-Beveland** 68 B5 *Island*, SW Netherlands
**Noordwijk aan Zee** 68 C4 W Netherlands
**Nora** 67 C5 C Sweden
**Norak** 101 F3 W Tajikistan
**Norddeutsches Tiefland** 81 A2 *Plain*, N Germany
**Norden** 77 B3 NW Germany
**Norderstedt** 77 C3 N Germany
**Nordfriesische Inseln** *see* North Frisian Islands
**Nordhausen** 77 C4 C Germany
**Nordhorn** 77 A3 NW Germany
**Nordkapp** *see* North Cape
**Norfolk** 47 D5 Nebraska, USA
**Norfolk** 43 I2 Virginia, USA
**Norfolk Island** 131 *Australian* ◇, SW Pacific Ocean
**Norias** 48 H6 Texas, USA
**Noril'sk** 94 E3 N Russ. Fed.
**Norman** 47 D8 Oklahoma, USA
**Normandie** *see* Normandy
**Normandy** 73 C2 *Cultural region*, France
**Normanton** 133 F2 Queensland, NE Australia
**Norrköping** 67 C6 S Sweden
**Norrtälje** 67 D5 C Sweden
**Norseman** 133 C5 W Australia
**Norsup** 137 G5 Malekula, C Vanuatu
**Northallerton** 71 E5 N England, UK
**Northam** 133 B5 W Australia
**North America** 38 *Continent*
**North American Basin** 14 *Undersea feature*, W Sargasso Sea
**Northampton** 71 E7 C England, UK
**North Andaman** 107 H4 *Island*, Andaman Islands, India
**North Bay** 35 D5 Ontario, S Canada
**North Canadian River** 48 G2 ≈ Oklahoma, USA
**North Cape** 135 C1 *Headland*, North Island, NZ
**North Cape** 67 E1 *Headland*, N Norway
**North Carolina** 43 F3 ⬖ *State*, SE USA
**North Channel** 44 E3 *Lake channel*, Canada/USA
**North Charleston** 43 G5 South Carolina, USA
**North Dakota** 47 B2 ⬖ *State*, N USA
**Northeim** 77 C4 C Germany
**Northern Cook Islands** 131 *Island group*, N Cook Islands
**Northern Dvina** 87 C4 ≈ NW Russ. Fed.
**Northern Ireland** 71 B5 *Political division*, Northern Ireland, UK
**Northern Mariana Islands** 131 *US* ◇ W Pacific Ocean
**Northern Sporades** 83 E5 *Island group*, E Greece
**Northern Territory** 133 D2 ⬖ *Territory*, N Australia
**North European Plain** 62 *Plain*, N Europe
**Northfield** 47 E3 Minnesota, USA
**North Frisian Islands** 77 B2 *Island group*, N Germany
**North Geomagnetic Pole** 139 A4 *Pole*, Arctic Ocean
**North Island** 135 B2 *Island*, N NZ
**North Korea** 103 C4 ◆ *Republic*, E Asia
**Northland** 135 C1 *Cultural region*, North Island, NZ
**North Las Vegas** 51 B7 Nevada, USA
**North Little Rock** 43 C4 Arkansas, USA
**North Platte** 47 B5 Nebraska, USA
**North Platte River** 47 B5 ≈ C USA
**North Pole** 139 C4 *Pole*, Arctic Ocean
**North Saskatchewan** 33 G6 ≈ S Canada
**North Sea** 62 *Sea*, NW Europe
**North Siberian Lowland** 94 E3 *Lowlands*, N Russ. Fed.
**North Taranaki Bight** 135 C3 *Gulf*, North Island, NZ
**North Uist** 71 B3 *Island*, NW Scotland, UK
**Northwest Pacific Basin** 15 *Undersea feature*, NW Pacific Ocean
**Northwest Territories** 33 D5 ⬖ *Territory*, NW Canada
**Northwind Plain** 139 B2 *Undersea feature*, Arctic Ocean
**Norton Sound** 54 D1 *inlet* Alaska, USA
**Norway** 67 A4 ◆ *Monarchy*, N Europe
**Norwegian Sea** 67 A4 *Sea*, NE Atlantic Ocean
**Norwich** 71 F7 E England, UK
**Noshiro** 103 F3 C Japan
**Nossob** 128 C6 ≈ E Namibia
**Noteć** 81 D3 ≈ NW Poland
**Nottingham** 71 E6 C England, UK
**Nouâdhibou** 124 A2 W Mauritania
**Nouakchott** 124 A2 ● SW Mauritania
**Nouméa** 137 G6 ○ S New Caledonia
**Nova Gorica** 77 E8 W Slovenia
**Nova Iguaçu** 115 G7 SE Brazil
**Novara** 79 B2 NW Italy
**Nova Scotia** 41 H2 ⬖ *Province*, SE Canada
**Novaya Sibir', Ostrov** 94 G2 *Island*, NE Russ. Fed.
**Novaya Zemlya** 87 E1 *Island group*, N Russ. Fed.
**Novgorod** 87 A4 W Russ. Fed.
**Novi Sad** 83 D1 N Yugoslavia
**Novoazovs'k** 85 G5 E Ukraine
**Novocheboksarsk** 87 C6 W Russ. Fed.
**Novocherkassk** 87 A7 SW Russ. Fed.
**Novodvinsk** 87 C3 NW Russ. Fed.
**Novokazalinsk** 94 B5 SW Kazakhstan
**Novokuznetsk** 94 E5 S Russ. Fed.
**Novolazarevskaya** 138 C3 *Russian research station*, Antarctica
**Novo Mesto** 77 E9 SE Slovenia
**Novomoskovs'k** 85 F5 E Ukraine
**Novomoskovsk** 87 B6 W Russ. Fed.
**Novorossiysk** 87 A8 SW Russ. Fed.
**Novoshakhtinsk** 87 A7 SW Russ. Fed.
**Novosibirsk** 94 D5 C Russ. Fed.
**Novotroitsk** 87 D7 W Russ. Fed.
**Novyy Buh** 85 E5 S Ukraine
**Nowogard** 81 C2 NW Poland
**Nowy Dwór Mazowiecki** 81 E3 C Poland
**Nowy Sącz** 81 F6 S Poland
**Nowy Tomyśl** 81 C3 W Poland
**Noyon** 73 D2 N France
**Ntomba, Lac** 128 B2 ◎ NW Dem. Rep. Congo (Zaire)
**Nubian Desert** 127 C1 *Desert*, NE Sudan
**Nueces River** 48 G5 ≈ Texas, USA
**Nueva Gerona** 61 B3 S Cuba
**Nueva Guinea** 59 E5 SE Nicaragua
**Nueva Ocotepeque** 59 B3 W Honduras
**Nueva Rosita** 57 E2 NE Mexico
**Nuevitas** 61 D3 E Cuba
**Nuevo Casas Grandes** 57 C2 N Mexico
**Nuevo, Golfo** 117 B7 *Gulf*, S Argentina
**Nuevo Laredo** 57 E2 NE Mexico
**Nui Atoll** 137 I2 *Atoll*, W Tuvalu
**Nuku'alofa** 131 ● Tongatapu, S Tonga
**Nukufetau Atoll** 137 I2 *Atoll*, C Tuvalu
**Nukulaelae Atoll** 137 J3 *Atoll*, E Tuvalu
**Nukumanu Islands** 137 E1 *Island group*, NE PNG
**Nukus** 101 D2 W Uzbekistan
**Nullarbor Plain** 133 D5 *Plateau*, S Australia/W Australia
**Nunavut** 33 F4 ⬖ *Territory*, NW Canada
**Nuneaton** 71 E7 C England, UK
**Nunivak Island** 54 C2 *island* Alaska, USA
**Nunspeet** 68 E4 E Netherlands
**Nuoro** 79 A6 Sardinia, Italy
**Nuremberg** 77 C6 S Germany
**Nurmes** 67 F4 E Finland
**Nürnberg** *see* Nuremberg
**Nurota** 101 E3 C Uzbekistan
**Nusaybin** 97 G4 SE Turkey
**Nyagan'** 94 D3 N Russ. Fed.
**Nyainqentanglha Shan** 105 C4 ⛰ W China
**Nyala** 127 B3 W Sudan
**Nyamtumbo** 127 D7 S Tanzania
**Nyandoma** 87 B4 NW Russ. Fed.
**Nyantakara** 127 C6 NW Tanzania
**Nyasa, Lake** 128 E4 ◎ E Africa
**Nyeri** 127 D5 C Kenya
**Nyima** 105 C4 W China
**Nyíregyháza** 81 F7 NE Hungary
**Nykobing** 67 B7 SE Denmark
**Nyköping** 67 D6 S Sweden
**Nylstroom** 128 D6 NE South Africa
**Nyngan** 133 G5 NSW, SE Australia
**Nyurba** 94 F4 NE Russ. Fed.
**Nzega** 127 C6 C Tanzania
**Nzérékoré** 124 B5 SE Guinea
**N'Zeto** 128 B3 NW Angola

## O

**Oahe, Lake** 47 C3 ⊡ N USA
**Oahu** 55 B1 *Island* Hawaii, USA
**Oak Harbor** 53 B2 Washington, USA
**Oakland** 53 B7 California, USA
**Oakley** 47 B6 Kansas, USA
**Oamaru** 135 B7 South Island, NZ
**Oaxaca** 57 F5 SE Mexico
**Ob'** 94 D3 ≈ C Russ. Fed.
**Oban** 71 C4 W Scotland, UK
**Ob, Gulf of** 94 D3 *Gulf*, N Russ. Fed.
**Obihiro** 103 G2 NE Japan
**Obo** 124 I5 E CAR
**Obock** 127 E3 E Djibouti
**Oborniki** 81 C3 W Poland
**Ocala** 43 F7 Florida, USA
**Ocaña** 75 D3 C Spain
**O Carballiño** 75 B2 NW Spain
**Occidental, Cordillera** 117 A2 ⛰ Bolivia/Chile
**Ocean** 55 New Jersey, USA
**Ocean Falls** 33 E6 British Columbia, SW Canada
**Oceanside** 53 D9 California, USA
**Och'amch'ire** 97 G1 W Georgia
**Ocotal** 59 D4 NW Nicaragua
**Ocozocuautla** 57 G5 SE Mexico
**October Revolution Island** 94 F2 *Island*, N Russ. Fed.
**Ocú** 59 G7 S Panama
**Odate** 103 G3 C Japan
**Ödemiş** 97 A4 SW Turkey
**Odense** 67 B7 C Denmark
**Oder** 77 E3 ≈ C Europe
**Oderhaff** 81 B2 *Bay*, Germany/Poland
**Odesa** 85 E6 SW Ukraine
**Odessa** 48 F4 Texas, USA
**Odienné** 124 C4 NW Côte d'Ivoire
**Odoorn** 68 F2 NE Netherlands
**Of** 97 F2 NE Turkey
**Ofanto** 79 E6 ≈ S Italy
**Offenbach** 77 B5 W Germany
**Offenburg** 77 B7 SW Germany
**Ofu** 55 *Island* Manua Islands, E American Samoa
**Ogaden** 127 F4 *Plateau*, Ethiopia/Somalia
**Ogaki** 103 F6 SW Japan
**Ogallala** 47 B5 Nebraska, USA
**Ogbomosho** 124 E5 W Nigeria
**Ogden** 51 D5 Utah, USA
**Ogdensburg** 41 D2 New York, USA
**Ohio** 44 E6 ⬖ *State*, N USA
**Ohio River** 44 F7 ≈ N USA
**Ohrid, Lake** 83 D4 ◎ Albania/FYR Macedonia
**Ohura** 135 D3 North Island, NZ
**Oil City** 41 B4 Pennsylvania, USA
**Oirschot** 68 D5 S Netherlands
**Oise** 73 D2 ≈ N France
**Oita** 103 D7 Kyushu, SW Japan
**Ojinaga** 57 D2 N Mexico
**Ojos del Salado, Cerro** 117 A4 ▲ W Argentina
**Okaihau** 135 C1 North Island, NZ
**Okanogan River** 53 C1 ≈ Washington, USA
**Okara** 107 D2 E Pakistan
**Okavango** 128 C5 ≈ S Africa
**Okavango Delta** 128 C5 *Wetland*, N Botswana
**Okayama** 103 E6 SW Japan
**Okazaki** 103 F6 C Japan
**Okeechobee, Lake** 43 F8 ◎ SE USA
**Okefenokee Swamp** 43 F6 *Wetland*, Georgia, USA
**Okhotsk** 94 H3 E Russ. Fed.
**Okhotsk, Sea of** 94 H4 *Sea*, NW Pacific Ocean
**Okhtyrka** 85 F4 NE Ukraine
**Okinawa** 103 A8 SW Japan
**Okinawa-shoto** 103 A8 *Island group*, SW Japan
**Oki-shoto** 103 D6 *Island group*, SW Japan
**Oklahoma** 47 C8 ⬖ *State*, C USA
**Oklahoma City** 47 D8 Oklahoma, USA
**Okmulgee** 47 D8 Oklahoma, USA
**Oko, Wadi** 127 D1 ≈ NE Sudan
**Oktyabr'skiy** 87 D6 SW Russ. Fed.
**Okushiri-to** 103 F2 *Island*, NE Japan
**Öland** 67 D7 *Island*, S Sweden
**Olavarría** 117 C6 E Argentina
**Oława** 81 D4 SW Poland
**Olbia** 79 B5 Sardinia, Italy
**Oldebroek** 68 E3 E Netherlands
**Oldenburg** 77 B3 NW Germany
**Oldenburg** 77 C2 N Germany
**Oldenzaal** 68 F4 E Netherlands
**Olëkma** 94 G4 ≈ C Russ. Fed.
**Olëkminsk** 94 G4 NE Russ. Fed.
**Oleksandriya** 85 E5 C Ukraine
**Olenegorsk** 87 B2 NW Russ. Fed.

**CAR** Central African Republic **FYR** Former Yugoslavian Rebublic **NSW** New South Wales **NZ** New Zealand **PNG** Papua New Guinea **Russ. Fed.** Russian Federation **UAE** United Arab Emirates **UK** United Kingdom **USA** United States of America

## P

◆ Administrative region  ◆ Country  ● Country capital  ◇ Dependent territory  ◎ Dependent territory capital  ▲ Mountain range  ▲ Mountain  ☒ Volcano  ◈ River  ◎ Lake  ▣ Reservoir

CAR Central African Republic   FYR Former Yugoslavian Rebublic   NSW New South Wales   NZ New Zealand   PNG Papua New Guinea   Russ. Fed. Russian Federation   UAE United Arab Emirates   UK United Kingdom   USA United States of America

155

◆ Administrative region  ◆ Country  ● Country capital  ◇ Dependent territory  ◎ Dependent territory capital  ▲ Mountain range  ▲ Mountain  ▲ Volcano  ➷ River  ☉ Lake  ▣ Reservoir

SURFERS PARADISE


Sélibabi 124 B3 S Mauritania
Selma 53 C7 California, USA
Semarang 109 D8 Java, C Indonesia
Sembé 128 B1 NW Congo
Seminole 48 E3 Texas, USA
Seminole, Lake 43 E6 ⊠ SE USA
Semipalatinsk 94 D5 E Kazakhstan
Semnān 99 E2 N Iran
Semois 68 D8 ≈ SE Belgium
Senachwine Lake 44 B6 ◎ Illinois, USA
Sendai 103 G4 C Japan
Sendai 103 D8 SW Japan
Sendai-wan 103 G4 Bay, E Japan
Senec 81 D7 W Slovakia
Senegal 124 A3 ◆ Republic, W Africa
Senegal 124 A3 ≈ W Africa
Seney Marsh 44 D2 Wetland, Michigan, USA
Senftenberg 77 E4 E Germany
Sênggê Zangbo 105 B4 ≈ W China
Senica 81 D6 W Slovakia
Senja 67 C1 Island, N Norway
Senkaku-shoto 103 A8 Island group, SW Japan
Senlis 73 D2 N France
Sennar 127 C3 C Sudan
Sens 73 D3 C France
Seoul 103 B6 ● NW South Korea
Sepik 137 A2 ≈ Indonesia/PNG
Sept-Îles 35 F4 Quebec, SE Canada
Seraing 68 D7 E Belgium
Serakhs 101 D4 S Turkmenistan
Seram, Pulau 109 G7 Island, Maluku, E Indonesia
Serang 109 C7 Java, C Indonesia
Serasan, Selat 109 D6 Strait, Indonesia/Malaysia
Serbia 83 D2 ◐ Republic, Yugoslavia
Seremban 109 B6 Peninsular Malaysia
Serengeti Plain 127 C6 Plain, N Tanzania
Serenje 128 D4 E Zambia
Sérifos 83 E6 Island, Cyclades, Greece
Serov 94 C4 C Russ. Fed.
Serowe 128 D5 SE Botswana
Serpukhov 87 A5 W Russ. Fed.
Sesto San Giovanni 79 B2 N Italy
Sète 73 D6 S France
Setesdal 67 B5 Valley, S Norway
Sétif 122 E1 N Algeria
Setté Cama 128 A2 SW Gabon
Setúbal 75 A4 W Portugal
Setúbal, Baía de 75 A5 Bay, W Portugal
Seul, Lac 35 A4 ◎ Ontario, S Canada
Sevan 97 H2 C Armenia
Sevan, Lake 97 H2 ◎ E Armenia
Sevastopol' 85 F7 S Ukraine
Severn 35 B3 ≈ Ontario, S Canada
Severn 71 D7 ≈ England/Wales, UK
Severnaya Zemlya 94 E2 Island group, N Russ. Fed.
Severnyy 87 E3 NW Russ. Fed.
Severodvinsk 87 C3 NW Russ. Fed.
Severomorsk 87 C2 NW Russ. Fed.
Sevier Lake 51 C6 ◎ Utah, USA
Sevilla see Seville
Seville 75 B5 S Spain
Seychelles 118 ◆ Republic, W Indian Ocean
Seydhisfjördhur 67 B1 E Iceland
Seydi 101 E3 E Turkmenistan
Seymour 48 G3 Texas, USA
Sfântu Gheorghe 85 C6 C Romania
Sfax 122 F2 E Tunisia
's-Gravenhage see The Hague
's-Gravenzande 68 C4 W Netherlands
Shache 105 A3 NW China
Shackleton Ice Shelf 138 E5 Ice shelf, Antarctica
Shahany, Ozero 85 D6 ◎ SW Ukraine
Shahrak 101 E5 C Afghanistan
Shahr-e Kord 99 D2 C Iran
Shahrud 99 E1 N Iran
Shamrock 48 F2 Texas, USA
Shanghai 105 G4 E China
Shangrao 105 G5 S China
Shannon 71 B6 ≈ W Ireland
Shan Plateau 109 B2 Plateau, E Myanmar
Shantou 105 G5 S China
Shaoguan 105 F5 S China
Shar 94 D5 E Kazakhstan
Sharjah 99 E4 NE UAE
Shark Bay 133 A4 Bay, E Indian Ocean
Sharon 41 B4 Pennsylvania, USA
Shashe 128 D5 ≈ Botswana/Zimbabwe
Shasta Lake 53 B5 ⊠ California, USA
Shawnee 47 D8 Oklahoma, USA
Shchëkino 87 A6 W Russ. Fed.
Shchors 85 E3 N Ukraine
Shchuchinsk 94 C5 N Kazakhstan
Shchuchyn 85 B2 W Belarus
Shebekino 87 A6 W Russ. Fed.
Shebeli 127 E4 ≈ Ethiopia/Somalia
Sheberghan 101 E4 N Afghanistan
Sheboygan 44 C4 Wisconsin, USA
Shebshi Mountains 124 F4 ▲▲ E Nigeria
Sheffield 71 E6 N England, UK
Shelby 51 D1 Montana, USA
Sheldon 47 D4 Iowa, USA
Shelekhov Gulf 94 H3 Gulf, E Russ. Fed.
Shendi 127 C2 NE Sudan
Shenyang 105 G2 NE China
Shepherd Islands 137 H5 Island group, C Vanuatu
Shepparton 133 F6 Victoria, SE Australia
Sherbrooke 35 E5 Quebec, SE Canada
Shereik 127 C1 N Sudan
Sheridan 51 E3 Wyoming, USA
Sherman 48 H3 Texas, USA
's-Hertogenbosch 68 D5 S Netherlands
Shetland Islands 71 D1 Island group, NE Scotland, UK
Shevchenko see Aktau
Shibetsu 103 G1 NE Japan
Shibushi-wan 103 D8 Bay, SW Japan
Shihezi 105 C2 NW China
Shijiazhuang 105 F3 E China
Shikarpur 107 C3 S Pakistan
Shikoku 103 E7 Island, SW Japan
Shilabo 127 F4 SE Ethiopia
Shiliguri 107 G3 NE India
Shilka 94 G5 ≈ S Russ. Fed.
Shillong 107 G3 NE India
Shimbiris 127 F3 ▲ N Somalia
Shimoga 107 D6 W India
Shimonoseki 103 D7 Honshu, SW Japan
Shinano-gawa 103 F5 ≈ Honshi, C Japan
Shindand 101 D5 W Afghanistan
Shingu 103 F7 Honshu, SW Japan
Shinjo 103 G4 Honshu, C Japan
Shinyanga 127 C6 NW Tanzania
Shiprock 48 C1 New Mexico, USA
Shiraz 99 D3 S Iran
Shivpuri 107 D3 C India
Shizugawa 103 G4 NE Japan
Shizuoka 103 F6 Honshu, S Japan
Shkodër 83 D3 NW Albania
Shoshoni 51 E4 Wyoming, USA
Shostka 85 E3 NE Ukraine
Show Low 48 C2 Arizona, USA
Shreveport 43 A5 Louisiana, USA
Shrewsbury 71 D7 W England, UK
Shu 94 C6 SE Kazakhstan
Shumagin Islands 54 C3 Island group Alaska, USA
Shumen 83 F2 NE Bulgaria
Shuqrah 99 C7 SW Yemen
Shymkent 94 B6 S Kazakhstan
Sialum 137 B2 C PNG
Šiauliai 67 E7 N Lithuania
Sibay 87 D7 W Russ. Fed.
Siberia 94 E4 Physical region, Russ. Fed.
Siberut, Pulau 109 A6 Island, Kepulauan Mentawai, W Indonesia
Sibi 107 B2 SW Pakistan
Sibiti 128 B2 S Congo
Sibiu 85 B6 C Romania
Sibolga 109 B6 Sumatra, W Indonesia
Sibu 109 D6 East Malaysia
Sibut 124 H5 S CAR
Sibuyan Sea 109 F4 Sea, W Pacific Ocean
Sichon 109 B5 SW Thailand
Sichuan Pendi 105 E4 Basin, C China
Sicilia see Sicily
Sicily 79 C8 Island, Italy
Sicily, Strait of 79 B8 Strait, C Mediterranean Sea
Siderno 79 E8 SW Italy
Sîdi Barrâni 122 H2 NW Egypt
Sidi Bel Abbès 122 D1 NW Algeria
Sidley, Mount 138 B5 ▲ Antarctica
Sidney 51 F2 Montana, USA
Sidney 47 A5 Nebraska, USA
Sidney 44 E6 Ohio, USA
Siedlce 81 F3 E Poland
Siegen 77 B5 W Germany
Siemiatycze 81 G3 E Poland
Siena 79 C4 C Italy
Sieradz 81 D4 C Poland
Sierpc 81 E3 C Poland
Sierra Leone 124 A5 ◆ Republic, W Africa
Sierra Madre 59 A3 ▲▲ Guatemala/Mexico
Sierra Madre Occidental 57 C3 ▲▲ C Mexico
Sierra Madre Oriental 57 E4 ▲▲ C Mexico
Sierra Morena 88 B4 ▲▲ SW Spain, Europe
Sierra Nevada 75 D6 ▲▲ S Spain
Sierra Nevada 53 B6 ▲▲ W USA
Sierra Vieja 48 E4 ▲▲ Texas, USA
Sierra Vista 48 C4 Arizona, USA
Sífnos 83 E6 Island, Cyclades, Greece
Sigli 109 A5 Sumatra, W Indonesia, Asia
Siglufjördhur 67 A1 N Iceland
Signal Peak 48 A3 ▲ Arizona, USA
Signy 138 A3 UK research station, South Orkney Islands, Antarctica
Siguatepeque 59 C3 W Honduras
Siguiri 124 B4 NE Guinea
Siilinjärvi 67 F4 C Finland
Siirt 97 G4 SE Turkey
Sikasso 124 C4 S Mali
Sikeston 47 G7 Missouri, USA
Siklós 81 D9 SW Hungary
Silchar 107 H3 NE India
Silesia 81 D4 Physical region, SW Poland
Silicon Valley 53 B7 Industrial and business region, California, USA
Silifke 97 D5 S Turkey
Siling Co 105 C4 ◎ W China
Silisili 137 A4 ▲ C Samoa
Silistra 83 F2 NE Bulgaria
Šilutė 67 E7 W Lithuania
Silvan 97 F4 SE Turkey
Silverek 97 F4 SE Turkey
Simav 97 B3 W Turkey
Simav Çayı 97 A3 ≈ NW Turkey
Simcoe, Lake 41 B2 ◎ Ontario, S Canada
Simeto 79 D8 ≈ Sicily, Italy
Simeulue, Pulau 109 A6 Island, NW Indonesia
Simferopol' 85 F7 S Ukraine
Simpelveld 68 E6 SE Netherlands
Simplon Pass 77 B8 Pass, S Switzerland
Simpson Desert 133 E4 Desert, Northern Territory/S Australia
Sinai 122 J2 Physical region, NE Egypt
Sincelejo 115 B2 NW Colombia
Sinclair, Lake 43 E4 ⊠ Georgia, USA
Sind 107 B3 Cultural region, SE Pakistan
Sindelfingen 77 B6 SW Germany
Sines 75 A5 S Portugal
Singapore 109 C6 ● SE Asia
Singapore 109 C6 ◆ Republic, SE Asia
Singen 77 B7 S Germany
Singida 127 D6 C Tanzania
Singkawang 109 D6 C Indonesia
Siniscola 79 B5 Sardinia, Italy
Sinmi-do 103 A5 Island, NW North Korea
Sinoie, Lacul 85 D7 Lagoon, SE Romania
Sinop 97 D2 N Turkey
Sinp'o 103 B4 E North Korea
Sinsheim 77 B6 SW Germany
Sint-Michielsgestel 68 D5 S Netherlands
Sint-Niklaas 68 C6 N Belgium
Sint-Pieters-Leeuw 68 B7 C Belgium
Sintra 75 A4 W Portugal
Sinuiju 103 A4 W North Korea
Sinujiif 127 E3 NE Somalia
Sion 77 A8 SW Switzerland
Sioux City 47 D4 Iowa, USA
Sioux Falls 47 D4 South Dakota, USA
Siping 105 G2 NE China
Siple, Mount 138 A5 ▲ Siple Island, Antarctica
Siquirres 59 F6 E Costa Rica
Siracusa 79 D8 Sicily, Italy
Sir Edward Pellew Group 133 E2 Island group, Northern Territory, NE Australia
Siret 85 C6 ≈ Romania/Ukraine
Sirikit Reservoir 109 B3 ◎ N Thailand
Sirjan 99 E3 S Iran
Şırnak 97 G4 SE Turkey
Sirte, Gulf of 122 G2 Gulf, N Libya
Sisimiut 139 A5 S Greenland
Sitges 75 G3 NE Spain
Sittang 109 A3 ≈ S Myanmar
Sittard 68 E6 SE Netherlands
Sittwe 109 A2 W Myanmar
Siuna 59 E3 NE Nicaragua
Sivas 97 E3 C Turkey
Sivers'kyy Donets' 85 F4 ≈ Russian Federation/Ukraine
Siwa 122 H3 NW Egypt
Six-Fours-les-Plages 73 E7 SE France
Siyäzän 97 J2 NE Azerbaijan
Sjælland 67 B7 Island, E Denmark
Skagerrak 67 B6 Channel, N Europe
Skagit River 53 B1 ≈ Washington, USA
Skalka 67 D2 ◎ N Sweden
Skegness 71 F6 E England, UK
Skellefteå 67 D3 N Sweden
Skellefteälven 67 D3 ≈ N Sweden
Ski 67 B5 S Norway
Skikda 122 E1 NE Algeria
Skopje 83 D3 ● N FYR Macedonia
Skovorodino 94 G5 SE Russ. Fed.
Skrīveri 67 E6 S Latvia
Skye, Isle of 71 B3 Island, NW Scotland, UK
Skýros 83 F5 Island, Vóreioi Sporádes, Greece
Slagelse 67 B7 E Denmark
Slatina 85 B7 S Romania
Slavonski Brod 83 C1 NE Croatia
Sławno 81 C2 NW Poland
Sliema 88 B6 N Malta
Sligo 71 B5 NW Ireland
Sliven 83 F3 E Bulgaria
Slovakia 81 E6 ◆ Republic, C Europe
Slovenia 77 E8 ◆ Republic, SE Europe
Slovenské rudohorie 81 E6 ▲▲ C Slovakia
Slov"yans'k 85 G4 E Ukraine
Słubice 81 B3 W Poland
Sluch 85 C4 ≈ NW Ukraine
Słupsk 81 D1 NW Poland
Slutsk 85 C3 S Belarus
Smallwood Reservoir 35 F3 ◎ Newfoundland, S Canada
Smara 122 B3 N Western Sahara
Smederevo 83 D2 N Yugoslavia
Smederevska Palanka 83 E2 C Yugoslavia
Smoky Hill River 51 H5 ≈ Kansas, USA
Smøla 67 B4 Island, W Norway
Smolensk 87 A5 W Russ. Fed.
Snake River 53 C2 ≈ NW USA
Snake River Plain 51 C4 Plain, Idaho, USA
Sneek 68 E2 N Netherlands
Sněžka 81 C5 ▲ N Czech Republic
Snina 81 F6 E Slovakia
Snowdon 71 C6 ▲ NW Wales, UK
Snyder 48 F3 Texas, USA
Sobradinho, Represa de 115 G5 ⊠ E Brazil
Sochi 87 A8 SW Russ. Fed.
Society Islands 131 Island group, W French Polynesia
Socorro 48 D2 New Mexico, USA
Socorro, Isla 57 B5 Island, W Mexico
Socotra 99 D7 Island, SE Yemen
Socuéllamos 75 E4 C Spain
Sodankylä 67 E2 N Finland
Söderhamn 67 D5 C Sweden
Södertälje 67 D5 C Sweden
Sodiri 127 B2 C Sudan
Sofia 83 E3 ● W Bulgaria
Sofiya see Sofia
Sogamoso 115 C2 C Colombia
Sognefjorden 67 A5 Fjord, NE North Sea
Sohag 122 I3 C Egypt
Sokch'o 103 B5 N South Korea
Söke 97 A4 SW Turkey
Sokhumi 97 F1 NW Georgia
Sokodé 124 D4 C Togo
Sokol 87 B4 NW Russ. Fed.
Sokolov 81 A5 W Czech Republic
Sokone 124 A3 W Senegal
Sokoto 124 E4 NW Nigeria
Sokoto 124 E4 ≈ NW Nigeria
Solapur 107 D5 W India
Sol, Costa del 75 D6 Coastal region, S Spain
Solec Kujawski 81 D3 W Poland
Solikamsk 87 D5 NW Russ. Fed.
Sol'-Iletsk 87 D7 W Russ. Fed.
Solingen 77 A4 W Germany
Sollentuna 67 D5 C Sweden
Solomon Islands 137 F2 ◆ Commonwealth Republic, W Pacific Ocean
Solomon Sea 137 C2 Sea, W Pacific Ocean
Soltau 77 C3 NW Germany
Sol'tsy 87 A4 W Russ. Fed.
Solwezi 128 D4 NW Zambia
Soma 103 G4 C Japan
Somalia 127 F4 ◆ Republic, E Africa
Somali Plain 15 Undersea feature, W Indian Ocean
Sombrero 61 J4 Island, N Anguilla
Someren 68 E5 SE Netherlands
Somerset 43 E3 Kentucky, USA
Somerset Island 33 H2 Island, Queen Elizabeth Islands, Nunavut, NW Canada
Somerton 48 A3 Arizona, USA
Somme 73 D1 ≈ N France
Somotillo 59 D4 NW Nicaragua
Somoto 59 D4 NW Nicaragua
Songea 127 D7 S Tanzania
Songkhla 109 B5 SW Thailand
Sonora 48 F4 Texas, USA
Sonoran Desert 53 D9 Desert, Mexico/USA
Sonsonate 59 B4 W El Salvador
Sopot 81 D2 N Poland
Sopron 81 C7 NW Hungary
Sorgues 73 E6 SE France
Sorgun 97 D3 C Turkey
Soria 75 E2 N Spain
Sorong 109 G6 E Indonesia
Sørøya 67 D1 Island, N Norway
Sortavala 87 A3 NW Russ. Fed.
Sotkamo 67 E3 C Finland
Sŏul see Seoul
Soúrpi 83 E5 C Greece
Sousse 122 F1 NE Tunisia
South Africa 128 C7 ◆ Republic, S Africa
South America 117 Continent
Southampton 71 E8 S England, UK
Southampton Island 33 I4 Island, Nunavut, NE Canada
South Andaman 107 H5 Island, Andaman Islands, India
South Australia 133 D4 ◐ State, S Australia
South Bend 44 D5 Indiana, USA
South Bruny Island 133 G7 Island, Tasmania, SE Australia
South Carolina 43 F4 ◐ State, SE USA
South China Sea 109 E3 Sea, SE Asia
South Dakota 47 B3 ◐ State, N USA
Southeast Indian Ridge 15 Undersea feature, Indian Ocean/Pacific Ocean
South East Point 133 F7 Headland, Victoria, S Australia
Southend-on-Sea 71 F7 E England, UK
Southern Alps 135 B6 ▲▲ South Island, NZ
Southern Cook Islands 131 Island group, S Cook Islands
Southern Cross 133 B5 W Australia
Southern Indian Lake 33 H5 ◎ Manitoba, C Canada
Southern Ocean 14 Ocean, Atlantic Ocean/Indian Ocean/Pacific Ocean
South Geomagnetic Pole 138 C5 Pole, Antarctica
South Georgia 138 A2 Island, South Georgia and the South Sandwich Islands, SW Atlantic Ocean
South Goulburn Island 133 E1 Island, Northern Territory, N Australia
South Indian Basin 15 Undersea basin, S Indian Ocean
South Island 135 C6 Island, S NZ
South Korea 103 A6 ◆ Republic, E Asia
South Lake Tahoe 53 C6 California, USA
South Orkney Islands 138 A3 Island group, Antarctica
South Platte River 51 G5 ≈ C USA
South Pole 138 C5 Pole, Antarctica
South Sandwich Islands 138 A2 Island group, SE South Georgia and South Sandwich Islands
South Sandwich Trench 138 B2 Undersea feature, SW Atlantic Ocean
South Shetland Islands 138 A3 Island group, Antarctica
South Shields 71 E5 NE England, UK
South Sioux City 47 D4 Nebraska, USA
South Taranaki Bight 135 C4 Bight, SE Tasman Sea
South Uist 71 B3 Island, NW Scotland, UK
South West Cape 135 A8 Headland, Stewart Island, NZ
Southwest Indian Ridge 15 Undersea feature, SW Indian Ocean
Southwest Pacific Basin 14 Undersea feature, SE Pacific Ocean
Soweto 128 D6 NE South Africa
Spain 75 C3 ◆ Monarchy, SW Europe
Spanish Town 61 D4 C Jamaica
Sparks 51 A5 Nevada, USA
Spartanburg 43 F4 South Carolina, USA
Spárti 83 E6 S Greece
Spearfish 47 A3 South Dakota, USA
Spencer 47 E4 Iowa, USA
Spencer Gulf 133 E6 Gulf, S Australia
Spey 71 D3 ≈ NE Scotland, UK
Spijkenisse 68 C4 SW Netherlands
Spin Buldak 101 E6 S Afghanistan
Spitsbergen 139 C5 Island, NW Svalbard
Split 83 B3 C Croatia
Spokane 53 D2 Washington, USA
Spratly Islands 109 D4 Disputed ◇ SE Asia
Spree 77 E4 ≈ E Germany
Spring City 51 D5 Utah, USA
Springer 48 E1 New Mexico, USA
Springfield 51 G6 Colorado, USA
Springfield 44 B6 Illinois, USA
Springfield 41 E4 Massachusetts, USA
Springfield 47 E7 Missouri, USA
Springfield 44 E6 Ohio, USA
Springfield 53 B4 Oregon, USA
Spring Hill 43 F7 Florida, USA
Springs Junction 135 C5 South Island, NZ
Springsure 133 G4 Queensland, E Australia
Springville 51 D5 Utah, USA
Spruce Knob 43 G2 ▲ West Virginia, USA
Sri Aman 109 D6 East Malaysia
Sri Jayawardanapura 107 E8 W Sri Lanka
Srikakulam 107 F5 E India
Sri Lanka 107 D8 ◆ Republic, S Asia
Srinagar 107 D1 N India
Srpska, Republika 83 C2 ◐ Republic, Bosnia and Herzegovina
Stabroek 68 C5 N Belgium
Stade 77 C3 NW Germany
Stadskanaal 68 F2 NE Netherlands
Stafford 71 E7 C England, UK
Stakhanov 85 G4 E Ukraine
Stalingrad see Volgograd
Stalowa Wola 81 F5 SE Poland
Stamford 41 E5 Connecticut, USA
Stanley 117 C9 ○ Falkland Islands
Stanthorpe 133 H5 Queensland, E Australia
Staphorst 68 E3 E Netherlands
Starachowice 81 F4 SE Poland
Stara Zagora 83 F3 C Bulgaria
Starbuck Island 131 Island, E Kiribati
Stargard Szczeciński 81 B2 NW Poland
Starkville 43 D4 Mississippi, USA
Starobil's'k 85 G4 E Ukraine
Starogard Gdański 81 D2 N Poland
Starominskaya 87 A7 SW Russ. Fed.
Staryy Oskol 87 A6 W Russ. Fed.
State College 41 C5 Pennsylvania, USA
Statesboro 43 G5 Georgia, USA
Staunton 43 G2 Virginia, USA
Stavanger 67 A5 S Norway
Stavropol' 87 A8 SW Russ. Fed.
Steamboat Springs 51 E5 Colorado, USA
Steenwijk 68 E3 N Netherlands
Steinkjer 67 C4 C Norway
Stendal 77 D3 C Germany
Stephenville 48 G3 Texas, USA
Steps Point 55 Headland W American Samoa
Sterling 51 G5 Colorado, USA
Sterling 44 B5 Illinois, USA
Sterlitamak 87 D6 W Russ. Fed.
Steubenville 44 F6 Ohio, USA
Stevenage 71 E7 E England, UK
Stevens Point 44 B3 Wisconsin, USA
Stewart Island 135 A8 Island, S NZ
Steyr 77 E7 N Austria
Stillwater 47 D7 Oklahoma, USA
Stirling 71 D4 C Scotland, UK
Stjørdal 67 B4 C Norway
Stockach 77 B7 S Germany
Stockdale 48 G5 Texas, USA
Stockholm 67 D5 ● C Sweden
Stockton 53 B7 California, USA
Stockton Plateau 48 E4 Plain, Texas, USA
Stoke-on-Trent 71 D6 C England, UK
Støren 67 B4 S Norway
Stornoway 71 C3 NW Scotland, UK
Storsjön 67 C4 ◎ C Sweden
Storuman 67 D3 N Sweden
Storuman 67 C3 ◎ N Sweden
Strabane 71 B5 W Northern Ireland,UK
Strakonice 81 B6 SW Czech Republic
Stralsund 77 D2 NE Germany
Stranraer 71 C5 S Scotland, UK
Strasbourg 73 F3 NE France
Stratford 135 D4 North Island, NZ
Stratford 48 F1 Texas, USA
Straubing 77 D6 SE Germany
Strehaia 85 B7 SW Romania
Strelka 94 E4 C Russ. Fed.
Strickland 137 A2 ≈ SW PNG
Stromboli 79 D7 ▲ Isola Stromboli, SW Italy
Stromeferry 71 C3 N Scotland, UK
Strömstad 67 B6 S Sweden
Strömsund 67 C4 C Sweden
Strymónas 83 E4 ≈ Bulgaria/Greece
Stryy 85 B5 NW Ukraine
Studholme 135 B7 South Island, NZ
Sturgis 47 A3 South Dakota, USA
Stuttgart 77 B6 SW Germany
Stykkishólmur 67 A1 W Iceland
Styr 85 C4 ≈ Belarus/Ukraine
Suakin 127 D1 NE Sudan
Subotica 83 D1 N Yugoslavia
Suceava 85 C5 NE Romania
Suckling, Mount 137 C3 ▲ S PNG
Sucre 117 B3 ● S Bolivia
Sudan 127 B3 ◆ Republic, N Africa
Sudbury 35 C5 Ontario, S Canada
Sudd 127 B4 Swamp region, S Sudan
Sudeten 81 C5 ▲▲ Czech Republic/Poland
Sue 127 B4 ≈ S Sudan
Sueca 75 F4 E Spain
Suez 122 I2 NE Egypt
Suez Canal 122 I2 Canal, NE Egypt
Suez, Gulf of 88 J6 Gulf, NE Egypt
Suğla Gölü 97 B4 ◎ SW Turkey
Suhar 99 E4 N Oman
Sühbaatar 105 E1 N Mongolia
Suhl 77 C5 C Germany
Sujawal 107 B3 SE Pakistan
Sukabumi 109 C8 Java, C Indonesia
Sukagawa 103 G5 C Japan
Sukhona 87 C4 ≈ NW Russ. Fed.
Sukkur 107 C3 SE Pakistan
Sukumo 103 E7 Shikoku, SW Japan
Sulaiman Range 107 C2 ▲▲ C Pakistan
Sula, Kepulauan 109 F7 Island group, C Indonesia
Sulawesi see Celebes
Sullana 115 A4 NW Peru
Sulphur Springs 48 H3 Texas, USA
Sulu Archipelago 109 F5 Island group, SW Philippines
Sulu Sea 109 E5 Sea, SW Philippines
Sulyukta 101 F3 SW Kyrgyzstan
Sumatra 109 B6 Island, W Indonesia
Sumba, Pulau 109 E8 Island, Nusa Tenggara, C Indonesia
Sumba, Selat 109 E8 Strait, Nusa Tenggara, S Indonesia
Sumbawanga 127 C7 W Tanzania
Sumbe 128 B3 W Angola
Sumeih 127 B3 S Sudan
Summer Lake 53 C4 ◎ Oregon, USA
Sumqayit 97 J2 E Azerbaijan
Sumy 85 F4 NE Ukraine
Sunch'on 103 B7 S South Korea
Sunda, Selat 109 C7 Strait, Java/Sumatra, SW Indonesia
Sunderland 71 E5 NE England, UK
Sundsvall 67 D4 C Sweden
Sungaipenuh 109 B7 Sumatra, W Indonesia
Sunnyvale 53 B7 California, USA
Suntar 94 F4 NE Russ. Fed.
Sunyani 124 D5 W Ghana
Suomussalmi 67 F3 E Finland
Suoyarvi 87 B3 NW Russ. Fed.
Superior 44 A2 Wisconsin, USA
Superior, Lake 44 C1 ◎ Canada/USA
Sur 99 F5 NE Oman
Surabaya 109 D8 Java, C Indonesia
Surakarta 109 D8 Java, S Indonesia
Šurany 81 D7 SW Slovakia
Surat 107 C4 W India
Sur, Cabo 137 C6 Headland, Easter Island, Chile
Sûre 68 E8 ≈ W Europe
Surendranagar 107 C4 W India
Surfers Paradise 133 H5 Queensland, E Australia


CAR Central African Republic  FYR Former Yugoslavian Rebublic  NSW New South Wales  NZ New Zealand  PNG Papua New Guinea  Russ. Fed. Russian Federation  UAE United Arab Emirates  UK United Kingdom  USA United States of America

## T

◆ Administrative region ◆ Country ● Country capital ◇ Dependent territory ○ Dependent territory capital ▲ Mountain range ▲ Mountain ⛰ Volcano ↗ River ○ Lake ▫ Reservoir

WANXIAN

Tsalka 97 H2 S Georgia
Tsarevo 83 G3 SE Bulgaria
Tsetserleg 105 E2 C Mongolia
Tshela 128 B2 W Dem. Rep. Congo (Zaire)
Tshikapa 128 C3 SW Dem. Rep. Congo (Zaire)
Tshuapa 128 C2 ~ C Dem. Rep. Congo (Zaire)
Tsu 103 F6 SW Japan
Tsugaru-kaikyo 103 F3 *Strait,* N Japan
Tsumeb 128 C5 N Namibia
Tsuruga 103 E6 SW Japan
Tsuruoka 103 F4 C Japan
Tsushima 103 C7 *Island group,* SW Japan
Tuamotu Islands 131 *Island group,* N French Polynesia
Tuapi 59 E3 NE Nicaragua
Tuapse 87 A8 SW Russ. Fed.
Tuba City 48 B1 Arizona, USA
Tubbergen 68 F3 E Netherlands
Tubize 68 C7 C Belgium
Tubmanburg 124 B5 NW Liberia
Tucson 48 B3 Arizona, USA
Tucumcari 48 E2 New Mexico, USA
Tucuruí, Represa de 115 G4 ⊠ NE Brazil
Tudela 75 E2 N Spain
Tufi 137 C3 S PNG
Tuguegarao 109 F3 N Philippines
Tuktoyaktuk 33 F3 NW Terr., NW Canada
Tula 87 A6 W Russ. Fed.
Tulancingo 57 F5 C Mexico
Tulare Lake Bed 53 B8 *Salt flat,* California, USA
Tulcán 115 B3 N Ecuador
Tulcea 85 D7 E Romania
Tulia 48 F2 Texas, USA
Tulle 73 D5 C France
Tulln 77 F7 NE Austria
Tully 133 G2 Queensland, NE Australia
Tulsa 47 D7 Oklahoma, USA
Tuluá 115 B3 W Colombia
Tulun 94 E5 S Russ. Fed.
Tulun Islands 137 D2 *Island group,* NE PNG
Tumbes 115 A4 NW Peru
Tumen 103 B3 ~ E Asia
Tumkur 107 D6 W India
Tunduru 127 D7 S Tanzania
Tungsten 33 F5 NW Terr., W Canada
Tunis 122 F1 ● NE Tunisia
Tunis, Golfe de 88 E4 *Gulf,* NE Tunisia
Tunisia 122 E2 ◆ *Republic,* N Africa
Tunja 115 C2 C Colombia
Tupelo 43 D4 Mississippi, USA
Tupiza 117 B3 S Bolivia
Turangi 135 D4 North Island, NZ
Turan Lowland 101 D2 *Plain,* C Asia
Turayf 99 B2 NW Saudi Arabia
Turbat 107 A3 SW Pakistan
Turda 85 B6 NW Romania
Turín 79 A2 El Salvador
Turin 79 A2 NW Italy
Turkana, Lake 127 D5 ◎ N Kenya
Turkestan 94 C6 S Kazakhstan
Turkey 97 C3 ◆ *Republic,* SW Asia
Turkish Republic of Northern Cyprus 88 D6 ◇ *Disputed Territory,* Cyprus
Turkmenbashi 101 B2 W Turkmenistan
Turkmenistan 101 B3 ◆ *Republic,* C Asia
Turkmenskiy Zaliv 101 B3 *Lake gulf,* W Turkmenistan
Turks and Caicos Islands 61 F3 *UK* ◇ N West Indies
Turku 67 E5 SW Finland
Turlock 53 B7 California, USA
Turnagain, Cape 135 D5 *Headland,* North Island, NZ
Turnhout 68 D6 N Belgium
Turnov 81 B5 N Czech Republic
Turpan 105 C2 NW China
Turtkul 101 D2 W Uzbekistan
Tuscaloosa 43 D5 Alabama, USA
Tuscany 79 C4 *Region,* C Italy
Tuticorin 107 D7 SE India
Tutuila 55 *Island* W American Samoa
Tuvalu 137 H2 ◆ *Commonwealth Republic,* SW Pacific Ocean
Tuwayq, Jabal 99 C5 ⛰ C Saudi Arabia
Tuxpan 57 E5 C Mexico
Tuxpan 57 D4 C Mexico
Tuxpán 57 F4 E Mexico
Tuxtepec 57 G5 S Mexico
Tuxtla 57 H5 SE Mexico
Tuy Hoa 109 D4 S Vietnam
Tuzla 83 C2 NE Bosnia and Herzegovina
Tuz, Lake 97 C3 ◎ C Turkey
Tver' 87 A5 W Russ. Fed.
Twin Falls 51 C4 Idaho, USA
Tychy 81 E5 S Poland
Tyler 48 H3 Texas, USA
Tympáki 83 F7 Crete, Greece
Tynda 94 G5 SE Russ. Fed.
Tyne 71 D5 ~ N England, UK
Tyrrhenian Sea 79 B6 *Sea,* N Mediterranean Sea
Tyumen' 94 C4 C Russ. Fed.
Tyup 101 I2 NE Kyrgyzstan
Tywyn 71 D7 W Wales, UK
Tuong Duong 109 C3 N Vietnam

## U

Ubangi 124 H5 ~ C Africa
Ube 103 D7 SW Japan
Ubeda 75 D5 S Spain
Uberaba 115 G7 SE Brazil
Uberlândia 115 F7 SE Brazil
Ubon Ratchathani 109 C3 E Thailand
Ubrique 75 C6 S Spain
Ucayali, Río 115 B4 ~ C Peru
Uchiura-wan 103 F2 *Bay,* NW Pacific Ocean
Uchquduq 101 E2 N Uzbekistan
Uchtagan, Peski 101 C2 *Desert,* NW Turkmenistan
Udaipur 107 D3 N India
Uddevalla 67 B6 S Sweden
Udine 79 D2 NE Italy
Udon Thani 109 B3 N Thailand
Udupi 107 D6 SW India
Uele 128 C1 ~ NE Dem. Rep. Congo (Zaire)
Uelzen 77 C3 N Germany
Ufa 87 D6 W Russ. Fed.
Uganda 127 C5 ◆ *Republic,* E Africa
Uglovka 87 A4 W Russ. Fed.
Uíge 128 B3 NW Angola
Uinta Mountains 51 D5 ⛰ Utah, USA
Uitenhage 128 D7 S South Africa
Uithoorn 68 D4 C Netherlands
Ujungpandang 109 E7 Celebes, C Indonesia
Ukhta 87 D4 NW Russ. Fed.
Ukiah 53 B6 California, USA
Ukmergė 67 E7 C Lithuania
Ukraine 85 C4 ◆ *Republic,* SE Europe
Ulaanbaatar *see* Ulan Bator
Ulaangom 105 D1 NW Mongolia
Ulan Bator 105 E2 ● C Mongolia
Ulanhot 105 G2 N China
Ulan-Ude 94 F5 S Russ. Fed.
Ulft 68 E4 E Netherlands
Ullapool 71 C3 N Scotland, UK
Ulm 77 C7 S Germany
Ulsan 103 C6 SE South Korea
Ulster 71 B5 *Cultural region,* Ireland/Northern Ireland, UK
Ulungur Hu 105 C2 ◎ NW China
Uluru 133 D4 *Rocky outcrop,* Northern Territory, C Australia
Ul'yanovsk 87 C6 W Russ. Fed.
Umán 57 H4 SE Mexico
Uman' 85 D5 C Ukraine
Umbro-Marchigiano, Appennino 79 D4 ⛰ C Italy
Umeå 67 D4 N Sweden
Umeälven 67 D3 ~ N Sweden
Umiat 54 E1 Alaska, USA
Umm Buru 127 A2 W Sudan
Umm Ruwaba 127 C3 C Sudan
Umnak Island 54 B2 *Island* Aleutian Islands, Alaska, USA
Umtata 128 D7 SE South Africa
Una 83 B1 ~ Bosnia and Herzegovina/Croatia
Unac 83 B2 ~ W Bosnia and Herzegovina
Unalaska Island 54 B3 *Island* Aleutian Islands, Alaska, USA
Uncía 117 B2 C Bolivia
Uncompahgre Peak 51 E6 ▲ Colorado, USA
Ungava Bay 35 E2 *Bay,* Quebec, E Canada
Ungava, Péninsule d' 35 D1 *Peninsula,* Quebec, SE Canada
Unimak Island 54 B3 *Island,* Aleutian Islands, Alaska, USA
Union City 43 D3 Tennessee, USA
Uniontown 41 B5 Pennsylvania, USA
United Arab Emirates 99 E4 ◆ *Federation,* SW Asia
United Kingdom 71 C5 ◆ *Monarchy,* NW Europe
United States of America 38 ◆ *Federal Republic,* North America
Unst 71 E1 *Island,* NE Scotland, UK
Ünye 97 E2 W Turkey
Upala 59 E5 NW Costa Rica
Upemba, Lac 128 D3 ◎ SE Dem. Rep. Congo (Zaire)
Upolu 137 B5 *Island,* SE Samoa
Upper Darby 41 D5 Pennsylvania, USA
Upper Klamath Lake 53 B4 ◎ Oregon, USA
Upper Lough Erne 71 B6 ◎ SW Northern Ireland, UK
Upper Red Lake 47 E2 ◎ Minnesota, USA
Uppsala 67 D5 C Sweden
Ural 94 B4 ~ Kazakhstan/Russ. Fed.
Ural Mountains 94 C3 ⛰ Kazakhstan/Russ. Fed.
Ural'sk 94 B4 NW Kazakhstan
Ural'skiye Gory *see* Ural Mountains
Urbandale 47 E5 Iowa, USA
Uren' 87 C5 W Russ. Fed.
Urganch 101 D2 W Uzbekistan
Urgut 101 F3 C Uzbekistan
Urmia, Lake 99 C1 ◎ NW Iran
Uroteppa 101 F3 NW Tajikistan
Uruapan 57 E5 SW Mexico
Uruguay 117 C5 ◆ *Republic,* E South America
Uruguay 117 C5 ~ E South America
Ürümqi 105 C2 NW China
Urup, Ostrov 94 I4 *Island,* Kurile Islands, SE Russ. Fed.
Uruzgan 101 F5 C Afghanistan
Usa 87 E3 ~ NW Russ. Fed.
Uşak 97 B3 W Turkey
Ushuaia 117 B9 S Argentina
Usinsk 87 D3 NW Russ. Fed.
Usol'ye-Sibirskoye 94 F5 C Russ. Fed.
Ussel 73 D5 C France
Ussuriysk 94 H6 SE Russ. Fed.
Ustica 79 C7 Sicily, SW Italy
Ust'-Ilimsk 94 F4 C Russ. Fed.
Ústí nad Labem 81 B5 N Czech Republic
Ustka 81 C1 NW Poland
Ust'-Kamchatsk 94 I3 E Russ. Fed.
Ust'-Kamenogorsk 94 D5 E Kazakhstan
Ust'-Kut 94 F5 C Russ. Fed.
Ust'-Olenëk 94 F3 NE Russ. Fed.
Ustyurt Plateau 101 C1 *Plateau,* Kazakhstan/Uzbekistan
Usulután 59 C4 SE El Salvador
Usumacinta, Río 59 A2 ~ Guatemala/Mexico
Utah 51 C5 ◐ *State,* W USA
Utah Lake 51 C5 ◎ Utah, USA
Utica 41 D3 New York, USA
Utrecht 68 D4 C Netherlands
Utsunomiya 103 G5 S Japan
Uttar Pradesh 107 E3 *Cultural region,* N India
Utupua 137 G3 *Island,* Santa Cruz Islands, E Soloman Islands
Uulu 67 E6 SW Estonia
Uvalde 48 G5 Texas, USA
Uvs Nuur 105 D1 ◎ Mongolia/Russ. Fed.
'Uwaynāt, Jabal al 127 B1 ▲ Libya/Sudan
Uyo 124 F5 S Nigeria
Uyuni 117 B3 W Bolivia
Uzbekistan 101 D2 ◆ *Republic,* C Asia
Uzhhorod 85 B5 W Ukraine

## V

Vaal 128 D6 ~ C South Africa
Vaals 68 E7 SE Netherlands
Vaasa 67 D4 W Finland
Vaassen 68 E4 E Netherlands
Vác 81 E7 N Hungary
Vadodara 107 C4 W India
Vaduz 77 C8 ● W Liechtenstein
Váh 81 D6 ~ W Slovakia
Vaitupu 137 J2 *Atoll,* C Tuvalu
Valdai Hills 87 A5 *Hill range,* Russ. Fed.
Valday 87 A4 W Russ. Fed.
Valdecañas, Embalse de 75 C4 ⊠ W Spain
Valdepeñas 75 D4 C Spain
Valdés, Península 117 B7 *Peninsula,* SE Argentina
Valdez 54 E3 Alaska, USA
Valdivia 117 A6 C Chile
Val-d'Or 35 D5 Quebec, SE Canada
Valdosta 43 F6 Georgia, USA
Valence 73 E5 E France
Valencia 75 F4 E Spain
Valencia 115 D1 N Venezuela
Valencia, Gulf of 75 F4 *Gulf,* Spain
Valenciennes 73 E1 N France
Valentine 47 B4 Nebraska, USA
Valjevo 83 D2 W Yugoslavia
Valkenswaard 68 D5 S Netherlands
Valladolid 57 I4 SE Mexico
Valladolid 75 D2 NW Spain
Vall D'Uxó 75 F4 E Spain
Vallejo 53 B6 California, USA
Vallenar 117 A4 N Chile
Valletta 88 B6 ● E Malta
Valley City 47 C2 North Dakota, USA
Válljohka 67 E1 N Norway
Valls 75 G3 NE Spain
Valparaíso 117 A5 C Chile
Valparaiso 44 C5 Indiana, USA
Valverde del Camino 75 C5 S Spain
Van 97 G3 E Turkey
Vanadzor 97 H2 N Armenia
Van Buren 41 G1 Maine, USA
Vanceboro 41 H2 Maine, USA
Vancouver 33 F7 British Columbia, SW Canada
Vancouver 53 B3 Washington, USA
Vancouver Island 33 E7 *Island,* British Columbia, SW Canada
Van Diemen Gulf 133 D1 *Gulf,* Northern Territory, N Australia
Vänern 67 C6 ◎ S Sweden
Vangaindrano 128 G6 SE Madagascar
Van Gölü *see* Van, Lake
Van Horn 48 E4 Texas, USA
Vanikolo 137 G3 *Island,* Santa Cruz Islands, E Solomon Islands
Vanimo 137 A1 NW PNG
Van, Lake 97 G4 *Salt lake,* E Turkey
Vannes 73 B3 NW France
Vantaa 67 E5 S Finland
Vanua Lava 137 G4 *Island,* Banks Islands, N Vanuatu
Vanua Levu 137 J5 *Island,* N Fiji
Vanuatu 137 E4 ◆ *Republic,* SW Pacific Ocean
Van Wert 44 D6 Ohio, USA
Vao 137 G6 S New Caledonia
Varanasi 107 F3 N India
Varangerfjorden 67 F1 *Fjord,* N Norway
Varangerhalvøya 67 E1 *Peninsula,* N Norway
Varaždin 83 B1 N Croatia
Varberg 67 B6 S Sweden
Vardar 83 E4 ~ FYR Macedonia/Greece
Varde 67 B7 W Denmark
Varese 79 B2 N Italy
Vârful Moldoveanu 85 B6 ▲ C Romania
Varkaus 67 F4 C Finland
Varna 83 G2 NE Bulgaria
Varnenski Zaliv 97 A1 *Bay,* E Bulgaria
Vasa *see* Vaasa
Vasilikí 83 D5 Lefkáda, Ionian Islands, Greece
Vaslui 85 D6 C Romania
Västerås 67 C5 C Sweden
Vatican City 79 C5 ◆ *Papal state,* S Europe
Vatnajökull 67 A1 *Glacier,* SE Iceland
Vättern 67 C6 ◎ S Sweden
Vaughn 48 D2 New Mexico, USA
Vaupés, Río 115 C3 ~ Brazil/Colombia
Vavuniya 107 E7 N Sri Lanka
Vawkavysk 85 B3 W Belarus
Växjö 67 C6 S Sweden
Vaygach, Ostrov 87 E2 *Island,* NW Russ. Fed.
Veendam 68 F2 NE Netherlands
Veenendaal 68 D4 C Netherlands
Vega 67 C3 *Island,* C Norway
Veisiejai 67 E7 S Lithuania
Vejer de la Frontera 75 C6 S Spain
Veldhoven 68 D5 S Netherlands
Velebit 83 B2 ⛰ C Croatia
Velenje 77 E8 N Slovenia
Velika Morava 83 D2 ~ C Yugoslavia
Velikiye Luki 87 A5 W Russ. Fed.
Veliko Turnovo 83 F3 N Bulgaria
Vel'ký Krtíš 81 E7 S Slovakia
Vella Lavella 137 D2 *Island,* New Georgia Islands, NW Solomon Islands
Vellore 107 E6 SE India
Velsen-Noord 68 C3 W Netherlands
Vel'sk 87 C4 NW Russ. Fed.
Vendôme 73 C3 C France
Venezia *see* Venice
Venezuela 115 C2 ◆ *Republic,* N South America
Venezuela, Gulf of 115 C1 *Gulf,* NW Venezuela
Venice 79 D2 NE Italy
Venice 43 C7 Louisiana, USA
Venice, Gulf of 79 D3 *Gulf,* N Adriatic Sea
Venlo 68 E5 SE Netherlands
Venta 67 E6 ~ Latvia/Lithuania
Vent, Îles du 137 A6 *Island group,* Archipel de la Société, W French Polynesia
Ventimiglia 79 A3 NW Italy
Ventspils 67 E6 NW Latvia
Vera 117 C4 C Argentina
Veracruz 57 F5 E Mexico
Vercelli 79 B2 NW Italy
Verdalsora 67 C4 C Norway
Verde, Costa 75 D1 *Coastal region,* N Spain
Verden 77 B3 NW Germany
Verkhoyanskiy Khrebet 94 G3 ⛰ NE Russ. Fed.
Vermillion 47 D4 South Dakota, USA
Vermont 41 E3 ◐ *State,* NE USA
Vernal 51 D5 Utah, USA
Vernon 48 G2 Texas, USA
Verona 79 C2 NE Italy
Versailles 73 D2 N France
Verviers 68 E7 E Belgium
Vesdre 68 E7 ~ E Belgium
Vesoul 73 F3 E France
Vesterålen 67 C2 *Island,* NW Norway
Vestfjorden 67 C2 *Fjord,* C Norway
Vestmannaeyjar 67 A2 S Iceland
Vesuvio 79 D6 ▲ S Italy
Veszprém 81 D8 W Hungary
Veurne 68 A6 W Belgium
Viacha 117 A2 W Bolivia
Viana do Castelo 75 B2 NW Portugal
Vianen 68 D4 C Netherlands
Viareggio 79 B3 C Italy
Viborg 67 B6 NW Denmark
Vic 75 G2 NE Spain
Vicenza 79 C2 NE Italy
Vichy 73 D4 C France
Vicksburg 43 C5 Mississippi, USA
Victoria 33 E7 Vancouver Island, British Columbia, SW Canada
Victoria 88 A6 NW Malta
Victoria 119 ● SW Seychelles
Victoria 48 H5 Texas, USA
Victoria 133 F6 ◐ *State,* SE Australia
Victoria Falls 128 C5 *Waterfall,* Zambia/Zimbabwe
Victoria Island 33 G3 *Island,* NW Terr/Nunavut, NW Canada
Victoria, Lake 127 C5 ◎ E Africa
Victoria Land 138 D6 *Physical region,* Antarctica
Victoria, Mount 137 I5 ▲ Viti Levu, W Fiji
Victoria River 133 D2 ~ W Australia
Victorville 53 D8 California, USA
Vidalia 43 F5 Georgia, USA
Vidin 83 E2 NW Bulgaria
Viedma 117 B7 E Argentina
Vienna 77 F7 ● NE Austria
Vienne 73 E5 E France
Vienne 73 C4 ~ W France
Vientiane 109 B3 ● C Laos
Vieques 55 E Puerto Rico
Vieques, Isla de 55 *Island,* E Puerto Rico
Vierzon 73 D3 C France
Vietnam 109 C4 ◆ *Republic,* SE Asia
Vieux Fort 61 K6 S Saint Lucia
Vigo 75 B2 NW Spain
Vijayawada 107 E5 SE India
Vila do Conde 75 B2 NW Portugal
Vilafranca del Penedès 75 G2 NE Spain
Viļaka 67 F6 NE Latvia
Vilalba 75 B1 NW Spain
Vila Nova de Gaia 75 B3 NW Portugal
Vila Real 75 B3 N Portugal
Vilhelmina 67 C3 N Sweden
Viliya 85 C2 ~ W Belarus
Villa Acuña 57 E2 NE Mexico
Villa Bella 117 B1 N Bolivia
Villacarrillo 75 E5 S Spain
Villach 77 E8 S Austria
Villacidro 79 A6 Sardinia, Italy
Villafranca de los Barros 75 C4 W Spain
Villahermosa 57 H5 SE Mexico
Villajoyosa 75 F4 E Spain
Villa María 117 B5 C Argentina
Villa Martín 117 A3 SW Bolivia
Villanueva 57 E4 C Mexico
Villanueva de la Serena 75 C4 W Spain
Villanueva de los Infantes 75 E4 C Spain
Villarrica 117 C4 SE Paraguay
Villavicencio 115 C2 C Colombia
Villaviciosa 75 C1 N Spain
Villazón 117 B3 S Bolivia
Villena 75 F4 E Spain
Villeurbanne 73 E5 E France
Villingen-Schwenningen 77 B7 S Germany
Vilnius 67 F7 ● SE Lithuania
Vilvoorde 68 C6 C Belgium
Vilyuy 94 G4 ~ NE Russ. Fed.
Viña del Mar 117 A5 C Chile
Vinaròs 75 F3 E Spain
Vincennes 44 C7 Indiana, USA
Vindhya Range 107 D4 ⛰ N India
Vineland 41 D6 New Jersey, USA
Vinh 109 C3 N Vietnam
Vinita 47 E7 Oklahoma, USA
Vinnytsya 85 D5 C Ukraine
Vinson Massif 138 A4 ▲ Antarctica
Viranşehir 97 F4 SE Turkey
Virginia 47 E2 Minnesota, USA
Virginia 43 H2 ◐ *State,* NE USA
Virginia Beach 43 I2 Virginia, USA
Virgin Islands (US) 55 *US* ◇ E West Indies
Virgin Passage 55 *Passage* Puerto Rico/Virgin Islands (US)
Virovitica 83 C1 NE Croatia
Virton 68 D9 SE Belgium
Vis 83 B3 *Island,* S Croatia
Visakhapatnam 107 F5 SE India
Visalia 53 C7 California, USA
Visby 67 D6 Gotland, SE Sweden
Viscount Melville Sound 33 G2 *Sound,* Arctic Ocean, N Canada
Visé 68 E7 E Belgium
Viseu 75 B3 N Portugal
Vistula 81 E2 ~ C Poland
Vistula Lagoon 81 E1 *Lagoon,* Poland/Russ. Fed.
Viterbo 79 C4 C Italy
Vitiaz Strait 137 B2 *Strait,* NE PNG
Viti Levu 137 I5 *Island,* W Fiji
Vitim 94 G5 ~ C Russ. Fed.
Vitória 115 H7 SE Brazil
Vitória da Conquista 115 H6 E Brazil
Vitoria-Gasteiz 75 E2 N Spain
Vitré 73 B3 NW France
Vitsyebsk 85 D2 NE Belarus
Vittoria 79 D8 Sicily, Italy
Vizianagaram 107 F5 E India
Vlaardingen 68 C4 SW Netherlands
Vladikavkaz 87 B9 SW Russ. Fed.
Vladimir 87 B5 W Russ. Fed.
Vladivostok 94 H6 SE Russ. Fed.
Vlagtwedde 68 F2 NE Netherlands
Vlieland 68 C2 *Island,* Waddeneilanden, N Netherlands
Vlijmen 68 D5 S Netherlands
Vlissingen 68 B5 SW Netherlands
Vlorë 83 C4 SW Albania
Vöcklabruck 77 E7 NW Austria
Vohimena, Tanjona 128 F6 *Headland,* S Madagascar
Voiron 73 E5 E France
Vojvodina 83 D1 *Cultural region,* N Yugoslavia
Volga 87 B7 ~ NW Russ. Fed.
Volga Uplands 87 B6 ⛰ W Russ. Fed.
Volgodonsk 87 A7 SW Russ. Fed.
Volgograd 87 B7 SW Russ. Fed.
Volkhov 87 A4 NW Russ. Fed.
Volnovakha 85 G5 SE Ukraine
Volodymyr-Volyns'kyy 85 B4 NW Ukraine
Vologda 87 B4 W Russ. Fed.
Vólos 83 E5 C Greece
Vol'sk 87 C6 W Russ. Fed.
Volta 124 D5 ~ SE Ghana
Volta, Lake 124 D5 ⊠ SE Ghana
Volturno 79 D5 ~ S Italy
Volzhskiy 87 B7 SW Russ. Fed.
Voorst 68 E4 E Netherlands
Vorderrhein 77 B8 ~ SE Switzerland
Vorkuta 87 E3 NW Russ. Fed.
Voronezh 87 A6 W Russ. Fed.
Võrtsjärv 67 E6 ◎ SE Estonia
Võru 67 F6 SE Estonia
Vosges 73 F3 ⛰ NE France
Vostok 138 D5 *Russian research station,* Antarctica
Vranov nad Topl'ou 81 F6 E Slovakia
Vratsa 83 E3 NW Bulgaria
Vrbas 83 C2 ~ N Bosnia and Herzegovina
Vrbas 83 C1 NW Yugoslavia
Vršac 83 D1 NE Yugoslavia
Vsetín 81 D6 E Czech Republic
Vukovar 83 C1 E Croatia
Vulcano 79 D7 *Island,* Aeolian Islands, S Italy
Vung Tau 109 C4 S Vietnam
Vunisea 137 J5 SE Fiji
Vyatka 87 C5 ~ NW Russ. Fed.
Vyborg 87 A4 NW Russ. Fed.

## W

Wa 124 D4 NW Ghana
Waal 68 D4 ~ S Netherlands
Waala 137 F6 W New Caledonia
Wabash 44 D6 Indiana, USA
Wabash River 44 D6 ~ N USA
Waco 48 H4 Texas, USA
Waddan 122 G3 NW Libya
Waddeneilanden *see* West Frisian Islands
Waddenzee 68 D2 *Sea,* SE North Sea
Waddington, Mount 33 E7 ▲ British Columbia, SW Canada
Wadi Halfa 127 C1 N Sudan
Wad Medani 127 C2 C Sudan
Waflia 109 G7 E Indonesia
Wagga Wagga 133 G6 NSW, SE Australia
Wagin 133 B5 W Australia
Wah 107 C1 NE Pakistan
Wahai 109 G7 E Indonesia
Wahiawa 55 B1 Oahu, Hawaii, USA
Wahibah Sands 99 E5 *Desert,* N Oman
Wahpeton 47 D2 North Dakota, USA
Waiau 135 A8 ~ South Island, NZ
Waigeo, Pulau 109 G6 *Island,* Maluku, E Indonesia
Waikaremoana, Lake 135 E3 ◎ North Island, NZ
Wailuku 55 C2 Maui, Hawaii, USA
Waimate 135 B7 South Island, NZ
Waimea 55 D2 Hawaii, USA
Waiouru 135 D4 North Island, NZ
Waipara 135 C6 South Island, NZ
Waipawa 135 D4 North Island, NZ
Waipukurau 135 D4 North Island, NZ
Wairau 135 C5 ~ South Island, NZ
Wairoa 135 E4 North Island, NZ
Wairoa 135 D2 ~ North Island, NZ
Waitaki 135 B7 ~ South Island, NZ
Waitara 135 C4 North Island, NZ
Waiuku 135 D3 North Island, NZ
Wakasa-wan 103 E6 *Bay,* C Japan
Wakatipu, Lake 135 B7 ◎ South Island, NZ
Wakayama 103 E6 SW Japan
Wakkanai 103 F1 NE Japan
Wałbrzych 81 C5 SW Poland
Walcourt 68 C8 S Belgium
Wałcz 81 C2 NW Poland
Wales 71 D7 *National region,* Wales, UK
Wales 54 D1 Alaska, USA
Walgett 133 G5 NSW, SE Australia
Walker Lake 51 A6 ◎ Nevada, USA
Wallace 51 B2 Idaho, USA
Wallachia 85 B7 *Cultural region,* S Romania
Walla Walla 53 C3 Washington, USA
Wallis and Futuna 137 I4 *French* ◇ C Pacific Ocean
Wallis, Îles 137 K4 *Island group,* N Wallis and Futuna
Walnut Ridge 43 C3 Arkansas, USA
Walvis Bay 128 B5 NW Namibia
Wanaka 135 B7 South Island, NZ
Wanaka, Lake 135 A7 ◎ South Island, NZ
Wandel Sea 139 C5 *Sea,* Arctic Ocean
Wanganui 135 D4 North Island, NZ
Wangaratta 133 G6 Victoria, SE Australia
Wanlaweyn 127 F5 SW Somalia
Wanxian 105 F4 C China

CAR Central African Republic FYR Former Yugoslavian Rebublic NSW New South Wales NZ New Zealand PNG Papua New Guinea Russ. Fed. Russian Federation UAE United Arab Emirates UK United Kingdom USA United States of America

◈ Administrative region   ◆ Country   ● Country capital   ◇ Dependent territory   ◎ Dependent territory capital   ▲ Mountain range   ▲ Mountain   ☒ Volcano   ✓ River   ◎ Lake   ▨ Reservoir

## NORTH AMERICA

 CANADA

 UNITED STATES OF AMERICA

 MEXICO

 BELIZE

 COSTA RICA

 EL SALVADOR

 GUATEMALA

## SOUTH AMERICA

 HONDURAS

 GRENADA

 HAITI

 JAMAICA

 ST KITTS & NEVIS

 ST LUCIA

 ST VINCENT & THE GRENADINES

 TRINIDAD & TOBAGO

COLOMBIA

 URUGUAY

 CHILE

## AFRICA

 PARAGUAY

 ALGERIA

 EGYPT

 LIBYA

 MOROCCO

 TUNISIA

 LIBERIA

 MALI

 MAURITANIA

 NIGER

 NIGERIA

 SENEGAL

 SIERRA LEONE

 TOGO

 BURUNDI

 DJIBOUTI

 ERITREA

 ETHIOPIA

 KENYA

 RWANDA

 SOMALIA

 SUDAN

 SOUTH AFRICA

 SWAZILAND

 ZAMBIA

 ZIMBABWE

## EUROPE

 DENMARK

 FINLAND

 ICELAND

 NORWAY

 MONACO

 ANDORRA

 PORTUGAL

 SPAIN

 ITALY

 SAN MARINO

 VATICAN CITY

 AUSTRIA

 BOSNIA & HERZEGOVINA

 CROATIA

 MACEDONIA

 YUGOSLAVIA (SERBIA & MONTENEGRO)

 BULGARIA

 GREECE

 MOLDOVA

## ASIA

ROMANIA

 ARMENIA

 AZERBAIJAN

 GEORGIA

 TURKEY

 IRAQ

 ISRAEL

 JORDAN

LEBANON

 IRAN

 KAZAKHSTAN

 KYRGYZSTAN

 TAJIKISTAN

 TURKMENISTAN

 UZBEKISTAN

 AFGHANISTAN

PAKISTAN

 SOUTH KOREA

 TAIWAN

 JAPAN

 BRUNEI

 INDONESIA

 MALAYSIA

 SINGAPORE

 BURMA

## AUSTRALASIA & OCEANIA

 MAURITIUS

 SEYCHELLES

 AUSTRALIA

 NEW ZEALAND

 PAPUA NEW GUINEA

 SOLOMON ISLANDS

 MARSHALL ISLANDS

 MICRONESIA